Adolescence:
A Social Psychological Analysis

THIRD EDITION

HANS SEBALD
Arizona State University

Prentice–Hall, Inc., Englewood Cliffs, New Jersey 07632

Library of Congress Cataloging in Publication Data

Sebald, Hans.
  Adolescence: a social psychological analysis.

  Includes bibliographical references and indexes.
    1. Youth—United States. 2. Adolescence. I. Title.
  [DNLM: 1. Adolescence. 2. Adolescent Psychology.
  3. Social Behavior—In adolescence. WS 462 S443a]
  HQ796.S423 1984   305.2'35   83-9547
  ISBN 0-13-008516-2

Editorial/production supervision
and interior design: Virginia Cavanagh Neri
Cover design: Diane Saxe
Cover photo: Marc Anderson
Manufacturing buyer: John Hall

Printed in the United States of America

10 9 8 7 6 5 4 3 2 1

ISBN 0-13-008516-2

Prentice-Hall International, Inc., *London*
Prentice-Hall of Australia Pty. Limited, *Sydney*
Editora Prentice-Hall do Brasil, Ltda., *Rio de Janeiro*
Prentice-Hall Canada Inc., *Toronto*
Prentice-Hall of India Private Limited, *New Delhi*
Prentice-Hall of Japan, Inc., *Tokyo*
Prentice-Hall of Southeast Asia Pte. Ltd., *Singapore*
Whitehall Books Limited, *Wellington, New Zealand*

To Karen
and her candidates for adolescence,
Michael, Kevin, and Sean

CONTENTS

Preface   ix

PART 1   INTRODUCTION

1

Adolescence: Its Time and Place in Civilization   1

Definitions: Adolescent, Teenager, Youth, and Juvenile   2
Historical Aspects: From Agricultural to Industrial Conditions   12
Postindustrial Conditions   16
Cross-Cultural Appearance of Adolescence   21
The Question of Universality of Adolescence   28
Summary   33

2

Adolescence: Its Time and Place in Personality Development   34

The Concept of Personality   35
Basic Assumptions of Personality Theory   35
Reference Group   39

The Significant Other 42
Culture and Role Learning 44
Changing Sex Roles 46
Identity: Moratorium, Diffusion, and Multiple Personae 55
Summary 64

PART 2 ANTECEDENTS OF ADOLESCENCE: THE SOCIAL MATRIX

3

Conditions of Postindustrial Life 66

Disjunction of Social Structure and Culture 66
Pursuit of Instantness 69
Separation of Home and Work 71
Education in Postindustrial Perspective 72
Mobility and its Disruptions 73
Home Away from Home 75
Adolescent Affluence 78
Sociosomatics: Societal Influences on Biological Development 82
Summary 87

4

American Culture Influences 89

Culture: A Sociological Emphasis 89
The Nature-Nurture Controversy 90
Pubescence and Cultural Values 92
Disparity Between Biological Adulthood and Social Adulthood 93
The Lack of Rite of Passage 94
Value Conflict: The All-American Dichotomies 96
Value Conflict: The Child-Adult Dichotomies 99
Anomie in American Life 102
Point of Order: The Problem of Selectivity 104
Summary 104

5

Social Change and Intergenerational Conflict 106

Conflict between Generations 106
Competing Authorities: Parents vs. Experts 111
Clash of Inferiority Complexes 113
Youth Cult: Not Bridging the Gap 113
The Sexual Revolution 114
Parental Reaction I: Permissiveness and Acquiescence 117
Parental Reaction II: Reassertion of Traditional Authority 120
Summary 126

6

The Modern Family 127

Changing Structure 128
Changing Functions 135
Momism: Inflicting Perpetual Adolescence 145
Parenthood: The Last Stand of the Amateur 150
The Quest for Alternative Structures 151
Summary 154

7

The Modern Educational Experience 156

Trends in American Education 156
Education: Nonfamilial, Longer, and Custodial 159
The High School Dropout 164
After School – The World of Work 175
American Education in Perspective 179
Summary 182

8

The Role of Television and Other Mass Media 184

Scope of Exposure 184
Prominent Ingredients: Violence and Unrealism 186
Questions of Imitation and Other Effects 190
Control Aspects 197
Other Fare and Functions 199
Summary 205

PART 3 CONSEQUENCES OF ADOLESCENCE: COMPENSATING COLLECTIVITIES

9

Etiology and Dimensions of Subculture 206

Definition and Dimensions 207
The Question of Etiology 209
Disagreements on the Existence of the Teenage Subculture 215
The Diversity of Teenage Subcultures 219
Adolescent Nonstatus and Teenage Status: A Paradox? 223
Summary 224

10

Inside the Teen Subculture 226

Norms and Values 227
Argot 250
Channels of Mass Communication 254
Fads and Styles 255
The Sense of Solidarity 263
Status Criteria 264
Hero Worship 267
Subcultural Institutionalization 273
Summary 276

11

Activism and Radicalism: The Making of Movements and Countercultures 278

Differences Between Subculture and Counterculture 278
Adolescence and Alienation 279
Search for Alternative Lifestyles 284
From the Counterculture to the New Age Movement 287
The True-Believer Movements 297
Common Features 306
Trends and Outlook 306
Summary 309

PART 4 SUMMARY AND OUTLOOK

12

Adolescence in Perspective 311

An Era of Youthful Dissent 311
Views of Adolescence 312
The Background 313
Research Needs 319
Outlook 321
What Price Adolescence? 324
Adolescence as Identity Growth: Crucible and Deliverance 325

Author Index 327

Subject Index 332

Preface

This book discusses adolescence as an individual as well as a collective phenomenon. On the individual level, the focus is on the adolescent's reaction to the urban-industrial conditions that have created an environment in which social roots are uncertain and personal identity is vulnerable. This aspect of the discussion is a social-psychological analysis. On the collective level, the focus is on adolescents' attempts to compensate for uncertainty and vulnerability by engaging in subcultural or even countercultural behavior. This aspect is a sociological analysis. On both levels, adolescent behavior can be understood as a groping—often anguished and drawn out—toward maturity, adulthood, and a stable identity.

A full examination of adolescence must be both *analytical* and *comprehensive* —analytical in the sense of showing the causes and consequences of adolescence, and comprehensive in the sense of describing the broader sociocultural context in which adolescence thrives. The text divides this task into four parts: (1) Introducing basic concepts and an historical perspective; (2) Identifying causes embedded in culture, technology, the social structure, and in psychological and developmental conditions; (3) Tracing the collective compensations that have evolved from the difficulties of going through adolescence; and (4) Summarizing and looking ahead.

In the course of portraying adolescence, I favor an interdisciplinary approach, which includes sociological, psychological, educational, anthropological, and family-life material, plus the occasional use of popular sources.

While most readers of this book are probably college students, it is equally well suited for the so-called layperson. This book is not written in academic lingo by professors for professors, but is a straight-forward analysis in plain English. Parents who are not in the mainstream of academic life should therefore find it intelligible and helpful.

The book is a guide through the tangle of social and psychological circumstances that have created and now perpetuate adolescence. The route of this journey is reflected in the structure of the book, which provides students with insight into a lifestyle barely outgrown, educators with a systematic introduction to the troubles and problems of modern youth, and parents with an understanding of the often disconcerting behavior of their offspring.

This is the third edition of *Adolescence: A Social Psychological Analysis.* Since the publication of the first edition in 1968, much has changed. Vehement uprisings of restless youth have shaken American society, indeed most of the Western world. Adolescence, as an ingredient of postindustrial society, has become a permanent fixture. The mass media have clamorously claimed more powerful positions in the socialization of the young; a new sexual morality has risen; patterns of drug use and abuse have shifted; roles (especially female) have been modified; colorful True Believer movements have soothed many of the weary survivors of the counterculture. The third edition reflects these changes and upheavals by modifying the previous editions in the following ways:

Reorganization of Part 1. The first part now introduces more discernibly the two parties to our analysis: society, if not civilization itself, and the individual. Chapter 1 focuses on the social environment, and Chapter 2 concentrates on the psychological and developmental experiences of the adolescent. This arrangement reflects the comprehensive nature of the social-psychological analysis, showing the relationship between social milieu and personality processes.

New emphasis added to the definition of adolescence. The importance of seeing adolescence as an increasingly normative phase of the life span in modern society is given special attention.

More balanced structural-functional analysis. This edition tones down the "problem approach" of the first edition and, thus, is freer to embark on an objective analysis.

Fuller examination of postindustrial conditions. Advanced urban-industrial life has been conceptualized as postindustrial, and the book discusses the ways in which late twentieth-century conditions reinforce adolescence.

Historical perspective on youth unrest. By now, standing in the wake of the counterculture, we have gained an historical perspective from which we can evaluate past disquiet.

Adolescence and the True Believer movements. True Believer movements attract anomie-tormented youth as a light draws moths. These havens, delusive as they may appear to many, welcome the youthful refugees from a freedom they could not bear.

Keener awareness of the impact of the mass media. Never ending armies of more or less artificial socializers constantly bedazzle the young in modern society.

Their daily procession across the TV screen is avidly absorbed by the youthful audience, and their power rivals that of traditional socializing figures.

Clarifying the definition of subculture. Because the definition of subculture has chronically suffered from ambiguity, this edition makes an effort to clarify eight generic dimensions that must be examined and measured when studying collective behavior.

Evaluation of the teen's collective behavior within subcultural dimensions. The colorful spectrum of collective behavior of American teenagers is sifted into subcultural dimensions. Chapter 10, "Inside the Teen Subculture," is a descriptive test of the dimensions' applicability to the youth scene.

Effects of changing roles. Young Americans, especially females, must cope with shifting social roles. This theme is discussed in the context of various topics throughout the book.

Rearrangement of the antecedents of adolescence. Part 2, including Chapters 3 through 8, proceeds from a discussion of basic postindustrial conditions to the intricacies of American culture, the speed of social change, the family, the modern educational experience, and the impact of the mass media.

Eliminating chapters on minority youth. Experience has borne out that racial, ethnic, and other minority groups are best dealt with in specialized books and courses, rather than tagged on to an analytic examination of modern adolescence. Hence, the chapters on black, Jewish, Indian, and lower-class youth of the first edition have been eliminated.

Eliminating chapters on specific problem areas. Again, experience has shown that such problems as the dropout, drug abuser, delinquent, and prematurely sexually and maritally involved teenager are best left to specialized books and courses. By eliminating this part, the current text has become more succinct in its analytic intention.

Reduced discussion of Momism. A previous chapter on Momism has been shortened and incorporated into the family chapter. The impetus for this change was the publication of *Momism: The Silent Disease of America*, which offers a more complete investigation than was possible within the limits of this book.

In addition to these major changes, this edition has of course benefitted from the usual updating and upgrading that are a consequence of new developments and the ongoing education of the author.

The preface is also the place to acknowledge contributions and say thanks. I very much appreciate the competent typing of revisions by Sandy Woodard. Many improvements are credited to Karen Y. Murray, who generously provided insight, new ideas, and an unfailing sense of style. In addition, she provided for me a natural workshop, allowing in-depth observations of young adolescents in action. My sincere thanks to her sons Michael, Kevin, and Sean, who consistently were more patient with me than I was with them.

Hans Sebald

Chapter 1

Adolescence:
Its Time and Place
in Civilization

Adolescence is an invention of modern civilization. It lacks the universality and naturalness that are innate to such statuses as childhood and adulthood. The societies affected are almost always urban-industrial countries, and hence if we want to understand the genesis of this modern occurrence we must scrutinize the typical conditions of industrial—particularly postindustrial—life. Somewhere within these conditions lies the answer to the question: Why adolescence in our time?

A poignant manifesto of adolescence was observed during recent decades, when youthful unrest exploded into a counterculture. While there was more to the counterculture than mere adolescent stirring, the vast segment of the urban-industrial population definable as adolescents provided followership, momentum, and the power of mass movement. Youthful unrest, in the form of subculture or counterculture, may well be the distinguishing mark that future historians of Western civilization will assign to the last decades of the twentieth century.

While probably no epoch of history has been entirely free of youthful tension —whether it be the normal trials and tribulations arising from the process of converting the young into culturized beings, or some degree of juvenile delinquency— our age witnesses a strikingly new development. We are confronted with an unprecedented recession of the young from the adult lifestyle. A youth subculture has arisen that developed into a veritable counterculture during the 1960s and 1970s. The extent, intensity, and, sometimes, ferocity of the new collectivity were astounding. The values, practices, and appearance of its members rocked and puzzled the United States and many other countries. In fact, youth unrest appears to have nearly global dimensions.

It was reserved for the American society, however, to be the prototype of an adolescence-troubled society. As Kenneth Boulding noted: "This is the first society that has ever segregated its youth."[1] Vast numbers of young Americans have evolved into a new class of native aliens. The analysis of adolescence throughout this book is therefore most appropriately based on the American experience. Crosscultural references are introduced only with the intention of deepening our perspective and helping us understand the adolescent conditions and symptoms found in our country.

The phenomenon we call adolescence is probably the most generic explanation for what is going on among young people today. It is assumed that adolescence underlies a good part, if not the vast majority, of modern youthful activities and expressions. Defense of this assumption requires examination of a field of complex interaction, and we shall try to identify in it the *causes* and the *consequences* of adolescence.

Since the causes are embedded in a myriad of urban-industrial conditions, only a number of the major ones will be selected for scrutiny. Identifying the consequences will lead to the youth subculture, a collective attempt at alleviating the difficulties of the adolescent experience. Basically, adolescence is an existential problem deeply felt by the individual. It is not a collective problem. The collective problem is the subculture that emerges as a consequence of adolescence. Only if this relationship is clearly understood can we recognize the essentially compensatory nature of the youth subculture — or even counterculture. The logical beginning of the analysis is therefore a discussion of precisely what adolescence means.

DEFINITIONS:
ADOLESCENT, TEENAGER, YOUTH, AND JUVENILE

During late 20th century, adolescence has *historically* "matured" to become a legitimate part of the life span. This does not mean, however, that it is an esteemed part or a well defined part. Rather, adolescence's moratorium on clarity of expectations is tolerated as an unavoidable phase. In a way, society now *expects* to find in adolescence poorly defined expectations and corresponding behavior. This invites the self-fulfilling prophecy and may well reinforce what we call adolescent behavior. It sounds like a paradox, but postindustrial conditions have evolved a structure of the life span within which we allow for a phase that expects confused expectations. Hence, adolescent behavior has become *normative* and is no longer considered random or unstructured. Adolescents are expected to reflect storm and stress, to be rebellious, and to have a subculture of their own.

---

[1] "A Conversation with Kenneth Boulding," *Psychology Today*, 6 (January 1973), 87.

The life span theory has been advanced by Glen H. Elder, Jr., who defines it as a "concern with the description and explanation of age-related behavioral changes from birth to death."[2] Accordingly, adolescents should be viewed in the light of their relationships to other phases of the life span. This text will try to keep this in mind. If this approach at times presents adolescence as if it were an isolated phase, it admittedly does so as a heuristic measure, i.e., in order to bring the portrait of adolescence into sharp focus, adjacent statuses must necessarily recede into a subdued background.

An additional problem in portraying adolescence deals with the spatial distribution of adolescence. Since adolescence typically is an urban phenomenon, what about rural youth? Depending on family background, adolescence is still a matter of degree for American youth. Hence portraying adolescence in temporal or spatial isolation creates certain violations of the true picture. This is the curse of working with an "ideal type" definition. Wherever possible, the reader will be alerted by modifications inserted in the discussions. With these caveats in mind, we will take a closer look at the definition of adolescence.

The word "adolescence" is derived from the Latin *adolescere*, which means "to grow into maturity." Since reference to growth is nonspecific, it could apply to physiological, psychological, or social growth. It is therefore necessary to agree on a more specific meaning. Adolescence in the *sociological* sense refers to the experience of passing through a phase that lies between childhood and adulthood. Historically it was thought of as a discontinuity of statuses, but now is better thought of as a *status with uncertain and diffuse guidelines*, engendering equally uncertain and diffuse behavior. In short, it means social existence without a clear blueprint for behavior.

The social scientist looks at the adolescent as going through a period of ambiguous role expectations. The young individual often cannot decide whether a situation calls for acting as a child or as an adult, and he or she frequently suffers uncertainty in relation to the adult world—the Establishment, as it is scornfully called. This confusion does not arise in relation to his or her peer group. In fact, adolescents evade uncertainty through involvement in the group activities of their agemates and by relying on the standards of the peer group, hence forming a teenage society estranged from the larger society.

The intensifying circumstances that make American society the epitome of an adolescence-troubled society include the extraordinarily long period between defining an individual as a child and as an adult. Further, there are no distinct rituals signifying the termination of childhood and entry into adulthood. Many societies have such rites of passage, and anthropologists believe that they provide guidance to the individual and serve an integrative function for society.

The purely sociological approach does not complete the portrayal of the adolescent experience. It illuminates only the social aspect. The *psychological*

[2] Glen H. Elder, Jr., "Adolescence in the Life Cycle," in Sigmund E. Dragastin and Glen H. Elder, Jr., eds., *Adolescence in the Life Cycle* (New York: Wiley, 1975), pp. 1–22.

aspect deals with the crisis of identity. The sociological and psychological definitions complement each other insofar as they call attention to the truism that an undefined social situation will have a corresponding repercussion in the personality of the individual who goes through it. It calls to mind a special meaning of the old adage that "no man is an island. A vacuous or inconsistent sociocultural environment is a poor bet for the development of a stable identity, whereas a clearly defined and consistent sociocultural environment is prone to yield a stable identity.

Erik H. Erikson's concept of *identity crisis* has been considered to be of as much relevance to our epoch as the problems of sex seemed to be to Freud's.[3] The concept deals with the relationship between what a person appears to be in the eyes of others and what he or she feels he or she is. It refers to the dynamics of the search for an inner continuity that will match the external social conditions. The reference was first used to explain a type of breakdown of inner controls observed among psychiatric patients. Similar control disturbances were found in young persons suffering from conflict and confusion. Gradually, the term *identity crisis* acquired a normative connotation and was applied to adolescents in general. As used by Erikson, *crisis* does not mean a breakdown or catastrophe but rather a "crucial period" when development must move one way or another and when stable reference points in and around the young person must be established. Generally, the identity concept focuses on the integration of a number of important elements—such as capacities, opportunities, ideals, and identifications—into a viable self-definition.

Adolescents differ in the tempo with which they establish an identity. Some may formulate a limited identity too early in order to avoid further confusion. In Eriksonian terms, such an early identity formation is called "identity foreclosure," and is usually due to parental ascription. Many delay such crystallization, are for many years incapable of a clear formulation, and exist in a psychosocial moratorium during which they try out various identities.

Certain developmental tasks complicate the identity struggle of adolescents. They include the necessity of the young to learn new ways of behaving, to acquire new ideas about themselves and other people, and to make important decisions that will affect the rest of their lives. Developmental psychologists emphasize how important it is that the young learn to master these tasks during their teen years. For example, Robert J. Havighurst felt that healthy unfolding of the personality demands mastery of the following skills, knowledge, and attitudes:

1. Accepting one's physique and learning to cope with a masculine or feminine role.
2. New relationships with agemates of both sexes.
3. Emotional independence from parents and other adults.
4. Achieving assurance of economic independence.
5. Selecting and preparing for a vocation.

[3] Erik H. Erikson, *Identity: Youth and Crisis* (New York: W. W. Norton, 1968).

6. Developing intellectual skills and concepts for carrying out the general civic responsibilities of an adult citizen.
7. Desiring and achieving socially responsible behavior.
8. Preparing for marriage and family responsibilities.
9. Cultivating values in harmony with a realistic and scientific world picture.[4]

While Havighurst's nine developmental tasks have been traditionally accepted as important or even natural, his reference to the learning of masculine/feminine role differences is no longer uncritically accepted by all people as necessary or "natural." Many modern Americans would prefer to substitute a new developmental task: the necessity for the young to develop communicative skill. Such skill, it is thought, would enhance young people's individualities, help them to accept others' individualities, and enable them to engage in more sensitive social relationships. Presumably, individualistic development, safeguarded by communicative ability, would be preferable over restrictive role learning. The extent to which such substitution will indeed be accomplished is a story to be told by future historians. In either case, the process will be most demanding—whether it means learning a role or learning communicative skill. At this time, gender-differentiated role learning is still pervasive.

The problems presented by developmental demands are intensified by *physiological* changes that occur during the earlier part of adolescence. This period is characterized by rapid biological growth. During pubescence, the changing proportions of the body tend to cause poor coordination, and the maturing of the endocrine system sharpens sexual interest. The young must learn to adapt to these biological changes. Within a relatively short time they find themselves endowed with primary and secondary sex characteristics and have reproductive capability. However, society discourages the enactment of these capabilities, insisting on postponement of their expression.

Even a general *legal* declaration of adulthood is only partially sufficient to end adolescence. Although 1971 federal legislation enfranchised the eighteen-year-old, the new political privileges do not necessarily abolish other conditions of nonadulthood. For example, the initial, early 1970s reaction to the federal legislation, when twenty-nine states lowered the drinking age, was reversed during the late 1970s, when twenty states reconsidered and raised the drinking age back up by one to three years. These reconsiderations continued during the early 1980s, when over twenty additional states planned to raise that age.

There is another abrogation, albeit an informal one, of full adulthood after age eighteen. What about the millions of young Americans who are between eighteen and twenty, and even older, enrolled in colleges and universities, and who are *economically* dependent on parents, relatives, and loans? Is it not a mark of adulthood to achieve a balance between production (making a contribution to the

[4] Robert J. Havighurst, *Developmental Tasks and Education* (New York: Longmans, Green, 1951), pp. 30-55.

division of labor) and consumption? Many, if not most, young Americans who attend institutions of higher education have not achieved symmetry between giving and taking. They are still being nurtured and receive support and care without making an equivalent contribution. *Full* adult status, although only informally and not necessarily legally, is tied up with a balance between producing and consuming. Being a full-time student after age eighteen is often a moratorium on full adult status. Allowance must of course be made for individuals using savings that are the result of their productive statuses and that are now used to balance the score. Participation in higher education under such circumstances does not disturb the production-consumption balance. Students who work as well as attend school to finance their studies likewise achieve balance and maintain adult status—at least in respect to the economic criterion.

The legislation declaring eighteen-year-olds responsible adults has nevertheless introduced greater clarity. For example, the tradition of educational institutions playing the *in loco parentis* role has been curtailed, and college students have achieved a modicum of independence.

In many societies, additional criteria bear on the definition of full adulthood. We are dealing here with informal *tradition*. For example, in a number of societies a man may assume full adult responsibilities only after he has a full-grown son. In other societies, such as traditional rural Greece, a young man must spend about ten years arranging his sisters' dowries before he is considered a man. Among Irish peasants, a son is not considered a mature adult until his father finally retires.

These, then, are the major elements that signal the termination of adolescence:

1. Sociologically, the termination of the unclear child/adult interim.
2. Psychologically, completing a number of developmental tasks and achieving a modicum of consistent identity.
3. Biologically, achieving physiological maturity.
4. Legally, reaching the age limit specified by law.
5. Economically, becoming self-supporting and maintaining a balance between production and consumption.
6. Traditionally, when informal customs lift the last restriction on adult privileges.

This list illustrates that there are various dynamic ingredients in the adolescent experience, all of them interrelated and culminating in a confounding experience. From a theoretical point of view, no agreement has been reached as to the relative importance of the various factors. Also, these variables are not conterminous; that is, each follows its own course and expires at different times. We may therefore speak of *degrees* of adolescence, or, conversely, of adulthood. For example, the onset of puberty normally signals the entrance into adolescence. This would set the modal entrance age at between twelve to fourteen years for girls and thirteen to fifteen for boys. But the termination of adolescence is not so readily determined.

There are no objective physiological indicators signifying the termination. While economic independence, stable employment, and marriage are adult indicators, they do not necessarily indicate psychological maturity. Moreover, the psychological and sociological meaning of such achievements must be viewed within the traditions of a given sociocultural environment. In tribal societies, the transition from childhood to adulthood may be swift, and adolescence is merely a brief interval that is clearly terminated by an initiation ritual. However, in American postindustrial society this transition is exceedingly protracted, and no rite of passage helps the young to drop an emotional anchor in adult life.

As has been mentioned above, in a strict legal sense adulthood in the United States is reached at eighteen years of age. At that age, full civil rights usually become available to young Americans. These privileges pertain to, among other things, voting, driving, drinking, employment, marriage, concluding contracts, criminal justice, etc. (As mentioned above, state and local statutes still defy uniformity about age levels, however.) But in a social-psychological sense, the termination of adolescence cannot be judged on the basis of chronological age. While the years of adolescence used to be fourteen through eighteen, in the late twentieth century these years extend into the twenties, and many young Americans remain adolescents until they are thirty.

The criteria for this assertion are embedded in at least two interrelated processes. Adolescence terminates *psychologically* with the establishment of realistic and relatively consistent patterns of dealing with internal conflicts and the demands of the social and physical environment. It terminates *socially* when the sociocultural environment yields sufficient consensus to declare the individual an adult. The progress of the two processes does not necessarily run in a one-to-one relationship, since one may precede the other. It is possible, for example, that a person has established realistic modes of problem-solving and is socially still not defined as an adult; and, vice versa, an individual may have entered adult status according to the general sociocultural definition but may still be lacking in realistic patterns of problem-solving. If the degree of inability to cope with the environment exceeds a certain limit, society can withdraw the status of adulthood from the individual regardless of chronological age and declare him or her mentally incapable. Such a person usually is placed under the supervision of a special institution, such as a mental hospital. However, psychological and social development are expected to coincide and produce a normally functioning young adult by the late teens.

Natural growth processes do not occur in distinct stages. Humans show considerable arbitrariness in defining life stages. They seem compelled to establish a stable structural order to facilitate social predictability and communication. In reality, life is a *continuous process*, and adulthood is the result of irregular and variable maturation that began with the fusion of the ovum and the sperm. It is, therefore, an arbitrary and heuristic practice to subdivide the period of adolescence into preadolescence, early adolescence, and late adolescence.[5] Whether these divisions

[5] E. B. Hurlock, *Adolescent Development* (New York: McGraw-Hill, 1949).

contribute to the overall understanding of the adolescent phenomenon is doubtful. Nonetheless, such divisions may be of clinical value for counseling teenagers at specific phases of their development.

It has been said that an adolescent is one who if not treated as an adult acts like an infant. There is truth in this aphorism: if role expectations are poorly defined — as they are during adolescence — the resulting confusion may induce a youngster to resort to one of the adjacent roles: either that of the adult or the child. Either alternative — as unfitting to the situation as it may appear — constitutes a solution and provides a clear form of reaction. This, of course, is merely a situational solution. In general, decision-making during adolescence is a most difficult process because the child's familiar forms of responding to a situation are no longer judged to be adequate, and new response patterns have not yet been developed.

The nomenclature for labeling young Americans often leads to miscategorizations. It is therefore advisable to distinguish between a number of references that are often improperly used as synonyms for *adolescent.* They are *teenager*, *youth*, and *juvenile.* Some of these terms capture certain aspects of the concept of adolescence, but more often they exclude essential qualities and include peripheral connotations.

A striking example of blurring distinctions comes from the writing of Eric Hoffer, who used *juvenile* and *adolescent* interchangeably.[6] Accordingly, both references center on persons, young or old, who are confused by change — *any* type of change. While it is true that an essential aspect of adolescence deals with drastic change, sharpness of focus is diminished when the concept is applied to all types of change. The concept should be reserved for one specific process: the change from child to adult. Hoffer's liberal application of the concept of adolescent to Pope Julius II, various heads of state, and the Ku Klux Klan loses the analytic benefit that a scientific concept holds.

Similarly, the term *juvenile* should be limited to matters of youthful law violations and enforcement, as in juvenile delinquency, juvenile court, juvenile detention center, juvenile officer, etc.

The term *youth* refers to the broad and non-specific "younger generation," including children, adolescents (in certain societies), and young adults. The concept is practically universally applicable, since all societies normally have a younger generation; if they did not, they would die out (an almost unheard-of reason for a society to disappear). Since adolescence is not necessarily a universal phenomenon, and some societies have youth but no adolescents, the two terms are not interchangeable. There are many societies, however, in which youth and adolescents are merged. These are the industrialized societies. The society typically free of adolescence tends to be rural or tribal. Its youth — younger generation — makes the transition from child to adult status without the adolescent interim.

---

[6] Eric Hoffer, "An Age for Juveniles," *Harper's* (June 1965), 18–21.

To complicate matters, some social scientists ascribe a highly specific meaning to the term. Kenneth Keniston, for example, studied the increasing numbers of young men and women who experience a particularly delayed entry into full adult status.[7] As he saw it, they moved into an emergent stage suspended between adolescence and adulthood. He called this stage "youth," and applied it to the eighteen-to-twenty-six age category. The reason for defining a postadolescent/preadult period was seen in the need to label the segment of America's young that consists of highly talented, affluent, and educated young people who defer entry into sociological adulthood. Presumably, these young adults are psychologically mature and meet the psychological criteria of adulthood: identity is resolved, capacity to work established, proficiency in a love relationship proven. However, they have not yet made commitments to the primary social institutions, such as marriage, family, and vocation. Hence, prime sociological characteristics of adulthood are lacking. While the great majority of young Americans move directly from adolescence to adulthood, these young individuals prolong experimentation with life's possibilities and their personal potentialities. The typical environments in which their activities unfold are college, graduate school, and, mostly in the past, the countercultural movement. Their identities are tied up with a generation and not with a tradition. The generations succeed each other quickly—as anyone over thirty-five has learned through rebuffs experienced when seeking association with youthful causes. Keniston called this phenomenon "youth culture;" Theodore Roszak called it the "counterculture."[8]

The significance of referring to Keniston's conceptualization is to make the reader aware of varying definitions. While Keniston's explorations produced insights, his choice of terminology could have been more felicitous. Retaining more descriptive terms for these eighteen-to-twenty-six-year-old Americans would increase the clarity of reference. The young adults who choose an extended moratorium could be more accurately described by such labels as "young adults," "young intelligentsia," "revolutionaries," members of the "New Left," "countercultural people," "dissident students," "young radicals," "older adolescents," and so forth—the choice of term depending on the particular nuance the communication means to accentuate. The term *youth*, as commonly used, has an inclusive connotation and should not be misappropriated for a highly specific segment of the younger generation. It is used throughout this book with the simple chronological denotation that is in harmony with common English language usage.

The term *teenager* is probably the most widely used word referring to young people in American society. While its denotation refers to an age bracket, its connotation suggests stereotypical behavior. This behavior is less than valued by the Establishment; and when adults talk of "teenage behavior," there is a trace of

[7] Kenneth Keniston, *Young Radicals* (New York: Harcourt Brace Jovanovich, 1968).

[8] Theodore Roszak, *The Making of a Counter Culture* (Garden City, N.Y.: Doubleday, 1968).

derogation and a tendency to label the behavior "immature." There is also the connotation of collectivity, suggesting that teenagers exist as a group rather than as distinct individuals. It is this latter connotation that is of sociological significance, since it purports to explain teenage behavior in terms of peer group norms.

The meanings ascribed to *adolescent* and *teenager* are closely related. Referring to a person as an "adolescent" means that we emphasize the peculiar interim between the statuses of child and adult; referring to a person as a "teenager" calls attention to age and the tendency to associate with peers and subcultural activities. Adolescence actually leads to the behavior typical of teenagers, since that behavior compensates for situational uncertainties.

Before we leave the matter of definitions, a few remarks should be made to put the discussion in its proper perspective. First, definitions must be understood as more than mere communicative labels. They reflect our particular view of reality and, at the same time, reinforce what we perceive as real. This means that our definitions tell us something about the way we think, categorize, and consequently behave. For instance, a somewhat one-sided view is presented by Joseph Kett, who thinks that "adolescence was essentially a conception of behavior imposed on youth, rather than an empirical assessment of the way in which young people actually behaved."[9] Admittedly, scientists are not immune to imposing their biases through seemingly objective definitions, and there is probably little reason to exempt the sociological definitions of *youth* and *adolescence* from this danger. Quite possibly we have invented labels and definitions because they appear plausible but actually are afflicted with bias. As a result, we risk the danger of responding not to stimuli but rather to our definitions of stimuli. This may sound pedantic; yet, unless we constantly check empirical conditions, we may lose ourselves in abstractions that have no real referents.

If losing oneself in abstractions were the only problem, it would have small consequence besides paying professors salaries for engaging in mental gyrations. But the problem is deeper. Definitions *act* on the persons labeled, making them meet our biases and expectations. In the case of *teenager*, for example, our definition (1) tells us how we perceive them and what kind of reality-view we have; (2) predicates the way we treat them; and (3) consequently elicits a reaction and style of behavior that, in a sense, fulfills our prophecy. The point may be exaggerated here —we hope! The purpose for doing so is to alert the reader to the possible tricks language in general and definitions in specific can play.

What can be done to control these tendencies? In the context of this book, I try to observe a number of safeguards against the definitional trap:

    [9] Joseph F. Kett, *Rites of Passage*, (New York: Basic Books, 1976), p. 327. Also see Benjamin Whorf, *Language, Thought, and Reality* (New York: John Wiley, 1956), and Clyde Kluckhohn, "Culture and Behavior," in *Handbook of Social Psychology*, vol. 2, ed. Gardner Lindsey (Reading, Mass.: Addison–Wesley, 1954).

1 *The interdisciplinary approach.* The behavioral sciences have been notorious in their subdivided and separate search for concepts, theories, and hypotheses. Various disciplines have divided up the person as if he or she consisted of discrete faculties; the results of this cognitive dissection have been incomplete and unreal portrayals of people. Throughout this book, an effort is made to merge sociological, psychological, anthropological, and some biological data to produce a fuller picture of the adolescent experience.

2 *Examination of a wide variety of data.* Many books in the social sciences are written by professors for professors and limit their exploration to theories propounded by colleagues. An attempt will be made to modify the sacred ritual of academic inbreeding by including "secular" sources, such as nonprofessional magazines (for example, *Seventeen*), travelogues, news reports, letters by teenagers, etc.

3 *Crosscultural illustrations.* To a remarkable extent we all are victims of the limited perceptual repertoire of our cultural background. Cross-cultural investigations are important to alleviate cultural myopia. Such studies have repeatedly demonstrated that our narrow frame of reference has a way of institutionalizing our own distortions of the truth. Throughout this book I shall make use of cross-cultural illustrations, although the main thrust of the analysis is directed toward the United States.

4 *The structural-functional approach.* Basically a method of analysis, this approach starts with the scrutiny of certain conditions and then, as objectively as possible, looks for their consequences. Thus adolescence is seen as a consequence of a constellation of circumstances (to be explored in Part II). This approach frees the writer from searching for adolescent "problems" and negative aspects of this period of life. Defining adolescence as a problem is an example of value judgment —most likely in line with the views of the Establishment. However, this book is *not* completely free from this tendency.

To refer to certain aspects of adolescence as problems is of course tempting since it seems plausible, for example, to label adolescent suicide a problem. The least we can do, then, is to also recognize aspects of adolescence that are positive. For example, adolescents have the opportunity to wait and grow. During this time, young individuals can make the best of a variety of experiments in lifestyle, education, and reflection. They have a chance to develop unique, independent, and integrated identities. To fully understand this point, it would be helpful to contrast the typical American adolescent with nonadolescent youth in other societies (or perhaps other times) and recognize the quality of life that emerges from the divergent lifestyles. The positive aspects of the adolescent moratorium might then become more apparent.

HISTORICAL ASPECTS:
FROM AGRICULTURAL
TO INDUSTRIAL CONDITIONS

Prior to and throughout the Middle Ages, children passed directly into the adult world between ages five and seven. The "younger generation" was hardly a recognizable concept. Barbara Tuchman's study of medieval conditions found that if children survived to age seven, their childhood was more or less over and they were treated as miniature adults.[10] Medieval artists appeared to be ignorant of what children even looked like, habitually portraying them as small adults. One twelfth-century painting illustrating Jesus' injunction to "suffer the little children to come unto me" shows Christ surrounded by a dozen undersized men. Schooling was of minimal importance and rarely extended into the teens. Teenagers of the Middle Ages sometimes made history at an age when modern teens are still going to high school. For example, Edward, the Black Prince, was sixteen when he triumphed at the Battle of Crécy; Joan of Arc was seventeen when she took Orléans from the English; and Ivan the Terrible was the same age when he commenced to make his name as the "Terrible" and had himself crowned czar of Russia. Work, in a strictly adult environment, came early. This rapid transition from childhood to adulthood was the norm prior to the Industrial Revolution and resembled the custom of primitive societies, in which children become full-fledged members of the tribe in one painful and often hazardous initiation. This swift transition compressed or even abolished the confusion and terror of stepping into adult life.

The certainty and swiftness of this transition gradually faded with the rise of the Industrial Revolution. Increasing urbanization and industrialization resulted in a slower and more ambiguous passage into adulthood. Greater concern for education and the occupational training of youth became evident. Most young people who lived in towns and cities went through apprenticeships, which prepared them for trades in the context of the guild system. Increasing numbers of young people traded the rural setting with its simple, observable work patterns for the urban milieu with its complex division of labor. This change divorced the place of residence from the place of work, and the working adult became progressively less visible to the young. A need evolved for formal education and vocational training, which in turn gave rise to new institutions. Concomitantly, ambiguity shrouded the status of the individuals who found themselves in the post-child and pre-adult phase which today we call adolescence.

With increasing industrialization, European societies developed a curious nostalgia about bygone pastoral days that were presumably more healthy and beautiful. As if to compensate for spreading industrial slums, Romanticism evolved. Romantics focused on children, and feared that the latter's assumedly pristine souls would be adversely affected by urban-industrial conditions. Society gradually

---

[10] Barbara Tuchman, *A Distant Mirror* (New York: Knopf, 1978), p. 52. Also see for comprehensive treatment Philippe Ariés, *Centuries of Childhood* (New York: Knopf, 1962).

accorded children their own activities. For the first time literature was created solely for the young by such 19th-century writers as Charles Dickens and Lewis Carroll. As parents began to see children's play as a natural, even educational activity, toys began to appear in artists' paintings, and children were shown in more informal and playful poses.

The romantic sentiment was particularly strong in England. Jean-Jacques Rousseau, in *Émile* (1762), declared humans good by nature but saw them as being corrupted by urban civilization. The Frenchman's writings and sojourn in England nurtured the English sense of protection toward children. It was in England, the front runner of the Industrial Revolution, where the conditions for such concern were ripe. Therefore, not surprisingly, England was the first nation to introduce compulsory education of children (1878). At that point, industrialization had progressed sufficiently to produce the first real indications of adolescence. Discontinuity between child and adult statuses became noticeable, with the causes rooted in the changing economy and technology (shifting from agriculture to industry) and in a new cultural attitude toward children. It was deemed necessary to protect children from death, sickness, adult sexuality, and the assumed immorality of the city.

Many historical documents portray early industrial conditions and the plight of the urban young. Lord Thomas B. Macaulay, for example, wrote about the London of the late 17th century:

> When the evening closed in, the difficulty and danger of walking about London became serious indeed.... Thieves and robbers plied their trade with impunity: yet they were hardly as terrible to peaceable citizens as another class of ruffians. It was a favorite amusement of dissolute young gentlemen to swagger by night about the town, breaking windows, upsetting sedans, beating quiet men, and offering rude caresses to pretty women. Several dynasties of these tyrants had, since the Restoration, domineered over the streets. The Muns and Tityre Tus had given place to the Hectors, and the Hectors had been recently succeeded by the Scourers. At a later period arose the Nicker, the Hawcubite, and the yet more dreaded name of Mohawk.[11]

Macaulay easily convinces us that there was much youthful villainy in earlier times. There is a striking similarity between adolescent gang activities in large modern cities like New York, Chicago, and Los Angeles and the actions of youthful gangs in London almost three hundred years ago. This casts doubt on the justifiability of the perennial complaint of many adults who negatively compare the youth of our day with the youth of previous generations. These complaints frequently conclude that youth has never been more degenerate than at present. Such reminiscing is more sentimental than factual. Socrates, nearly 2400 years ago, talked in a fashion that one finds repeated ever since—and one that possibly ante-

[11] Thomas B. Macaulay, *History of England*, vol. 2 (Boston: Houghton Mifflin, 1899), p. 81.

dated him. He referred to the children of his time as being infatuated with luxury, behaving with bad manners and with disrespect for authority, and as being tyrants of their households.

While complaints about the behavior of the young appear timeless, they reached a crescendo during the Industrial Revolution. It was that era that convinced every major industrial society that it had a youth problem. Consequently, as Edgar Z. Friedenberg has pointed out, young people were given the "colonial treatment," which included (1) the attempt to persuade them to abandon their "barbaric" ways; (2) the assumption that they had no traditions of their own; (3) the conviction that they were economically dependent, and the corresponding efforts to keep them that way; and (4) the failure to provide an adequate job market for them.[12] Children were safekept in schools—more for custodial than for educational purposes; in other words to keep them off the streets. Industrialized societies began to insist on segregating their young, on shutting them away from realistic life. Over generations, such practices created an artificial environment, a moratorium on adult life. Introduction of compulsory education in early industrial society thus constituted the chrysalis that eventually hatched into modern youth's subculture with its separate values, rebellion, and dissidence.

English—or, for that matter, *general industrial*—conditions, laws, and lifestyle were reflected in the New World, and American society of the mid-nineteenth century manifested typical youth problems. Reports concerning gang violence during the middle of the last century have a striking resemblance to today's headlines. The only difference seems to be that the names of the gangs are different. In 1857 the *New York Times* printed articles concerning the activities of New York City gangs with such names as the Dead Rabbits and the Bowery Boys. It was even necessary to call out the state militia in 1857 to squelch the street fighting between rival gangs and reestablish peace.[13] New Orleans, likewise, reported the activities of teenagers who roamed the streets beating, stabbing, and robbing innocent citizens.[14]

The influx of immigrants into the United States during the early 1900s did nothing to reduce the adolescent phenomenon. Anomie and marginality tinged the struggle of the immigrants' first-generation American children. While immigrant parents continued to draw their identity and response patterns from a background in the Old World, their children could choose between the values of their Old World oriented parents and the demands of American society. Choosing and adjusting was not easy for the young of various ethnic minorities. Ernest W. Burgess and

[12] Edgar Z. Friedenberg, *Coming of Age In America* (New York: Random House, 1965). Also see John R. Gillis, *Youth and History: Tradition and Change in European Age Relations, 1770-Present* (New York: Academic Press, 1981); Paula Fass, *The Damned and the Beautiful: American Youth in the 1920s* (New York: Oxford University Press, 1977).

[13] Reported in David Gottlieb and Charles Ramsey, *The American Adolescent* (Homewood, Ill.: The Dorsey Press, 1964), p. 4.

[14] Ibid., pp. 4-5.

Harvey J. Locke illustrate the youth problem of immigrant families using the example of an Italian family:

> ...The third son is in Leavenworth: He is an original "42" [a notorious criminal gang that was located on the West Side of Chicago]. He finished two years of high school. At this point his family moved only about three blocks but into the midst of the "42" gang. Here the boy picked up delinquent cronies, cultivated new pleasures and habits, became delinquent and ended up as a big-time robber, the accomplice in professional stick-ups, the pal of notorious, big gangsters. There was nothing the family could do to save the boy.[15]

Another social movement that aggravated the problem of adolescence in the United States was rural-urban migration. In the early decades of this century, there were conspicuous indications that uprooted rural youth had to make difficult adjustments to city life. One such adjustment involved becoming accustomed to less parental supervision and fewer family obligations. Former farm youths found themselves financially and morally independent. Many observers—then as well as today—judged such rural-urban migration dangerous and undesirable. City life was viewed as incompatible with the "wholesome" living seen as necessary for youth. Here is an example of this concern:

> One has only to compare the broken, bent, and depraved youth of the city with the honest and firm farm child to see what evil the city offers. On the farm the young person learns to respect work and to disregard evil influences. The air about him is fresh and he does not breathe the stench of the factory or narcotics. He can take pride in the accomplishments of his work and the pleasures of his family. In the city, youth are always subject to the wicked...[16]

The adjustments demanded of ex-rural youth living in urban centers are not necessarily problems of the past. As the evidence indicates, these problems are timeless and still exist in the United States today. Youths with farm or rural-slum backgrounds who have migrated from Appalachia to the big cities of the Midwest are current examples. The following statement, made in 1910, could be easily applied today and would describe contemporary situations in such cities as Columbus, Cleveland, Philadelphia, and Indianapolis, all of which receive an influx of youth from the hills of Kentucky, West Virginia, and Tennessee:

> Never before in civilization have such numbers of girls been suddenly released from the protection of the home and permitted to walk unattended upon city streets and to work under alien roofs; for the first

[15] Ernest W. Burgess and Harvey J. Locke, *The Family: From Institution to Companionship* (New York: American Book, 1945), p. 124.

[16] "Annual Report of the Ohio State Board of Agriculture," *Agriculture Record, 1912,* p. 476.

time they are being prized more for their labor power than for their
innocence, their tender beauty, their ephemeral gaiety...
    Never before have such numbers of young boys earned money inde-
pendently of the family life, and felt themselves free to spend it as they
choose in the midst of vice deliberately disguised as pleasure.[17]

While value judgment inherent in the statement tends to obscure the technical
aspects of the sociological process, the report nevertheless succeeds in conveying a
picture of the situation.
    In sum, the historical sketch shows that adolescence is not a newcomer to our
era. It has been growing along with increasing urbanization and industrialization –
in the United States as well as elsewhere. In essence, when the agricultural way of
life gave way to the urban-industrial lifestyle, simple social structure was jolted and
a fissure developed between childhood and adulthood. This fissure has become ever
wider; indeed, it has developed into a gap.

POSTINDUSTRIAL CONDITIONS

While the industrial society produced the plain and simple adolescent, postindustrial society has created whole armies of adolescents with causes (or pseudocauses).
To understand this development, a description of postindustrial conditions is in
order.
    Economic and technological progress can be divided into three sequential
types: (1) agricultural; (2) industrial, or manufacturing; and (3) service-oriented, or
postindustrial. Although most economic systems include a mixture of the above,
they can be distinguished by their emphasis on a particular economic-technologic
style. As societies become industrialized, an inevitable trajectory manifests itself.
An ever-increasing proportion of the labor force concentrates on manufacture, and,
as national incomes rise, there evolves an ever greater demand for services. Service
orientation is established when the majority of the labor force no longer works in
agriculture or manufacturing but in services like health, recreation (including
entertainment, tourism, sports, mass media, etc.), research, education, government,
transportation, the military, finance, and trade. Most countries in the world,
especially in Asia and Africa, are still dependent on their raw labor power and
natural resources. Russia and some of her satellite nations, Japan, and most of
Western Europe engage the majority of their labor forces in industry and the
manufacture of goods.
    The United States has been the first nation in history to shift the greater
portion of its labor force to the provision of services. In 1970 this proportion
amounted to 60 percent and by 1980 it had risen to 70 percent. To select just one

[17] Jane Addams, *The Spirit of Youth and the City Streets* (New York: Macmillan, 1910),
pp. 5–6.

example from the pool of services, there are about 3 million civilian employees in charge of running the vast federal bureaucracy of this country. In addition, there are state, county, and municipal government employees, comprising the single largest salaried group in the United States.

Daniel Bell's definition of *postindustrial society*[18] is presently enjoying wide acceptance among social scientists, despite its misleading choice of word, since we are obviously *not* living "post"industrial. On the contrary, our industrial complex has developed to the extent where goods can be manufactured in such expedient ways so as to assure their abundance —meaning elimination of the scarcity that was a principle of preceding economic systems. Methods have improved productivity to the point where a huge industry can be run by relatively few workers. The ultimate of scientific industrialization, the manufacture of "intelligence" through computers, enables a radical cutback in the number of employees and creates dispensable labor. This adds to the reason why a society is able to shift attention to service: it can shift labor surplus to this sector. In fact, the various services are industrialized themselves. The health industry, for example, includes medical research centers, government supervisory agencies, hospitals, physicians' associations, drug firms, and so on. Retention of the industrial mode of manufacture and rendering service in our age is the reason why Alvin Toffler, in *Future Shock*, preferred the more plausible expression *super-industrial society* to describe late twentieth-century American society.[19]

The rise of the postindustrial system is an historical turning point. If we have failed to visualize this clearly, it is due to its gradual emergence and to the blind spots we develop toward what is closest and most immediate to us. Other Western societies are on the verge of turning into postindustrial service-oriented systems, with resultant changes in social relations and power structure imminent as well.

Cultural elements primarily affected are those related to the Protestant ethic: the notion of hard work, deferred gratification, and constant reinvestment of the fruits of one's labor. Since scarcity of goods has been drastically reduced by the use of advanced industrial means and since such reduction is accomplished by relatively few workers and relatively easy work, the old work ethic appears no longer meaningful to the younger generation. Automation has created the ethic-eroding impression that work may some day be eliminated, that machines will eventually take over society's chores. John Kenneth Galbraith proclaimed: "The greatest prospect we face is to eliminate toil as a required economic institution."[20]

Material security has become commonplace to the young, especially to those in the middle class. Therefore the adult preoccupation with material pursuits invites their scorn. Purpose or need for it is no longer understood. Why worry about resources for a "rainy day" when such days are virtually unknown! The role of new

---

[18] Daniel Bell, *The Coming of Post-Industrial Society* (New York: Basic Books, 1973) and *The Cultural Contradictions of Capitalism* (New York: Basic Books, 1976).

[19] Alvin Toffler, *Future Shock* (New York: Bantam Books, 1971), p. 491.

[20] *Time* (October 30, 1972), 96.

social welfare practices adds to the alleviation of fear of hard times. For example, for nearly two decades, until the early 1980s, young people could devote their time to formal education relatively easily because they could draw from a variety of grants, loans, and welfare supplements. Policymakers have even discussed the possibility of every American citizen receiving a guaranteed annual income. It came as a dumbfounding surprise to many students when, in the '80s, the federal government tried to tighten educational loans and grants. Here was a generation that had already taken for granted that society owed them education and training. The reaction of shock poignantly illustrated that the "hardship values" of the older generation had lost their meaning to the young. It will have to be seen whether the Protestant ethic is going to be rejuvenated by the economic crisis of the '80s and whether the younger generation will have to relearn traditional work values. If postindustrial conditions progress as they have over the past decades, they will continue to dismantle the old work ethic. For the majority of the young, deferment of gratification is as odious as it is odd and is a "hang-up" of the old; immediate gratification is "natural" and thus a righteous demand.

While the generating powers of these value changes are primarily found in scientific progress and technological innovations, this is not to say that an unmodified Marxian interpretation, which insists that the substructure of the means of production totally determines the superstructure (including the various cultural dimensions), has to follow. Some aspects of Western culture are undergoing changes relatively independent of technological conditions. Some of these shifts in thinking, albeit not necessarily coherent or compatible with Western Culture, enlarge the sense of individualism, the search for a new mystique, the quest for identity, and concerns in civil liberties.

Postindustrial conditions involve a number of important *social-structural* changes. One concerns the need to reduce the labor force. This is manifested by the educational institution playing a custodial role and expanding the adolescent experience as long as possible, and by early retirement that increases the need to entertain and care for the "elderly." Perhaps the most important alteration in the social structure has to do with increasing specialization. Modern roles isolate individuals by defining for them extremely limited modes of behavior. Life becomes largely a positional experience, with limited opportunities to interact on a casual and general-cultural basis. While the incumbent of the position may find a modicum of personal identity—a positional identity—and thus a compensation for the anomic nature of the general culture, he or she also experiences a notable degree of isolation.

Other changes in human relationships deal with the ascent of technological experts, who have profound influence over national policymaking. Theodore Roszak painted a vivid picture of the rule of the experts and their "objective consciousness," which is, in effect, the new technocracy of America. Related to this change is increasing government control over the goals of science. Government control of science is a corruption of a process that traditionally was apolitical. While government used to represent ideology—the emotional and the expressive—, science dealt with the instrumental and calculative. As the government began to assume custody of the technical, it became a technocracy whose high priests were the scientific experts. This shows up the anomic nature of late twentieth-century America: a preoccupation with the mastery of instruments but a poverty of values concerning their application, a characteristic of a society emphasizing instrumental norms and neglecting basic cultural values.

Into what roles do the different economic-technological systems cast their young? In a typical agricultural society we find *youth* but no adolescents; in a typical industrial society we find *adolescents*; and in the postindustrial society we have *adolescents* and a *youth subculture*, which, in its advanced metamorphosis, becomes a *counterculture.*

Postindustrial society, then, has widened the distance between child and adult statuses. While the gap and the structural conditions that created it already existed in the plain industrial society, the gap widened and the conditions intensified in postindustrial society. Major *structural conditions* responsible for this gap are: (1) Long periods of education, partly necessitated by the need for extensive preparation for the complex urban-industrial structure, and, partly, by the custodial function of the educational institution to delay youth's entry into the labor market. (2) Separation of the location of work from domicile, making adult work invisible to the young. (3) Highly specialized division of labor. (4) Youth's considerable share of affluence. (5) Relatively high social and geographic mobility to which young individuals are exposed. (Chapter 3 will elaborate on these conditions.)

In addition, some new cultural emphases accentuate the adolescent experience in the United States. Large numbers of young Americans expect society to provide a career and lifestyle that is both economically secure and psychologically rewarding. The attitude can be summed up as the "philosophy of entitlement," referring to the development of a pervasive feeling of being entitled to all sorts of material and psychological benefits and that the provision of these benefits is the responsibility of society. This departs from the traditional American "rugged individualism" and represents a shift toward a welfare mentality.

The shift was and still is disguised as social reform, social equality, and a more equitable distribution of power, wealth, and status. Most of these demands and efforts were at the core of the counterculture and provided material for varying interpretations. Writers like Theodore Roszak, Jack Newfield,[21] Philip Slater,[22] Charles A. Reich,[23] and to some degree Kenneth Keniston[24] arrived at an optimistic interpretation of youth's unrest and dissidence. They saw their rebelliousness directed against the broken promises of authority and the insensitivity of the

---

[21] Jack Newfield, *A Prophetic Minority* (New York: Signet Books, 1966).

[22] Philip Slater, *The Pursuit of Loneliness* (Boston: Beacon Press, 1970).

[23] Charles A. Reich, *The Greening of America* (New York: Random House, 1970).

[24] Kenneth Keniston, *Youth and Dissent* (New York: Harcourt Brace Jovanovich, 1971). The inclusion of Keniston in the category of writers who render an optimistic value judgment of youth's activism should be modified. Keniston, unlike the others, bases his opinion less on intuition than on empirical studies.

American system. Roszak was particularly vocal in dignifying youthful resentment and interpreted it as a countermanifesto against technocracy. In his classic, *The Making of a Counter Culture*, he described what he felt are the insidious ingredients of modern American society, in which impersonal technocracy rules the lives of its members. These conditions have presumably dulled and dehumanized Americans. Roszak believes that youth has risen against technocratic tyranny, attempting to introduce sensitivity, humaneness, and mystique to life. While this attempt may have been sincere, it abated and by the early 1970s the countercultural movement had lost momentum.

The argument of these writers, that our materialistic and technologized culture is responsible for the rise of youthful dissent, is extremely tenuous. Western societies have been materialistically oriented for hundreds of years. Technological innovations must have appeared overwhelming to people of every epoch, but there was hardly a youth countermovement to contend with as well. Thus the roots of dissent are at best only partly explained by this argument, and the significance of the period of moratorium is brought back into focus. It is this period that creates *the time and the collectivity* that make possible the offering of new ideas and the expression of dissent and criticism. These activists, whatever their impressive slogans or quasi-platforms, are essentially adolescent. They have largely refused to join adult institutions and to work in any substantive sense toward the betterment of society. John Aldridge reminded us that for about two decades we may have been "brainwashed by the doctrine that whatever is young is right."[25]

This does not mean, however, that all youthful causes have no substance. Many of the demands and suggestions are valuable and insightful. But these contributions toward a just and beautiful lifestyle are selected out of a vast range of contributions, many of which are immature and destructive. The selective perception of many idealistically minded writers, in their fervent desire to perceive civilizational progress, has chosen only the positive aspects of youthful activism and ignored such behavior as unintelligent drug use, problems of hygiene and health, refusal to work, and delinquency and crime. What is disputable with the type of interpretation offered by Roszak, Newfield, and others, is therefore not *what* they say but what they *do not* say.

It is undoubtedly true that rebellious adolescents constitute dynamic elements in society and function as stagnation-preventing catalysts. When considered within the progress-oriented ethos of our Western civilization, these effects can be interpreted as a positive function.

---

[25] John W. Aldridge, *In the Country of the Young* (New York: Harper's Magazine Press Book, 1970), p. 75.

CROSS-CULTURAL APPEARANCE
OF ADOLESCENCE

The theory that industrial or postindustrial conditions have a characteristic effect on young individuals in any country is supported by cross-cultural survey. In the industrialized world we are witnessing various expressions of adolescence—some of them in the form of harmless fads, some in the form of delinquency, and some in the form of serious efforts to advance social change. This section presents an international sampling of youthful stirring that puts the discussion of American adolescence into universal perspective.

England has experienced an upsurge in youth-style and adolescent-gang activities since the middle of the century. It began with the elegantly dressed but often aggressive Teddy boys of the late 1950s. They were followed by the gentle Mods and the tough Rockers in the 1960s, forming opposing camps. The Rockers derived their name from rock 'n' roll, which the Mods rejected for what they thought were more refined styles. Mod was short for "modish" and "modernist." Rockers wore black leather and rode powerful motorcycles. Mods went for stylish clothes, long hair, high-heeled shoes, and motor scooters. Each group defined the other as the out-group, and each was visibly identifiable, forming a ready target for the other. Significant of English-teenagers is their remarkable affluence, which they use to acquire their subcultures' material identifications in terms of "in" clothes, scooters, and motorcycles.

During the late 1960s and early 1970s, England made its contribution to the international hippie movement. Similar to the American counterparts, English hippies drew antagonism from the Establishment, mostly on account of appearance. Large contingents of bearded and drug-using British flocked to such favorite grounds as the Netherlands, where they found greater tolerance in Amsterdam's Vondel Park than in London's Hyde Park, and along the beaches of the Mediterranean. These English youths assumed a moratorium on adulthood by experimenting not only with lifestyles but also with life-locations. Many of them oscillated between wanderlust and academic pursuit—periodically returning to school in England and elsewhere in Europe.

Besides the activities of generally nondelinquent teen subcultures, juvenile delinquency has sharply increased in England—a typical trend for most European countries since the 1960s. The most extreme expressions were reported from London, where organized groups engaged in violent behavior that was obviously normative for the group and functioned to reinforce in-group sentiments.

Among the gangs were the Skinheads of the 1970s, who recruited primarily from lower-class neighborhoods and were responsible for initiating a new style. These teenagers, mostly boys, shaved their skulls, dressed in oversized workpants held up by thin, red suspenders and wore hobnailed, steel-toed boots, which they used as weapons to kick and trample. Some grew their hair a trifle longer and identified themselves as Suedeheads. Skins and Suedes were lineal descendants of the Rockers and specialized in terrorizing hippies, homosexuals, and immigrants from the Orient. Extensive Skinhead violence prompted mass demonstrations by Pakistanis in front of No. 10 Downing Street. Police were prompted to confiscate bootlaces and suspenders of suspicious Skinhead packs on the theory that it is difficult to kick if one's boots are flapping and trousers sagging.

The sadistic Skinhead style gave impetus to the sadomasochistic Punk style in the late 1970s, a style that assumed international dimensions and became noticeable in the United States by the early 1980s. Its initially rather crude British form transmuted into a more sophisticated style in America and, at least for specific subgroups, filled the want of style created by the demise of the mod and the hippie styles. American Punk, dubbed "the hippies' revenge," attracted mostly disturbed teenagers, who substituted sadomasochistic symbolism and mock violence on the dance floor for actual violence in the streets. A spin-off from Punk during the 1980s was New Wave, reintroducing bizarre mod styles, expressing less violence, and separating itself from Punk.

Germans refer to their adolescents as *Teenagers*, an addition to the German vocabulary accepted as if it were of perfect Teutonic origin. The word has been incorporated into regional dialects and, for example, is often used in Bavaria with an added *l* to produce *Teenagerl*, suggesting a diminutive version of teenager. However, an unfavorable image of teenager is reinforced by the frequently antisocial conduct of German adolescents. Destructive conduct is not necessarily the domain of delinquent gangs, but is often the byproduct of nondelinquent teenage fads. In the 1960s, when Britain's Rolling Stones performed in West Berlin, the aftermath of the performance included a rampage by teenage fans that cost the city $150,000 in damages.[26]

Excesses of teenage fads proclaim the existence of an adolescent collectivity. But they fail to leave a lasting imprint on society's social structure and institutions. Other segments of the youth population leave a more serious impression. For example, West Germany's students have manifested their moratorium on adulthood with particular force. Caught in the margin between family background and adult status in a complex industrial society, they have demanded more say in the environment in which they spend many years of their lives. During the late 1960s and early 1970s, hardly a campus escaped their riotous demands. There were strikes, occupations of buildings, the taking of hostages, marches, sit-ins, and destruction of government property. The demands concentrated on obtaining a voice in structuring the curriculum, hiring and firing of faculty, distributing funds, and arranging various campus facilities. In addition, international matters, particularly the Vietnam War, played an important role in student protests. In 1973, for example, students stormed Bonn's city hall, smashing furniture and looting official files, to protest the visit of South Vietnam's President.

The Vietnam war had added a rationale to youth's outbursts the world over, but after its termination in 1972, an apparent paucity of causes created a lull in youthful activism throughout most countries. The lull came to an end in most

[26] UPI report (Berlin, September 17, 1965).

European countries when new political and social concerns arose during the early 1980s. A new cause, uniting hundreds of thousands of young European protesters, came with the Reagan administration's abrupt and unilateral announcement in 1981 that it intended to deploy advanced nuclear weaponry on European soil. The announcement created, virtually overnight, a new peace movement and caused European youth to rush to antiwar and antiAmerican rallies in numbers not seen since the Vietnam war. Other concerns stirring up young Europeans, as well as their American peers, focused on nuclear power generators and their dangers to human life and the ecosystem.

One cause that degenerated into violent activism attacked housing policies in big cities such as Berlin. Young people, many of them students and rootless adolescents, illegally occupied condemned residences, staged mass demonstrations, and marched into planned battles against police. While many of the participating youths were sincerely motivated by social concerns, many participated out of nihilistic hostility against an anomic moratorium that prevented them from being meaningful members of a prosperous society. Indeed, alienation had driven a number of adolescents to the point of totally rejecting their society—a rejection based on irrational hatred without the benefit of ideology or coherent philosophy (thereby differing from political terrorists). These blindly destructive youths were called *Chaoten* and their professed purpose was to create as much chaos in society as they possibly could.[27] The fact that such a label came into existence tells us about a new phenomenon: the ultimate manifestation of nihilistic adolescence that holds no stock in the adult world. Although the majority of activist youths were not necessarily violent themselves, they protected the *Chaoten* at demonstrations and in street fights by forming protective phalanxes around them whenever the police charged or attempted to reach these usually masked individuals. It is a telling symptom of a civilization lopsided with adolescents when masses of young people choose to side with deliberate chaos-makers rather than with law and order.

The lull was broken in the United States during the early 1980s by several political and social innovations. Among them were the reintroduction of draft registration for young men (which had been suspended after the Vietnam war), the administration's cutting of student loans and grants, and the government's overtures toward interfering with rebel movements threatening the status quo of a Central American country. Each of these events caused protests, rallies, and demonstrations. However, compared with reactions to the government's Vietnam policy, the responses were mild-mannered. Nonetheless, they signaled an end to American youth's political apathy, which had set in after the end of the Vietnam conflict, and heralded the political awakening of a new generation. Aspects of the reawakening are more properly discussed in the framework of social movement and activism and are presented in Chapter 11.

France's adolescent problems were expressed in terms of the *blousons noirs* and *teenagers*. The latter term—again an untranslated innovation from American

[27]"Widerliche Auswüchse," *Spiegel*, August 17, 1981, pp. 31–32.

culture —was frequently branded by patriotic Frenchmen as an undesirable example of "Franglais," the intrusion of English words into French. The opponents of such innovations object to them on the assumption that with the introduction of English words, *"l'American* way ot lite" was also introduced, since new concepts stimulate new behavior patterns. Their analysis was correct—the typical teenager as we know him or her in the United States has become a way of life in France. The country also experienced a share of the countercultural uprisings that swept through Western Europe and North America during the late 1960s.

In Sweden there is concern about the *raggare* (alienated, subcultural youths) and Swedish young people in general. As Swedish society perplexedly stands by, their young people manifest rising rates of alcoholism, drug abuse, and suicide. It seems as if it were part of the old "Scandinavian puzzle." The youth of one of the world's most advanced and secure countries, protected by social welfare practices of every imaginable sort, are listless and desire to immigrate to other countries where they believe opportunities would challenge their wits and life would not be regulated to the point of boredom and meaninglessness.

Austrian society watches with consternation as boys and girls abandon yodeling and dirndls and turn to rock music and hippie-type clothes. The older generation condescendingly calls them *Halbstarke,* "half-growns." Australian society is confronted with growing numbers of adolescents who have formed, as in America and Western Europe, a distinct collective power vis-à-vis the Establishment.

Expressions of adolescence can no longer be hidden even in Communist countries. As in Western societies, industrialization has progressed to create discontinuity between child and adult statuses. Although Communist governments have attempted to fill this interim, use it for their ideological goals, and create a national youth organization, enough deviance in fads and interests has been observed to warrant suspicion that the efforts were only partially successful. Increasingly over the past decades, news has reached the West about the activities of the *stilyagi,* "style chasers," imitating Western fashions and setting teenage styles in Russia. Part of *stilyagi* jargon is the use of American nicknames, a practice supported by the use of black-marketed American rock 'n' roll records. The musical styles of Western youth (condemned by Soviet officialdom as "shouts, roars, and hysteria") hold paramount attraction for the *stilyagi,* and they tune into Western broadcasts to tape music. They also function as black marketeers and as the "center-boys" (referring to the centers of large cities) who trade counterfeit icons for foreign tourist clothes. Blue jeans used to be one of the most lucrative underground trading items—until 1975, when the first Soviet-made jeans appeared. The typical long hair of Western male youth appeals immensely to Soviet boys but is disapproved of by the Establishment. Drug use is not (yet) a social problem. Only on large university campuses does one occasionally encounter rumors that someone has used marijuana, heroin, or a psychedelic agent. Alcohol is a different story: even officials admit that it is a national problem.[28]

[28] Walter D. Connor, *Deviance in Soviet Society: Crime, Delinquency, and Alcoholism* (Irvington, N.Y.: Columbia University Press, 1972).

⌈A sure indication of the existence of a teenage subculture is the development of <u>teenage slang</u>⌋ Such argot has been spreading among Soviet youth, with the press labeling it *stilyagi-ism* of speech. It is particularly the creeping "Americanization" of Russian teenage slang that causes concern to Russian officials. *Votch, bathon,* and *fahzer* illustrate phonetic adaptations of watch, button, and father.⌈A complaint in *Pravda* accused Soviet teenagers of talking like alien visitors from such places as Michigan, Texas, or California.[29] Officials fear that the lingo might spread from teenagers and students to workers, and the officials, in their campaign to define it as vulgar and unpatriotic, have marshalled the power of press releases⌋ reprimands by Comrade Courts, and life-sized posters ridiculing young offenders. As a more stringent measure, 500 students were expelled in 1981 from Ukrainian medical schools—some for failing grades, others for violating principles of "Soviet morality."[30]

To the horror of Soviet authorities, even Punk entered the Russian teenage scene during the 1980s. Moscow teenagers were observed imitating the jerky arm-and-leg movements characteristic of a Walkman wearer, adorning their hair with spikes and wearing black leather pants punctured by safety pins.[31]

Besides teenage subcultural styles, Russia is troubled by serious delinquency. News reaching the West indicates widespread adolescent drinking, assaults, rapes, and other delinquency among urban Soviet youth. The scope of delinquency is illustrated by the decision of various cities to impose curfews on teenagers, prohibiting them to be on the street after 9:00 p.m. In 1974, the Supreme Court of the Soviet Union called for "unwavering struggle against hooliganism."

⌈A more significant indicator of adolescence is less visible and deals with the drawn-out period during which Soviet youth must prepare for positions in the industrial complex. Soviet sociologist Alexandre Kotlyar reported widespread dissatisfaction among Soviet youth, who felt that the industrial positions they had entered did not match the professional qualities they had achieved in institutions of education. As a consequence, young workers change jobs twice as often as do their fathers.[32] To remedy the situation and prevent later disillusionment, a program initiated in 1981 in the Ukraine required medical students to take internships. As an almost immediate consequence, 60% of the interns decided that they had chosen the wrong profession.[33]

It is true that Communist authorities have succeeded in curbing the "perennial student syndrome" (young people excessively extending the period of their education), but at the same time pay dearly for it. By means of a centralized system, they strictly enforce a numerus clausus, which regulates how many students are allowed to major in certain fields. Unlike the United States, Soviet authorities plan and project future societal needs for professions, and admit stu-

---

[29] "Moscow Beat," *World Press Review*, 29 (February 1982), 16.

[30] "Moscow Beat," *World Press Review*, 29 (April 1982), 14.

[31] "Pizza and Punk on Gorky Street," *Time*, (August 1982), p. 40.

[32] Agence France-Presse (Geneva, November 1974).

[33] "Moscow Beat," (April 1982), p. 14.

dents to majors accordingly. For example, applications for majoring in medicine, biology, psychology, teacher's education, and architecture far exceeded the figures allotted for majoring in these areas in East Germany during the early 1980s. Unlike previous years, no substitutions, even in related areas, were permitted.[34] Such regimentation avoids prolongation of the educational process and prevents unemployment after graduation, but it is hard on individual desires. As a consequence, young people's career satisfaction and general happiness is as much endangered in Communist countries as it is in Western ones, albeit for different reasons.

Even Communist China has come face to face with youth problems. Blaming urban conditions (overcrowding and unemployment), Chinese officials have admitted that juvenile delinquency has become a major national problem. Supreme Court President Jiang Hua announced that a fourth of the inmates of Peking's prisons are under eighteen. A high proportion of murderers, thieves, rapists, drug traffickers, and racketeers are juveniles. For example, "in Hokiang a band of delinquents were convicted of 96 felonies: burglaries, robberies, rapes, and a bank robbery in which 60 people were held hostage." As in the Soviet Union, Chinese officials try to stem the tide of Western influence that threatens, particularly in urban areas, to give impetus to subcultural behavior among the young. Referring to Western music and dance styles, authorities have not merely chided young Chinese for performing "vulgar dances to unhealthy music in dimly lit rooms," but even arrested and jailed a score of them in an attempt to halt the spread of "bourgeois culture."[35]

The situation in other Communist societies is similar. Attempts to "protect" youth from "bourgeois decadence" had to make concessions and grant adolescents some style of their own. In East Germany, for example, underground discotheques, playing "decadent" Capitalistic rock music, burgeoned beyond the control of the regime. The government therefore decided to nationalize the discotheques, license disc jockeys (insisting on non-English terminology, he or she became *Schallplatten-unterhalter*), distribute their own socialist-made records, and pass detailed laws regulating behavior in such places. Additional concessions to subcultural youth included manufacturing indigenous "Socialist" jeans to curb blackmarketeering in Western jeans, tolerating punk style, and toning down the Puritanical criticism of youth's sexual expressiveness.

The Bulgarians, intent on outdoing the Russians in Communist puritanism, established in the early 1970s an official barbershop in their capital where police force-sheared the locks of teenagers they hauled off the street. The government felt that alarming numbers of young Bulgarians had succumbed to Western styles and morals.

Hair-trimming campaigns of course only scratch the surface of adolescence as a growing societal phenomenon. The more serious aspects are hidden in the con-

---

[34] *Mitteilungen*, Deutscher Akademischer Austauschdienst, Bonn, March 1982, p. 2.

[35] "Chinese Juveniles," *World Press Review*, 29 (April 1982), 10; and Daily Telegraph, London, April 20, 1982.

stantly extending period of education and training to prepare for a place in the increasingly industrial lifestyle. Reports from other Communist societies are similar in that there are solid indications that the younger generation wants to establish its own style, lingo and philosophy. The repressive actions of the governments are only partially successful. In addition, all Communist countries struggle with increasing juvenile delinquency.

Adolescence has evolved also in non-European societies that have developed an industrial potential. In the Far East, for example, Japan and Taiwan have undergone adolescent stirrings. Japan has achieved industrialization to the point of post-industrial conditions, and the moratorium on adulthood has become a way of life. Concern was aroused by indications of an astonishingly high degree of youthful alienation from the economic and political system. A 1973 survey by Gallup International, which included responses from 22,000 eighteen to twenty-four-year-old Japanese, Americans, English, West Germans, Brazilians, French, Yugoslavs, Swedes, Filipinos, Swiss, and Indians, found Japanese youth's dissatisfaction and alienation to be the highest. Only about 10 percent answered "yes" to the question "Do you think your government protects the welfare and rights of the people?" Figures from other countries ranged from 30 percent in France to as high as 83 percent in West Germany. The study also showed that young Japanese were less interested in religion, had fewer close friends, were more inclined to believe that human nature is evil, and were less interested in kindness to others than youth in other countries.[36] Youthful crime in Japan has jumped over 10 percent during the early 1980s, with juveniles accounting for nearly half of all criminal offenders. Violence on school grounds increased over 40 percent during this time, and most of the crimes were directed against teachers.[37]

The political, economic, and industrial development of Taiwan has given rise to adolescence. Most notable are the *tai-paus*, gang members with largely middle-class backgrounds who have formed a subcultural environment within which they develop an identity. Over one hundred *tai-pau* units have been identified, each with its own name and fiercely loyal following. Their activities are nonutilitarian and merely serve to maintain group solidarity. Delinquent behavior, like gang fighting, assaults, car theft, truancy, and teasing police, is to be understood in this light.[38]

The list of countries experiencing adolescence includes most, if not all, urban-industrial nations. The above examples illustrate what can happen in a society with a division between generations.

The country internationally viewed as the prototype of an adolescence-troubled society is the United States, and many observers of the international scene regard the American teenage subculture as the cause of the development of the

[36] *New York Times*, August 5, 1973, p. 12.

[37] "Education: Japanese Students are Driven by Shiken Jigoku," *Time*, March 15, 1982, pp. 80–81.

[38] You-Yuh Kuo, "Identity-Diffusion and Tai-Pau Gang Delinquency in Taiwan," *Adolescence*, 8 (Summer 1973), 165–70.

various vernacular versions. It is undoubtedly true that American youth has had "form-inspiring" influence on youth in other societies through the mass media, which have effectively permeated international boundaries. However, it is questionable whether the American influence is *responsible* for the youth movements that are springing up everywhere in the world. It is more accurate to say that similar social and cultural conditions have arisen in these societies and that these are responsible for the development of adolescence.

The development of adolescence is basically due to (1) a finely divided division of labor, which produces a very technical and complex social structure, and (2) the failure of a culture to provide its members with a compelling ideation that would result in a strong identity and a feeling of purpose. The combination of these two variables, one having to do with the nature of the social structure and the other with the weakness of the culture, form the requisite and sustaining conditions for adolescence.

The nature of American social structure and American culture is probably more adolescence-inducing than that of most societies. A social structure that produces discontinuity between the status of the child and that of the adult would cause only minor forms of adolescent expression *if* the culture were able to compensate for the ensuing structural vagueness; that is, if the culture were able to infuse a sense of identity and meaning into the interim between the two statuses. The assumption is that in a typical urban-industrial environment the interim between child and adult statuses is usually unstructured and consequently lacks the type of meaning and identity that evolves from a definite career or from a goal-oriented apprenticeship. The burden of providing meaning during these interim years falls therefore on the overall ethos of the culture. If the culture fails to compensate for the social-structural limbo, adolescence is bound to express itself.

It is interesting to observe the progress that many of the developing nations have made toward the urban-industrial lifestyle and the concomitant development of juvenile and adolescent problems. Normally, adolescence is a symptom of a well developed and relatively affluent society. If this is true, many of the rural and semiurban societies may anticipate the development of adolescence along with technological maturation.

THE QUESTION OF UNIVERSALITY
OF ADOLESCENCE

While it is true that a high correlation exists between urban-industrial conditions and the growth of adolescence, the correlation is not absolute. To understand the exceptions, it is necessary to recognize the interaction between *social-structural conditions* and *cultural forces*.

Structural conditions are found in institutional structure, group affiliation, authority hierarchy, socioeconomic stratification, and the division of labor, all which form the basis of human relationships. For adolescence to evolve, the social structure, especially the division of labor, must be complex enough to exact a long transition from child to adult status. The social-structural circumstances can therefore be called the *necessary* cause of adolescence. The inability of culture to infuse enough meaning into the interval becomes the *sufficient* cause. This is analogous to the situation in which the necessary cause for disease X is the presence of X bacteria. But the presence of the necessary cause alone does not mean that the disease manifests itself. If the attacked organism provides enough resistance, the bacteria may be powerless, and the organism will not exhibit the symptoms of disease X. But if the organism cannot rally sufficient resistance, it falls victim to the bacteria. The analogy is applicable to the phenomenon of adolescence and clarifies the causal process. If cultural resistance is strong and provides the "antibiotics," adolescence may not express itself. However, if the cultural ideation and identity-forces are weak and nondescript, adolescence will appear.

Adolescence can be curbed, or possibly altogether avoided, if a society provides a compelling and convincing ideology or religion for its members and succeeds in indoctrinating the young. The most reliable and lasting social-control mechanism is the internalized fervor and conviction that become part of the "conscience." Little or no external enforcement is needed to obtain firm adherence to cultural norms and values once people have internalized them as convictions. If a society succeeds in implanting an identity that rises above the narrow frame of social-structural arrangements and creates a feeling of meaningful belonging to a cultural tradition, symptoms of adolescence will be minimal.

This minimization is especially noticeable where a specific youth program is designed to infuse ideological directives. As a result, the void created by the structural interim between child and adult statuses is filled with meaning. The feeling of belonging to the general culture and the exposure to specific youth programs create an identity in the young independent of specific positions in the division of labor. The young individual obtains the status of a meaningful and vital member of society and cannot be classified as adolescent.

Some examples in recent history illustrate the ideological compensation for adolescence-inducing urban-industrial structures. The *Hitler-Jugend* of Nazi Germany, the *Pioneers* and the *Komsomol* in the Soviet Union, the *Freie Deutsche Jugend* (FDJ) in East Germany, and the *Red Guard* in China were, or in some instances still are, organizations that successfully combated the urban-industrialized conditions that produce adolescence.

Reference to these historical events is not to be interpreted as an endorsement of totalitarian systems that convert adolescents into cooperating and goal-oriented members of society. The purpose of presenting these situations is to elucidate the structural-functional principle that assumes that if certain cultural dimensions prevail, certain behavioral consequences follow. The German, Russian, and Chinese examples depict modifications of the generalization that adolescence is a universal trait of modern urban-industrial societies.

But these examples are, or are in the process of becoming, historical examples. They refer to situations that have lost ideological purity and have acquired adolescent symptoms. As noted earlier, subcultural and delinquent youth-activities have increased in Russia, while youth's ideological commitment appears to have decreased since the Stalinist era. Nevertheless, for about 23 million Soviet youths between the ages of fourteen and twenty-eight, the Communist Youth League, or *Komsomol*, still provides a tangible environment in which they receive guidance, fellowship, and a sense of belonging.

The FDJ of Russia's German satellite is modeled after the *Komsomol* and subjects a large segment of East German youth to Communist indoctrination. In addition to this Communist youth organization, East Germany has developed another important state-run youth movement, the *Gesellschaft für Sport und Technik* (GST), the Society for Sport and Technology, with a membership of about 650,000, representing almost two thirds of the nation's fourteen to eighteen-year-old population. The GST functions primarily as a paramilitary organization in which boys and girls learn to drive jeeps, shoot, operate radio transmitters, and parachute. These organizations are financed by the government, have monthly publications, and hold members to an oath of absolute obedience.

The nature of the *Red Guard* movement has greatly changed. Originally used by Mao Tse-tung in the Great Cultural Revolution and the purge of dissident elements, the Red Guard became expendable and was dispatched to the hinterland to work with peasants. An estimated 40 million youths were removed from cities and sent to the countryside to become the "first generation of educated peasants." Rather than adjusting to rural and isolated lives, these millions became a disaffected and potentially subversive mass, ready to follow any leadership that would rescue them from rural exile.

In totalitarian societies, the political philosophy of the state imposes an identity on the younger generation that neutralizes social-structural features containing status-discontinuing potential. Youths in this type of situation do not have a moratorium on identity or commitment. Their commitment is a product of contrivance and persuasion; their identity a carbon copy of mass identity; and their individuality lacks the eventual benefits that come with the struggle of learning personal judgment—an essential part of the adolescent experience. Rather than facing adolescence, the young in these societies are relegated to a socially approved and well organized position such as the "youth of the nation" or "youth of the leader."

To achieve and maintain the mass position, the totalitarian leadership employs a range of stratagems including uniforms, marches, songs, slogans, pageantry, hero worship, oratory, and paramilitary games and plays. Many a national leader (for example Hitler) showed intuitive skill as a social psychologist in manipulating and inspiring masses of young people. The well defined status of youth created clear standards, predictable behavior, rights and obligations that were, or had to be, respected by the community. This public status alleviated, if not eliminated, the crisis of discontinuity between the status of the child and of the adult. As a result, there was an absence of the adolescent symptoms and expressions so typical of the more democratic societies.

Because of modern urban-industrial youths' intense need for clear identity, they can easily fall prey to demagogues' promises, charismatic leaders' calls to action, and the various appeals of "the true belief." The development of many totalitarian regimes was possible because a leader or a power elite had success in winning the enthusiasm and loyalty of the nation's adolescents. Psychiatrist Maurice N. Walsh feels that the rise of Nazi Germany was possible partially because of the National Socialists' success in indoctrinating the nation's adolescents:

> It is a mistake to assume that the Nazis gained control in Germany solely by means of brutality and terror. No one who knows Germany can believe such a myth. Control was gained by seduction, and seduction of adolescents was a powerful tool in preparing the young Germans, through the Hitler Jugend, for their sacrifice in the coming war. Seduction of many of their parents was also carried out, but the older generation is never so easily seduced as is the younger. The reasons reside in the emotional instability of the adolescent, who is passing through a critical period in his emotional life and development.[39]

Pitirim Sorokin's classification of types of societies, or the specific phases through which most societies pass, may be helpful in this context.[40] A society with a salient ideation will find it relatively easy to extend a consistent and logically integrated identity to every member of the social system, even though the immediate social-structural position may lack clarity. This lack of structural specificity may not even be noticed or found disturbing, since the overall cultural identity and the feeling of belonging are ample compensation. Belonging to a national movement may be perceived as a position in its own right—the position of being a member of the totalitarian society. This membership enables the young to satisfactorily answer the question "Who am I?" The situation during the Middle Ages exemplifies the point. Millions of people would have answered the basic question of identity by saying: "I am a member of the Church" or more basically: "I am a child of God." The "true believer," who feels that he or she is a child and envisages a powerful "Father," possesses an identity as strong as or even stronger than any specific social position that he or she could ever occupy.

In effect, the tenets of the religio-cultural ethos were sufficiently meaningful to involve the believing member regardless of social differentiation factors, such as age, position in the division of labor, or socio-economic status. In an *ideational* society, the central creed offers identity and belonging at any phase in the life cycle of the individual.

But societies do not remain forever in the ideational phase. Sorokin's theory holds that the subsequent stage is the *idealistic* period, during which the previously

---

[39] This article first appeared in *The Humanist*, March/April 1967, and is reprinted by permission.

[40] Pitirim A. Sorokin, *The Crisis of our Age: The Social and Cultural Outlook*, (New York: Dutton, 1941).

unambiguous creed breaks up into factions. The religious character of the ideation proliferates into philosophies that are more this-worldly than other worldly. The Renaissance marks the idealistic phase of Western civilization and the weakening of the ideational forces that could have functioned as a check on the development of adolescence. The cultural forces that had extended basic identity lost persuasiveness.

The idealistic period is followed by the *sensate* period, which, according to theory, includes the present. The unified cultural credo has declined, if not disappeared altogether, and rather than being concerned with ideational precepts we are now intent on satisfying immediate sensate cravings. Priority of values and ideas is determined by material and pleasurable results. Cultural norms and values have become nonspecific and allow increased individual freedom. This individual freedom has been held responsible for our current anxiety about, and confused searching for, identity. *The most striking sociological effect of this loss of basic cultural identity is the burdening of the social structure with the demand for an identity that is no longer available from culture.* A shift in identity-genesis has occurred: What the general culture can no longer provide is now expected from specific social positions. This means that members of contemporary society depend more strongly than ever before on a social position for identity. The specific role of a given social position, be it that of an auto mechanic or a physician, has become the core of identity.

Cut off from such social-structural anchors, adolescents tend to suffer problems of identity. Distress symptoms can be observed among the youths who have not yet chosen an occupation and among retired persons who are no longer actively involved in their identity-reinforcing occupation. However, unlike adolescents, the latter can at least draw on an identity associated with years in a given occupation.

Finally, the universality of adolescence in urban-industrial societies can also be challenged on the intranational level. In large modern societies the heterogeneity of the population allows for enclaves within which the young can remain relatively unaffected by the adolescence-inducing elements of the larger society. Not all American teenagers experience the same degree, or for that matter any degree, of adolescence. Young people who experience relative immunity to adolescence usually belong to such ethnic, racial, religious, or socioeconomic groups as the Hutterites, Amish, American Indians, and upper socioeconomic stratum. While the Amish and the Hutterites are nearly totally free of adolescence, the other groups experience adolescence in varying degrees and styles.

While the thrust of this book aims at identifying the typical adolescent experience of the American middle class, deviations from this norm are acknowledged and examined elsewhere.[41]

[41] The limits of this book preclude treatment of the diversity of the adolescent experience, and the interested reader is advised to consult specialized works on racial, ethnic, and other minority groups, as, for example: B. Eugene Griessman, *Minorities* (Hinsdale, Ill.: Dryden, 1975); Elton Long, *American Minorities* (Englewood Cliffs, N.J.: Prentice–Hall, 1975); Dale S. McLamore, *Racial and Ethnic Relations in America* (Boston: Allyn & Bacon, 1980).

SUMMARY

Adolescence refers to the ambiguously defined child/adult interim and has become part of public life in many contemporary societies. It is a period in the life of the young individual when the status of child has vanished and the status of adult is not yet available. Interim ambiguities may reach such an extent that the label *identity crisis* is justified. This crisis, since it is shared with peers, has evolved into the collective compensations we label youth subcultures.

While the definition of *adolescent* is based on the experience of an interim between the statuses of child and adult, the term *juvenile* has legal implications. *Teenager* is more than just a denotation of age; it connotes immaturity and a collective style. *Youth* is a term used broadly to refer to the "younger generation" or to young adults.

Adolescence as a collective phenomenon is nearly universal in the modern world. Some countries exhibit it to a greater degree than others, usually depending on their degree of urban-industrial development. There seems to be a direct correlation between the degree of urban-industrial advancement and the extent of adolescence. Therefore, adolescence should not be described—let alone explained—as an exclusively American characteristic that has spread to other countries, but rather as an outgrowth of certain social and cultural conditions that can be found in many societies today.

Causal conditions of adolescence include the structural disruption of the child-to-adult progression as the *necessary* cause and a weak cultural idiom as the *sufficient* cause. Only when the two conditions coincide can adolescence develop.

Historically speaking, juvenile delinquency is not new. Chroniclers of all ages have commented on this particular youthful problem. However, it was not until the onset of the Industrial Revolution that the social structure made for discontinuity between the statuses. Likewise, it was not until the Renaissance that the ideational forces of medieval Christendom weakened. As a result, the social structure became a more effective source for identity than the general culture.

In the few cases where totalitarian states succeeded in indoctrinating youth with compelling convictions, the social-structural void between statuses was filled with meaning and purpose, and adolescence was prevented. However, in most contemporary urban societies teenagers find themselves in an ill-defined interim: adolescence.

CHAPTER 2

Adolescence:

Its Time and Place

in Personality Development

A social psychological analysis of adolescence must never forget that two parties are involved: on one side is *society*, if not civilization, and on the other side is the *individual*. The parties do not always share identical interests, goals, and needs, but they are intricately interrelated. An investigation aspiring to completeness must attend to both. In the preceding chapter, the societal and civilizational setting was brought into focus. The present chapter shifts levels of examination and focuses on the individual's personality processes as they take place during the adolescent phase of his or her life span. While this appears to be an abrupt change of level, it is justified by the fact that societal and personal realities fail to manifest themselves in identical ways. Hence I feel that both parties must be introduced at the beginning of the book.

Nonetheless, readers or instructors who prefer to continue on a strictly sociological plain or wish to save the discussion of personality processes for later can go from Chapter 1 directly to Chapter 3 and continue with the conditions of postindustrial life. These conditions focus more on social and technological antecedents of adolescence than on personality processes as such.

Among the major processes that occur in personality development are the learning of roles and the crystallization of a personal identity. The stirring of these intimately intertwined elements is at its most intense during adolescence, and this chapter discusses processes that go into the making of the human personality.

THE CONCEPT OF PERSONALITY

The frameworks for referring to personality can range from the biological to the sociocultural. Gordon W. Allport surveyed the professional literature and extracted fifty different definitions of personality.[1] They can be grouped into sociological, biological, psychological, juridical, or cultural categories. For example, E. Faris proposed a sociocultural definition by calling personality "the subjective aspect of culture." Ernest W. Burgess held that "personality is the integration of all the traits which determine the role and status of the person in society. Personality might therefore be defined as social effectiveness." C. H. Prince thought of personality as "the sum-total of all biological innate dispositions, impulses, tendencies, appetites, and instincts of the individual, and the acquired dispositions and tendencies— acquired by experience." Arnold Gesell saw personality as "the pervasive super-pattern which expresses the integrity and the characteristic behavioral individuality of the organism." Allport added that "personality is the dynamic organization within the individual of those psychological systems that determine his unique adjustment to his environment."[2]

These illustrations show that the concept of personality has been used to emphasize appearance, traits determining status, individual uniqueness, sum totals of innate or acquired traits, impulses, dispositions, style of life, adjustment to environment, and the subjective aspect of culture. Since the concept can refer to literally any type of human behavior and is a concern of behavioral scientists of different disciplines, diversity is inevitable. It is hardly possible to synthesize all definitions currently in use. Rather than asking *what* personality is, it might be more fruitful to first determine *which aspect* of personality is to be discussed.

BASIC ASSUMPTIONS OF PERSONALITY THEORY

In spite of the wide terrain covered by the concept of personality, there are a few basic assumptions generally accepted by social psychologists:

Personality as social product. The aspects of personality in which a social scientist is primarily interested are those that are socially learned. The etymology of the word *personality* suggests learned behavior. It is derived from *persona*, which, in Latin, refers to the theatrical mask used by Roman actors in Greek dramas. Allusion to "actor" implies that personality is a product of the social setting, of the social "stage," and not of some biogenetic process.

[1] Gordon W. Allport, *Personality: A Psychological Interpretation* (New York: Holt, Rinehart & Winston, 1973).

[2] Ibid., pp. 25–54.

Personality as process. Personality is continuously affected by new social experiences, so that many behavioral scientists consider it more realistic to think of personality in terms of process than in terms of completed product. One of the reasons why American sociologists are critical of Freudian theory is its heavy emphasis on personality as a product of childhood experiences. Sociologists prefer to think of personality as an ongoing process, constantly patterned and repatterned by social and cultural stimuli. The facile sociological view of personality as a carbon copy of the sociocultural surrounding contrasts with the orthodox psychoanalytic view of personality as the end product of childhood years. Neither view is trustworthy, and the truth probably lies somewhere in the middle.

The findings of one of the very few longitudinal studies ever done on this issue supports the Freudian view. Between 1966 and 1974 the Institute for Social Research at the University of Michigan followed 2000 young men from tenth grade until five years after high school. During that period, researchers conducted five data collections to detect changes in attitudes, aspirations, and self-concepts. Marked differences in self-concept were found between persons who achieved educational and/or occupational success and those who were failures—*but* "these differences were largely in place by the tenth grade." Graduate students' high self-esteem simply mirrored their good self-image as high-school sophomores. Similarly, the poor self-image of the dropouts had existed before they abandoned school. The study also discredited the assumption that education has a powerful socializing effect on students. Racial attitudes are a striking example: "Our study found that racial attitudes were already set by the 12th grade. Something that was supposed to be the effect of college was really set before."[3]

Personality as developmental phases. While psychologists largely agree that personality development does not occur in one big step but rather through certain phases, the specific division, labeling, and interpretation of these phases differ widely. (Compare the differing theories of Sigmund Freud, Carl Rogers, Erich Fromm, Jean Piaget, Erik Erikson, and others).

It is primarily for exemplification that Abraham Maslow's theory of hierarchical needs of human beings is briefly described. According to Maslow, humans exhibit a hierarchy of needs, and their fulfillment must proceed from primary physiological needs (for example, hunger, thirst, temperature control) to secondary needs (safety, protection, stability). After these come needs for affection and social belonging. Beyond these needs are those for self-esteem (success, competence, and independence). Maslow suggested that there is another group of needs he called "metaneeds" or growth needs. They include the need for knowledge, justice, and beauty. Metaneeds are not hierarchical like the basic needs, that is, one can be substituted for another. But they cannot be satisfied before basic needs are satisfied. However, both types must be satisfied, or psychological maladjustment arises.

[3] "Dogmatic Teens, Entrenched Attitudes at an Early Age," *Human Behavior*, October 1978, p. 32.

Maslow believes that the healthy individual progresses from the fulfillment of one need to the next, steadily moving toward self-actualization. A supportive environment is imperative for achieving need fulfillment and resultant self-actualization.[4]

Piaget's theory that all experience is organized by intelligence is another notable example of the idea that personality has discrete developmental phases. Children construct and constantly revise their models of reality, and do so in a regular sequence. Mental growth, according to Piaget, proceeds through four major stages. During the first two years of life, the child is limited to the comprehension of only physical objects. For about the next four years, the child is preoccupied with symbols and the learning of language. Starting around age six, the child comprehends abstractions, masters numbers, and understands relationships. Finally, starting at about thirteen years, the youngster begins to understand purely logical thought and can analyze his own thinking processes. With that ability comes the understanding of double messages contained in irony, satire, double entendre, and aphorism. In explaining human behavior, Piaget would rank midway on the nature-nurture continuum, since he allowed for innate structuring and for biological timing of developmental abilities.[5] Hence he is not sociology's favorite personality theoretician.

Personality as Gestalt. Normal behavior does not consist of unrelated fragments and discrete processes. Separate acts are parts of a response system integrated in a manner lending continuity and meaning to behavior. Gestalt emphasizes the meaningful integration of behavioral elements, using the concept of *Prägnanz* to denote major structural features that offer direction and orientation.

Personality and physiological prerequisites. The development of personality is severely impeded if an individual's brain functions are damaged, unbalanced, or undeveloped. The abnormality can be defined as retardation, feeble-mindedness, or mental illness.

Personality and the primary group. The type of social interaction in which the young individual is enmeshed is of utmost significance to personality formation. If, for example, the primary family environment is disturbed, or partially or totally absent, virtually indelible marks will be impressed on the personality. Kingsley Davis reported on the case of Isabelle, an illegitimate child, who had lived in seclusion with her deaf-mute mother until she was nearly seven years old. When she was discovered, her behavior was that of an unsocialized animal. She had not learned language and could make only inarticulate sounds. At first it was thought she was

---

[4] Abraham Maslow, *Motivation and Personality* (New York: Harper & Row, 1970), and *Toward a Psychology of Being* (Princeton, N.J.: Van Nostrand, 1968).

[5] Jean Piaget, *The Origins of Intelligence in Children* (New York: International Universities Press, 1952), and *The Grasp of Consciousness: Action and Concept in the Young Child* (Cambridge, Mass.: Harvard University Press, 1976).

feeble-minded. However, after careful training, Isabelle was able to progress, join the public school system, and achieve normalcy.[6]

A similar case of a "wild" child came to the attention of social scientists in the 1970s. They tried to rehabilitate "Genie," but succeeded only partially. It appears that if childhood years are not utilized for language development, a certain brain capacity atrophies and later teaching attempts will not rehabilitate it entirely.[7]

Such extreme cases are rare, and presented merely to make a point. There are less extreme instances in evidence every day. For example, subtle personality deficiencies can develop in the thousands of orphans and parent-neglected children who grow up in institutional homes resembling more a secondary than a primary group environment. Observations in the Junior Village at Washington, D.C., revealed that institutional youths suffer from anonymity and fears of abandonment. Educators believe that adult-child verbal exchanges are needed at an early age if the children are to learn the fundamentals of language. However, because the institution was not only crowded but also segregated by age, the two-year-olds could only speak with other two-year-olds. These conditions caused regressions in language skill and physical accomplishments.[8]

A New York study compared children in foster homes who had spent the first two to three years of their lives in an institution with children whose total experience had been in foster homes. The study found that children placed in foster homes after a period of institutional rearing evidenced greater problem behavior than children with complete foster-home experience. Institutionally raised children were found to be less secure, less proficient in entering into relationships, emotionally retarded, and often destructive and cruel without apparent cause.[9]

Another study showed that institution children had great difficulty in adjusting to foster homes. Compared with children who were placed in foster homes immediately after birth, institutionally raised children were more frequently replaced because of problem behavior. "Deviant" and "strange" behavior were the most common reasons for the replacement of such children, while similar symptoms were rare in the exclusively foster-home group. The problems leading to replacements in the institution group can be categorized into (1) aggressive, hyperactive; (2) bizarre and disoriented, and (3) emotionally unresponsive. In addition, institution children displayed greater speech deficiencies, more serious school difficulties, and more frequent mental retardation. The researchers concluded that

[6] Kingsley Davis, "Final Note on a Case of Extreme Isolation," *American Journal of Sociology*, 5 (March 1947), 432–37, and "Extreme Isolation of a Child," *American Journal of Sociology*, 45 (January 1940), 554–65.

[7] Maya Pines, "The Civilization of Genie," *Psychology Today*, September 1981, pp. 28–34.

[8] J. W. Anderson, "A Special Hell for Children in Washington," *Harper's*, November 1965, pp. 51–56.

[9] William Goldfarb, "Infant Rearing and Problem Behavior," *American Journal of Orthopsychiatry*, 13 (April 1943), 249–65.

institutional children tend to remain limited in their intellectual and emotional progress by a fixation on the more primitive levels of abstraction and conceptualization.[10]

Many studies support these findings, maintaining that removal of the primary group environment, normally represented by the family, tends to be detrimental to the personality of the young.[11] Since group environment is so highly instrumental in forming personality, the group's imprint can be traced to even less extreme cases of deprivation than those of institutional children. Research has shown delinquency rates and divorce rates later in life to be significantly higher for children whose family environment has been disturbed by separation or divorce.[12]

REFERENCE GROUP

While it is true that the young child depends heavily on an immediate group environment for physical survival, this does not mean that a young person, once he or she has learned how to relate to abstract ideas and images, must remain on the relatively primitive level of relating only to physically present persons. People's effort to understand themselves and their universe is not limited, although highly influenced, by membership groups. *Direct* physical contact with other persons is not necessary to absorb ideas, philosophies, and religions. An actual example is that of a young man with no social connections to Greeks or corresponding ethnic subgroups in the United States, who decided to embrace Greek Orthodox Christianity. His decision was based not on social interaction but entirely on reading and abstract reflecting.

This example illustrates the difference between the reference group and the membership group. Human ability to abstract can free them from face-to-face interaction for information and acquiring values. The concept of reference group was developed mainly to define the process whereby individuals derive norms and values without necessarily being in physical contact with those persons holding the emulated view. Normally, however, most of a person's membership groups also function

[10] William Goldfarb, "The Effects of Early Institutional Care on Adolescent Personality," *The Journal of Experimental Education*, 12 (December 1943), 106–29.

[11] See R. A. Spitz, "Anaclitic Depression: An Inquiry into the Genesis of Psychiatric Conditions in Early Childhood," in *Psychoanalytic Study of the Child* (New York: International Universities Press, 1946); Lauretta Bender and H. Yarnell, "An Observational Nursery," *American Journal of Psychiatry*, 97 (March 1941), 1158–74; and D. Beres and S. J. Obers, "The Effects of Extreme Deprivation in Infancy on Psychic Structure: A Study in Ego Development," in *Psychoanalytic Study of the Child*.

[12] William J. Goode, "Family Disorganization," in *Contemporary Social Problems*, ed. Robert K. Merton and Robert A. Nisbet (New York: Harcourt Brace Jovanovich, 1961), p. 549, and *The Family* (Englewood Cliffs, N.J.: Prentice-Hall, 1982), p. 166. Daniel Amneus, *Back to Patriarchy*, (Ithaca, N.Y.: Cornell University Press, 1979), p. 18. Michael E. Lamb, "Paternal Influences and the Father's Role," in John Keating, ed., *Social Psychology 82/83* (Guilford, Ct.: Dushkin, 1982), pp. 68–73.

as reference groups. In the cases where the two groups do not coincide, serious conflicts may arise for the person involved in both.

The relationship between adolescent behavior and reference groups is complex. Modern urban-industrial environment offers youth a heretofore unknown number of potential reference groups, and value derivation can proceed through ubiquitous images and models presented in the mass media. As a result of the diversity of reference groups, the adolescent's personality development is beset with a number of complications:

Shifting reference groups. A significant aspect of adolescence is the gradual shift in orientation from teenage standards to adult norms and values. Usually, the adolescent has no choice but to ultimately accept adult behavior patterns.

Multiple reference groups. Often because of personal preference, but more often because of mandatory conditions, the adolescent is involved in a number of membership groups, which usually constitute reference groups at the same time. Examples of such combinations for the adolescent are family, school, church, and peer group.

Sebald and White's 1980 study found teenagers divided on reference groups and unevenly aligned with peers and parents. Suburban high schoolers clung to their peers' advice on matters of whom to date, which clubs to join, how to dress, choice of hobby, and reading material. Only 10 percent or fewer of the teenagers would turn to parents in these matters. (This was particularly true of boys; significant boy-girl differences will be mentioned later.) On the other side, approximately 50 percent sought parental guidance in matters of choosing a career, going to college, and how to spend money. Comparison with 1960 data shows that this juxtaposition has sharpened and nearly polarized, with teenagers of the '70s and '80s drawing distinct demarcation lines as to which issue belongs to which reference group.[13]

Conflicting reference groups. Multiplicity of reference groups frequently leads to conflict. Most conflicts stem from the clash between standards of the peer group and those of the parents. Peers represent a powerful reference group, and researchers have found that the clique's expectations often take precedence over norms and values held by family and adults. "The clique, then, acts as a protective structure which may oppose and evade adult authorities and sanctions."[14]

James S. Coleman, studying high school youth, found considerable conflict when a teenager had to choose between standards of peers and demands of parents.[15] The researcher presented the subjects with a hypothetical situation, asking them what they would do if they were asked to join a particular club to

[13] Hans Sebald and Becky White, "Teenagers' Divided Reference Groups: Uneven Alignment with Parents and Peers," *Adolescence*, 15 (Winter 1980), 979–984.

[14] Ernest A. Smith, *American Youth Culture* (New York: Free Press, 1962), p. 9.

[15] James S. Coleman, *The Adolescent Society* (New York: Free Press, 1963), pp. 138–40.

which they had always wanted to belong but at the same time were faced with a request by parents not to join. The response pattern of the students depended on the type of community in which they lived. Responses, gathered from ten different schools, had between 45 to 80 percent of the boys and 60 to 85 percent of the girls stating that they would probably or definitely not join the club against their parents' wishes. Greatest regard for the parents' demands was shown in the smallest school, in "Farmdale," a rural community; the least regard was apparent in "Executive Heights," a large suburban school. The four schools in which 70 percent or more of the boys preferred the parents' advice and the three schools in which 80 percent or more of the girls chose the parents as reference persons were located in smaller, nonurban communities. The schools in which girls and boys were least willing to conform to parents' ideas were two suburban schools, "Newlawn," a working-class suburb, and "Executive Heights," an upper middle-class suburb. The findings indicate that in "Farmdale" and "Marketville," the two smallest schools in a predominantly rural area, teenagers enter adult responsibilities earlier and are more familistically oriented, while in "Executive Heights," adolescents assume adult responsibilities later and remain more peer-oriented. These differences between a small farm community and an upper middle-class suburb illustrate the differential influence of the adolescent reference group. "Executive Heights" reflects a style of life that is spreading in the United States. "Farmdale" and "Marketville" reflect a more familistic style that seems to be gradually disappearing.

Conflicting reference groups tend to interfere with the formation of a unified and unambiguous self-conception. A young woman, for example, on being accepted into a sorority, may yield to informal pressure and develop modes of conduct like smoking and social drinking that would cause her family's disapproval. Another example would be the conflict experienced by a teenager simultaneously involved in a delinquent gang and in a family of law-abiding parents and siblings, or the conflict caused by holding membership in a religious congregation and at the same time being a member of a delinquent group.

Unclear reference groups. A majority of modern youths experience difficulty in deciding between different, and often incompatible, reference groups, and are frequently torn between them, unable to clearly identify with any single one. This inability to identify completely with any reference group tends to thwart the formation of a clear and stable identity. In a sense, the social environment functions as a mirror showing the person an image of her- or himself. The powerful influence of social repercussion on the person's identity or "self" has been widely accepted as a basic principle of social psychology.[16] If social images are blurred, distorted, or markedly divergent, personality formation will probably reflect these ambiguities.

[16] George H. Mead, *Mind, Self, and Society* (Chicago: University of Chicago Press, 1934), p. 164; Charles H. Cooley, *Human Nature and the Social Order* (New York: Scribner's, 1902), p. 184; and Alfred R. Lindesmith, Anselm L. Strauss, and Norman K. Denzin, *Social Psychology* (New York: Holt, 1977), pp. 312–348.

THE SIGNIFICANT OTHER

One might insist it is not groups and their standards but rather individuals and their attitudes that significantly influence attitudes. Social scientists, in an effort to capture the meaning of this relationship, have suggested the concept of "significant other." H. S. Sullivan[17] first coined this concept and believed that significant persons have decisive influence on the perception (including self-perception) of the socializee. Robert K. Merton also tried to conceptualize this influence and suggested the term "reference person."[18] However, the term can be taken to imply volition, consciousness, and choice of reference on the part of the socializee—an assumption that would limit the application of the concept. The concept of significant other does not convey such limitations and thus allows for a greater variety of types of socializer-socializee relationships.

Those having the greatest impact on personality development are parents. Parental behavior constitutes a potential model for role learning. Since many roles can be learned only by observing others, observability of role enactment is important. In cases of general roles, such as the feminine, masculine, and marital, role taking is largely an informal and unconscious process. Specific roles, such as professional ones, are learned more formally and consciously.

Generally, the young acquire their role perceptions by unconsciously internalizing norms and values reflected by the behavior of models. The importance of this social psychological process can hardly be exaggerated, since role perceptions form the core of one's identity. It is the internalized roles and their degrees of clarity and meaningfulness that make up one's identity. It follows that individuals who are expected to exemplify certain roles possess an immense influence and, to a large extent, bear responsibility for role behavior of the next generation. Role learning and role transmitting may be influenced or disturbed by acts of commission and/or acts of omission. Acts of commission refer to definite instances exhibiting role behavior, such as exerting parental authority, engaging in adult work, and carrying out adult responsibilities. Acts of omission imply absence of exemplification of role behavior, as, for example, chronic father-absence affecting the child. Failure to provide role models is of concern to many behavioral scientists, since role confusion may arise when important norms are neither formally taught nor informally visible. An extreme example would be the feminine self-perception and feminine behavior of young boys whose mothers have served as near-exclusive role models.[19]

Children are highly dependent on their parents' example in acquiring sex role and marital role. These role concepts are part of the cultural heritage; that is, they

---

[17] As reported by Dorothy R. Blitsten, *The Social Theories of Harry S. Sullivan* (New York: William-Frederick Press, 1953), pp. 74–75.

[18] Robert K. Merton, *Social Theory and Social Structure* (Glencoe, Ill.: Free Press, 1957), pp. 302–4.

[19] Paul S. Ullman, "Parental Participation in Child Rearing as Evaluated by Social Deviates," *Pacific Sociological Review*, 3 (Fall 1960), 89–95.

are *learned* ways of behaving and thinking. In many modern societies, the norms that distinguish between masculinity and femininity are no longer as distinct as they were. Vagueness in sex-role definitions and decreasing visibility of parental models have contributed to problems of identity. Young males in the American middle class seem to be particularly vulnerable to the effects of cultural anomie and father-absence. The traditional family—characterized by patriarchal authority, familistic attitudes, and domicile-work combination—has almost vanished in favor of the modern equalitarian family, which emphasizes individualism over familism. Father-absence from the home has become frequent, and the young male has little or no opportunity to observe his father at work. Home life, *at least from the boy's perspective*, has become matriarchal.[20]

Social scientists have disputed the Freudian distinction between love-object and identification-object, preferring to view the relationship between infant and mother as identification and not as love.[21] Thus, learning of cultural norms of masculinity necessitates a shift from the original identification-object—mother—to a culturally more acceptable identification-object—father, or some other adult male image. This is not necessary for the girl. As several social scientists have pointed out, the young female has an initial advantage in progressing toward appropriate sex-role identity.[22] The boy faces a more precarious situation for if he does not make the shift of identification early enough during childhood, it may be difficult for him to achieve a masculine identity. Father-absence complicates the shift in identification, and the boy finds himself learning his role more by trial and error than by consistent imitation. As a result, boys more than girls seek and obtain instruction outside of the family and tend to identify with a general cultural image, or with the male *position* in general, while girls identify with the mother as a *person* and not with an impersonal image or position.

Social scientists seem to agree that physical absence of the father, or presence of a father not providing a clear role model, impedes the development of such traits as independence and achievement orientation.[23] Boys lacking adult role models develop more dependent and submissive personality features. In contrast, father-dominated socialization promotes assertive traits in young males.[24]

[20] Talcott Parsons, "Age and Sex in the Social Structure of the United States," *American Sociological Review*, 7 (October 1942), 604–16.

[21] Orvall H. Mowrer, *Psychotherapy: Theory and Research* (New York: Ronald Press, 1953).

[22] Daniel G. Brown, "Inversion and Homosexuality," *American Journal of Orthopsychiatry*, 28 (April 1958), 424–29; David B. Lynn, "Learning Masculine and Feminine Roles," *Marriage and Family Living*, 25 (February 1963), 103–5; and David B. Lynn, "The Process of Learning Parental and Sex-Role Identification," *Journal of Marriage and the Family*, 28 (November 1966), 466–70.

[23] Talcott Parsons and Robert F. Bales, *Family, Socialization and Interaction Process* (Glencoe, Ill.: The Free Press, 1955); Urie Bronfenbrenner, "Socialization and Social Class Through Time and Space," in *Readings in Social Psychology*, ed. Eleanor E. Maccoby, et al. (New York: Holt, Rinehart & Winston, 1958), pp. 400–425; and Ullman, "Parental Participation in Child Rearing."

[24] Lois W. Hoffman, "The Father's Role in the Family and the Children's Peer Group Adjustment," *Merrill-Palmer Quarterly*, 7 (April 1961), 97–105.

A word of caution: These traditional assumptions and findings must be reconsidered in the light of at least two major developments. First, progress made by the women's liberation movement has modified the traditional role definitions and stereotypical behavior. Hence, future social-psychological research may come up with different findings, necessitating modification of theory. Second, increasing power and scope of exposure to mass media, particularly television, constitute a change in socialization patterns that calls for modification of the conventional assumption that physically present role models are irreplaceable. For example, studies have found little evidence that father-absent boys are more feminine, dependent, and less aggressive.[25] It is possible that mass media heroes increasingly function as objects of identification.

CULTURE AND ROLE LEARNING

Humans are role-learning animals. They lack innate knowledge or feeling as to what their roles are to be and must rely on culture to provide blueprints specifying how to behave in certain places in the social structure. To achieve role skills takes years of effort, persuasion, and even coercion. Much of what is taught meets with initial resistance, for it thwarts the child's natural impulses. Freud expressed a social psychological principle when he said that the id forces must be replaced by the superego, meaning that the unrefined hedonistic approach to gratification must be replaced by culturally acceptable behavior.[26] The time during which this conversion to cultural standards takes place is turbulent and involves emotions of love and hate, conflict and anxiety, rejection and acceptance. Personality emerges not on the basis of the autonomous *action* of the organism, as orthodox instinctivists maintain, nor solely on the basis of the *reaction* to external stimuli, as many behaviorists claim, but on the basis of *interaction* with other individuals.

The human obligation to learn positional blueprints applies even to the most basic roles, such as the sex roles. It would be a misconception to equate biological maleness and femaleness with learned masculinity and femininity. Crosscultural studies reveal that perception of masculinity and femininity depends on cultural definitions. Each culture postulates values and norms, defining actions and interactions of males and females.

Role definitions are premises from which specific actions and reactions can be deduced, thus allowing prediction of behavior. Role premises and their application in everyday life therefore become integral parts of the social order—in fact, the

[25] Hans Sebald, "Parent-Peer Control and Masculine-Marital Role Perception of Adolescent Boys," *Social Science Quarterly*, 49 (September 1968), 229–36; Alan J. Crain and Caroline S. Stamm, "Intermittent Absence of Father and Children's Perception of Parents," *Journal of Marriage and the Family*, 27 (August 1965), 344–47; and Joan McCord, William McCord, and Emily Thurber, "Some Effects of Paternal Absence on Male Children," *Journal of Abnormal and Social Psychology*, 54 (May 1962), 361–69.

[26] See Sigmund Freud's discussion of the repressive and often frustrating aspects of group life in his *Outline of Psychoanalysis* (New York: Norton, 1949), pp. 19, 121.

foundation of social order. For the sake of social order, it does not matter greatly *how* the role premise is formulated, just as long as there is consensus. The variety of formulations is exemplified by natives on some Polynesian islands who virtually reverse Western concepts of masculinity and femininity. Men tend the hearth and the children, while females perform the more strenuous outdoor work.

Definitions often change over time, especially in dynamic urban-industrial societies. Many qualities looked on as strictly masculine or feminine fifty years ago are not considered so today. Such changing conceptions invalidate instruments of behavioral scientists that try to measure sex-differentiation criteria. Examination of one of the earliest (1936) sex-differentiating instruments, the M-F (masculinity-femininity) inventory,[27] shows that many items are no longer relevant in determining masculinity or femininity. Cultural conceptions have been modified — generally in the direction of more diffused standards. One researcher found that in order to devise a valid and reliable instrument applicable today, more than one-half of the test items of the original M-F inventory would have to be discarded or modified.[28]

Learning to interact in terms of social roles is probably the most important function of socialization. To achieve adequate social participation, the young must internalize role prescriptions as cognitive and affective predispositions; that is, they must look at the world in certain ways and experience certain prescribed emotions. A young boy thus comes to see manliness in terms of courage and physical prowess and experiences profound emotional reactions should he be asked, for example, to wear girls' clothes. However, in order to perform any social role adequately, the boy must also be familiar with the other social roles in his environment. Understanding this network of interacting roles has been conceptualized as the "generalized other."[29] Personality grows concomitantly with role understanding. In fact, internalization of roles is almost synonymous with growth of personality, and internalized roles with which one identifies form the core of one's personality, the "self."

To avoid the mistake of looking for sameness of personality features where two individuals have internalized the same roles, it must be emphasized that a role is characterized by *personal* meaning and by the place it occupies among the other internalized roles and attitudes. The motivation it commands in a particular personality will not be the same as in other personalities. Thus the uniform role requirements are modified by idiosyncracies. For example, the role of girl in a given society is part of the cultural blueprint, but the role internalization of any particular girl is a specific variant and more than just a mirror image of the blueprint.

Another way of looking at the process of role internalization is through a theory describing the relationship between social structure and the personality

[27] Lewis M. Terman and Catherine C. Miles, *Sex and Personality* (New York: McGraw-Hill, 1936).

[28] Sebald, "Parent – Peer Control."

[29] Mead, *Mind, Self, and Society*, p. 154.

system as *isomorphic interpenetration.*[30] The theory assumes that cultural norms interpenetrate both the personality system and social structure. In the personality system these norms manifest themselves as motivations, and in the social system they are known as role expectations attached to positions. In an "ideal-type" society, motivations and roles are isomorphic; that is, both exhibit themselves in the same form.

However, "ideal-types" seldom exist in reality. In American society there is considerable confusion concerning the specifics of male and female roles. For example, roles prescribed for college women tend to be contradictory. One study, dealing with college coeds, found that some attitudes necessary for a woman to successfully play the "feminine" role tended to interfere with her performance in the role of "modern" woman with emphasis on efficiency, independence, and self-assertion.[31] At times it is the independent "modern" female who will chafe under the pressure to conform to the "feminine" pattern, while at other times family and college will thrust the "modern" role on the girl. Generally speaking, American culture confronts the young female with powerful challenges to excel in competitive endeavors and to adopt techniques identical to those of the male. Later in life, however, the very success in meeting these challenges can cause frustration. Psychiatric opinion maintains that the early-learned habit of competing with the opposite sex can cause sexual and marital maladjustments as competitive attitudes are carried into the realm of sexual relations.[32]

The American teenager's task of learning basic roles is complicated not only by absence or rejection of visible models, but also by vagueness of role definition. Vague role concepts seem to be related to at least two conditions: (1) Parents suffer from "cultural lag" and have difficulty in conveying role definitions that fit the technological and social environment of their children. (2) The general culture is nonspecific, emphasizing personal choice.

In sum, the American ethos of individual freedom acts as an agent of uncertainty, leaving the young without clearly differentiated sex-role definitions, requiring them to take extra time to search for clarity. The matter of changing roles applies most acutely to today's young women. Their roles are undergoing more alteration than any other role, and this phenomenon merits additional discussion.

CHANGING SEX ROLES

Traditionally, American society, as most societies, has upheld polarized images of male and female each with contrasting attitudes and behavior. But postindustrial conditions have forced people to question these images. Modern science and tech-

---

[30] Talcott Parsons, "Psychology and Sociology," in *For A Science of Social Man*, ed. John Gillin (New York: Macmillan, 1954).

[31] Mirra Komarovsky, "Cultural Contradictions and Sex Roles," *American Journal of Sociology*, 52 (November 1946), 184–89.

[32] Bruno Bettelheim, "Growing Up Female," *Harper's*, October 1962, pp. 120–28.

nology have affected the traditional division of labor between the sexes and brought about a reconsideration of thinking in terms of two essentially different lifestyles. The women's liberation movement feels that there is neither biological nor social justification for dividing humanity into feminine and masculine categories. The movement gained momentum to the point where many young Americans, especially young women, abandoned stereotypical role behavior.

What is happening in essence is rejection of age-old cultural blueprints, according to which previous generations have patterned their interaction, and inauguration, at least during the transitional stage, of a pronounced degree of interpersonal anomie.

Reference to a "transitional stage" raises the question of what the end (or next) stage will be. In other words, what will be the nature of human interaction after the typical sex-role interaction has been abandoned or radically modified? The answer emphasizes a nonsexist style of *human* interaction expected to replace a sex-stereotyped lifestyle. Some find this starkly individual-centered prospect utopian, while others defend it only as feasible and necessary.

Whatever the future, at this time there is a significant eroding of the traditional stereotypes. Sex-role blueprints have become blurred, and prediction of a person's behavior on the basis of gender is no longer as reliable as it used to be.

The brunt of the change has been felt by the female. While the traditional role of the male has changed little (the old masculine rigidity is largely still with us), the female role has undergone considerable reorientation. A number of important laws have been instrumental in furthering change in the female role, the most obvious being those concerning equality in employment, income, education, and training. Other changes are manifested by the blossoming of daycare centers and the greater emphasis being placed on bipartisan child-rearing.

One of the most telling indicators of women's changing role has been sexual liberation and the erosion of the traditional double standard. The sexual revolution was much more real for the female than for the male. Several studies support this contention. For instance, while the percentage of college men having premarital sexual intercourse increased between 1965 and 1975 from 65 to 74 percent the college women's percentage increased from 28 to 57 percent.[33] The Zelnik and Kantner surveys corroborate these findings and show that between 1971 and 1979 premarital intercourse for teenage girls increased from about 30 to 50 percent. In addition, *frequency* of intercourse had significantly increased. Mostly as a consequence of growing numbers of teenage girls becoming sexually active, the premarital pregnancy rate doubled between 1971 and 1975, going from 8 to 16 percent.[34]

While the majority of studies still report higher rates of premarital intercourse for men, a few studies have found women outrating men. For example, the 1975

---

[33] K. King et. al., "The Continuing Premarital Revolution among College Coeds," *Journal of Marriage and the Family*, 39 (1977), 455–459.

[34] "Contraception," *Psychology Today*, November 1980, pp. 100–101.

Jessor and Jessor study discovered 85 percent of college women but only 82 percent of college men as having had premarital intercourse.[35] The 1972 Sarrel and Sarrel survey reports 75 percent of the college women compared with 62 percent of the men as having had premarital coitus.[36]

Other indicators of women's sexual liberation include growing numbers of women opting for cohabitation instead of marriage. The Glick and Norton analysis of US Census Bureau data shows that two million persons cohabitated in 1977, 80 percent more than in 1970.[37] Single status, alone or in cohabitation, has become a real alternative to marriage in the United States. In fact, Peter Stein's study found the prevailing theme among the young to be that marriage was "a restriction and obstacle to human growth." A significant number of young women believed that "one central relationship as an exclusive source of emotional support and social identity was both unrealistic and confining."[38]

Most postindustrial societies exhibit similarly liberal sexual standards. For example, a 1979 survey of Swedish women married since 1971 showed that 99 percent of them had cohabitated prior to getting married.[39] The Allensbach Institute for Opinion Polling in West Germany found that premarital coitus among German women under age thirty-one rose from 61 percent in 1963 to 96 percent in 1978; the rate for German teenagers under age seventeen rose from 10 to 30 percent during that same period. Finally, heightened expectations and corresponding feelings of deprivation brought on by liberalization are reflected in the decrease of marital satisfaction among German women: while in 1949 62 percent of the wives were "very satisfied" with their marriages, in 1978 only 36 percent felt that way.[40]

Another area in which the young woman has changed is in her competition with men. Traditionally, the female tried to understate her intellect and tone down "success" when compared with men. Psychologists termed this attitude "fear of success." Presumably this fear was motivated by fear of deviating from the cultural blueprint, which stressed noncompetition and nonaggression vis-à-vis men. Traditional sex roles had tasks divided in such a fashion that competition was minimal. Postindustrial conditions, however, have brought the sexes closer together in career possibilities and allowed men and women to compete against each other.

[35] S. Jessor and R. Jessor, "Transition from Virginity to Nonvirginity among Youth: A Socio-psychological Study over Time," *Developmental Psychology*, 11 (1975), 473–484.

[36] L. Sarrel and P. Sarrel, "The College Subculture," in M. S. Calderone, ed., *Sexuality and Human Values* (New York: Association Press, 1974), pp. 71–84.

[37] Paul C. Glick and Arthur J. Norton, *Marrying, Divorcing and Living Together in the US* (Washington, D.C.: Population Reference Bureau Inc., 1977).

[38] Peter J. Stein, "Singlehood: An Alternative to Marriage," *The Family Coordinator* 24 (October 1975), 493.

[39] "Sexuality," *Psychology Today*, February 1980, p. 104.

[40] AP Report, July 24, 1978.

Two related studies explored role diffusion and the connected anxieties in a sample of medical students in the 1960s[41] and early 1970s.[42] Whereas the earlier study found that 65 percent of the women had "fear of success" as compared with 10 percent of the men, the more recent study (using the same variables and the same school) found, somewhat puzzlingly, an unchanged percentage of the women but now 77 percent of the men afflicted with achievement anxiety. Details of the study disclosed, however, that the nature of "fear of success" was essentially different between the sexes. While for women the motive to avoid success was in both studies primarily based on the fear of experiencing social rejection or being found unfeminine, for the men the motive was primarily the questioning of the value of the achievement per se, especially in regard to academic and professional success. This type of anxiety had not been found in the 1965 study. Since the follow-up study was conducted in|1971, at the height of countercultural agitation, the heightened sense of questioning the traditional masculine role, the old career definition, and materialism in general may well have been reflected in the phenomenal increase in men's fear of success.

The philosophical base for men's fear of success was apparently still solid after the counterculture years. A late 1970s study supported the earlier findings of women's fear being based on personal-relational considerations, while men's fear was more abstract and philosophical. The latter feared their lives might become one-sided and unfulfilled and that they might sacrifice humanitarian concern for self-advancement.[43]

Woman's fear of success was more narrowly based and dealt with fear of affiliative loss, specifically with the fear of being rejected by peers. These peers were mostly female associates (roommates, friends) and so, unlike males, anxiety arose more from same-sex ingroup relations than from female-male interaction or competition. This finding introduces a sour note to the hopes of the women's liberation movement since serious obstacles to the free unfolding of talent are apparently generated *within* the female peer group and not necessarily (at least not directly) from the outside by a male group. It seems the Trojan horse of the women's movement is their own in-group.

That women's fear of success is no longer (if it ever was) determined by overwhelming concern as to how they might appear to men is illustrated by Mirra Komarovsky's longitudinal study comparing attitudes of the 1950s with those of the 1970s. In response to the question "When on dates how often have you pre-

[41] Matina Horner, "The Motive to Avoid Success and Changing Aspirations of College Women," in *Readings on the Psychology of Women*, ed. J. Bardwick (New York: Harper & Row, 1972), pp. 62–67.

[42] Lois W. Hoffman, "Fear of Success in Males and Females: 1965 and 1971," *Journal of Consulting and Clinical Psychology*, 42 (June 1974), 353–58.

[43] Phoebe K. Schnitzer's study reported in *Human Behavior*, August 1977, pp. 51–52. Another study, surveying 20,000 teenagers, corroborates that girls indeed are consistently more interpersonally and affiliatively oriented, have more empathy for their friends, and place greater emphasis on sociability; Daniel Offer, Eric Ostrov, and Kenneth I. Howard, *The Adolescent: A Psychological Self-Portrait* (New York: Basic Books, 1981), pp. 75, 95f.

tended to be intellectually inferior to the man?" 32 percent reported "very often," "often," or "several times," 26 percent reported "once or twice," and 42 percent said "never" in 1950, as compared with 15 percent, 30 percent, and 55 percent respectively in 1971.[44]

Indeed, a study in the early 1980s discovered a new trend in which men, *not* women, tended to more often play "dumb" and knowingly underplay their intelligence and knowledgeability. The findings showed that more men than women underplayed their intelligence in almost all situations, including interactions with friends, strangers, bosses, coworkers, dates, and children. Understating was most common among persons with more education and high-status careers.[45]

This finding radically deviates from results of previous studies, in which women were consistently found to fake inferior capabilities. Further research is needed to establish whether this indeed is a reversal of a gender-differentiated attitude and whether it is perhaps a sort of male "reaction formation" to changes in women's roles.

Yankelovich's national survey corroborated the trend visible in the above mentioned studies. For example, the traditional image of what it means to be a man seems to have undergone a change in the eyes of young adults. The old emphases on "good masculine looks," "physical strength," and "being handy around the house" come in last in a list of twelve qualities. The new major preferences heading the list are (1) concern with the sexual satisfaction of the woman, (2) the ability to be a good economic provider, and (3) having strong moral views about what is right and wrong.[46]

Similarly, the view of women's role has undergone change. In a four-year follow-up study of college students, a marked decline in the endorsement of a traditional role definition for women was found. At the time of entry into college in 1967, a national sample of freshmen were asked their opinions concerning the statement "The activities of married women are best confined to the home and family." At that time, 66 percent of the men and 44 percent of the women indicated agreement ("agree strongly" or "agree somewhat"). A resurvey of the same respondents in 1972 showed a sharp decline in endorsement of the traditional position, with only 30 percent of the men and 15 percent of the women agreeing with it.[47]

Statistics indicate that young women are also catching up with men in areas that are eminently destructive—signaling, possibly, that they are now exposed to the same tensions typical of the male role. Such tensions lurk particularly in urban

[44] Mirra Komarovsky, "Cultural Contradictions and Sex Roles: The Masculine Case," *American Journal of Sociology*, 78 (January 1973), 873–84, and *Dilemmas of Masculinity: A Study of College Youth* (New York: Norton, 1976).

[45] Michael Hughes and Walter G. Gove, "Playing Dumb," *Psychology Today*, 15 (October 1981), 74.

[46] Daniel Yankelovich, *The New Morality: A Profile of American Youth in the 1970s* (New York: McGraw–Hill, 1974), p. 39.

[47] Alan E. Bayer et al., "Four Years After College Entry," *ACE Research Report*, 8 (Washington, D.C.: American Council on Education, 1973).

centers. For instance, metropolitan areas across the country have experienced a phenomenal rise in the female suicide rate during the decade of the mid 1960s to the mid 1970s. Los Angeles County, for example, reported that the suicide rate for males under twenty years of age went from 3 to 10 per 100,000 population, a more than threefold increase. However, for females in the same age group the change was from .4 to 8, a twentyfold increase. Similarly, while the suicide rate for males between twenty and thirty years of age slightly more than doubled, the rate for females of the same age increased over fourfold.[48] Girls particularly vulnerable to suicide were "those whose fathers have been either uncaring or long absent from home, and first-born girls, particularly those with younger brothers."[49]

However, it must be noted that the mid 1970s ushered in a general downward trend in suicide for both males and females. It can only be speculated whether this change, coinciding with the fading of the counterculture and the cooling of collective dissidence, had anything to do with the steadying of the collective mood of young Americans and the beginning of a less disturbed period in American life.

An "empathic ecological explanation" of the fluctuations of suicide rates was offered by psychiatrist Daniel Offer and his coworkers, who studied the suicide rate among adolescents over several decades. They hit upon a significant positive correlation between adolescent suicide rates and changes in the proportion of adolescents in the U.S. population. Apparently, density of youth population is significant insofar as "it may be more difficult for an adolescent to gain a sense of self-worth and to find friends in the large impersonal high schools of today than in the smaller schools of the past."[50] The researchers suspect that an isolated and depressed youth may interpret his or her efficiently bubbling environment as a sign that everybody is functioning fine while he or she is not. Observing seemingly well-functioning peers, and assuming they are such without knowing for certain, may further lower already low and vulnerable self-confidence and push him or her into withdrawal. A resulting sense of hopelessness may plunge the youth into attempted or completed suicide.

The ecological explanation may explain why suicides in urban centers are strikingly higher than elsewhere. It may specifically explain the extreme increases in suicides among women in urban settings. Persons with greater affiliative and relational needs — as women are found to have according to pertinent studies — may react more acutely to urban isolation.

In addition, the Offer team found that girls consistently feel worse about themselves on *all* self-image scales, particularly on the self-esteem scale.[51] As if that were not enough, the girls of the 1970s surveys felt worse than those in the 1960s surveys. It is possible that the generally worsening self-image of young

[48] "Young Suicides," *Society*, 9 (June 1972), p. 12.

[49] Pamela Cantor's research at Boston University reported in *Time*, January 3, 1972, p. 57.

[50] Offer, Ostrov and Howard, p. 124.

[51] ibid., p. 95.

women, for whatever reason, contributes to the "catching up" with the male suicide rate.

Another conspicuous symptom of changing life conditions of the American woman is reflected in the number of violent crimes performed by women, which has increased at rates six and seven times greater than that of crimes of violence committed by men. Rutgers University Professor of Criminal Justice Freda Adler did a study of the impact of political and social changes on the criminality of women and found that the "new woman" in crime — from the liberated prostitute to the revolutionary terrorist — is responsible for the striking ascent of the female crime rates especially in homicide, armed robbery, embezzlement, and aggravated assault.[52]

On the positive side of the women's liberation movement, an influx into formerly male-dominated training and professions, such as medicine, dentistry, law, engineering, and politics, has been noted. For example, female enrollment in medical schools increased from 13 percent in 1972 to about 25 percent in the fall of 1974, and more male than female medical students are dropping out during the first crucial year. Similarly, female enrollment in law schools has progressively increased, from 3.6 percent in 1960 to 9.3 percent in 1971 to 20 percent in 1974. The American Bar Association reported that the proportion of practicing female attorneys is sharply increasing, rising from 2.8 percent in 1972 to 7 percent in 1975.[53]

While an upswing in female careerism was sharply noticeable during the early 1970s, the late 1970s and the early 1980s have seen a slowing down of this trend. Taking the decade of the '70s as a whole, nearly all careers experienced increases in the percentage of female participants. Here are a few examples:

Engineers, .8 to 2.9
Lawyers and judges, 3.6 to 12.4
Physicians, dentists, and related practitioners, 9.3 to 11.9
Social scientists, 21.3 to 34.5
Managers and administrators, 17.6 to 24.6
Construction laborers, .5 to 2.7
Truck drivers, .6 to 2.1[54]

Female influx into professional careers is significantly encouraged by educational achievement — a relationship illustrated by the diminishing differential in male/female completion of higher education. For example, in 1950, 329,000 men

[52] Freda Adler, *Sisters in Crime: The Rise of the New Female Criminal* (New York: McGraw–Hill, 1975).

[53] "Women: Still Number Two but Trying Harder," *Time*, May 26, 1975, pp. 40–41.

[54] *Statistical Abstracts of the United States*, 101st ed. (Washington, D.C.: U.S. Dept. of the Census, 1980), pp. 418–420.

and 103,000 women earned Bachelor's degrees, the difference being 206,000. The difference has consistently decreased since then, and in 1978 it amounted to only 53,000, with 487,000 men and 434,000 women obtaining college degrees.[55]

The essence of the ongoing changes seems to be that many young women are no longer playing the traditional female role but are working out various types of role combinations and innovations. Teenage girls demand a great deal more than just marriage and motherhood. While they expect to experience some aspects of the old domestic role (spouse, children, home), they *also* want to complete their education and pursue a meaningful career. Hence the erstwhile dilemma of choosing between one or the other lifestyle is now replaced by the dilemma of trying to combine both. To come to grips with this expanded lifestyle, today's young women must be goal-directed, self-assertive, and highly adaptable. In order to make the combination of instrumental and expressive roles a creative and happy experience, young women must learn to cope with the tension and confusion that role experimentation usually produces and must be resourceful enough to resolve conflict.[56]

A suggestion was offered by educator Susanne M. Shafer on how to overcome difficulties of role combinations. She suggested a sequential model, whereby girls should plan their lives in phases, for example, school, work experience, career choice, college, marriage, motherhood, reeducation, and reentry into productive work.[57]

The 1980s have seen increasing numbers of women align themselves with this theoretical model. However, some significant deviations are emerging. After college, more and more women prefer to firmly establish themselves in a career, pursue it for an *extended* period, and finally, in their thirties or even forties decide on motherhood—with or without benefit of being married. The proportion of women aged 25 to 29 years who are still childless has jumped sharply. For example, among women born in 1950 (the cohort of 1950), 25 percent had had no children as of 1980 at age thirty, compared with just 14 percent for comparably aged women born ten years earlier. The rate for mothers in their thirties having a first child increased 66 percent, rising from 7.3 first births per 1000 women aged 30 to 34 in 1970 to 12.1 in 1980. The rate for women aged 35 to 39 rose by 33 percent during this period, from 1.8 to 2.4. The steady increase in first-birth rates for women in their thirties has occurred at a time when birth-rates for women of other ages have generally fallen, including rates for the traditionally high first-birth categories of women in their teens and early twenties. The desire of many women to complete their education and become established in a career appears to be the important factor in accounting for the high levels of postponed childbearing. In 1979, nearly half of the

---

[55] *Statistical Abstract of the United States* (Washington, D.C.: Government Printing Office, 1980), p. 165.

[56] See extensive treatment: David R. Matteson, *Adolescence Today: Sex Roles and the Search for Identity* (Homewood, Ill.: Dorsey, 1975).

[57] Susanne M. Shafer, "Adolescent Girls and Future Career Mobility," in Robert E. Grinder, ed., *Studies in Adolescence* (New York: Macmillan, 1975), pp. 114–125.

first-time mothers aged thirty to thirty-four had completed four or more years of college, compared with just 28 percent in 1970.[58]

These postcareer mothers tend to treat motherhood as a sort of second career and attach the dimensions of careerism to the motherhood experience. As a consequence, the child is often metamorphized into a "project" that must prove "successful motherhood" just as the preceding career was meant to yield success and self-realization. It would be worthwhile to speculate whether or not these post-career mothers will swell the ranks of those mothers who have come to be defined as "momistic."[59]

While it is true, as we said initially, that the male role has hardly changed, the male nevertheless has had to make adjustments to the more liberated female role. While his options have not changed, those of women have, and the man must adjust to them. Women, on the other side, may evolve their options without needing to consider a changed male role. Their task is to expand their role, and men's task is to adjust. Both tasks require time and patience, and will inevitably produce their share of confusion, frustration, and even animosity.

Mirra Komarovsky introduced the findings of an important study on men's role perceptions by acknowledging that "gender roles today reflect massive institutional and cultural disorganization."[60] She found that although most college men idealistically espouse men's liberation, just as they support women's liberation, they suffer from a dilemma she calls a "double bind." While the young men seem to genuinely favor women's liberation and express a verbal and ideological commitment to it they experience apparent difficulties in translating this idealism into reality—and, all the while, are unaware of the gap between ideal and real. The double bind arises when they desire a partner who is an equal but who, at the same time, never threatens them or has divergent or contradictory needs—an equal, in short, who is willing to be subordinate. However, by definition, once a woman subordinates herself she is no longer an equal. This contradiction manifests itself in such incongruous expectations as men wanting women to pursue a challenging and creative career, but simultaneously assuming that she will leave her career upon the birth of the first child and, from then on, be a full-time mother and homemaker. Komarovsky concludes that the path of men toward "liberation" is infinitely more complex than that of a mere "escape" from the traditional male role.

In view of the adjustments men have to make, the findings of a study scrutinizing what happens when young men and women meet are pertinent. Overriding the traditional assumption that achieving men and expressive women get along better with each other than men and women whose personalities are less complementary, the study found that it is the androgynous man and the androgynous woman (measured on the sex-role scale by Stanford University psychologist Sandra

---

[58] U.S. Department of Health and Human Services, *Monthly Vital Statistics Report*, 31 (May 27, 1982).

[59] Hans Sebald, *Momism – The Silent Disease of America* (Chicago: Nelson-Hall, 1976).

[60] Mirra Komarovsky, *Dilemmas of Masculinity: A Study of College Youth* (New York: Norton, 1976), p. 2.

Bem) who, when meeting a person for the first time, prove more flexible, communicative, and rewarding. Androgynous people among a sample of college students talked, gestured, smiled, and looked at each other more often than did the traditionally male and female people. The researchers concluded that androgyny makes for more comfortable interaction.[61] However, the study does not conclude that this initially more comfortable interaction will necessarily result in predictable interaction later on.

From this data follows a number of implications for the new man-woman interaction: (1) A decrease in predictability of how one or the other party will act; (2) an increase in the necessity to establish a self-definition that is not merely grounded in gender identity; and (3) a demand to base decisions not on rigid role images but on genuine personal feelings and preferences.

In summary, the modern teenage girl will be exposed to a score of changes and will have to orient herself accordingly:

1. She will experience a decrease in the protection traditionally accorded to women and will be more "on her own" than her mother's generation. As a transitional temptation, she may attempt to juggle the old and the new roles to her advantage – often unfairly so.
2. She will be faced with a rapid increase of options and can expand her preferences nearly infinitely. This includes possibilities in professional careers, education, and lifestyles. Within the latter, she is able to choose among the single status, marriage, family, divorce, abortion, birth control, cohabitation, and so forth.
3. She will be faced with a vastly more complex life that is based less on predictable, rigid blueprints and more on uniquely personal encounters and feelings. The skill to make personal decisions will demand independent thinking.
4. She will become involved in an intense search for her true self, since a cultural matrix based on gender will no longer spell out her identity.
5. She will experience a definite increase in demands on her intellect and responsibility. Having to make independent decisions calls for knowledge, insight, and accountability for the consequences.
6. She will have to learn to cope with increasing frustration and anxiety. While frustrations due to inequality will decrease, frustrations due to life's complexity and the loss of the security of the old role will more than replace the old frustrations.

IDENTITY: MORATORIUM, DIFFUSION, AND MULTIPLE PERSONAE

The core of personality is self-perception and the answer to the fundamental question, "Who am I?" This question directly challenges the person's identity – in fact, predicates it. It is a question that can be examined on at least two levels: (1) On the

[61] William Ickes and Richard Barnes, "Boys and Girls Together – and Alienated," *Journal of Personality and Social Psychology*, 36 (July 1978), 669–683.

personal, psychological level; and (2) on the social, if not civilizational, level. The psychological examination dwells directly on an individual and limits itself to his or her self-perception, possibly including the history thereof. The sociological examination explores the larger social and societal processes that influence identity formation, trying to show how societal conditions pattern identity processes in such a pervasive manner as to produce similar identity residues in members of society. This is the search for possibly endemic features in the identity Gestalts — a search in harmony with the goal of sociology to validly generalize. The following discussion explores these two approaches and relates them to the adolescent phase in the life cycle. Erik H. Erikson, in the context of ego-psychoanalytic theory, believes that the development of identity is the distinctive psychosocial task of adolescence.[62]

The psychological approach. James E. Marcia's definition of identity refers to "an existential position, to an inner organization of needs, abilities, and self-perceptions as well as to a sociopolitical stance."[63] He links this definition to four basic identity statuses: (1) *Identity achievement* refers to individuals who have mastered a decision-making period and have self-chosen pursuits and ideological goals. (2) *Foreclosure* pertains to people who are also committed to occupational and ideological positions, but whose decisions were made for them by parents and other authorities. They show little evidence of going through or having gone through a "crisis." (3) *Identity diffusion* is experienced by youth who have no set occupational or ideological orientation, regardless of whether or not they went through a decision-making period. (4) *Moratorium* describes persons struggling with occupational and/or ideological issues and being in an identity crisis. The typical identity statuses experienced during adolescence in America are moratorium and identity diffusion. In line with the life span theory (as introduced in Chapter 1), enactment of these two statuses, or a mixture thereof, is virtually expected of young Americans today. A host of personality characteristics of these statuses were discovered by psychological research, and some examples are presented here.[64]

Typical emotional symptoms of identity diffusion and moratorium are anxiety and low self-esteem. Moratorium youth, predictable from their "in-crisis" position, are the most anxious and foreclosure youth the least anxious. Identity-diffused teenagers displayed the widest discrepancy between self-concept and the concept of how others perceived them. Identity development seems to be correlated with the development of moral reasoning, and it was found that youth with a more definite sense of identity had a clearer sense of ethics and empathy than identity-diffused individuals. In the area of intellectual performance, identity-

---

[62] Erik H. Erikson, "Identity and the Life Cycle," *Psychological Issues*, 1 (1959), Monograph #1; *Childhood and Society* (New York: Norton, 1963); *Identity: Youth and Crisis* (New York: Norton, 1968).

[63] James E. Marcia, "Identity in Adolescence," in Joseph Adelson, ed., *Handbook of Adolescent Psychology* (New York: Wiley, 1980), pp. 159.

[64] ibid., pp. 159–187.

achieved individuals showed better study habits and achieved higher grades than individuals in other identity statuses. A study of college dropouts showed that identity-diffused students usually dropped out because of low grades, while identity-achieved individuals left for more positive and self-initiated reasons. Moratorium individuals and identity-diffused individuals frequently manifest divergent traits, probably because moratorium individuals had a higher sense of identity. For example, in terms of cultural sophistication (interest in art, music, and literature), the moratorium individuals were clearly superior. The Eriksonian hypothesis that intimacy ability depends on a stable identity has been substantiated by research disclosing that identity-diffused persons score lowest on intimacy scales and are least self-revealing in intimacy tasks.

Studies have also revealed interesting gender differences: (1) In contrast to men, the level of identity diffusion among college women was as great in the senior year as it had been in the freshman year; that is, women showed less evidence of a regular progression toward identity achievement. (2) Among moratorium youth, boys appear to be engaged in an inner struggle to free themselves from their mothers' influence (if not domination). In general, moratorium youth seem to be less willing to give in to their parents than individuals in other statuses. (3) Identity-diffused boys seem to come from families with active mothers and passive fathers; identity-diffused girls come from families with the pattern reversed. (4) As a general rule, the primary concerns of most adolescent girls are not with occupation and ideology, but with the establishment and maintenance of interpersonal relationships. On the other hand, boys aim at life decisions that frequently lead to interpersonal conflict with family and authority. Experiencing such conflict often is an identity-confirming event for boys, but not for girls. Girls tend to see themselves as having failed if they do not succeed in establishing the all-important relationships and, hence, conflict proves confusing and stunting to their identity process.

While these separate psychological studies do not yet add up to a complete portrait of the adolescent identity status, they at least give us an idea of what is going on during that phase.

The sociological approach. This approach to the understanding of identity dwells on the larger sociocultural conditions and, in its social-psychological slant, tries to identify how these conditions impinge on the personality. Sociologists assume that personality in general and personal identity in particular are influenced by our reference groups, significant others, and the roles we derive from our cultural heritage. The crucial point at which all these influences converge and culminate is the guiding principle of personality: the basic identity. The personal identity is the agent that must be known, or at least sensed, before actions, reactions, and motivations of a person can be understood.

Adolescence is the time when the basic question "Who am I" is asked with unrelenting force and insistence and when reference groups, significant others, and roles are avidly scanned in an attempt to derive a meaningful answer. Hence, the answer intimately depends on these social and cultural involvements, and the unique nature of the involvements contributes to the unique nature of the individual personality. If, then, we want to make sense of modern adolescents and understand their identity, or relative lack of it, we must examine the nature of these sociocultural conditions.

The *traditional* social psychological theory of the process of identity formation contains a number of assumptions. It maintains, first, that identity is a holistic phenomenon that normally is relatively integrated and is grounded in a few fundamental precepts held by the person; second, that clarity and comfort with which an individual views him- or herself depend on how clear and free of conflict the important sociocultural conditions were to which the youth was exposed; and third, that a person's behavior patterns are thoroughly influenced, if not determined, by how the person perceives him- or herself. If the sociocultural conditions surrounding the young during the period of socialization do not add up to a unitary lifestyle without inconsistency and conflict, then failure to produce a unitary identity is anticipated. Such failure used to be judged as "pathology" of both the social environment and the personality troubled by ongoing identity crisis.

Earlier writers, concerned with the relationship between social interaction and personality formation, made an understandable assumption of their time; namely, that the various roles a person carries out are compatible. James M. Baldwin, Charles Cooley, George H. Mead,[65] and others took as their point of departure the small community where a member was known as a total person and whose actions exhibited logical and ethical coherence. These notions of personality growth presupposed the small-town environment characteristic of nineteenth-century America, where the primary group was the consistent and almost exclusive influence on the development of the social nature of the individual. These early social psychologists described the rise of the social self as the process of taking over integrated sets of attitudes by way of role-playing, role-taking, and internalization of the "generalized other." The product of this process was normally an integrated personality system.

Although contemporary social psychologists usually agree with the logic of this learning principle, they believe that since the social environment has undergone significant structural changes, the process and product of personality development have also changed. The typical socialization environment of the urban-industrial era is no longer the small, intimate community where a basic set of values and norms was the orienting force; it is now the anonymous city, with compartmentalized positions and roles no longer uniformly coordinated by a value premise. The typical member of modern society no longer develops a uniform outlook on life, but rather learns situational ways of solving problems. Absence of an overall personality premise is related to what psychiatrists have come to define as "problems of identity." Since role performances normally have formative impact, absence of coherence among the roles an individual enacts can result in lack of sufficient

[65] James M. Baldwin, *Social and Ethical Interpretations in Mental Development* (New York: Macmillan, 1897); Cooley, *Human Nature and the Social Order*; and Mead, *Mind, Self, and Society*.

Prägnanz (major structural dimensions) in a personality *Gestalt*. Uncertainty about one's place in life has a concomitant reflection in one's self-perception.

Max Lerner sees modern Americans engaged in intense search for models and called the symptoms of this groping the "neurosis of the ego."[66] Lerner assumes that this type of mass neurosis is a novel symptom of Western people and quite different from previous mass problems. A previous endemic neurosis of Western civilization was the "neurosis of the id and the superego," which arose primarily from the patriarchal family setting in Europe, with its strict values and discipline, causing widespread repression of personal desires. In other words, while the causality of the modal European neurosis lay in patriarchal authoritarianism prompting various types of repression, the more recent American problem lies in the lack of models and compelling convictions.

The reason for the lack of personal models can be traced to the nature of modern social structure, which contains discrete and almost mutually isolated sets of interaction. Performing on various and often incompatible "stages" of social life has been described in terms of "off-stage" and "on-stage," "team," "script," "front," "audience," and "performance." These terms of the theater can easily be translated into social-structural concepts, such as positions, private vs. public, group, role, social behavior, the public, and role enactment. Use of dramaturgical imagery paints a vivid picture of modern persons as multi-*personae*, as opportunists, supersensitive to every ephemeral demand in the social environment.

Life in society is described as analogous to an infinite array of different "stage plays" where every social situation calls for its own script and character. The individual who is the character must keep one set of motives secret from the other. He or she compartmentalizes not only conduct but also the *reasons* for it. There is always a different audience; there is always a different set of actors; and, finally, there are always different goals and different motivations. The purpose of the performance is to influence others and gain success. This is usually done cooperatively by a team under the management of impressions. Hence, according to a number of modern sociologists, in lieu of the concept of the self as an autonomous moral agent or as the humanistic person of taste, the self is now viewed as an opportunistic agent observing, at best, purely discretionary rules.

It is easy to see that according to the traditional theory most modern youths suffer from lack of unitary identity, since the sociocultural environment in post-industrial America is not unitary and integrated. What are some of the modern features that cause the lack of unitary environment? One trait, ubiquitous in the lives of nearly all young Americans, is the mass media, especially television.

Most characters of the mass media exert influence on development of personality traits in an extremely situational fashion; that is, they depict situations that are often unrealistically isolated from the overall life context of the person portrayed. Limited character portrayal is responsible for a novel type of learning.

[66] Max Lerner, *America as a Civilization* (New York: Simon & Schuster, 1957), pp. 694–97.

Instead of presenting a holistic "significant other," whose various actions follow logically from basic values and norms, enabling generalization and prediction about other possible actions, the mass media present characters who exhibit behavior forms applicable to only a specific situation. In effect, the model depicts only a *situation* and not a total person. A child continuously exposed to the mass media tends to adopt such situational styles of problem solving and, as a result, may come to exhibit incompatible behavior forms. In crisis situations the youth may recall a style of problem-solving that was shown by the hero or the successful villain of the mass media, and he or she may be induced to act accordingly. Hence the manner of solving a problem in one moment may be logically and morally incongruent with the manner of solution in another moment, since they are not derived from a common premise. The overly influenced youth, who has only minimal live models, tends to have no common premise but only unrelated stereotypes by which to determine solutions.

In a sense, the youth behaves like a different person in each situation, and the question of who the "real" person is becomes hypothetical. The youth is equipped with a number of different *personae*, which can change from situation to situation with no one *persona* more important than any other.

Lest this type of individual be confused with an abnormal or mentally disturbed person, it should be emphasized that reference is being made to the normal member of society, very much the same sort of person whom David Riesman described as the other-directed personality, who presumably is the prevailing personality type in modern American society.[67] Professor Riesman described this typical member of society as a gregarious creature, highly sensitive to the opinions and ideas of other people, constantly scanning the social horizon with a "radar screen" to pick up acceptable modes of conduct. Ultimately, dependence on other-directedness creates a social atmosphere where actions are defined more by social sensitivity than by premises.

It would be misleading to suggest that other-directedness is the sole product of the mass media's characters and models. An equally prolific source of multiple *personae* is the social structure. Youth living in a modern urban-industrial environment are ensconced in a social structure that patterns life into discrete multipositional segments, thereby producing a world view that reflects confusion and conflict. For example, as members of the family they are expected to respect parents and to conform to a way of life that is partially obsolete in the light of what they learn in school. In their religious congregations they are taught dogmas and assumptions that are difficult to reconcile with scientific training and understanding. When they enter occupational positions, they are expected to interact differently with superiors than with colleagues. In sum, the different environments —family, job, school, church, peers and military—call for different manners and values. In a sense, these different environments call not only for different behavior, but virtually for different persons.

[67] David Riesman, *The Lonely Crowd* (New Haven: Yale University Press, 1950).

Traditional social psychological theory is largely obsolete and a more flexible model of modern identity formation is needed. Actually, the revision might be more radical than that—perhaps *any* theory of identity has become superfluous and has lost applicability.

This is exactly what sociologist Erving Goffman argued: A style of social interaction has arisen that no longer requires—or could even profit from—a unitary identity.[68] The new interactional mode is *situational performance.* Such performance is too transient to be couched in terms of roles, since the concept of role connotes consistency and permanence. By 1982, when he died, Goffman had exhibited an increasing tendency to get away from the old labels and interpretations that suggested a simpler and more unitary life style. Starting in his first book, *The Presentation of Self in Everyday Life,* Goffman used the language of the theater to describe the multi-"stage" life of modern urban persons. In his earlier writing, Goffman agreed with sociologist Robert E. Park, who felt that most social behavior consists of role-playing and of following a consensual script and that "it is in these roles that we know each other; it is in these roles that we know ourselves."[69]

In his subsequent writings, Goffman deemphasized role as the prompting device for behavior, and moved "appearance" and "interpersonal manipulation" to center stage. He called his data-gathering methodology "observations of a participant witness of contemporary urban America," and proceeded to describe what he thought was the prevailing mode of modern social interaction: the face-to-face interaction in daily settings. Contemporary Americans, he felt, put a premium on mutual manipulation under protected and consensual ground rules. These rules use body language and social ritual—eye contact, regard for personal space, ceremonies of apologies and explanations, vocabulary of embarrassment, and ceremonial profanities—more than abstract principles to govern the ubiquitous and ephemeral encounters in public life (*Relations in Public* and *Interaction Ritual*). Goffman reminded us of the myriad calculative, gamelike elements in our mutual dealings, which manifest themselves in even the shortest-lived encounters (*Strategic Interaction*). Governed by unspoken and unwritten understandings, these "games" are carefully polished frontstage performances (meticulously prepared by impression management) that testify to humans' need to maintain social appearances. Goffman was convinced that by looking at these sociological aspects we can derive greater understanding of modern humans than by examining purely psychological attributes.

In *Frame Analysis* and *Forms of Talk,* Goffman went much farther than in his previous writings and suggested that we are always putting on performances

[68] Erving Goffman's most important works pertaining to this question include: *The Presentation of Self in Everyday Life* (Garden City, N.Y.: Doubleday, 1959); *Interaction Ritual* (Garden City, N.Y.: Doubleday, 1967); *Strategic Interaction* (Philadelphia: University of Pennsylvania Press, 1969); *Relations in Public* (New York: Basic Books, 1971); *Frame Analysis: An Essay on the Organization of Experience* (Cambridge, Mass.: Harvard University Press, 1974); *Forms of Talk* (Philadelphia: University of Pennsylvania Press, 1981).

[69] Robert E. Park, *Race and Culture* (Glencoe, Ill.: The Free Press, 1950), p. 249.

even in situations where we believe we "are ourselves." To explain these behavior patterns in terms of the old role concept would constitute a bias in the direction of wholeness and authenticity, which is not at all contained in such behavior. What is really taking place is a series of one-person shows that pragmatically change according to the contingencies of the various situations. Apparently, Goffman came to the conviction that "real life activities" are nothing but dramatic realizations—which means that there is no substance behind the show. Goffman was thus saying that we all wear social masks, and if we take off one mask, we will not discover a real self but only additional masks. This implies that the nature of the *situation* determines the character of the self.

The interpretation of humans as "appearances" rather than abiding selves or consistent identities is partly supported by other social scientists. Erik Erikson has argued that "ego identity" is not a fixed entity but rather a dynamic process that continues throughout the life cycle.[70] Growth and change of identity are related to a person's affiliations and identifications. Since in our modern age such collective influences are subject to turmoil, identity processes have become labile. In recent writings, Erikson has downgraded the value of these groups, referring to them as dangerous "pseudospecies" that maintain their own uniqueness by dehumanizing others. Each of these groups enforces a "normalcy" that may, in fact, be pathological.

The most outspoken proponent of Goffman's brand of the "new look" social psychology is Kenneth J. Gergen, who feels that the traditional assumption, that a firm and coherent sense of identity is necessarily a measure of normalcy, is an obsolete bias standing in the way of taking a fresh and unencumbered look at post-industrial interaction as it actually is.[71] The maintenance of a rigid, unidimensional identity would prove highly dysfunctional in our society; it would impede the smoothness and expedience with which flexible and pragmatic "appearance"-oriented modern humans interact and satisfy their needs. In fact, the old rigidity with which the traditional social psychologist predicated healthy and happy human beings would render them stifled and unhappy. Perhaps the old emphasis on "identity" has become a forced question that artificially conjures up some kind of imagined need to perpetuate the concept.

In sum, we have thus two theoretical interpretations of the relationship between modern social interaction and the personality system: the traditional one, upholding a unitary identity as a measure of normalcy, and the new multi-*personae* theory, rejecting the old rigidity and seeing functionality in the new flexibility. The impact of modern social interaction (with its ingredients of multiple and inconsistent reference groups, significant others, and roles) on adolescents can therefore be interpreted in two ways:

[70] Erik H. Erikson, *Life History and the Historical Moment* (New York: Norton, 1975).
[71] Kenneth J. Gergen, "Multiple Identity: The Healthy, Happy Human Being Wears Many Masks," *Psychology Today*, 5 (May 1972), 31–66.

(1) According to the traditional theory, a holistic identity is of paramount significance, and modern social interaction is seriously stunting its growth. The impact of situational character portrayal via the mass media and the diverse and discrete "stage lives" of people enmeshed in modern social structure have aggravating effects on adolescence. If adults suffer identity problems from the influence of such compartmentalized and ephemeralized social situations, how much more must adolescents, who are intensely involved in the process of identity formation. If identification situations, positions, and roles are isolated from each other, situationally defined, and often incompatible, isomorphic reflections become noticeable in the personalities of the young.

Situational definitions make learning difficult because the young individual can generalize only minimally and must learn the "proper" style for each separate situation. To accomplish such situational adroitness requires a longer period of learning than the simple and old-fashioned specific-action-follows-general-premise style of learning. Adolescence can become a lifelong condition if a young individual is unable to find a common denominator, a basic premise for specific behavior, among or beyond the multiple *personae* that modern society demands from him or her. For most adolescents, performing multiple characters will be a confusing problem of identity.

(2) According to the new multi-*personae* theory, the question of identity is a white elephant inherited from a bygone era that does not apply to modern society. Humans involved in a postindustrial system must rely on communicative and interactional skills and not on rigid principles. In essence, personality development has become part of the activities of the marketplace, of the web of "strategy of success" within the manipulative process of interpersonal relations. Goals, norms, roles, and definitions fluctuate from one social situation to the other, and identity has lost its functionality. The modern person has become a *persona dramatis* — an actor of many scripts.

The problem of adolescents lies therefore more in learning skills to eliminate interpersonal friction than in learning basic roles and principles. Rather than integrity, adolescents must learn sensitivity; rather than proceeding by chart and principled plan, they embark on their life-journeys equipped with "social radar" that will tell them situational circumstances and help them to circumnavigate barriers and dangers.

Perhaps this novel type of human interaction is already visible in the relations between the sexes. Rather than proceeding according to traditional sex-role definitions, many young Americans embark on a course of interaction relatively unfettered by sex stereotypes and try to come to terms with each other on an individual level.

The future of identity formation, with which adolescence is so intimately associated, depends largely on which theory will prove to be true. At this time prognosis is difficult. Perhaps, indeed, we are facing the emergence of a new type of *Homo sapiens*, one who is conditioned by the postindustrial system to be skillful, communicative, and more concerned about practical problem-solving than about how basic purposes and principles should pattern the world.

SUMMARY

In spite of confusion about the definition of *personality*, there is consensus of its social, processual, phasic, and *Gestalt* nature. In addition, development of normal personality depends on physiological prerequisites and adequate care in human group environment.

Behavioral orientation is not limited to membership groups, but can be a product of identification with abstract reference groups. Understanding of the behavior of modern adolescents is difficult because of their exposure to multiple, shifting, conflicting, and sometimes unclear reference groups. This accounts for misunderstood and unexplained behavior patterns, including deviations from adult norms, and confused and situationally compartmentalized behavior.

Significant others are models influencing personality development. Traditionally, parents served as such important figures, but modern conditions have diminished the effectiveness of personal models. Among these conditions are the abundance of available reference groups, the relative invisibility or absence of personal models, and exposure to characters portrayed in the mass media.

The traditional sex-specific expectations have become blurred. Nonspecificity has created new freedoms. However, the price for freedom of individuality is uncertainty and anxiety. Erosion of traditional sex-role definitions has come to greatly affect the boy-girl interaction and the personality of the teenage girl. Young women manifest their role change by altered behavior in many areas; for example, in sexual activities, intellectual expression, competition, and such negative phenomena as crime and suicide.

The question of identity formation as the core process of personality presents extraordinary difficulties. Traditional theory emphasized identity as the stabilizing, guiding, and integrating function of the person. Its stability depends, however, on the stability and consistency of the social environment. Concern has been expressed that this environment has become fragmented and inconsistent, thus effecting an isomorphic repercussion in the individual's identity. The characters of the mass media as well as the nature of modern social structure, with its multipositional life situations, induce modern humans to act in terms of isolated sets of social interaction. The various "scripts" and ethics that are part of modern social existence tend to endow the individual actor with multiple *personae*. This has repercussions for the person's identity, since the basic question "Who am I" demands a unitary answer.

A more recent social-psychological formulation deemphasizes the importance of identity and ascribes greater importance to the learning of communicative and interactional skills. Humans are thought of as functioning more efficiently without the rigidity of traditional roles. Adolescents, therefore, would do better to concentrate on learning skills rather than rigid principles.

The future will show which theory earns greater credibility. Future generations of adolescents will either display greater identity confusion or will adjust to the new "games" of social interaction that require less "script" and more intuition.

There is an escape hatch open to the young: they can get away from some of the confusion and conflict by seceding to subcultures with norms and values that lend temporary orientation.

Chapter 3

Conditions

of

Postindustrial Life

The structure of postindustrial society is eminently adolescence-inducing. Super-industrialization has accentuated the discontinuity and the isolation of social positions, converted education into a custodial institution, depersonalized the authority hierarchy, and altered cultural attitudes toward the meaning of work and material achievement. The impact of these conditions on young people is discussed in this chapter.

DISJUNCTION OF SOCIAL
STRUCTURE AND CULTURE

Probably the most striking feature of postindustrial society is its complex network of positions. The division of labor, the way society distributes the functions necessary for its maintenance, includes such fine subdivisions that most people would be unable to identify all of them. An example is the network that regulates automobile use: the operator-licensing office, the auto-licensing office, laws, courts, law-enforcement agencies, the highway department, driver's education classes, insurance companies, and so forth.

Since American working conditions rarely give the individual a chance to do a "whole" job, a sharp discontinuity arises between the life of the child and the life of the adult. The life of the child is more holistic, in that his or her early education and training usually take in the broadest range of different curricula and activities. In late adolescence, when a youth begins a job, this broad range abruptly narrows, and the individual must focus on one particular activity for which he or she probably was not specifically prepared and may require new training and education. The job may be so specialized that, as a child or teenager, he or she may not have had a model or role definition to aid in understanding the new situation. As a result, thousands of teenagers who enter the labor force immediately after, or even before, graduation from high school are unable to decide which vocation will provide personal fulfillment. Their reactions often take the form of discontent, frequent job changes, and even delinquency.

To see the multispecific nature of modern social structure in the right perspective, it is necessary to elaborate on two interrelated phenomena. One is the nature of the general culture and the other is the process of achieving personal identity. As already mentioned in the introductory chapter, there seems to be a gradual shift of identity-genesis from the culture to one's specific social position. This trend was brought about by diminishing persuasiveness of the culture and, at the same time, by an increasing social-structural specialization. The multispecific social system makes it increasingly difficult to interpret its variegated life experiences into generally understandable terms.

Sociologist Daniel Bell recognized this development and saw the general cultural plateau of postindustrial society undergoing a kind of atrophy because of the outgrowth of technical specialization.[1] He understood culture as the symbolic expression of the common social processes in which people are involved in everyday life. People need such symbolic expression to communicate and share their experiences with one another. But superindustrialization impedes such sharing, and the common ground for symbolic expression is eroding away under the growth of a highly specialized division of labor. Consequences have been felt in all sectors of life and have been symptomized as political alienation, work dissatisfaction, and the general feeling of ignorance and powerlessness vis-à-vis an unfathomable and amorphous industrial-scientific complex. In short, culture is failing in its function to serve as a forum through which people can find common expression. Our advanced technology, with its finely divided and isolated work patterns, inhibits the formulation of common symbolic expression and fosters isolation and alienation.

What modern society fails to provide in terms of ideational guidance it tries to make up in bureaucratic guidance. But this effort is of little help. Indeed, it worsens the situation because it adds to *anomie* an element of unfreedom that blocks the search for new principles and prohibits experimentation with new behavior patterns. Thus, as Peter Berger, Brigitte Berger, and Hansfried Kellner

---

[1] Daniel Bell, "The Post-Industrial Society," in *Technology and Social Change*, ed. Eli Ginzberg (New York: Columbia University Press, 1964), and *The Cultural Contradictions of Capitalism* (New York: Basic Books, 1976).

pointed out, alienation through bureaucratization turns modern humans into "homeless minds" in search of a meaningful culture.[2]

As a consequence, people depend on discrete social positions for personal identity and partially ignore a culture that is too general to represent the wide spectrum of life experiences. In fact, in this type of society, culture *cannot afford* to be specific, since it would violate, contradict, or discriminate against the life experiences of many members.

It is true, however, that the superficial and sensate ingredients of postindustrial culture are widely shared, creating the impression of a culture of substance and viability. But a close look reveals that most messages and images are geared toward sensate appeals or common anxieties and not toward an ideational union or commitment. The common cultural denominator intelligible to the masses of the postindustrial society is the sensate. (Echoes of Sorokin's philosophy of history!). Postindustrial people compensate for *anomie* and superficiality by clinging to social positions for directions and goals.

This situation creates identity problems for youth. While still generalists, dependent on vague and nonspecific cultural "blueprints," young people suffer from *anomic* conditions that create difficulty in answering "Who am I?" unless parental guidance and value indoctrination compensate for cultural nonspecificity. It is not until the young person enters and feels at home in a specific position that a sense of trustworthy identity develops. This, then, is the dilemma of modern adolescents.

The above generalizations, applicable as they may be to the majority of American youth, require at least two modifications. The first deals with the institution of apprenticeship, a process whereby the young are systematically introduced into the adult division of labor. Apprenticeship became a common practice in the Old World with the development of urban and industrial conditions and helped to introduce the young into a craft and an adult position. An apprentice had a defined status, with rights and obligations specified in a contract, and spent from three to six years under the supervision of a master. After successful completion, he or she was initiated (by rite of passage) into the rank of journeyman and henceforth regarded as an adult.

The United States tried to encourage the tradition of apprenticeship through the National Apprenticeship Act of 1937, wherein the Secretary of Labor was "authorized to formulate and promote the labor standards necessary to safeguard the welfare of apprentices, to encourage the inclusion of such standards in contracts, to bring together employers and labor for the formulation of programs of apprenticeships."[3] About 420,000 Americans benefited from this legislation in 1980 and were trained as carpenters, electricians, iron workers, barbers, butchers, painters, printers, roofers, and in many other skills. The number of such registered apprentices had substantially increased over the preceding ten years which was

---

[2] Peter Berger, Brigitte Berger, and Hansfried Kellner, *The Homeless Mind* (New York: Random House, 1973).

[3] *United States Congressional Record*, Chapter 663, Washington, D.C., August 1937, p. 664.

only 155,000 in 1962.[4] The Bureau of Apprenticeship and Training of the United States Department of Labor suggested a composite portrait of the "typical apprentice": He is a "married 25 year old male high school graduate with no physical handicap, presently in his third year of apprenticeship, and whose father does not work in the same trade. Prior to his apprenticeship he did have a full-time job, and his chances of being a veteran are about even."[5] While apprentices are still predominantly male, the 1981 Report shows that the proportion of women is steadily increasing; it was 4.3 percent in 1978 and 6.4 percent by 1980.

The second qualification deals with the widespread custom of teenagers working part-time during their school years. This practice sometimes prepares them for positions and hence reduces the "culture shock" when entering the adult position. The important functions of part-time work experience for a teenager include: (1) a feeling of economic independence; (2) a feeling of self-reliance; (3) a strengthening of self-respect; (4) acceptance of proper sex-role behavior; (5) rehearsing and practicing socially responsible behavior; and (6) facilitating the process of selecting and preparing for a final occupation.

PURSUIT OF INSTANTNESS

One of the most cherished goals of supertechnology is *instantness* of result and gratification. One may view the achievement of instantness as the acid test of a postindustrial society's capability of providing goods and services. The rationalization of processes of manufacture and service creates a soaring productivity, and postindustrial economy holds out at least two promises: the promise of instantness of gratification and the promise of elimination of scarcity.

Given the American obsession with time and efficiency, it comes as no surprise that this society has become the prototype of *technological instantness* and has assumed virtual world leadership in this capacity. Promises of instant results abound and have become an ever present feature of consumerism. Numerous products and services are promoted with the adjective *instant*. Examples include drugs ("instant relief" through Dristan/Aspirin/Excedrin/Rolaids/etc., "instant sleep" through Sominex), food ("instant" coffee/rice/breakfast/pudding/potatoes/etc.), transportation ("instant transportation" through Boeing 747), communication ("instant communication" through satellite relay), finance ("instant credit" by supermarkets), religion ("instant prayer" by dialing a number), cosmetics ("instant hairsetting" by Clairol), recreation ("instant dancing through dance studios), and so forth.[6] The range of modern instancies has created the impression

---

[4] U.S. Department of Labor, *Employment and Training Report*, Government Printing Office, Washington, D.C., 1981, pp. 45, 46.

[5] U.S. Department of Labor, *Apprentice Survey*, Code 321, Government Printing Office, Washington, D.C., March 1975, p. 8.

[6] See details in Hans Sebald, "The Pursuit of Instantness in Technocratic Society and Youth's Psychedelic Drug Use," *Adolescence*, 7 (Fall 1972), 343–50.

that instancy is unlimited. This is an illusion. While in many sectors of modern life the expectation for immediacy is realistic, in some sectors it is unrealistic. Hence the vision of and the insistence on instantness in *all* aspects of life are delusory.

Modern adolescents are particularly receptive to this delusion. The inventions and miracles of modern science are no longer awesome to adolescents; they are taken for granted and expected to be available whenever desired. In short, youthful attitudes include the naive belief in and the unabashed demand for instantness in *all* areas of life. This includes the extrapolation of the principle of *instant results* from the feasible to the nonfeasible.

One area where instancy is not feasible is mental achievement and psychological maturity. There are no instant "knowledge pills." Yet many American youths continue to experiment with psychedelic drugs, trying to legitimize their habit by claiming to derive such benefits as "mystic" experiences, keen insights, and the more efficient performing of mental tasks. There is no reliable study to support this claim. At best, the user *perceives* but does not really *achieve* improvement or solution. The greatest danger of the psychedelic-drug habit is not the uncertain or detrimental chemical reaction caused by the active ingredients — although they can indeed present formidable problems — but the fostering of a pervasive psychological condition: the conviction that psychological problems have instant solutions, that problem solving can be achieved through chemistry rather than by coping. The ironic aspect of this assumption is that it is close to the habit of the adult Establishment, presumably despised by the members of the psychedelic-drug culture, of seeking solutions to personal problems through a nearly endless array of drugs: a pill for falling asleep, a pill for waking up, a pill for calmness, a pill for nonpregnancy, and so forth. The youthful drug culture is in perfect harmony with the assumptions of the American drug syndrome that make drug dependence for instant results an entirely acceptable lifestyle.

Adolescents are involved in an intense process of mental development. They must learn a culture, memorize a vast body of technical knowledge, and, at the core of all these mental tasks, form a personal identity. Our technocracy's ethos of instantness seduces them into believing that shortcuts and instant achievements can be had in these intricate processes. The attitudes emanating from such a broad conviction are naive, if not outright unrealistic and immature. In the process, the American ethos of the right to the pursuit of happiness becomes corrupted into the assumption of the right to *instant happiness.* Deferment of gratification has become largely unintelligible and repugnant to American youth. When they encounter the demand for it, they tend to become outraged and suspect something basically wrong with "the system."

The postindustrial promise of instantness and youth's natural hedonism coalesce into the tenacious inclination to eschew delay and tedious effort. Compared with previous generations, postindustrial adolescents grow up with a vastly diminished concept of the scarcity of goods and services. The pioneer era and the hardships of the Great Depression are to them mere historical anecdotes, encountered only when an instructor insists that they read assignments or when a grandfather relates "stories." Emphasis in American life is no longer on producing, but on consuming. These changes have had their impact on the mentality of the younger generation: (1) the traditional work ethic (to see value in work per se) is seriously challenged; (2) tedium in work patterns is found intolerable; and (3) deferment of gratification is interpreted as unnatural.

The nation's approximately 25 million workers under thirty years of age may in fact be too educated, too expectant, and too antiauthoritarian for many of the positions that the postindustrial economy offers. Affluence, the rise in hedonism, and the rejection of the Protestant ethic have turned many young people against their parents' dedication to work.

These new attitudes have become conspicuous in all sectors of American life. The institution of education is one example. College education is increasingly viewed by the young as just another "right." They demand that it be made palatable and added to the list of "fun and instantness." If it fails to live up to this syndrome, something is wrong and should be changed instantly. Modern youth, accustomed to instantness in life, experience difficulty in coping with exceptions. The educational institution is such an exception, and American youth try to impose their search, if not demand, for "instant education." Bruno Bettelheim observed: "The expectation is that education can hand over knowledge and skill, and this nearly instantly."[7]

SEPARATION OF HOME
AND WORK

In industrialized societies, the setting for raising children and the setting for employment have become separate realms. The practice of commuting from the home to the place of employment seems to be directly correlated with the degree of a country's industrial development. For example, in the 1950s West Germany had roughly 3 million people commuting to jobs in communities outside their own. In 1965, with progressing technology, industrialization, and affluence, the number of such commuters was 6.3 million.[8]

Most urban families no longer practice the tradition whereby the son takes on the occupation of his father and the daughter that of her mother. (However, most girls still learn the wife-mother role through the mother.) James S. Coleman found that in the city and the suburbs less than one out of ten boys intended to pursue the occupation of his father.[9] In most cases, the children are not familiar with the specific type of work their fathers do, and when they assume their own vocational activities they are received into a completely new surrounding. The

[7] Bruno Bettelheim, "Student Revolt, The Hard Core," *Vital Speeches of the Day*, 35 (1968–69), 406.

[8] *The Bulletin*, Press and Information Office of the Federal Republic of Germany, Bonn, November 9, 1965, p. 6.

[9] James S. Coleman, *The Adolescent Society* (New York: Free Press, 1963), p. 7.

abrupt change from primary socialization in the nuclear family to secondary socialization in the job can create considerable confusion.

Conditions of modern society have gradually changed the family from a production unit to a consumption unit. Each member is *individually* engaged in the production process. This is strikingly different from the tribal or folk societies where the consanguine family is a production unit as well as a consumption unit and where only the most elementary division of labor exists. The network of positions may comprise merely a few simple status definitions, such as hunters, warriors, chiefs, housekeepers, etc. This type of social structure prevents discontinuity between the position of the child and of the adult, since children experience early involvement in visible and imitable work. Primary and secondary socialization are merged into one process.

In contrast, in a rapidly changing and highly rationalized society education within the family has been replaced by formal institutions covering an ever longer span of time. Nonfamilial education and training has resulted in a byproduct: the evolution of *social systems* that resemble subcultures with norms and values of their own. As a result, not only have education and job training been removed from parental supervision, but so has youth. They now belong to a society of peers, a society whose natural habitat is the campus of the high school or college.

The population of this youth habitat has risen sharply over the last decades. In 1900, only 11 percent of America's high school-aged youth were *in* high school; in 1930, the proportion was 51 percent[10]; today it is estimated at well over 90 percent. The emphasis on formal education is directly correlated with industrial development—a correlation observable the world over.

EDUCATION IN POSTINDUSTRIAL PERSPECTIVE

The modern educational institution plays a salient role in the lives of the young and calls for a separate examination. Hence the major discussion is deferred to Chapter 7, The Modern Educational Experience. A brief summary preview is offered at this time for the purpose of indicating that the topic has an important place in the array of postindustrial conditions.

Nonfamilial education. Modern education has assumed a ghetto existence away from most adult institutions. This is particularly true of high school campuses, the Teenland America, where students pursue their own values, styles, and lingo. Never before have the institutions of the family and of education been such separate experiences. Many families do not see the values they cherish reflected in the schools. Such nonfamilial education has aroused opposition in ethnic groups, who fear their children might be unduly exposed to worldly and decadent influences. One example is the Amish, who have opposed "worldly" education persis-

---

[10] James S. Coleman, *Adolescents and the Schools* (New York: Basic Books, 1965), p. 7.

tently enough to persuade the authorities to grant them their own Amish-run schools. Obviously, the vast majority of American school-aged children do not have such a privilege. They continue to experience a parallel socialization process with family and school remaining separate, if not opposing, institutions.

Longer education. There has been a steady increase in years added to the formal education of Americans. Roughly half of the American population now has finished high school *and* spent some time in college. The question arising parallel to longer educational affiliation concerns the sociological and psychological status of the students. Prolonging the sojourn in academia also means prolonging adolescence by offering a moratorium on social responsibilities, allowing time for psychological growth, and delaying career decisions.

The extended segregation of the young from adult life unintentionally created a setting conducive to: (1) peer influence and subculture formation; (2) freedom of sexual experimentation; and (3) mate selection beyond the constraints of parental control.

Custodial education. While longer education is in part a function of the necessary preparation for sophisticated careers, it is in part also a holding pen to keep the young from invading the labor market too soon and adding to unemployment pressure. The increasing concern voiced over the educational dropout is motivated less out of awe for the presumed knowledge disseminated through the educational process than out of worry of not knowing what else to do with the masses of America's young.

MOBILITY AND ITS DISRUPTIONS

Urban-industrial Americans are among the world's most mobile people. Precisely how this trait affects American youth and their adolescent experience is not yet fully understood. Probably the best that can be done is to suggest plausible hypotheses.

First, what is meant by *mobility*? The term has several meanings. One refers to *movement within the social structure*, either *vertically* or *horizontally*. Changing from the occupation of waiter to that of doctor would be an example of vertical mobility, while changing from factory worker to construction worker would be an example of horizontal mobility.

Mobility can also refer to geographic movement—a kind of mobility that is remarkable among Americans. For example approximately 20 percent of the American population changes address each year, compared with about 12 percent in Europe and 8 percent in Japan.[11] If we accept the theory that development of a stable personality depends on consistent environment, disruption of life patterns

[11] U.S. Department of Labor, *Economic Forces in the United States* (Washington, D.C.: Government Printing Office, 1973); and AP report (Washington, Oct. 20, 1975).

through frequent moving should negatively influence the adolescent experience, prolong it, and aggravate confusion. Research has revealed that children and adolescents whose families move are dismayed about losing friends, worried about making new ones, and show a decline in scholastic achievement. Highly mobile youths (who have moved twice or more) exhibited notable maladjustment to peers and were less frequently chosen as playmates than youths with local roots.[12]

Military families are prototypes of this mobility, and their children have been found to be characterized by social and psychiatric troubles. Psychiatrist Don M. LaGrone found 12 percent of all children and adolescents on a base in need of psychiatric help and diagnosed 4 percent of them as psychotic. Causal to these conditions, he felt, were extensive father-absence, the families seeing themselves as transients with no roots, and children moving from school to school so frequently that they had to break into peer groups repeatedly as the "new kid" and were often the school's scapegoats.[13]

Vance Packard takes this contention a step further and, in *A Nation of Strangers*, expresses concern that too many Americans move too often, become rootless, and contribute to the decline of a sense of community.[14]

While the effects of frequent moving can be interpreted as disruptions of identification processes, they can also be interpreted as providing the young with extra opportunities for learning and greater variety of reference persons. One could argue that adolescents subject to mobility acquire more information and better insight. This may make the process of identity growth more complex (compared with the process of the nonmobile youths who stay in one community), but not less valid or stable in its final outcome. In fact, one might argue that for the nonmobile, roots become ruts. At this time, the statistical question waiting to be researched is: How many people adapt easily to and grow emotionally and intellectually by moving, and how many suffer and how seriously?

Vertical mobility either compares members of one generation with those of the next (generational mobility) or compares different stages in the life of one individual (career mobility). The focus here is on generational mobility and the resulting discontinuities. Part of the American heritage is the Protestant ethic, which includes a mobility ethic that encourages Americans to achieve "success" in life. Hence, the young are not necessarily encouraged to follow in parental footsteps, but to improve on the latter's lives.

In most industrial societies, the placement function of the family has declined. While it is true that children identify and are identified by status and prestige of their families, as teenagers and young adults they become detached from familial influence, and social standing depends increasingly on personal achievements. The status eventually achieved may be on a different level from that of the

---

[12] Joseph Schaller, "The Relation Between Geographic Mobility and School Behavior," *Man-Environment Systems*, 5 (May 1975), 185–87.

[13] Don M. LaGrone, "The Military Family Syndrome," *American Journal of Psychiatry*, 135 (September 1978), 1040–1043.

[14] Vance Packard, *A Nation of Strangers* (New York: David McKay, 1972).

parents. In postindustrial society, family origin affects the status of the individual only indirectly, by influencing opportunities for educational and occupational achievements.

Research in American generational mobility has shown widespread discontinuity between the careers of the parents and the offspring. Sociologists Cecil C. North and Paul K. Hatt surveyed sons' deviations from fathers' occupations and revealed that, with the sole exception of farming, no occupational category achieved more than one-third generational continuity.[15] It should be noted that those who classified their occupation in the same general class as their fathers' did not necessarily occupy the *same specific* occupation, implying that a great deal of horizontal mobility existed *within* the broad occupational classes. Coleman found that few boys planned to follow in the occupational footsteps of their fathers. His survey showed 23 percent of boys in small towns and only 9.8 percent of boys in city and surburban schools planning to enter their fathers' occupation.[16]

The mobility ethic can have a devastating impact on those adolescents who fail, as some must, in the process of status striving. In a society that encourages all to strive and that promises success to those who are capable, failure is considered evidence of personal inadequacy. For those who achieve upward mobility, difficult adjustments are required. This problem is frequently evident in both the research literature and the popular "success" story, describing the situation of the rich and successful but unhappy and maladjusted man or woman.

Lack of family continuity and tradition may present teenagers with an obscure future for which they have no visible models. They are called on to make one of the most vital decisions in life—choosing a career. The mobility ethic, expecting the teenager to go beyond the family's level of achievement and improve his or her level of social prestige, contributes additional pressures. By ruling out parents as occupational models, a familiar sociocultural orientation is rendered irrelevant. Most teenagers who choose an occupation or vocational training that differs significantly from their parents' undergo a shift in life orientation often comparable to "culture shock." Symptoms of this shock emerge as feelings of anxiety.

HOME AWAY FROM HOME

Many American children are raised, partially or wholly, away from the parental home. Some children are entrusted to the care of a *partial* home while their mothers are employed full-time. Others are victims of disabled or delinquent parents and grow up in welfare institutions. Still others are delinquent youths who serve time in a penal or rehabilitative institution. This discussion deals with those children in day-care centers part-time and those in welfare institutions full-time.

[15] Cecil C. North and Paul K. Hatt, "Jobs and Occupations: A Popular Evaluation," *Opinion News*, 9 (September 1947), 3–13.

[16] Coleman, *The Adolescent Society*.

The day-care center enables mothers to simultaneously pursue motherhood and an occupation outside of the home. Although estimates vary, figures indicate that day care is available for nearly 1 million of the almost 6 million preschool children whose mothers work. Since the 1940s, the number of working mothers has climbed 700 percent, while the population has increased 50 percent. The number of working mothers with children under age five is expected to increase to over 5 million during the 1980s.[17]

Effects of maternal employment on children's personalities have been studied by many investigators. Examination of the research literature by Edith H. Grotberg revealed a diversity of findings regarding the correlation between mother's employment and children's delinquency, school and personal adjustment, and academic achievement.[18] While some studies demonstrated the positive functions of day care, such as increased language skill and a sense of security within a group setting, others concluded negatively, pointing up reduced capacity for emotional attachment, diminished sense of autonomy, and stifled creativity.[19]

The findings fail to add up to a consistent picture, and suspicion is warranted that research has ignored important variables. There are many relatively unexamined conditions that play an intermediary role between a mother's work away from home and the personality formation of the child. For example, one study discovered that a mother's liking or disliking of her job is significantly associated with how she interacts with her children. Mothers liking their work had more positive relationships with their children, though their children exhibited nonassertive and dependent attitudes. Mothers who disliked their work had more negative relationships with their children, and their children exhibited assertive and hostile attitudes.[20]

Correlations of this nature remind us of the complexity of the matter and of the many variables that enter into the picture. Such variables must be explored before we can obtain a clearer view of maternal employment and its impact on children.

The full-time institution is for youths who have no, or no adequately functioning, parents. Information derived from studying youths in such settings is more conclusive than that concerning day-care center children. Clinicians have long agreed that substituting the parental home with the anonymous crowd in an institution has detrimental effects on children.

The case has been stated by Dr. Lauretta Bender, who observed approximately six thousand children in New York's Bellevue Hospital for more than a

---

[17] Richard B. Zamoff and Jerolyn R. Lyle, "Who Needs What Kind of Day-Care Center," *Child Welfare*, 52 (June 1973), 351.

[18] Edith H. Grotberg, *Review of Research, 1965-69, of Project Head Start*, U.S. Department of Health, Education, and Welfare, Office of Child Development, 1969.

[19] Bruno Bettelheim, *The Children of the Dream* (New York: Macmillan, 1969).

[20] Lois W. Hoffman, "Effects of Maternal Employment on the Child," *Child Development*, 32 (March 1961), 187-97.

decade and noted that children parentally deprived for one or more years were rarely able to adjust in foster homes: They all appear retarded, untrained, and impulsive in their behavior. As they grow older and the demands of society increase, their behavior becomes progressively more asocial.[21]

Another study reported the transfer of thirteen orphaned children, less than three years old, from the state institution where they had been living to a home for retarded women.[22] Two years later, the children showed a surprising increase in intellectual proficiency, while children who had remained at the state orphanage retained marked impairment of mental abilities. A follow-up study showed that the transferred children grew up to be normal members of the community, while most of the children in the orphanage were retarded and spent the major part of their lives in institutions. The explanation for the different outcomes was ascribed to the love and attention that the thirteen children received from the retarded inmates. The two reports are typical of numerous observations of what can happen to children reared in institutions.

A crucial shortcoming of institutional homes is the number of youths per adult supervisor or nurse. The Child Welfare League of America recommended no more than approximately six children per adult. In most institutional settings, this suggestion remains utopian. Consequences of serious understaffing and parental deprivation include the following:

1. With understaffing, anonymity is unavoidable. The child with its needs, opinions, and dreams does not receive sufficient attention *to feel known*. In fact, it is usually necessary for the nurse or supervisor to avoid emotional involvement with individual children. To carry the emotional burden of each child would be beyond the staff member's endurance.

2. The child may be disturbed by the perfunctory atmosphere of the institution and wonder whether he or she is really wanted. The feeling of *full acceptance* is immensely significant to a child, and its absence can result in feelings of personal worthlessness.

3. The experience of *physical affection* is of utmost significance in the development of a healthy personality. The effect of the caressing touch has been demonstrated in laboratory animals. In experiments with two sets of rats, all variables were kept constant, except that the experimental group received physical caresses daily. The fondled rats gained weight faster, matured earlier, appeared healthier, and generally expressed greater vitality than the rats in the control group.[23] The basic condition underlying this finding can be extrapolated to humans. Its significance applies to the institutional setting insofar as it rarely affords conditions where the child finds sufficient physical intimacy.

[21] Lauretta Bender, *Aggression, Hostility and Anxiety in Children* (Springfield, Illinois: Thomas, 1953), p. 153.

[22] Stephen A. Richardson, "Retarded Children," *Trans-Action*, 6 (September 1969), 6.

[23] Victor H. Denenberg, "Animal Studies on Developmental Determinants of Behavioral Adaptability," in *Experience, Structure and Adaptability*, ed. O. J. Harvey (New York: Springer Publishing Co., 1966), pp. 123–47.

4. Children have an interminable need for *question-answer* interaction. Their constant "why," "how," and "what-is-this" can hardly draw adequate responses in an institutional environment and their curiosity must go unsatisfied. This may generate indifference, dullness, and, in extreme cases, even retardation.

5. Human qualities appear to be the product of the primary family group — a sense of loyalty, cooperation, affection, and consideration. As Charles H. Cooley pointed out, these qualities are universal because of the universal primary-group experience and constitute essential elements of what is loosely called "human nature."[24] The question arising in conjunction with the substitution of institutional homes for the primary familial home is: What modifications, if any, does the institutional substitute have on the *human nature* of the child? Will the child's sense of kindness, sympathy, and affection be reduced? Will the child develop characteristics of the sociopathic personality, showing little regard and sympathy for suffering of others? A vast amount of research findings, a few of them already mentioned above, point to example after example of sociopathic products of institutional child-rearing.

6. Institutional upbringing may add complications to the process of transition from child to adult status. A common criticism of subjecting the child to constant adult supervision is that it *prolongs dependency*. The child is deprived of the opportunity to make independent decisions, lacks opportunity to roam about, cannot escape from constant adult supervision — conditions that are inimical to developing an independent personality. Under constant supervision, the child becomes passive and prefers to let others take the initiative. Such attitude patterns cause serious problems when the individual tries to assume adult responsibilities.

7. Institutional upbringing may fix the child's loyalty and value-orientation on the institutional *peer group*. They learn early to adhere to norms and values different from those of the home and the adult world.

ADOLESCENT AFFLUENCE

The influence of teenage affluence on their subculture was recognized years ago. Sociologist Jessie Bernard went as far as seeing the relationship in terms of strict causation: "Our teenage culture is a product of affluence. It is possible because our society can afford a large leisure class of youngsters not in the labor force but yet consumers on a vast scale, or, if in the labor force, free to spend their earnings on themselves."[25]

The causative implication of this statement is overdrawn. Affluence does not cause the teenage subculture; it has its origin in adolescence. While the affluence of late twentieth-century America causes neither adolescence nor the subculture, it effectively promotes the spread and survival of the collective expression of adoles-

[24] Charles H. Cooley, *Social Organization* (New York: Scribner's, 1915), pp. 23-24.

[25] Jessie Bernard, "Teenage Culture: An Overview," *Annals of the American Academy of Political and Social Science*, 338 (November 1961), 3.

cence – the teenage subculture. This is achieved through teenagers' buying patterns, the interests of the business world, and reinforcement of stereotypical teenage behavior.

Reinforcement of teenage behavior is primarily the result of rewards obtained through conforming to peer norms. These rewards are popularity and prestige in the peer group. Adherence to peer patterns often necessitates material implementation and may involve a car, "in" clothes, electronic gadgets, cosmetics, recreational paraphernalia, and other leisure-class goods and services. In order to buy the latest fads and fashions of the subculture, a teenager must have financial means. Statistics indicate that such means are available and modern teenagers control a large share of society's affluence.

Estimates from national surveys show that spending by teenagers (thirteen to nineteen years old) grew from $29 billion in 1977 to about $39 billion in 1980.[26] "From cosmetics to pizzas and from electronic games to records, teenagers and young adults make up a huge market...that seems resistant to recession and inflation."[27] The majority of youngsters enjoy parental safeguarding of their basic needs (housing, food, insurances, clothing) and hence are free to spend their money on leisure and luxury. The University of Michigan's Institute for Social Research found that about 40 percent of college-bound high school graduates already owned cars and that 50 percent of those not going to college owned theirs. The presumedly financially struggling American college student has, on the average, $173 per month to spend on pleasure, after room and board are paid.

High school youngsters also have an impressive consumption record. While it is impossible to cover all the market habits of American teenagers, studies have provided enough data to form a general picture. Some of these data are mentioned below. The *Media Book '79* lists the following items:

About half of the teenagers own cameras (40 percent of the boys, 55 percent of the girls)

80 percent go to movies on a more or less regular basis (Gallup Report 1981 indicates that only 2 percent of American teenagers "never attend")

15 percent have traveled abroad within three years prior to the survey

over 40 percent play tennis

about 20 percent ski

86 percent of the boys and 77 percent of the girls have driver's licenses

39 percent of the boys and 53 percent of the girls buy records

in comparison, a relatively low 29 percent of the boys and 43 percent of the girls buy books

52 percent of the boys and 62 percent of the girls have bicycles

42 percent eat at fast food restaurants once or more a week, with eight out of ten of them buying hamburgers[28]

---

[26] "Youth on the Move," *U.S. News and World Report*, January 5, 1981, pp. 72–76.

[27] Ibid., p. 77.

[28] *The Media Book '79* (New York: Barlow & Papazian, 1979), pp. 469, 471.

Do teenagers spend their *own* money on such consumption? Not necessarily. The Sacramento Metropolitan Teenage Market Study disclosed that teenagers usually pay out of their own pockets for records, radios, and entertainment. This tendency increased during the 1970s, with 19 percent of the teenagers spending "parents' or others' money" in 1970, but only 10 percent did so by the mid 1970s. On the other hand, the proportion of parents or others buying jewelry, shoes and clothes for teenagers sharply increased during that period, going, for example, from 33 to 43 percent for jewelry, 37 to 52 percent for shoes, and 54 to 70 percent for clothes.[29]

As a group, parents spend many billions of dollars each year on their children. The Agriculture Department has estimated that parents spend approximately 70 thousand dollars to raise a child through age seventeen in moderate circumstances. They pay about $9,000 more to send the youngster to an average public university for four years. A private university would increase the price tag for a degree to about $20,000.[30]

Even the government helps to free youth from a number of serious expenditures. In 1980 at least 20 percent of total public expenditures, or $172 billion, went to education, welfare, and Social Security benefits for people twenty-one and younger.[31]

To what extent do teenagers make their own buying decisions? Over 90 percent of the teenagers themselves—and not their parents—make buying decisions for almost all items.[32]

How do teenagers acquire their financial resources? One of the most common sources is the weekly allowance. The Sacramento surveys indicate that allowances have kept pace with inflation. During the 1960s, 95 percent of high school students received up to $15 a week; in 1970 and 1974, 92 and 80 percent, respectively, fell into this category. Conversely, the proportions receiving $15 or more increased from 5 percent in the 1960s to 8 percent in 1970 to 20 percent in 1974. There were no significant allowance differences between boys and girls.[33] Many students hold part-time jobs to boost their finances. Surveys in 1964, 1970, and 1974 found weekly earnings up to $15, respectively, for 67, 45, and 42 percent of those responding. Conversely, again reflecting inflation, the over $15 group increased from 33 to 55 to 58 percent. There were significant gender differences in income: 77 percent of the boys earned above $15, but only 28 percent of the girls fell into this category.[34] Another estimate of teenagers' (fifteen to nineteen years old)

[29] H. Nicholas Windeshausen and Paul A. Williams, *Sacramento Metropolitan Teenage Market Study* (Sacramento: California State University Center for Research, '74), p. 26.

[30] "Youth on the Move," p. 78.

[31] ibid.

[32] Windeshausen and Williams, p. 22.

[33] ibid., p. 8.

[34] ibid., p. 7.

income put it at $2,370 per year during the early 1980s—all of it discretionary income that could be spent on leisure and luxury.[35]

It is interesting that girls outspend boys early in life, a lead they apparently never relinquish. In a Rand Youth Poll's charting of twenty years of fiscal habits of America's youth, girls have consistently held a spending lead over their male counterparts. In the late teens, the gap is widened further. This raises intriguing questions. Since they earn *less* but spend *more* than boys, where and how do they get their finances? A plausible answer may be that parents buy more of the necessities for girls than boys. In addition, their boy friends pay certain luxury and social expenses for them. Thus they can more freely spend the money they have.

Aware of the teen buying potential, the American business world is trying to cater to youth's tastes. It would be misleading, however, to understand the teenage influence as a one-way causality. Merchants, ad writers, and market researchers grasp the enormous potential available for exploitation and are manipulating, if not actually creating, the tastes and styles of the young. Therefore the marketing system consists of a complex interrelationship between preferences of teenagers and manipulations of the marketeers. In exactly which proportions the etiology of styles evolves is not known at this time. In any case, the teen market is a volatile one. Sometimes, a few youngsters will suddenly wear somthing to school, and then everybody has to have it. Sometimes the fad is grubby work pants ("gas station" pants), and a year later it is printed turtlenecks.

Predictably, the American business establishment tries to profit from teenagers' buying power and their apparent need for their own styles and fads. What are the industry's means of exploring and exploiting? A premium is on sheer inventiveness. For example, in the early 1980s a San Francisco firm came out with rock concert souvenirs such as T-shirts selling for $8.00 a piece to the crowds worshiping their idols. Signifying that their necessities are somehow taken care of, teenagers provide an immensely profitable market for sports equipment. Some of the best-selling items during the early 1980s were skis and equipment for racquetball, jogging and exercising. Of perennial profitability are soft drinks and manufacturers, while addressing all ages, direct their appeal particularly at the young. The Coca-Cola Company developed Mello Yello, a low-carbonated drink, to sell to teenagers who are into sports. Marketing experts seem to agree on the principle that if you want to capture youth, you must lure them with a gimmick. Hence theaters and pizza parlors have pinball machines, arcade and video games; department stores use disco music, blinking lights, and space-age displays; fast food restaurants almost exclusively use children and teenagers in their advertisements; sports stores use champion skaters, skiers, swimmers in their commercials; beer brewers display hardy, youthful outdoor people "slamming down" a Lite; ads in college papers read "You didn't get the courses you wanted. But you got Friday off...Now comes Miller time."

---

[35] "Youth on the Move," p. 78.

This brings into play the power of the mass media. Many advertisement specialists believe the best way to reach teenagers is via the radio. Rock stations still draw the biggest audiences and hence are favorites for advertisers. Of course, there is also the advertising power of TV. In any case, an enticing mass-medium depiction of consumption patterns can establish and sustain the marketing plans of the industry.

The economic power of teenagers is not limited to their actual financial means; it includes their psychological power, manifesting itself through the peculiarly youth-oriented market in the United States. Teenagers stimulate most mass buying trends by functioning as persuasive agents in their families. For example, surveys have indicated that teenagers have weighty influence on their parents' purchases of automobiles in 69 percent of the cases, on 68 percent of vacation plans, 66 percent of the food buying, and 54 percent of television purchases.[36]

In summary, adolescents' expenditures are not made randomly but are selectively invested in goods and services that enhance popularity among peers. The selections are usually in accord with short-lived fashions of the subculture and create a feeling of belonging. Material implementation furthers identification with subcultural standards and in this way promotes the survival of the subculture. Also, material implementation facilitates communication within the subculture — communication that does not have to be verbal, but can speak through the visible common style and fashion. Faded jeans, therefore, are not just clothes but a symbol.

It is through this reinforcement that adolescence has obtained structure and internal statuses and become a way of life. This way of life is not wholly acceptable to the adult world and is viewed with ambivalence. In the final analysis, adolescent "status" is paradoxical in that it is relatively structured from the *inside* of the subculture, but is uncertain *within* the adult world.

SOCIOSOMATICS:
SOCIETAL INFLUENCES
ON BIOLOGICAL DEVELOPMENT

The sociological view of human beings is regrettably limited. It tends to regard them as interactional units or status entities but rarely as biological creatures. And, yet, we are both. Because of this neglect, the relationship between societal (social, cultural, and technological) factors and the human body is insufficiently studied. While psychologists and clinicians study the relationship between mental states and physiological responses (classified as *psychosomatic*), few social scientists have explored the impact of social and cultural conditions on the human body. One might call this influence *sociosomatic*, referring to sociocultural variables on one

---

[36] "Millions of Young Adults, A New Wave of Buyers," *U.S. News & World Report*, 72 (January 17, 1972), 16.

side and the human body on the other. Sociosomatic processes accelerate and become noticeable under conditions of rapid social change or cultural innovation.

Since young people are always in the chronological front line, they are the first to experience the impact of innovation—not only as social units but also as biological organisms. The following discussion attempts to recognize some of the important influences on the biological development of adolescents.

The most significant biological process during the period of adolescence is *pubescence.* (*Pubescence* is derived from Latin *pubertas,* "age of manhood," and *pubescere,* "to grow hairy.") While adolescence refers to the period of social maturation, pubescence refers to the physiological development during which the reproductive system matures. Pubescence normally corresponds with early adolescence and ends with the appearances of secondary sex characteristics and the achievement of reproductive ability. These changes usually take place over approximately two years. The exact age at which reproductive maturity is achieved varies widely and is influenced by many factors.

Of these factors, gender difference plays a major role. Girls mature about two years earlier than boys. Climate, however, seems to make little difference. It was once thought that girls who grew up in a hot climate developed earlier than those who grew up in a cold one. Actually, researchers found a tendency toward earlier maturation in the *temperate* zone rather than in either tropical or arctic regions.[37] In general, however, scientists reject assumptions of climatic determination. Race seems to have even less effect than climate. In two studies, age at menarche (first menstruation) for black girls did not vary significantly from that of white girls who lived in the same places and had similar socioeconomic backgrounds.[38]

The most influential factors seem to be nutritional and medical ones.[39] This is where sociosomatic processes enter the picture, where social and cultural conditions have marked influence on biological development and age of maturity. A social environment that uses recent scientific insights in these areas—as is typical of postindustrial society—usually lowers the age of pubescence. Among the various aspects of scientific progress, *better nutrition is the most significant factor.* Scientific standards of nutrition, hygiene, and medication are more common in urban-industrial societies than in tribal or agricultural societies and more common in the middle and upper socioeconomic classes than in lower classes. This is why a consistent difference of menarcheal age exists between higher and lower socioeconomic classes, a difference verified by international studies. Menarcheal difference between higher and lower classes was found to be two months in Copenhagen,

[37] David P. Ausubel, *The Theory and Problem of Adolescent Development* (New York: Grune and Stratton, 1954).

[38] Comradge L. Henton, "A Comparative Study of the Onset of Menarche among Negro and White Children," *Journal of Psychology,* 46 (July 1958), 65–73; and N. Michelson, "Studies in Physical Development of Negroes, Onset of Puberty," *American Journal of Physical Anthropology,* 2 (June 1944), 151–66.

[39] Ann C. Petersen, "Can Puberty Come any Earlier?" *Psychology Today,* February 1979, p. 45.

Denmark; three months in Bristol, England; eight months among blacks in New York; six months among Hindus; ten months in Durham, South Africa; and five months among South African Bantu.[40]

A related study found Japanese girls born in Japan but reared in California to be one-and-a-half years ahead of Japanese girls born in California but reared in Japan. The racial factor was constant between the groups, and the groups were large enough to include comparable cross sections of social stratification. The researcher concluded that the difference was due to the better diet of the girls who grew up in California.[41]

Heredity contributes to the determination of the time a girl experiences menarche. Daughters of early-pubescent mothers tend to reach menarche earlier than those of late-pubescent mothers.[42]

Effects of various factors reinforce each other and at other times neutralize each other. For example, if a German girl whose mother matured at eleven was brought up during the war and experienced nutritional deficiences, she may have started menstruation at a later age. But the daughter of a late-maturing mother of a poor family may reach menarche earlier if the family moves up the socioeconomic ladder and provides a better diet. A double effect is experienced by the daughter of a late-maturing mother deserted by the husband and living under depressed economic standards. The girl is prone to reach menarche at an even later age than her mother.

Intergenerational comparisons of menarche reveal an ever-decreasing menarcheal age in most societies. This especially is true of societies that have improved standards of nutrition and sanitation. Complete sets of records are available in Norway, covering the period from 1840 to 1950. Average menarcheal age in 1840 was seventeen years, one month. This age decreased consistently, until in 1950 it arrived at thirteen years, three months—a decrease of almost four years.[43] Similar changes have been found in Sweden, Germany, Denmark, England, Finland, Japan, and the United States.

In the United States, a study comparing mothers and daughters found the average menarcheal age for the mothers to be 13.99 years and for the daughters

[40] K. W. Boylen, G. Rasch and M. Weis-Bentzon, "The Age Incidence of Menarche in Copenhagen," *Acta Obstetrica et Gynecologia Scandinavica*, 33 (1954), 405–33; R. C. Wofenden and A. L. Smallwood, *Annual Report of the Principal Medical Officer* (Bristol, England: City and County of Bristol Education Committee, 1958); E. Kark, "Puberty of South African Girls, III, Social Class in Relation to the Menarche," *South African Journal of Laboratory and Clinical Medicine*, 2 (1956), 84–88; and A. G. Oettlé and J. Higginson, "Age at Menarche in South African Bantu Girls," *Human Biology*, 33 (May 1961), 181–90.

[41] Paul D. Ito, "Comparative Biometrical Study of Physiques of Japanese Women Born and Reared under Different Environments," *Human Biology*, 14 (September 1942), 279–351.

[42] Harley N. Gould and Mary R. Gould, "Age of First Menstruation in Mothers and Daughters," *Journal of the American Medical Association*, 98 (April 1932), 1349–52.

[43] V. Kiil, "Menarche-alderen hos skolepeker i Oslo og sammenhengen mellom menarche-older og fysiskutwicklung statistiche," *Kvartalashelft*, 43 (1954), 84–88.

13.61 years.[44] Another study found that American college women born around 1920 reached menarche six months earlier than those born around 1900.[45]

The reason why reference is made almost exclusively to the pubescent process of girls is that there is no clearly defined method for determining the onset of pubescence among boys. There is no equivalent sign as unmistakable as menstruation. Indications of male pubescence are appearance of pubic hair, voice change, and nocturnal emission. However, not all of these male pubescent characteristics appear at the same time; several may go unnoticed for some time.

Conditions of urban-industrial society have influenced not only timing of maturation but also quality. In 1961, researchers compared measurements of thirteen-year-old white Iowa schoolgirls with those of girls of the same age taken in 1880, 1899, 1916 to 1919, and 1937 to 1939.[46] Comparison showed progressive increase in all physical aspects except head width. Comparison of measurements taken in 1880 and in 1960 showed that girls of 1960 were taller by four inches in mean stature, heavier by twenty-two pounds in mean weight, and not different in head width.

The average boy of mid-twentieth century is five inches taller and twenty-four pounds heavier than his counterpart of 1880.[47] The average soldier in the United States army during World War II was three-fifths of an inch taller, almost ten pounds heavier, and better nourished than the average World War I soldier.[48] College students today are taller and heavier than their counterparts of twenty-five year ago. Today's athletes outstrip yesterday's stars in nearly every discipline. In the eighteenth century, the king of Prussia, Frederick the Great, had to search all over Europe to find enough men six feet tall to serve as his special guards. Today, he could find that many in almost every large high school. Visitors to museums are frequently astounded by the size of armor and other garments worn by medieval knights; they give the impression that twelve-to-fourteen-year-old children went on the Crusades. Actually, armor was worn by adults who on the average were several inches shorter than today's adults. The measurements of recruits in countries that have had universal military draft show consistent increases in both height and weight over the past generations.[49]

The examples given show that these increases are due to greater availability of food, a more balanced diet even among the poor, more equitable distribution of the countries' wealth, improved medical care, the resulting decrease in illness and epidemics, and virtual elimination of child labor.

[44] Gould and Gould, "Age of First Menstruation."

[45] Clarence A. Mills, "Further Evidence on the Reversal Human-Growth Tide," *Human Biology*, 13 (September 1941), 365.

[46] Howard V. Meredith and Virginia B. Knott, "Descriptive and Comparative Study of Body Size on United States School Girls," *Growth*, 26 (December 1962), 283–95.

[47] Luella Cole and Irma N. Hall, *Psychology of Adolescence* (New York: Holt, Rinehart & Winston, 1965), p. 23.

[48] Ibid.

[49] Ibid.

"Natural experiments" tested the role of nutrition in the maturation process and revealed a direct correlation between quality of nutrition and physical development. Adverse effects of inadequate nutrition were observed during three socioeconomic upheavals: World War I, the Great Depression, and World War II. All three catastrophes had a direct impact on the growth of children and teenagers. During World War I, there was a slowing of growth among the children of nations that were intensely involved in the war.

Reliably documented correlations between nutrition and physical measurements come from Stuttgart, Germany, where children were measured every year since 1910, with records available for both the *Volksschule* (elementary school) and the *Oberschule* (secondary school).[50] The records show marked reductions in weight and height during times of national crisis. For example, around 1925, the average weight for all age levels declined sharply. These were years of severe inflation. Concomitantly with recovery from the national economic disaster, there was an upswing in physical measurements. During the first years of World War II there was an increase in weight, probably because Germany acquired food supplies through conquest. Over the subsequent four years, however, the average weight declined rapidly and remained low for two or three years after the end of the war.

An additional insight grew out of this study. There was a consistent difference between pupils in the two types of schools. Since the German system allows youths of the same age to attend either the *Volksschule* or the *Oberschule*, comparison between pupils of the same age was possible. The *Oberschule* draws enrollment primarily from upper socioeconomic classes. Although the impact of the national crises affected the pupils of both school systems, the average measurements of the *Oberschule* pupils *always* remained above those of the *Volksschule* pupils.

The direct correlation between socioeconomic background and physical growth has been verified in Germany as recently as the 1980s. A survey showed that students from unskilled working-class families had the smallest measurements, while those from professional and business families had the largest. Students from the middle of the socioeconomic range—from skilled working-class and farm families—had inbetween measurements.[51]

The influence of a national crisis on the growth pattern of children was observed in America during the Great Depression. The greatest impact was among the children of middle-class parents, who met the crisis by reducing the quality of food rather than relying on public relief. Interestingly, the children of the lowest income groups actually gained weight during those years, probably because the

---

[50] Paul E. Howe and Maria Schiller, "Growth Responses of the School Child to Change in the Diet and Environmental Factors," *Journal of Applied Physiology*, 5 (August 1952), 51–61.

[51] "Karlsruhe: Studenten immer länger," DAAD *Mitteilungen*, Bonn, November 1982, p. 17.

food given to them in public kitchens or through charities was better than the diet their parents had been able to provide.[52]

Rate and quality of growth correlate positively with socioeconomic status. The differences are small but consistent from one study to another. Children of professionals or business executives are on the average taller and heavier than those from middle-class homes, who, in turn, exceed in all aspects of growth the children from the lowest socioeconomic class.

American society is characterized by factors favoring earlier maturation and superior physiological development, with a concomitant intensifying effect on adolescence. Earlier maturation creates a longer period of adolescence, and superior maturation produces a youth with the capabilities and physical appearance of an adult, but he or she is not allowed to act as an adult.

Although the age of pubescence has begun to level off in the United States, we can assume that the teenage subculture will soon include ten-to-nineteen-year-old youths rather than thirteen-to-nineteen-year-old youths.

Postindustrial society is delaying adulthood for educational, economic, and other reasons, while improved biological care shortens the period of childhood. Inbetween lies an expanding period of contradiction, a no man's land in which a person's physical and sexual endowments are out of phase with his or her social position.

SUMMARY

Postindustrial life aggravates the adolescent experience. Most influential in this aggravation is the complex network of positions making continuity from child to adult status difficult. The division of labor in postindustrial society requires specialists to occupy a vast range of highly specific positions. Children are "generalists." When they enter adolescence, the generalist standing becomes dysfunctional and they must choose a specific but relatively unknown position. Most teenagers know little about their parents' occupational responsibilities, and only a small proportion follow the occupation of their parents. This situation calls for nonfamilial preparation for the adult position. High schools and other institutions have replaced traditional preparation within the family setting and assumed *in loco parentis* authority. Since technological progress is continuously eliminating the need for unskilled manual labor and creating new technical and managerial positions, training and education of adolescents have become more complex and time consuming. This adds more years of poorly defined status to the adolescent experience.

American schools have become detention camps that try to prevent an onrush of millions of sixteen-year-olds into the labor market. The holding-pen nature of

[52] C. E. Palmer, "Height and Weight of the Depression Poor," *United States Public Health Reports*, 50 (1935), 1106–13.

modern education has been sensed by the students and has created among them a sense of meaninglessness and resentment. The students' resentful attitudes are compounded by many young Americans' unrealistic expectation that postindustrial society's promise of "instantness" can be applied to mental tasks.

In addition to geographic mobility, extensive generational mobility increases uncertainty by inducing the teenager to improve, strive, and enter a career with prestige.

Frequently, socialization of the young takes place in nonfamilial institutions. Clinicians have found that parental deprivation disables the young, inducing defects in achievement, identity, assumption of adult responsibilities, and acquisition of normal emotions.

The most conspicuous aspect of modern adolescents is their affluence, which allows them to materially implement peer standards. By signifying membership in the subculture, material implementation reinforces collective identity.

Modern medicine, technology, and especially nutrition have lowered the age of puberty. Since the upper limit of adolescence is not lowered, increasing proportions of America's youth experience adolescence.

Chapter 4

American Culture Influences

CULTURE:
A SOCIOLOGICAL EMPHASIS

While the preceding chapter discussed the impact of major structural, technological, and biological conditions on the adolescent experience, this chapter explores the influence of a more abstract phenomenon: culture.

The concept of culture varies with the frame of reference. For example, the colloquial connotation usually deals with the "finer things" in life, such as art, music, theater, dance, literature, etc. Anthropologists refer to either physical or nonphysical culture or to both, including *all* human creations. Physical aspects of culture refer to the products of technology; nonphysical aspects to ideas, knowledge, and common symbolic expressions.

The latter dimensions of culture are important to the sociological discussion, since they emphasize *rules, expectations, and values of society*, making up the "blueprint" for behavior that society imposes on its members. This blueprint consists of cultural dicta and is enforced by social sanctions (by punishment for deviation, reward for conformity). It is a powerful force, capable of evoking compelling reactions, such as guilt and shame in cases of violation, and pride and self-esteem in cases of adherence. The following discussion uses the term *culture* primarily in the sense of a blueprint for behavior maintained by formal as well as informal sanction systems.

THE NATURE-NURTURE
CONTROVERSY

Although social scientists agree that modern teenagers are characterized by restless and confused behavior, they differ in explaining this behavior. While most sociologists and psychologists argue for an environmental, primarily cultural, explanation, a few opt for a biogenetic hypothesis. The question of whether *nature* (biological conditions) or *nurture* (social environment) is responsible for a given behavior pattern is an old one and has been asked in relation to various stages of life. The assumption that a causal relationship exists between the physiological, especially endocrinological, changes during pubescence and the adolescent's behavior has been largely discarded in favor of the cultural explanation.

It is for historical interest that we refer to G. Stanley Hall, frequently called the father of the psychology of adolescence. He promoted a biogenetic theory that became well known in the 1910s and 1920s and became the credo of many educators and psychologists.[1] In fact, the concept of adolescence was brought to the attention of the public through Hall's writing, starting during the last two decades of the nineteenth century.

Hall's psychology of adolescence assumed a causal relationship between pubertal changes and social-psychological adjustment problems. It translated Darwin's concept of evolution into a psychological theory of individual recapitulation, asserting that the experiential history of the human species had become part of the genetic structure of each individual. The law of recapitulation maintained that the individual organism, during its development, passes through phases that simulate the developmental stages of the human race from early animal-like primitivism through an era of savagery to the more recent, allegedly more civilized, ways of life that characterize maturity. "Ontogeny recapitulates phylogeny" is the famous adage derived from this theory.

Hall's first major developmental phase includes the first four years of life, when the child is still crawling. Presumably this corresponds to the animal stage of the human race, when the species was using four legs. The period of childhood, ranging from about four to eight, corresponds to the epoch when hunting and fishing were humans' main activities. This primitive way of living is reflected in children's play preferences, such as playing cowboys and Indians, using toy weapons, and building caves, camps, and other hiding places. The latter activities putatively parallel the cave-dwelling culture of early history. Youth, from eight to twelve, recapitulates the life of savagery of several thousand years ago. Hall considered children in this stage to be receptive to learning skills and discipline. Adolescence ranges from puberty to the attainment of full adult status, which occurs between twenty-two and twenty-five years of age. Hall ascribed the idiom *Sturm und*

---

[1] G. Stanley Hall, *Adolescence*, 2 vols. (New York: Appleton–Century–Crofts, 1916).

Drang[2] (storm and stress) to this stage and likened it to the time when the human race was in a turbulent, transitional stage. In late adolescence, the individual recapitulates the initial phase of modern civilization and enters the end phase of the process: maturity.

These developmental stages are presumably brought about by biologically innate forces that control growth and behavior. Human behavior was thought to manifest itself therefore in unchangeable patterns regardless of the cultural environment.

Cultural anthropologists challenged this assertion in the light of crosscultural observations.[3] They pointed to societies where adolescence did not exist, thereby invalidating Hall's claim that the adolescent's dispositions are universal expressions of innate drives.

However, Hall and his followers continued to insist that socially unacceptable behavior, the type held analogous to earlier historical phases, must be tolerated by parents and educators, since it is part of unavoidable stages in the social development of the individual. These psychologists reassured parents and teachers that objectionable behavior would vanish of its own accord in subsequent stages of development and that corrective measures were neither necessary nor advisable. Remnants of this theory still occupy a place in American educational philosophy embedded in such ideas as Gesell's concept of maturation.[4] In fact, Hall's theory played a role in the formation of the educational philosophy of permissiveness—a style that has become widespread in America. Like Rousseau, whose educational philosophy is illustrated in *Émile*, Hall believed that the adult should not interfere with the natural course of development, which is determined by directional forces innate to humans.

Although G. Stanley Hall has almost been forgotten, if not rejected, he has left his mark on the theories of adolescence. His critics denied the validity of conceptualizing personal growth in terms of "stages," yet this is still done. His critics charged him with exaggerating the "storm and stress" symptoms, yet this is the preoccupation of many psychologists of adolescence today.

---

[2] Hall was strongly influenced by a movement in German literature that was led by Schiller and Goethe. The literary trend extolled idealism, search for goals, revolution against the old, expression of personal feelings, passion, and suffering. Hall drew an analogy between the objectives of this group of youthful writers at the beginning of the eighteenth century and the psychological characteristics of adolescence.

[3] One of the first and most incisive challenges was Margaret Mead, *Coming of Age in Samoa* (New York: William Morrow, 1983). However, recent reexamination of Mead's data revealed her "nurture" bias and her consequent misrepresentation—albeit unintentional—of growing up in Samoa. See Derek Freeman, *Margaret Mead and Samoa: The Making and Unmaking of an Anthropological Myth* (Cambridge, Mass.: Harvard University Press, 1983).

[4] Arnold Gesell maintained that maturation and growth is a process that should not be interfered with. He assumed that time alone will solve most of the normal problems of the child and that difficulties and deviations will be outgrown. Arnold Gesell and Frances L. Ilg, *Infant and Child in the Culture of Today* (New York: Harper & Row, 1943).

A realistic assessment of the nature-nurture question will probably result in neither an extreme environmental nor an extreme biogenetic statement, but rather in a balanced view Without doubt, the physiological upheavals during early adolescence are capable of profoundly influencing the psychological processes and the social behavior of the young individual. However, the vast majority of modern behavioral scientists ascribe greater influence to the cultural environment that offers *interpretations* of this physiological turbulence than to the physiological processes per se.

Cultural interpretations establish the meaning of an event, thing, or physiological process. Humans, as creatures who interpret symbols, do not react to things and happenings as such, but mainly to the *meanings attached* to them. From a cross-cultural point of view, it is possible to observe a nearly endless *differential interpretation of neural impulses*; that is, one and the same physiological process can be perceived in totally different ways.

PUBESCENCE AND CULTURAL VALUES

As mentioned in the preceding chapter, urban-industrial society causes earlier onset of pubescence and extends the adolescent period into younger age groups. This implies that concomitant sexual needs occur at a progressively younger age.

The young adolescent's awareness of physiological changes—even if they were not accompanied by any particular cultural interpretation—would be enough to cause him or her alarm. Bodily changes take place too rapidly to give the child enough time to adjust. When a negative cultural interpretation of the sexual maturation process is added, it leaves a powerful and often lasting impression.

American culture turns pubescence into an adolescence-reinforcing event by making the young feel that they go through a stage that should not be mentioned. Both girl and boy develop ambiguous perceptions of their bodily changes that often result in nonacceptance of themselves.

In contrast, in many so-called primitive tribal societies, pubescence is celebrated. For example, the Apache Indian girl's menarche is celebrated by a priest who kneels before her to obtain her blessing.[5] Four ceremonial days honor the Navajo girl's puberty. She is bathed and decorated; relatives bake corn cake; songs and chants are offered; and young men run the dawn races.[6]

---

[5] Ruth Benedict, *Patterns of Culture* (New York: New American Library, 1950), p. 26.

[6] Charlotte J. Frisbie, *Kinaaldá: A Study of the Navajo Girl's Puberty Ceremony* (Middletown, Conn.: Wesleyan University Press, 1967).

DISPARITY BETWEEN BIOLOGICAL
ADULTHOOD AND SOCIAL
ADULTHOOD

American culture prescribes sexual neuterness at a time the young have just achieved sexual potency and are characterized by intense sexuality. Biologically, the vast majority of adolescents are as capable of the reproductive act and as much in need of erotic release as the adult. But, while adolescents are sexually adult, they are not yet socially adult. This cultural norm is legally edged: Not one state in the union permits marriage under the age of eighteen without the consent of the parents.

The social immaturity ascribed to teenagers has serious implications for their sex lives. American mores discourage young adolescents from expressing their sexual interests; sexual expression, be it heterosexual, homosexual, or autoerotic, is disapproved. Yet the majority of adolescents have been both sufficiently informed and encouraged by mass media fare to choose actual sexual experimentation over passively limiting themselves—as utopian cultural standards would seek—to fantasies or nocturnal emission. Without exception, survey data have shown increasing rates of masturbation, petting, sex play, and intercourse.

Representative survey findings of 1979, collected by U.C.L.A. sex researcher Aaron Hass and based on samples across the nation, show that among fifteen-to-sixteen-year-olds 43 percent of the boys and 31 percent of the girls have had intercourse. Approximately 28 percent of the boys and 7 percent of the girls report ten or more sexual partners. In the same age group, 80 percent of the males and nearly 50 percent of the females report they masturbate at least once a week. Nearly 70 percent of the girls and 90 percent of the boys approve of oral sex, and among seventeen-to-eighteen-year-olds, over half of each group has performed it.[7]

The Kantner-Zelnik surveys, corroborating many others, show that teenage sexual activities have increased over the past decades. National samples indicate that the proportion of fifteen-to-nineteen-year-old girls having premarital intercourse has grown from 30 to about 50 percent in 1979.[8] These figures confirm the findings of various surveys showing increases in premarital intercourse rates for all groups of young Americans, but particularly for women, who now roughly match the men's rate.

Since premarital sexual behavior deviates from cultural norms, most sexually active teenagers experience feelings of guilt and shame. Recognizing that they have violated standards imposed by adults, they develop a sense of alienation. Feelings of shame and guilt are easily converted into feelings of rejection and hatred against those causing the self-punishing emotions. Ultimately, a reinforcing vicious cycle forms between the rejector and the rejectee. This holds especially true when the parties involved are collectivities, since feelings of rejection toward outsiders thrive

---

[7] Aaron Hass, *Teenage Sexuality* (New York: Macmillan, 1979), pp. 53, 54, 67, 68, 86.

[8] "Contraception," *Psychology Today*, November 1980, p. 100.

most vigorously if an in-group supports and rewards hostile attitudes. The rejection that teenagers perceive because of their sexual attitudes and activities is in this way transformed into feelings of belonging to the peer group, which accepts them as they are.

THE LACK OF RITE
OF PASSAGE

Life in society consists of a series of passages from one age group to another, from one occupation to another, from one institutional membership to the next—in other words, from one status to another. In parts of the world, the progression from one status to the next is accompanied by ceremonies publicly proclaiming entry into the new status. Sometimes the ceremonies are of a sacred nature, suggesting divine sanction of the new role and entrusting the individual with rights and obligations. In all cases, these rites are public rituals, manifesting the consensual quality of the transition.

Certain transitions are universal. Birth, puberty, assumption of adult responsibility, marriage, parenthood, and death are examples of universal experiences. These and other crises are usually accompanied by *rites of passage*, designed to carry the individual from one phase of human experience to another. Although the celebrations may differ in detail and manner from one culture to another, wherever they are present they essentially serve the same three functions:

Informing.   The initiate is informed of his or her new rights and obligations. Sometimes this may involve a special period of training and indoctrination supervised by qualified elders of the community.

Announcing.   The community is alerted to the fact that a given person assumes a new status and that the actions and reactions of its members must now fall in line with new role interaction.

Emotionally anchoring.   Humans respond to rituals profoundly. More persistent loyalty and commitment can be elicited through them than through almost any other means. Taking on a new role in the eyes of the public and witnessing its decisive approval presents the young with a validated reinforcement that gives him or her a feeling of "belonging" to the new status. The initiate does not *play* the new role; he or she *becomes* the role. (Points 1 and 3 are obviously not implemented in birth and death. where the rite is soley for the benefit of the community.)

The rite of passage in the context of adolescence concerns the transition from the status of child to the status of adult. It is popularly held that the transition is indicated, if at all, by puberty rite. However, it is necessary to distinguish between the rite of passage concerning physiological puberty and "social puberty;" they are different and only occasionally converging phenomena.

Many privileges, such as sexual expression, marriageability, and adult responsibilities, do not depend on puberty but may be experienced earlier or later,
depending on the individual and the social environment. Nonsynchronization of
physiological puberty and social puberty can be illustrated by many examples, such
as the fact that in Italy girls are legally marriageable at age twelve, when barely 10
percent of Italian girls have started menstruating. In France it is legal to marry at
sixteen and one-half years of age, but the average age of puberty is around fourteen.[9] Thus, in Italy social puberty precedes physiological puberty, while in France
it follows.

Among the Salish Indians of British Columbia, membership in an endogamous
adult class begins with a name-giving ceremony, which always comes later than the
ceremony of puberty. The father prepares an elaborate feast and invites the relatives. When all have gathered, the father leads his son, together with sponsors, onto
the roof of the house and begins a prescribed dance and song. This is followed by
distribution of gifts in the name of ancestors. Then the father asks forty nobles to
act as witnesses, while two elder chiefs step forward with the young man between
them and announce the name and the titles of that ancestor after whom the father
wishes the son to be named. In most cases it is the grandfather. The crowd expresses consent through hand-clapping. Once more, gifts are distributed, and a meal
follows; afterward the young man is known by the name and title received at the
ceremony.[10]

This custom is not as unique as it may appear. For example, in Japan and
Europe during the Middle Ages, the coat of arms corresponded to the totem and
sacred symbols and tatoos for age groups or secret societies. Bestowing of the coat
of arms, like that of the totemic emblem, is a rite of passage into an adult group.[11]
Among the Masai of Kenya, circumcision as a ritual of social puberty occurs as soon
as boys are considered strong enough to undergo the elaborate rite, usually between
twelve and sixteen. The date sometimes depends on the affluence of the boy's
family. Circumcision may be performed earlier if the parents are rich; if the parents
are poor, the ceremony is delayed until they can pay the cost. The ritual of circumcision takes place every four to six years; all boys who are circumcised at one time
belong to an age group bearing a special name chosen by the chief. Simultaneously
with or prior to the rite of passage for the boy, the father must undergo the rite of
"passing the fence," signifying acceptance of the status of "old man," after which
he is called "father of (name of his offspring)."[12]

Another example of the independence of initiation rite from puberty is the
bar mitzvah. It takes place when the Jewish boy is thirteen and presumably enters
the age of responsibility and religious duty, thereby acquiring adult status. The bar

---

[9] Arnold van Gennep, *The Rites of Passage* (Chicago: University of Chicago Press,
1960), p. 66.

[10] Ibid., p. 101.

[11] Ibid., pp. 101-2.

[12] M. Merker, *Die Massai, Ethnographische Monographie Eines Ostafrikanischen Semiten-
Volkes* (Berlin: Reimer, 1904), p. 55.

mitzvah has been reduced to mere religious ceremony with little or no bearing on the public and secular life of the boy. Obviously, a thirteen-year-old boy is not eligible for marriage and may not assume adult status.

Because of discrepancy between physiological maturation and ascription of adult status, it is incorrect to refer to *initiation rites* (entry into adult status) as puberty rites. In virtually all societies the age at which young men and women are allowed to marry does not coincide with physiological puberty; and if one day the two moments, one social and the other physiological, come to coincide, they will do so only as a result of deliberate planning.

American culture lacks *both* puberty and initiation rites. Puberty is a taboo issue and is not accompanied by a public ritual with status-clarifying effect. Likewise, there is no definitive rite of initiation into the adult world, although a legal age is set for marriageability and franchise. However, prior to these particular privileges, there is partial assumption of adult responsibilities and privileges through military service, employment, driving an automobile, etc. One cannot speak, therefore, of a *certain age* at which the young of our society move from one status to the other.

Clarity of one's social position and integration into the system is a recognizable human need. To meet this need, a number of prerequisites must be completed, one being a clear introduction into one's status. Absence of a transition rite reduces awareness and clarity of one's status and can create maladjustment.

If society is to prevent this type of maladjustment, it must (1) clearly define roles, (2) cultivate consistent responses toward role incumbents, (3) respect the importance of each role, and (4) observe a transition procedure that clearly signals the change of role.

Unfortunately, these principles are not applied to American teenagers. There is role confusion, condescension toward their age group, inconsistent response patterns on the part of the larger society toward the young, and lack of transition procedure.

VALUE CONFLICT:
THE ALL-AMERICAN DICHOTOMIES

Although dualism in value patterns can be observed in most modern societies, American society appears to subject its members to extreme contrasts. Some deserve special mention because they cause confusion and uncertainty for Americans in general and youth in particular:

Competition vs. cooperation. American society maintains the value of fierce competition and glorifies a "winner"—whether it is a beauty queen or a farmer raising the finest cattle. The goal of economic success has been heavily stressed and has strained institutional regulations and the permissible means for its attainment. In extreme instances, only questions of technical effectiveness have entered into the choice of means for the goal, and "business is business" has been the apology of robber barons, organized crime, and racketeering.

However, the generosity of the American people is proverbial. There exists an enormous range of voluntary humanitarian activities in America such as the Community Chest, service clubs, public welfare agencies, religious charities, private philanthropies, and the Peace Corps.

The polarity of competition and cooperation is part of many situations involving young people. In school, boys and girls become aware very early that they are competing with one another. The typical American grading system, the "curve" method, automatically converts students into competitors. Yet students are expected to cooperate when it comes to other aspects of interaction, such as dating, courting, and marriage. Necessity of frequent, abrupt switches from one attitude to the other and unclearness of when and how to do so introduce confusion into the boy-girl, and later the man-woman, relationship.

Work vs. leisure. Puritan tradition gave secular work activities religious sanction and viewed successful work as a sign of divine grace. The metaphysical directive to work was the norm in the older rural culture of America and is still extant in rural areas and subcultures that have not yet assimilated postindustrial attitudes toward leisure and consumption.

Modern American youth's attitude toward work mirrors the economic conditions of the nation. During the early 1970s, propelled by idealistic counterculture philosophy, youth took material security for granted and looked for psychological rewards ("self-realization") when choosing a career. The attitude was reflected in Yankelovich's survey findings: 57 percent of college and 52 percent of noncollege youth felt confident that they would "make as much money as they want." Yet their confidence apparently was not based on the Protestant ethic, since their belief in "hard work always pays off" declined from 79 percent in the 1960s to 56 percent in the 1970s.[13]

With worsening economic conditions, including increasing inflation and unemployment, the early 1980s saw a return to basic material concerns by American youth. College students no longer spouted confidence and idealistic slogans, but realized that they were facing hard times in which the work ethic again played a role. But a modification had also developed: Young people expected the work ethic to be supplemented, if not replaced, by social welfare programs. In spite of the efforts by the federal government to curb proliferation of welfare benefits, the austere 1980s still have not entirely recovered the traditional work spirit.

At the same time, we have observed continuing conspicuous consumption. For example, despite gas prices, hotel fees, and import duties, America's lakes still teem with speed boats, hotels still show "no vacancy" signs, and young people are saturated with foreign-made goods. The 1980s, more so than the 1970s, reveal the

[13] Daniel Yankelovich, *The New Morality: A Profile of American Youth in the 70s* (New York: McGraw–Hill, 1974), pp. 84, 87, 103.

contrasting values of hard work and of consumption patterns anchored in post-industrial affluence.

Piety vs. freethinking. Public opinion polls have shown that freedom is repeatedly mentioned as one of the most cherished advantages of American life. Most Americans are proud to remember such freethinkers as Walt Whitman, Ralph Waldo Emerson, and Henry Thoreau. When it comes to concrete instances, however, "free thought" rapidly loses its appeal. It is often said that America is a land of freedom of religion, but hardly *from* religion. For example, one who publicly admits being an atheist often meets with suspicion and rejection. This conflict between "free thought" and Christian piety has been visible in long, drawn-out battles and polemics concerning prayer in public schools.

Individualism vs. conformity. The "individual" in American life is conceptualized as an independent and inventive agent, morally responsible only to him- or herself. While theoretically this idea is still maintained, considerable dependency and conformity has developed in American life. Regulations have been introduced, presumably guaranteeing economic well-being for all, including social security, Medicare, and obligatory retirement funds. Critics call these measures "welfare state practices" and claim that freedom is no longer tied to a system of private property and passive government.

American youth are introduced to many glorified, historical exposés of "rugged individualism" and encouraged to emulate this "truly American" trait. On the other hand, they are constantly challenged to conform to national and patriotic standards. Although conflicting values have been part of any era, they were particularly visible during the 1960s and early 1970s when dissent against the Vietnam war ran high. A powerful faction of public opinion, the "silent majority," recognized dissent not as an expression of individualistic thinking but as subversive and unAmerican. It is interesting to note that factionalism also split the youth population, dividing them into "hawks" and "doves."[14]

With the Vietnam war over, American youth declined in militancy, yet sustained a great deal of the counterculture-generated individualism, manifested by experimentation with communal living, cohabitation, and cults. The 1980s ushered in a generally placid attitude by youth toward political life. A few relatively minor upheavals disturbed the calm. One was the sporadic (mostly individual) protest against the renewal of the draft registration; the other was a new peace movement opposing the Reagan administration's nuclear armament policy.[15] The latter had international dimensions, and the rally of 700,000 concerned Americans in New

[14] Hans Sebald, "Voices of War and Peace – What Do They Know? Attitudes and Knowledge about the War in Southeast Asia," *Pacific Sociological Review*, 14 (October 1971), 487–510.

[15] "Campuses vs. the Bomb," *Newsweek*, March 15, 1982, p. 19; "New Peace Movement," *World Press Review*, March 1982, p. 43; "Full ahead, Course uncertain. Antinuclear Groups still Lack Direction," *Time*, June 28, 1982, p. 37.

York City's Central Park on a summer day in 1982 was matched in numbers and fervor by youth in several European countries.

New national and international issues will continue to challenge youth. They will have to decide whether to adhere to or dissent from governmental policies. Each generation of young Americans will have to learn anew that the cultural blueprint for individualism is ambiguous and situational—imposing on them the nongeneralizability that prevents simplicity and predictability in social life.

Sex vs. chastity. One of the most notorious confusions within the blueprint of American society concerns sex. On the one side, sex and "love" are eulogized *in abstracto* and, on the other side, there ensues furtive and guilt-ridden apprehension. Sex education is an unwelcome task often evaded and passed from one institution to another, and it is rare that any of them accomplish adequate instruction. It is unclear whether the family, school, doctor, minister, or mass media should enlighten the young.

During this pedagogic impasse, movies and literature continue to invite teenagers to participate in a type of love that magnifies the erotic and exploitative. Sex has become part of the American "fun" concept, although law, religious tradition, and public opinion condemn premarital sex. Such condemnation has proved ineffectual and hypocritical, since the ubiquitous fact is that the adult world's preoccupation with sex has saturated the adolescent's environment with images that encourage sexual activities.

It appears, then, that American culture is beset with schizoid values concerning sexual matters. These inconsistent polar concepts cause confusion and anxiety among adolescents, who are trying to arrive at a consistent blueprint for sexual behavior.

One could extend the list of conflicting values and point out the effects they have on young individuals trying to integrate their life experiences. If the theory is accepted that a healthy personality requires an integrated *Gestalt* of views and attitudes, then cultural conflict will have confounding effects.

VALUE CONFLICT:
THE CHILD-ADULT DICHOTOMIES

No culture ascribes the same blueprint to all participants. Humans at different chronological stages have different needs and capabilities; nowhere is a child required to act like an adult, neither is a mature and healthy adult allowed to act like a child for any length of time. The differences that various cultures have in respect to time of role transition and to degree of role distinction vary greatly. In some societies, mostly the small and so-called primitive societies, children assume adult roles at an early age, while in the large and modern societies children grow in adulthood via a nondescript phase that separates adulthood from childhood by as much as ten years. In respect to degree of role differentiation, American culture goes to

great lengths to emphasize contrasts between the roles of child and adult, pre-
scribing for each distinct sets of expectations. This principle can be exemplified by
a number of specific opposing role expectations.[16]

Responsibility vs. nonresponsibility.   As an illustration of more relaxed role
differentiation, the Canadian Ojibwa allow their children to engage in adult activities as soon as they are physically capable. The boy accompanies the father on
hunting trips and brings in his catch to his sister as his father does to his mother. It
is the girl's responsibility to prepare the meat and skins for her brother just as the
mother does for her husband. By the time the boy reaches twelve years of age, he
usually operates a line of traps on a hunting territory of his own and returns to his
parents' house only occasionally to bring the meat and skins to his sister. A child
of this tribe is taught at an early age to rely on him- or herself and to see the world
of the adult as not much different from the world of the young.

Child-rearing practices of American culture differ. The inside worlds of industry, business, professions, and labor are relatively inaccessible and largely unknown
to the child. Children do not contribute to the division of labor until they are in
their late teens or early twenties; then they are expected to assume adult responsibilities in an abrupt fashion.

In many tribal societies, child-rearing techniques achieve a continuity of
activities that is not limited to daily nurturing patterns but is extended to include
responsibilities that, in our society, are reserved for adults. For example, in the
United States a child is declared nonresponsible in respect to serious adult work.
Americans consider it a rule that the child wants to play and that the adult has to
work, forgetting that in many societies the mothers take their babies along to their
daily work, carrying them in shawls or baskets close to the body. The child thus has
an opportunity to observe adult work and, as soon as the child is old enough, he or
she takes on tasks that are important and yet suited to his or her strength—thereby
precluding formation of a dichotomy between work and play.

In American society, the law enforces the child/adult dichotomy. For example, a child cannot be accused of a crime but only of "delinquency." The legal
and moral burden is the parents' because the child presumably has not yet reached
the "age of legal responsibility." The question of *when* the social and legal reaction
to a child's "delinquency," either in terms of penalty or correction, is commensurate with the child's understanding raises a difficult issue. There has been suspicion that permissive and "understanding" attitudes and counseling will only
reinforce the delinquent pattern. What is needed, according to some psychiatric
experts, is "reality therapy" that makes social reactions commensurate with the
juvenile's understanding of his or her acts.[17] Readjustment of the legal machinery

---

[16] Based on Ruth Benedict, "Continuities and Discontinuities in Cultural Conditioning,"
Psychiatry, 1 (May 1938), pp. 161–67.
   [17] William Glasser, *Reality Therapy* (New York: Harper & Row, 1965).

in this direction would mean that the juvenile would be held more responsible for his or her deeds.

Jerome S. Bruner, head of the center for cognitive studies at Harvard, thinks we grossly underestimate the perceptual and comprehensive capability of children. Bruner holds that children can learn any subject at any stage of their development and advocates that they be required to perform far more complicated tasks than they do. By not expecting much from children, we in fact condition them not to give much, thereby perpetuating the American myth that nonresponsibility for children is necessary.[18]

Sex vs. sexless. Sexual attitudes and activities are the most complicated discontinuities in cultural learning. In virtually all societies the child must seriously modify his or her behavior at puberty or at marriage—these two occasions representing universal discontinuities in both sexual capability and sexual standards. At such times, the cultural prescriptions for sex may, for example, change preadolescent sexual license to marital fidelity or, as in a few societies, premarital virginity in either male or female to marital status with considerable sexual license.

Although some degree of discontinuity in sexual behavior is a universal condition, there can be continuity in one aspect: *continuity in sexual expression means that the child is taught nothing he or she must unlearn later.* Therefore, in spite of the universal conditions of puberty and marriage one can classify some societies as facilitating continuity and others as imposing discontinuity.

For example, adults among the Dakota Indians observe great privacy in sex acts and in no way encourage children's sexual activities.[19] Yet one cannot speak of discontinuity, since the child is not indoctrinated in ways he or she must unlearn later. In a culture with this type of sex pattern, adults view children's sexual experimentation as in no way wicked but rather as innocuous play.

But the same *laissez-faire* attitude may be taken by adults in societies where such play is encouraged among young children. This is true of Melanesian cultures where adults exhibit sexual permissiveness and children feel free to indulge in sex play that is autoerotic, homosexual, or heterosexual. Although modified by marital regulation, the same open and hedonistic style is carried over into adult status, and no discontinuity is experienced.[20]

If society's emphasis is on reproduction, as for instance it is among Zuñi Indians, sexual expression among children is not encouraged. Although the Zuñi child is impressed with the prohibition of premature sex, the prohibition is not associated with sex itself but only with sex at a young age.[21] In Anglo-American

---

[18] Jerome S. Bruner, *The Process of Education* (Cambridge, Mass.: Harvard University Press, 1963), pp. 33ff.

[19] Benedict, "Continuities and Discontinuities," pp. 164–65.

[20] Ibid.

[21] Ibid.

culture the association is with sex as such and the adult often fails to unlearn the evil connotation of sex.

Dominance vs. submission.   Americans tend to accept as universal the custom of viewing the adult-child relationship as dominant-submissive. This ethnocentric assumption has been exposed by anthropologists who studied cultures with different modes of intergenerational relations. In some cultures the terminology of address between father and son reflects a reciprocal relationship; the two are equal and the terms of their relationship will never change. When the son becomes a parent, he will establish the same relationship with his child. In societies with this type of equalitarian father-son relationship, the figure with a disciplining function usually is a close male relative, such as the mother's brother.[22] Such kinship conventions provide the individual with a behavior code he or she can follow from childhood through adulthood with minimal discontinuities.

In American society the child lives under parental authority by informal custom and formal law, reinforced by religious dictates of the Judeo-Christian heritage that threaten with damnation everyone who disobeys parents. This generational polarity raises questions for young people about when and how to shift from one mode of the relationship to the other.

The above list of value discontinuities could probably be extended to include work vs. play, independence vs. dependence, inhibition vs. impulsivity, etc. However, these additions probably would be less mutually exclusive than the ones discussed above. The point is that cultural values vary on a continuum of age-differentiation, with certain values in complete opposition and others overlapping.

In conclusion, American culture contains enough child-adult dichotomies to exert strain on both the individual personality and the interpersonal process. The main impact of this situation is felt by young persons at a time when they find themselves *between* two relatively well-defined roles. During the transition they struggle with ambiguity, trying to decide which set of behaviors they should enact.

ANOMIE IN AMERICAN LIFE

Effects graver than those caused by conflicting values can result from a culture's failure to spell out *any* values or norms. Deviation from known norms or compromise between conflicting norms seems to be less destructive to personality and the social system than vagueness or lack of norms, since deviation or compromise at least starts with a stable point that potentially provides direction.

Humans need structure, a *Gestalt* that conveys a sense of direction, orientation, and stability. Such guides are intimately dependent on clear norms and expectations. A person not realizing any norms would be shiftless and unstable. Emile

[22] Reference is to the Trobriand Islanders. Bronislaw Malinowski, *Magic, Science, and Religion, and Other Essays* (New York: Doubleday, 1954).

Durkheim recognized this principle in his classic study on suicide, and conceptualized one type of suicide as *anomic*, the result of a person feeling meaningless in a normless environment.[23] Anomie, derived from the Greek *anomia*, originally meant "lack of order" and was used by Durkheim to describe a social milieu in which control over the members has broken down. This breakdown liberates the individual from moral authority of the community, but at the same time results in personal disequilibrium manifested by a variety of antisocial behavior patterns that may include suicide, delinquency, and formation of subcultures.

Values, usually tied up with general cultural goals suggesting *what* is to be valued, and norms, more specific rules of conduct spelling out *how* to go about achieving the values, can be considered two different phenomena. The relationship between them varies and can be classified in a number of ways. Robert Merton developed a typology and showed anomie to be a result of preoccupation with cultural goals in the absence of clear norms and means. In terms of American culture, values are suggested, but feasible ways of achieving them are not indicated. As a general example, American culture stresses monetary success, but fails to extend "a corresponding emphasis upon the legitimate avenues on which to march toward this goal."[24] This type of anomie can cause apathy, manifested by the rejection of goals and norms altogether. A prominent type of apathy results after a cultural goal is not attained in spite of intense striving. Reaction to failure may be anxiety expressed in moral fatigue and indifference. The individual may be left in a social vacuum, without direction or meaning.

The significance of anomie for adolescence is that it strikes hardest when social-structural security is not yet obtained, when the young individual is still a "generalist" trying to find orientation in the *general* culture. "General" is emphasized because youth lacks *specific* norms and directives, which come with adult positions. It is in the general culture that anomie operates, and the teenager is bound to suffer anxiety when attempting to derive direction from it.

Adults are faced with the same anomic condition when trying to orient themselves by abstract cultural features. However, adults have established clarity by means of concrete living patterns — patterns that are guided by positions in the social structure. Since the young are largely excluded from the division of labor of the adult world, they tend to group together and compensate for cultural vacuum by forming a culture of their own.

In conclusion, the psychological reaction to anomie is *anxiety*, the feeling of being lost in an amorphous surrounding. The reaction to conflict, on the other hand, is *frustration*, the feeling of anger against opposing points. American teenagers suffer from both. The attempt to escape from them leads to subculture formation, where teenagers find norms and values that fit together, thereby eliminating, at least temporarily, anomie and anxiety.

[23] Emile Durkheim, *Suicide: A Study in Sociology*, trans. J. A. Spaulding and G. Simpson (Paris: F. Alcan, 1897; reprint ed., Glencoe, Ill.: The Free Press, 1951).

[24] Robert K. Merton, "Social Structure and Anomie: Revisions and Extensions," in *Social Theory and Social Structure* (Glencoe, Ill.: The Free Press, 1949), p. 133.

POINT OF ORDER:
THE PROBLEM OF SELECTIVITY

This chapter attempted to identify causes of adolescence as they exist in American culture. To accomplish this, I focused exclusively on negative aspects of our culture to extract examples necessary to accomplish the analysis. The task can be compared to the job a medical doctor has to do when tracing the causes of a certain condition. The report may point to several physiological problems to explain the illness. For example, he or she may diagnose a malfunction of a certain organ, a deficiency in nutrition, and low resistance. The illness can be understood as the result of the constellation of these factors, and the diagnosis will fail to list all the healthy and normal aspects of the organism since they are of no importance to the diagnosis.

Similarly, in searching for the causes of the adolescent condition, a negative selectivity prevails and only those circumstances are reported that seem to explain it. We investigated the "organ" of culture and found certain characteristics that help us understand the development and persistence of the adolescent condition. Obviously, there are many cultural factors that do not contribute to this condition, but they are not our concern here since they contribute nothing to the diagnosis.

Hence, the picture that emerges from our examination is grimmer than the total reality. Not all aspects of culture work against the adolescent, and not all adolescents stand outside the Establishment's blueprint for behavior. Many American teenagers are sufficiently adjusted, and American culture is no more an ogre to the young than most other cultures. Before they know it, the vast majority of adolescents have grown up and adjusted—and the erstwhile ogre has become a reasonably comfortable habitat.

America has many teenagers who have made a comfortable and even creative adjustment to their culture, enjoy its various institutions, and participate in its programs. A later discussion will illuminate some of these aspects.

SUMMARY

American culture, as culture everywhere, is responsible for interpreting life's experiences and issuing blueprints for behavior. The blueprints of our culture contain a number of elements that add complexity to adolescence. The discussion dwelled selectively on several major negative aspects.

Theories of tracing adolescent "storm and stress" to physiological maturation have largely been replaced by anthropological principles emphasizing the role of cultural relativity in perceiving such organic changes. In American society pubescent changes create adjustment problems because culture avoids giving adequate explanation for them. Youth is thus left unaided to cope with new growth patterns. Social adulthood is not synchronized with biological maturation. During the time teenagers are sexually mature but socially underprivileged, cultural interpretations cause them to feel guilty about sexual expressions. Teenagers' reactions to the negative cultural interpretation are hostility and withdrawal, partially explaining the subcultures.

American culture lacks a definitive rite of passage into adulthood. Transition unclarity creates maladjustments.

Americans are subject to such value dichotomies as competition and cooperation, piety and free thinking, sex and chastity, work and leisure, individuality and conformity. It is difficult for adults to decide which value applies in certain situations and even more difficult for teenagers still working on a basic orientation. Another schism of values breaks the continuity between child and adult roles. Children are kept from continuous involvement in responsibilities and decision-making. They have to relearn or unlearn many modes of thinking and behaving when entering adult positions.

Adolescents are particularly vulnerable to anomie in American life because they do not yet have access to specific positions in the productive sector that would help them derive identity and stability.

In the final analysis, reactions of teenagers to characteristics of American culture develop into *typically adolescent* behavior patterns. Their emotional reactions include: (1) *embarrassment* due to pubescent changes negatively evaluated; (2) *resentment* because of the disparity between sexual and social maturity; (3) *uncertainty* because there is no rite of passage to signify entry into adult status; (4) *confusion* as a result of schismatic values; and (5) *anxiety* as a consequence of anomie.

Chapter 5

Social Change
and
Intergenerational Conflict

CONFLICT BETWEEN GENERATIONS

Conflict between older and younger generations is a perennial force. The social dynamics of every society undergoing change promote tension between generations. Postindustrial society seems singularly afflicted, and a number of points show how this unprecedented disharmony has come about.

Uneven social change. Postindustrial American society is far from being an integrated and "organismic" entity. As Daniel Bell asserts in *The Cultural Contradictions of Capitalism*, three realms within society have different rhythms of change: *techno-economic structure*, *polity*, and *culture*.[1] Rather than enjoying harmonious connections, they drift apart as if wedges were driven between them. A center of gravity is apparently missing; each sector is propelled by its own force.

Traditionally, the techno-economic order was wedded to a compatible ethos that emphasized work, production, investment, and ascetic lifestyle—in short, the Protestant ethic. Now the techno-economic order finds itself increasingly confronted by a sensate ethos that stresses hedonism, insistence on "self-realization," and a novel psychology of entitlement. The latter takes for granted services rendered by the techno-economic system without regard to the recipient's real needs

[1] Daniel Bell, *The Cultural Contradictions of Capitalism* (New York: Basic Books, 1976).

(*wants* now override *needs*) and without respect for costs required to produce the services.

In the forefront of the psychology of entitlement and hedonism stand the young, advancing the new sensate ethos with bravado. However, the new morality transcends generational boundaries to a significant extent. Over time, generational differentiation with respect to new cultural features will probably erode. At this time, the main thrust of hedonistic advance is carried by the young. A large proportion of the older generation still adheres to the Puritan ethic that clashes with the ethos of the younger generation. The elders call the young disrespectful of work and service, and the young refer to adults as rigid and obsolete.

Comparison of Gallup Poll data from 1955 and 1980 revealed that there is indeed substance to the stereotypical complaint that "workers just don't care about their jobs the way they used to." Analysts found that the shift in attitude is not due so much to changes in the nature of work as it is to the retirement of persons who had learned to value work. When the question "Do you enjoy your work so much that you have a hard time putting it aside?" was submitted to a cross section of American workers in the 1950s, 52 percent said yes. A repeat in 1980 yielded only 34 percent. Analysis of the decline showed that one generation sampled in both surveys was still working in 1980: people fifty to sixty-four, who were in their twenties and thirties in the 1950s. Their enjoyment of work was the same in *both* surveys; the declining enjoyment occurred in the younger generation.[2] Older, highly work-oriented people were replaced with less work-oriented people.

Traditionalists sense the ongoing change and accuse the young of consuming the fruits of the techno-economic structure while declining to cooperate in maintaining the structure. Modern youth, they think, adhere to values and norms that must necessarily result in atrophy and, eventually, demise of the structure. Daniel Bell, among others, feels strongly that unless we revitalize our culture and prevent a slide into a superficial, hedonistic ethos, our capitalistic society as we have known it for the last two hundred years will disintegrate.

Rapid social change.   Part of the explanation of the generation gap lies in the pace of social change. In a rapidly changing society, established and respected norms of one generation become obsolete to the next. The older generation may greet innovations with mixed emotions ranging from caution to hostility. Nostalgia for the "good old days" is the universal reaction of elders to unfamiliar behavior patterns. The older generation's lack of familiarity with new styles frequently labels innovations as "weird," "immoral," or "subversive." These epithets, describing the younger generation, can be found in the diaries of virtually all eras. Exceptions to this rule are limited to a few simply-structured tribal societies in isolated localities in which the pace of social change is almost imperceptible.

The tempo of sociocultural change varies from society to society and can be measured on a continuum ranging from near-stagnancy to revolutionary reorganiza-

---

[2] "Work," *Psychology Today*, April 1982, pp. 17–18.

tion. One way of classifying societies by their internal dynamics is in terms of the folk-urban continuum, with slow-changing societies at one end and dynamic urban-industrial societies at the other. Tempo of change is directly correlated with imbalance of perceptions and behavior patterns between the generations. This means that the faster a society changes, the wider the psychological distance between the older and the younger generations. In a nearly unchanging society, the young follow the norms and goals of the older generation so faithfully that the socio-cultural fabric of society remains unchanged. Conversely, in dynamic society one would find the young clashing with the older generation, whose norms and goals have become obsolete.

Modern American society is a prime example of a rapidly changing social system. The turnover of technological and social innovations is rapid enough to create a milieu for each new generation notably different from that of the preceding generation, thus inviting adults to perceive youth as "rebellious" and youth to perceive adults as "old fashioned."

The explanation for the unusual amount of adult-youth conflict in modern society can be summed up by a few interrelated propositions:

1. Each generation learns culture early, and as its members get older, they have difficulty changing their views of right and wrong.
2. Cultural content in American society is changing rapidly.
3. Culture learned by the parental generation was different from that learned by the offspring, insofar as the adolescent learns from peers and from specific adults who are more current in their thinking.
4. Therefore there is a culture conflict experienced by parents and their offspring.[3]

Functionality of conflict. Many observers of symptoms of strain between generations regard these dynamics as dysfunctional. This is a biased view that has to be balanced by pointing to functional aspects of youth unrest and agitation. Since young people are not committed to, and so are less likely to settle for, the *status quo*, they are able to function as a prime factor of innovation and societal improvement.[4] The young have not yet developed the vested interests that their parents are likely to have in either the ongoing economic system or the value structure, and thus are less likely to plead for the *status quo*. Being new-comers to the established order makes young people apt to sympathize with social movements that voice dissatisfaction with society. Being young in a modern society means, among other things, being "marginal," not yet having vested interests in the existing social order and not yet being integrated in the economic and psychological fabric of society. The position of "outsider" explains youth's fascination with movements that are at the fringe of society.

---

[3] Kingsley Davis, "The Sociology of Parent-Youth Conflict," *American Sociological Review*, 5 (August 1940), 523–36.

[4] Karl Mannheim, *Diagnosis of Our Time* (New York: Oxford University Press, 1944).

Youth's lack of commitment to the existing order can be interpreted as a potential resource. Static or slowly evolving traditional societies do not call on this resource and may even suppress it. However, dynamic societies often use it and even organize it for social progress.

Dangers of conflict. One might conclude from this discussion that all youth movements are progressive or liberal, if not downright radical. But surely not all youth movements are progressive. The Nazi youth movement was certainly not politically liberal, at least not in the sense of opposing the regime in power.

Youth is in great need of security and stability, and its search for this type of psychological reward is so unrelenting that it can be exploited. Although young people often rebel against the reality in which they find themselves—and nearly all of them are sooner or later tempted to resent their primary family environment— they almost immediately want to replace it with another form of social reality. (Freedom from norms is unbearable!) Karl Mannheim noted that "dissociation from one's previous reality and the seeking of distance from the primary environment are principal impulses. It is with a sense of liberation that the adolescent discovers alternative interpretations and new values. Self-assertion and defiance accompany this experience."[5]

If a suitable replacement of social reality is prepared for adolescents—as a clever nationalistic demagogue could easily provide—they may embrace it wholeheartedly and so, paradoxically, support the *status quo* by means of their rebelliousness.

It seems that the young find it difficult to endure multiple possibilities and loyalties since such diffuseness might confuse their identities. If they arrive at an extrafamilial loyalty, a schism may develop between them and their parents. As Mannheim saw it, youth's desire to attain distance from the family culture often leads them to embrace opposing values. Those who grow up in a rigorously traditional home may develop revolutionary leanings, while those with a liberal background may choose a conservative course. However, it must be noted that his theory was not supported by Richard Flacks' study of activist students, who generally came from liberal homes (see discussion under Parental Reaction II). It is, then, with a great deal of caution that we accept the slogans and complaints that youth uses to legitimize rebelliousness against the Establishment. Is it invariably the true reason? Or is it an idealized excuse (a typical rationalization) to marshal legitimacy for one's alienation and disturbance? One could defend the notion that the criticism and outspokenness on the part of adolescents is not so much a function of the dismal state of society but rather a normal and almost universal expression of trying to strike roots in a bewildering world.

[5] Karl Mannheim, *Essays on the Sociology of Culture* (New York: Oxford University Press, 1956), p. 165.

Socializing the young: universal conflict. Aristotle commented over two thousand years ago, in a society far less subject to change than ours, that young people have exalted notions because they have not yet been humbled by life's trials and tribulations. All their mistakes are in the direction of doing things excessively. They would always rather do noble deeds than useful ones; their lives are regulated more by feeling than reasoning. They overdo everything—they love too much, they hate too much, and the same with everything else.

Aristotle noted that older people usually differ in such characteristics. After many years of struggles and mistakes, they have become more ponderous, see things in less than black and white, always "think" but never "know," and in their hesitation always add "perhaps" or "maybe," so that all their statements are of this kind: never unqualified.[6]

In other words, the changes through which society goes may not be the sole reason for conflict. Simply that the young are going through socialization contributes to the generation of friction between the old and the young.

Conflict and subculture. It is youth's often very convincing complaining, and successful bluffing, that has cowed the Establishment into making apologies and concessions. Many social scientists have interpreted youthful agitation as symptomatic of a subculture apart from the adult culture, and they have come to be known as "great gap" theorists.[7]

But others have taken issue with this interpretation, maintaining that youth has no real value integration of its own. Thus there is no real subculture causing the generation gap, and the guilt-ridden Establishment is merely reacting *as if* there were a youth subculture and a generation gap.[8] A representative opinion was expressed by Joseph Adelson, who felt that his survey findings refuted the existence of such a gap.[9]

[6] Aristotle, *The Art of Rhetoric*, trans. John H. Freese (Cambridge, Mass.: Harvard University Press, 1959), book 2, chs. 7–13.

[7] Advocates of the "great gap" theory include Theodore Roszak, *The Making of a Counter Culture* (New York: Doubleday, 1969); Charles A. Reich, *The Greening of America* (New York: Random House, 1970); Margaret Mead, *Culture and Commitment: A Study of the Generation Gap* (New York: Basic Books, 1970); James S. Coleman, *The Adolescent Society* (New York: Free Press, 1963); and Edgar Z. Friedenberg, "The Generation Gap," *Annals of the Academy of Political and Social Science*, 382 (1969), 32–42.

[8] Researchers who refute the "generation gap" theory include Joseph Adelson, *Handbook of Adolescent Psychology* (New York: Wiley, 1980); Denise B. Kandel and Gerald S. Lesser, *Youth in Two Worlds* (San Francisco: Jossey-Bass, 1972); Vern L. Bengtson, "Generation and Family Effects in Value Socialization," *American Sociological Review*, 40 (June 1975), 358–71; Daniel Yankelovich, "The Generation Gap: A Misleading Half Truth," Paper presented at the meeting of the Eastern Sociological Society, 1970; Frederick Elkin and William A. Westley, "The Myth of Adolescent Culture," *American Sociological Review*, 20 (December 1955), 680–84; Daniel Offer et al., *The Adolescent: A Psychological Self-Portrait* (New York: Basic Books, 1981); and Majda Thurnher et al., "Value Confluence and Behavioral Conflict in Intergenerational Relations," *Journal of Marriage and the Family*, 36 (May 1974), 308–19.

[9] Joseph Adelson, "Adolescence and the Generalization Gap," *Psychology Today*, February 1979, p. 33.

The trouble with these refutations lie in their violation of the social-psychological principle which says that a situation is real if the participants *perceive* or *define* it as real. Hence it become superfluous to question the existence of a youth subculture. If youth *behaves* as if it holds distinct values and has a subculture, then indeed it has one. And youth does in fact behave differently—whether on the basis of clearly understood values or not—and therefore has a subculture that bears its share of the responsibility for the existence of the generation gap.

Many dimensions must be taken into consideration in order to understand the generation gap. One deals with the "normal" condition of being young and, as already noted by Aristotle, having "exalted notions." Another deals with the disjuncture of the techno-economic and the cultural realms, which results in uneven changes that muddle relations between the generations. A third concerns the pace of society's innovations, scientific progress, and "knowledge explosion." A fourth dimension consists of unique political events that cause a reaction on the part of young people, provoke their scorn, anger, or fear. (A recent example in American history was the war in Vietnam.) A fifth factor deals with cultural images, such as the American youth cult that invites feelings of inferiority among adults and fosters the tendency to accept youth's complaints as correct descriptions of societal malfunctions. We will examine some of these dimensions in the following section.

COMPETING AUTHORITIES: PARENTS VS. EXPERTS

In primitive societies, social change is slow enough for a child to live the same kind of life his or her parents did. In more advanced societies that have more noticeable change, children often abandon their parents' ways and model their behavior on teachers and friends. However, changes fostered by postindustrialism have eroded even these models. Modern youth are like children of wilderness pioneers—the first natives in a new world. For the first time in history there are no elders who know all that the young know. In fact, parents who desire to keep up with current knowledge will have to reverse the traditional pattern and let their children teach them.

This creates an ironic situation. On the one hand, parents are charged with the obligation of introducing children to society, of proceeding with the necessary training, of exerting the necessary control to make the child conform to the demands of culture. On the other hand, parents suffer from cultural lag that leaves them a few paces behind in knowledge in many areas of modern life.

Science and technology are constantly changing, modifying, and adding information in all branches of endeavor. Postindustrial life imposes a premium on the ability to constantly reorient and modify. In order to accomplish this with some degree of adequacy, an almost full-time dedication would have to be invested. Parents can rarely do this. Children, however, attend school, are exposed to the latest information, and *are* involved in this full-time pursuit. Students are at the frontier of knowledge—a frontier that is advanced by experts who are preparing the young for a future that comes faster for each generation.

As any professor knows, it has become exceedingly difficult to keep abreast of the publications and research reports in one's area of expertise. In addition, any particular area has shrunk to an amazingly narrow focus, and is continuing to shrink further. It is no longer possible, for example, to ask a sociologist about just any sociological problem and expect an answer. If the question involves religious behavior, the harried instructor might refer the student to a colleague who is a *sociologist of religion*; if the question concerns population shifts, the student is sent to a *demographer*; if it involves criminal behavior, a *criminologist* is suggested; and if it deals with adolescents, a *sociologist of youth* is consulted. But even within these narrow foci, publications and research reports pile up and drive even the bravest scholar to despair.

The division of expertise has rendered parents helpless and increasingly poorly informed. It is normally impossible for parents to be specialists in more than one or two fields. Children and teenagers therefore obtain instruction and advice from specialists and experts. Through the schools, modern youth has access to the most recent discoveries in nearly all branches of science and knowledge, and can acquire insights and up-to-date information that ordinarily never reach the parents. Parents are preoccupied with making a living and providing their children with an education, and learn about the latest developments and discoveries—often inadequately—via secondary channels, such as popular magazines, newspapers, radio, and television. As a novelty in human history, parents are now instructed by their children.

The socialization function of parents was of course never limited to mere factual instruction and scientific information, but included such aspects as ethical guidance, religious indoctrination, and practical advice. Yet the often conspicuous inability of parents to offer the latest piece of scientific knowledge has had a generalizing effect on the children, inducing them to disregard other aspects of parental competence. In line with this "halo effect," evidence of incompetence in one area tempts children to suspect incompetence in other areas and makes them doubt the ability of parents to introduce them to the adult world.

Extrafamilial "experts" are now doing a substantial part of the rearing and instructing of children. The controversy of *in loco parentis* shows the increasing transfer of socialization function and accompanying authority to schools. Modern teachers with their expanded socialization function, including counseling and advising in matters of personal problems, such as sex and vocational plans, have unintentionally promoted parental obsolescence and reduced parental authority.

Modern adolescents resent parents who wield authority over them when they feel that the latter are not qualified to do so; they insist on being independent decisionmakers in areas previously under parental sovereignty. Authority based merely on position and power—such as the parents'—is increasingly branded by young people as "irrational," while authority based on knowledge (expertise) is defined as "rational." The tendency to engage in the "halo effect" increases the chances that the offspring will view his or her parents' decisions and advice as irrational and overbearing.

Youth finds it difficult to make the distinction between emotional maturity and intellectual acuity—a distinction that must often be drawn between parents and experts. By not drawing this distinction, the young often create confrontations. Parents who, in spite of cultural lag, insist on traditional authority, complete the ubiquitous drama (or comedy, as the case may be) of intergenerational friction and further alienate their offspring.

CLASH OF INFERIORITY COMPLEXES

American culture is responsible for the evolution of two mutually reinforcing complexes that have become elements in intergenerational conflict. They are the inferiority complex of teenagers and the inferiority complex of the parents. These emotional dispositions frequently lead to considerable tension and misunderstanding between the generations. Sociologist Clifford Kirkpatrick has conceptualized this interaction as "clash of inferiority complexes."[10]

The concept describes the subtle dynamics whereby offspring try to dethrone parents. Young people feel inferior because they are untried and lack experience. Feeling this deficiency keenly, they overcompensate by aggressiveness and pseudo-sophistication. Parents often feel a sense of inferiority because they believe they have passed their prime in life, are declining in youthful attractiveness and sexual prowess, and look back on a life of relatively minor achievements. When they look ahead, they perceive themselves as declining in importance.

When such opposite attitudes encounter each other, as they often do, they reinforce each other—sometimes to the point of exploding in animosity. It is a process of mutually reinforcing and cumulative social response. Youth's cockiness begets renewed insistence by parents that their authority must be upheld. As the final result, alienation between the generations emerges. This estrangement is often superficial and temporary, but occasionally it is of tragic duration.

It is important to understand that the collision of inferiority complexes *reinforces* the inferiority feelings of the two parties and consequently generates more tension. We have here a social psychological *perpetuum mobile* that, at least theoretically, continues the parent-youth conflict forever.

YOUTH CULT: NOT BRIDGING THE GAP

An element of the American ethos relating directly to the inferiority complex of parents is the cult of youth. American culture minimizes the role of the aged as a source of wisdom and a center of authority, and values the activism of youth,

---

[10] Clifford Kirkpatrick, *The Family as Process and Institution* (New York: The Ronald Press, 1955), pp. 266-67.

assuming that middle or old age hinders persons from being active and inventive. Old age connotes passive contemplativeness, the nemesis of youthful activism. Trial and error procedure is closer to the hearts of Americans than theory. The "doers" are thought of as young people who have physical vigor to experiment and create. For example, at forty or forty-five years of age, highly trained and experienced pilots are grounded because "they are too old for flying." The practice of "defunctioning" middle- and old-aged citizens may result in "no-longer-needed" attitudes. The aged are "cared for" and kindly entertained—but safely away from the mainstream of life, in physical and mental isolation.

The youth cult focuses on the active young, allowing them to set the pace, themes, goals, and tastes of society. Older people can frequently be observed imitating the practices and the crazes of the young generation. It is an almost entirely new historical occurrence that dances and music are passed from teenagers to adults. This trend has evolved over the past few decades and was highlighted by such figures as the Beatles, who created music by the young for the young—creations that eventually were avidly absorbed by adults.

It is virtually impossible to determine the causal direction between the youth cult and the parental inferiority complex. Has the youth cult created parent inferiority feelings, or are the parents compensating for bygone youthful attractiveness by adoring and imitating the ways of youth? The question of causal direction can probably never be answered. It is more important at this time to study the mutually reinforcing relationship between the two phenomena.

Manifestations of parents' obsession with youth are not well received by teenagers. They do not care to be imitated. In order to understand the negative reaction, it must be remembered that teenagers feel inferior about themselves and about many of their activities. Persons who perceive themselves as inferior are likely to look down on others who show similar behavior patterns. A college freshman was quoted complaining that his parents were trying to behave like teenagers: "When you see yourself reflected in your folks, it's just awful." Adolescents, by definition uncertain, find their lives directionless in a social environment that decides to rely on their tastes. Adolescents need parents who are adult models and not buddies or imitators of their styles. The teenage peer group already provides companionship among like-minded trial-and-error oriented friends. Adults who try to join the ranks of the young are considered unwelcome renegades from the ranks of potentially helpful adult models.

THE SEXUAL REVOLUTION

The social and technological innovations that took place during the first half of the twentieth century were profound enough to change basic perceptions of the functions of sex and the role of women. The label Sexual Revolution is thus not out of place as a description of these changes. Traditional sex codes as correlated to religious dogma came under severe attack and were undermined by important new developments. At least seven major forces of social change can be discerned:

Female emancipation. Most noteworthy has been the liberation of women from the traditional description of being sexually passive. The so-called Sexual Revolution applies in fact more to women than to men, with the male sexual behavior remaining relatively unchanged—except in areas where it would interfere with the female's rising demands and sexual expressivity. The game of seduction is largely replaced by frank, equal participation in mutually desired sex. Most of America's young women will no longer retreat to coyness and a false facade, but will take the Pill and destroy once and for all the illusion of female passivity.

The female no longer pretends. She now admits that she enjoys sex as much as the male, knows as much as he, and believes that males and females represent physical but not emotional or psychological differences. The male has been made aware of past chauvinism and of its vestiges in institutional arrangements. Vast changes and adaptations have followed, and studies indicate that women have largely dispatched the sexual double standard to history. (Studies illustrating this development have been described in previous chapters.)

Sexual equality diminished women's dependency on marriage and on males in general. Formerly indispensable for her sustenance, the male figure had shifted directly from father to husband. Now she is able to remove herself from the influence of the father and yet not enter immediately into a dependency relationship with a husband. This interim provides the woman with a period of freedom and independence heretofore unknown.

Medical and technological innovations. Probably nothing decreased inhibition and fear of sexual activities for the woman more than the availability of contraceptives. A woman freed from the old moral compunctions did not imperil her future by unwanted pregnancy and could enjoy with impunity the physical and psychological pleasures of sex. The aspect of pleasure was possibly the most revolutionary feature in the Sexual Revolution: the female now openly regarded sex as enjoyable.

Secularism. There has been a general shift in the perception of the institutions of marriage and the family. These primary institutions had been viewed as sacred, inviolable arrangements. The secular philosophy and attitude, in contrast, saw such institutions as arrangements that should be changed when human needs and desires call for such changes.

The decline of familism correlated with the rise of secularism: the focus of concern shifted from the family to the individual. Modern American life grants to both males and females the right to seek personal pleasure and satisfaction without the impediment of control by the parental family. Another way to characterize secularism is to note the modern preference for sensate pleasures over ascetic and orthodox religious principles. Gratification of personal needs has become a major goal. This social change is greatly relevant to the female who, for example, can now easily obtain a divorce if she feels that her personal needs, sexual and otherwise, are not fulfilled in a given marriage.

Legal reorientation. A by-product of secularism was a new trend in legislation concerning sexual behavior, marriage, divorce, and family matters. New laws granted the individual more personal choice and greater independence. For example, sexual behavior previously defined as law violations, such as adultery, sodomy, and homosexuality, were decriminalized. Safeguards were also established to protect equality of the sexes in such areas as jobs, income, sexual expression, and education.

Significantly, birth control became legal, as did availing oneself of pertinent means and devices. The 1972 *Baird* vs. *Massachusetts* conflict reached the U.S. Supreme Court, which struck down as unconstitutional the state's ancient prohibition of the distribution of contraceptives to *unmarried* people. The high court's decision rested on the 14th Amendment's guarantee of equal protection before the law. This meant that whatever the rights of individuals to access to contraceptives may be, the rights must be the same for unmarried and married. As a result, other states voided similar discriminatory laws.

Broadening adolescent period. Improved medication, sanitation, and nutrition led to earlier onset of puberty. At the same time, the progressively more complicated expansion of the division of labor and the social structure in general caused delay in reaching fully acknowledged adult status. The sum effect of the two developments is a longer span of adolescence. During these years, the youth is physiologically mature and characterized by fully developed sexual needs.

It is unrealistic to expect that the adolescent can or will defer gratification of sexual needs until completing schooling, which may extend into the twenties if college is attended. As long as youth are affiliated with an educational institution, it is difficult to accord them full adult status. Not until establishing themselves occupationally and earning a living do they achieve major criteria of adult status.

Despite the prolonging of the period between child and adult statuses, no socially acceptable provisions have been made to allow sexual needs to be fulfilled outside of marriage. To some degree, premarital chastity still is a social value. Technically, *any* form of sexual gratification during adolescent years constitutes a deviation from the blueprint. Whatever sexual gratification does takes place – autoeroticism, hetero- or homosexuality – is defined as illicit, or at least improper, and burdens the majority of adolescents with strain and conflict. Prolonged adolescence is in part responsible for the increased rate of premarital sexual activities over the past few decades.

Titillating mass media. Ubiquitous American mass media also weakened traditional norms. The sexual stimuli presented in various media grossly contradicted traditional values of chastity and asceticism. Female "sexiness" became an established value, attracting emulation by the teenage girl and fervent endeavors of conquest by the teenage boy. Considering the sexual insecurity that is normally an important part of adolescence, it is hardly possible to overestimate the sex-encouraging influence of movies, TV, advertisements, and a vast range of reading material.

Not knowing exactly the part sex was to play in their lives, youth became suscep-tible to imitating the characters that the mass media presented.

Credo of instantness of fulfillment. Postindustrial conditions markedly fostered a belief in instant fulfillment of needs. Sharp resentment and insistence on an instant remedy are the response to any slackening of society's ability to come to the individual's aid and provide an effective and immediate answer to any desire that is defined as a need. Moreover, need and frustration are blamed on society's failure to prevent such unpleasantness in the first place. Individual sexual frustrations have now entered the list of such societal failures. The Sexual Revolu-tion is strongly supported by the demand for instantness and, conversely, by the rejection of the old Protestant ethic that includes deference of gratification.

This new credo is part of the new psychology of entitlement. Accordingly, more and more Americans assume, first, that they have a right (not merely a chance) to self-actualization, economic security, and general comfort and, second, that this right must be implemented and materialized by society.

PARENTAL REACTION I:
PERMISSIVENESS AND ACQUIESCENCE

Many parents have become aware of their cultural-lag position and seek remedy. Willingness to communicate with their teenage children is evidenced by a wave of self-effacing literature that can be described as a "parents-are-problems" campaign. Personally and through the mass media, some parents have shown eagerness to learn from, adjust to, and listen to teenagers.

The status of parent is unabashedly labeled a social problem, and parents are often apologetic about being parents. Examples of educational literature, often aimed at teenagers to help in the "upbringing" and "understanding" of their parents, include such books as *Raising Children in a Difficult Time*[11] or articles such as "Children as Agents in Socializing Parents," "Parent-Teen Education – An Exercise in Communication," and "Expectations of Youth in Relating to the World of the Adult."[12]

The cultural-lag condition of the parents has also been appraised in popular teenage songs, advising more seriously than facetiously that teenagers should try to understand parents in spite of all the "foolish things they are doing," since they are at a difficult stage in life and need youth's understanding and forgiveness. Other indications that the socialization process has undergone considerable change come from interviewing teenagers. Their suggestions to remedy the communication gap typically demand of parents that they (1) must listen before teenagers can tell them anything; (2) must want to cooperate before there can be communication;

[11] Benjamin Spock, *Raising Children in a Difficult Time*, New York: Norton, 1974.
[12] In *The Family Coordinator*, 19 (July 1970).

(3) must update their views; (4) must think as teenagers think; (5) must make themselves available; and (6) must be more understanding.[13] Such expressions indicate that the direction of condescension and instruction has been reversed, proceeding now *from young to old.*

This modification of the age-old socialization process was stimulated by postindustrial conditions but also helped by the American ethos, which emphasizes equality, usually in regard to sex, race, religious affiliation, etc., but now also included (young) *age.* In addition, American culture has little reverence for old age and hence has induced parents to be willing to learn from their children and even to adjust to their way of life. Innumerable articles, books, conferences, and PTA meetings vie with one another for the attention of parents, with the intention of educating them for their children and teenagers.

Other evidence of the parental (or general adult) effort to establish *rapprochement* with the teen world includes the adoption of teenage customs, fashions, and modes of behavior. In various social institutions, adults have promoted teen styles to retain adolescents' loyalty.

Innovations can even be observed in religious institutions, traditionally the most conservative bastions of culture. Services have been employing the type of music, prayer, and dance preferred by modern youth. Tunes of folk songs and the beat of jazz and rock 'n' roll have become acceptable in worship services. In 1967 the Roman Catholic Church relented in its nearly two thousand-year-old adherence to sacred liturgy and Pope Paul VI issued a revolutionary document that allowed the use of secular tunes and rhythms in the Mass. The churches' adaptations to teenage styles include clothes, lingo, philosophy, and nonabstract communication. Churches have emphasized their adaptability by headlining newspaper ads with "Geared for Teenagers." Others invite the young to come and "wear anything you feel comfortable in."

Prayers are adjusted to teenage lingo, exemplified by *Treat Me Cool, Lord,* a collection of prayers by teenagers; and sermons refer to "hangups," "uptight," "let your hair down."[14] The Bible's bucolic imagery, with its reference to sheep, shepherds, fields, sowing, and harvesting, is thought to be largely meaningless to them. When a minister told a group of boys in Buffalo about the lilies of the field that neither toil nor spin, he encountered laughter—later he found out that in their argot a "lily" meant a homosexual. The minister subsequently encouraged the boys to rephrase biblical parables and adapt them to the conditions and the argot of their environment. In this way, the Good Samaritan became the "cool square" who helped a "mugged" victim after a "hood" and a "sneak" (not so "cool" as a "hood") had "passed by." The Christmas story was modified to show the setting in Buffalo during a convention when all hotel rooms were taken and the Savior's stable was a hot dog stand in some municipal park. The parable of the lost sheep

---

[13] UPI report (New York, November 3, 1965.)
[14] Carl F. Burke, *Treat Me Cool, Lord* (New York: Association Press, 1970).

was rephrased to be understood as a used-car lot owner who goes looking for the "heap" that someone "snitched."[15]

The Reverend Clarence J. Rivers of the Catholic Archdiocese of Cincinnati defended the use of teen vernacular in church by saying that there is nothing wrong with entertaining churchgoers, that liturgy's main function is to entertain, and that the reason for a visible church is "to show something: it must be a show."[16] Religion's adaptation includes the musical *Godspell*, which uses clowns, jokes, and soft-shoe dancing to portray the life of Christ in American vaudeville style: "an 18-year-old youth, portraying Jesus Christ, ran down the aisle and leaped on the stage. He wore a Superman shirt and had clown make-up on his face."[17]

The institution of the theatre has exhibited similar acculturation to teenage style. It found profit in paying homage to the Age of Aquarius and raising curtains on such rock operas and youth musicals as *Hair, Jesus Christ Superstar*, and *Tommy*.

Many of those in the literary establishment, with Arthur Miller as spokesperson, adulated youth's style and presumed values, and referred to them as precursors of a new humanism: "Can anyone doubt that if everyone over thirty vanished tomorrow, there would be racial peace in this country in a year and a way found to end the Vietnam war?"[18]

Persons in various professions have similarly endorsed, or at least acquiesced to, youth's way of life. A federal judge, for example, sides with youth's criticism of "adult hypocrisy";[19] a professor advocates the "open family" with children as "voluntary" members;[20] and some sociologists call on adults to fulfill youth's expectations: "Continuity of social support is most needed during the transitional stage of adolescence. But if support in the form of guidance is to come from adults (as it should), it must be they who fulfill youth's expectations and not the reverse."[21] The sociologists' suggestion means that youth may set standards and expectations and that adults are obliged not only to tolerate them but to actively assist in carrying them out. Maybe this is the epitome of what the Hechingers warned of in their ominous book, *Teenage Tyranny*.[22]

[15] "The Bible," *Time*, March 5, 1965, p. 44.

[16] "Father River's Songfest Hikes Beat," *Arizona Republic*, February 20, 1971, p. 8.

[17] "Youth Group Presents Modern Version of the Life of Christ," *Arizona Republic*, December 9, 1972, p. 48.

[18] Arthur Miller, "The War between Young and Old," *McCall's*, July 1970, p. 32.

[19] Charles E. Wyzanski, Jr., "It is Quite Right that the Young Should Talk About Us as Hypocrites. We Are," *Saturday Review*, July 20, 1968, p. 14.

[20] Larry L. Constantine, "Open Family: A Lifestyle for Kids and Other People," *Family Coordinator*, (April 1977), 113–121.

[21] George Won and Douglas Yamamura, "Expectations of Youth in Relating to the World of Adults," *The Family Coordinator*, 19 (July 1970), 219.

[22] Grace Hechinger and Fred M. Hechinger, *Teenage Tyranny* (New York: William Morrow, 1963).

Permissiveness has increased spectacularly in the college setting. The combined forces of lowering the legal adult age to eighteen and the inroads forged into institutional rigidity by the counterculture of the early 1970s have caused *in loco parentis* authority to decline. Students not only want more personal autonomy (as achieved through abolition of curfew rules, for example), but also codetermination of institutional policy, including academic expectations. In the wake of the counterculture, taxing students' academic aptitudes provoked students enough to have them proclaim their own version of "No taxation without representation." Hence, students' demands included having "relevant" courses and representation on faculty and administration committees. Their demands met largely with compliance by faculty and administrators.

Two interpretations of increased student freedom can be observed throughout the country: (1) as a welcome opportunity for youth to accept responsibility and to grow; (2) as a spilling over of adolescence into formerly adult-run institutions, resulting in lowering the value and maturity of institutional functions. The latter view is aligned with the goal of reasserting traditional authority and curbing social-structural implementation of adolescent thinking and behavior.

Similar permissiveness prevails in high schools. Within a decade, most of the rules have been swept away. Today, in almost all schools, students dress as they please, in class and out. Various fads in clothes and grooming are tolerated, including boys' shoulder-length hair, which used to be the most disputed and most severely persecuted item of teen styles. Many boys were prohibited from attending class or were even expelled from school because of long hair, while a drug conviction or other delinquency had much less consequence on continuing with school life.

In summary, many adults as well as institutions have attempted *rapprochement* with reproachful and alienated youth. The strategies employed seem to add up to a three-pronged thrust: *democracy*, *communication*, and *information*. Most adult-initiated programs purporting to bring about understanding between the generations were based, explicitly or implicitly, on these three concepts. The concept of democracy was applied to remind parents to consider teenagers as equals. The emphasis on communication was meant to encourage parents to keep in touch with teenagers and diligently work out misunderstandings. The emphasis on information stimulated parents to remedy the knowledge gap and acquire up-to-date information.

PARENTAL REACTION II: REASSERTION OF TRADITIONAL AUTHORITY

The permissive response of parents, and adults in general, to teenagers' invasion of public life has not met with unanimous approval. The American population is too heterogeneous to react uniformly to anything.

There are forceful voices challenging youth's inroads on adult authority. It is helpful to discuss three "reactionary" responses. One is the *turn-about reaction* of frustrated parents who have tried the utopian approach of bridging the generation gap by pursuing the ideals of democracy, communication, and information. Another is the relatively unwavering philosophical conviction of many Americans that *adults should naturally wield authority and impose limitations* on the young. A third discussion deals with historical *fluctuations between permissiveness and authoritarianism* that appear almost cyclically in American society.

Many parents have suffered spectacular defeat in idealistic endeavors toward *rapprochement.* Their offer of equality, willingness to communicate, and eagerness to acquire information did not succeed in narrowing the gap, and many of them suffered disappointment. As a result, they are reconsidering strategy, recalling "traditional rights," and demanding a new respect from adolescents.

Many have conceded that the notion of equality between parents and offspring is utopian. Their suspicion was borne out by such studies as Richard Flacks', which explored family backgrounds of rebellious students. He found that almost all of them had grown up in liberally oriented (equalitarian) homes but were among the least adjusted and satisfied youths.[23] In other words, the expectation that equalitarian treatment and child-rearing would prevent generational strife was not supported. However, extremely alienated youth did not share this type of family background and were even more estranged from both family and society.

Parental attempts at communication fared no better. Some observers, such as Paul Goodman, felt that the attempts failed not because the message did not get through (indeed, it was understood loud and clear) but because it was unacceptable to the young.[24] However, John W. Aldridge regarded the typical intergenerational communication as an exercise in futility because youth used it to rationalize hedonism and immaturity.[25] It became a substitute for the hard look at oneself and for the search for solutions in one's own mental repertoire. Communication also served as reinforcement of in-group ideas by repetitively voicing slogans and criticisms and hearing peers do the same.

Other obstacles to fruitful communication include parents' limitation in finding time needed for resolving basic differences between generations. Moreover, it is doubtful whether *intellectual* communication can resolve basic *emotional* differences. It may be possible to establish an intellectual understanding of certain differences in tastes or convictions and still not arrive at *rapprochement* between the parties.

Finally, the vast majority of parents found it impossible to keep abreast of children's advanced scientific knowledge. To keep up with well-informed students would require parents to literally go to school with their offspring, listen to the

---

[23] Richard Flacks, "The Liberated Generation: An Exploration of the Roots of Student Protest," *Journal of Social Issues,* 23 (July 1967), 52–75.

[24] Paul Goodman, *Growing Up Absurd* (New York: Random House, 1960).

[25] John W. Aldridge, *In the Country of the Young* (New York: Harper's Magazine Press, 1970), p. 101.

same lectures, study the same lessons, and read the same up-to-date books and research reports. Few parents can afford such efforts. In general, then, many parents, frustrated in their campaign to promote "equality, communication, and information," began to reverse their attitudes and became more authoritarian.

Vociferous Americans have assumed an authoritarian stance from the very beginning and insist that the traditional pattern of adults being the *socializers* and the young the *socializees* not be changed. They feel that this universal practice is necessitated by the fact that children are born culturally "unprogrammed," thus requiring socialization. It would be totally unrealistic to believe that the young always submit willingly to the manifold enculturation pressures exerted by their elders. Adult society determines standards of "right" and "wrong," and it is virtually impossible to discuss and explain the societal codes to the young in every situation of intergenerational controversy. Rather, it is frequently necessary to overrule the offspring without giving them equal opportunity. For example, children are not given a choice when a decision is made about going to school or not, or about playing with toys or with fire. If necessary, adults will coerce children to comply with standards and regulations. Thus, by definition, the socialization process implies inequality.

But American civilization tends to overrate and overrespect teenagers because of a deep-seated adoration of youth. A number of critics fear that, as a result, teenage influence has permeated public life and imposed teen standards. It is this adolescence-expanding process that has caused concern among critical observers and has led them to call "corruption of adulthood" a "creeping disease." The symptoms of this disease presumably are immature goals in music, art, and literature, replacement of adult English with limited vocabulary of the teen culture, and teen invasion of newspapers, television, and movies.

These voices deplore that so many concessions have already been made to youth's barbarism and warn that it is time to reverse the trend. An early alarm was sounded by the Hechingers in *Teenage Tyranny*, charging American society with surrender of adult standards to superficial teenage tastes and urging adults to reassert themselves. They do not believe that adolescents should be left in charge of their own lives, much less in control of the lives of any adults they can persuade or intimidate.

An eloquent indictment of youth's barbarism was made by John W. Aldridge, who feels that adults are bluffed into self-accusation about being hypocrites, while it is the young who are the hypocrites. The young are remarkable for a number of inconsistencies, usually overlooked by guilt-preoccupied adults. The young profess an interest in improving society, but are actually only showing a parasitic interest; they are preoccupied with style, but show an endless appetite for banality; they are quick with moral severity when it comes to adults, but exhibit irresponsibility in their personal lives; they talk obsessively about the quality of university instruction, but are disinterested in ideas, imaginative literature, and the values of the Humanistic tradition; they are collectively vociferous and militant, but individually inarticulate and limp in manners; they proclaim a passion for individuality, but hew close to collective action and fashion; they flaunt their desire to "communicate" and to "relate," but suffer from lack of communicative substance; they sound a mystical belief in the primacy of intense feelings and profound intuition, but have neither the know-how nor the courage to implement their impulses in a creative lifestyle; and although they have more freedom of action and experimentation than any previous generation, they are quick to complain of restrictions.[26]

Among the prominent personalities who have supported the reassertion movement is psychoanalyst Peter Blos, who advises against permissiveness toward the sexual expression of teenagers, in spite of the fact that they mature earlier than previous generations.[27] Many parents respond to their offspring's maturation by condoning early dating, and some even by encouraging use of the pill by girls barely in their teens. To Blos, the young adolescent is psychologically still a child, regardless of his or her biological maturation. Allowing hasty sexual-emotional involvement may preclude emotional growth and stability. Blos even favors sex-segregated schooling for a while after puberty and disagrees with the argument that thwarting the young's evolving sex drive will be harmful. On the contrary, the young adolescent's personality will not only tolerate it but even profit from delay and repression, since it will channel youthful bravado into creative sublimations. Adults must set limits, deny youth's clamor for adult privileges, and refuse to be intimidated by charges of authoritarianism. While such steadfastness will cause tension and antagonism between parent and adolescent, it is the only way for healthy growth. The young need resistance and confrontation to acquire a realistic view of life and to work out a durable identity.

Psychologist Bruno Bettelheim warns that overpermissive parents create in offspring senseless uncertainty about identities and that resultant confusion and frustration will generate enough resentment to deepen the generation gap. Radical attacks on real evils have misled many well-meaning adults into overlooking the underlying motive: it is hate, not desire for a better world.[28] Bettelheim encourages the universities to act like firm but understanding parents and adhere to guidelines that will help students cope with inner conflicts.

M.I.T. Professor Thomas J. Cottle zeroes in on the common misconception that taking it easy with adolescents is doing them a favor. He feels that tremendous harm can result when superordinates—the parents, teachers, and elders—try to equalize what must remain an asymmetrical relationship. Asymmetry refers to relationships wherein the services exchanged are of unequal and therefore noncomparable content, and the behavior of one party is not the cue for identical behavior in the other. It applies to situations where authority must be maintained in order to preserve clarity of interaction and promote success in the pursuit of common goals. Such situations include the parent-child, teacher-student, and doctor-patient

[26] John W. Aldridge, *In the Country of the Young.*

[27] Peter Blos, "The Child Analyst Looks at the Young Adolescent," *Daedalus*, 100 (Fall 1971), 961; and *The Young Adolescent; Clinical Studies* (New York: Free Press, 1970).

[28] "Youth: Confused Parents, Confused Kids," *Time*, September 5, 1969, p. 58.

relationships. In order to achieve goals, the participants must often carry out different functions. If they do not, and mistakenly assume that identical behavior will get them to the finish line, they will fail in the common project, become confused, and often face each other with mutual disgust. Young people's attack on authority, as healthy as it may be most of the time, should not obscure the service that authority renders. Authority is not to be toned down to the level of the young, "it is to remain firm in its commitment to preserve the essential asymmetry and the indelible generational separation, even if this means being seen as a 'square.'"[29] Relinquishing authority would deprive the young of the necessary resistance against which they test themselves and of the guidance they desire.

Sociologist Robert A. Nisbet calls for the reassertion of faculty and administration authority and wants to restore the old identity of the university.[30] Students must relearn to accept their proper places and to recognize the function of school not as a political forum or sounding board for criticisms but as a place where learned disciplines are taught.

Even some clergymen have joined the criticism of youth's lifestyle. Reverend Paul D. Urbano barely tolerates teen music and dancing, but condemns their "tribal language" as intolerably "dull," saying it conceals youth's refusal to learn subtleties and nuances because it requires effort and concentration.[31] Teen jargon is a coverup for laziness in learning English and cultivates nondiscrimination of differences in experience, feelings, and nature. As a consequence, teen jargon has an impoverishing effect, keeping imagination and descriptive ability of the young at a minimum.

Finally, the animosity that many parents hold toward youth was brought out during the aftermath of the killing of several Kent State University students in 1970. When James Michener interviewed parents, a surprising number of them approved of the action of the National Guard.[32] In fact, many of them called for more bloodshed if necessary to keep the students in line. In the interviews, many housewives revealed that they resented the bralessness and presumed promiscuity of today's young women, and many men seemed to resent (or envy?) the sexual freedom they did not know as youths.

Limiting the discussion of adult reactions toward the "invasion of centaurs"— as Roszak analogized modern youth's assertiveness—to two types, the permissive and the authoritarian, is somewhat arbitrary. There is of course also the level-headed *authoritative* stance, which is less a reaction than an even tempered self-assurance that has no need for defensive counteraction. This is the authority expressed by persons who feel secure in their knowledge, understand the motives

[29] Thomas J. Cottle, "Parents and Child—The Hazards of Equality," in *Children's Liberation*, ed. David Ramsey (Englewood Cliffs, N.J.: Prentice-Hall, 1973), p. 90.

[30] Robert A. Nisbet, "The University Had Better Mind Its Own Business," *Psychology Today*, 4 (March 1971), 22–37.

[31] Paul D. Urbano, "Tribal Language," *Arizona Republic*, June 20, 1970, p. 37.

[32] James Michener, *Kent State, What Happened and Why* (New York: Random House, 1971).

behind youth's stirrings, and perhaps show more compassion than passion. This is also a minority. The majority engages either in acquiescence or authoritarianism.

The majority reaction is understandable. Youth's extreme criticisms bring out extreme responses and seldom promote a balanced view. This is why the authoritative response is rare—it is an attitude anchored in self-confidence and is unswayed by attack; it feels neither the need to fight back nor surrender. We may have to admit that the vast majority of people are less self-confident and that attacks on them elicit defensive reactions, such as authoritarianism.

Some social scientists believe that the rising and ebbing of authoritarianism does not depend on specific national events but is an almost rhythmic or cyclic recurrence. While the etiology of this societal pendulum is not clear, we know something about the duration of the stages. Sociologist Seymour Lipset has calculated that each American social obsession or preoccupation—be it McCarthyism, student apathy, or the counterculture—has a lifetime of about five years.[33] After that it quickly fades.

Public moods concerning child-rearing philosophy seem to fluctuate in the same manner. While the last years of the counterculture were associated with a lessening of control and an increase in permissiveness (possibly shown by the 1971 legislation to lower legal adult age to eighteen), the mid- and late-1970s showed signs of tightening of control and movement back to authoritarianism. The late-1970s were a period of reemerging harmony, when the young were less critical of the old and the old were relatively reassured of their position. Both parties relaxed intergenerational warfare.

The permissive element will not disappear, regardless of chronological fluctuation or the authoritative voices of traditionalists. Major reasons are the shifting lifestyles of middle and working classes. While the former seems to tighten the reins on youthful excesses, the latter shows symptoms of trying to imitate the middle class with its affluence, careerism, small families—and permissive child-rearing.[34] It seems to be a historical truism that when a *nouveau* class is ascending to a coveted social level, imitation of the new social status is thorough and indiscriminate. Hence, the old middle-class permissiveness will probably experience a rebirth.

---

[33] Quoted in "The Graying of America," *Time*, September 17, 1973, pp. 76–77; also see Seymour M. Lipset, *Rebellion in the University* (Boston: Little, Brown, 1972).

[34] A sociological investigation into the fluctuating child-rearing practices in the United States was conducted by Urie Bronfenbrenner, "Socialization and Social Class Through Time and Space," in *Readings in Social Psychology*, ed. Eleanor E. Maccoby et al. (New York: Holt, Rinehart, and Winston, 1958). Child-rearing practices were found to vary among social classes and likely to change most quickly in those segments of society that have closest access to the agencies of change—mass media, clinics, physicians, counselors, books. Accordingly, it was concluded that middle-class parents are usually forming the modes and standards of child-rearing, while lower-class and rural families lag behind. Evaluation of various sociological researches led Bronfenbrenner to conclude that before World War II, working-class mothers were markedly more permissive than those of the middle class. After World War II, middle-class mothers developed more permissive and equalitarian attitudes, while working-class mothers gradually assumed a stricter and more disciplinary attitude.

In summary, socialization attitudes are in constant flux, and it is difficult to make accurate forecasts. There is constant polarization of pedagogic philosophies, with the permissive and the authoritarian vying with each other. What would probably help to calm the rough waters of intergenerational relations is greater self-acceptance on the part of America's middle- and older-aged population, finding greater meaning in their life-stages, and *acting* on the basis of their true identities and sincere preferences rather than *reacting* frantically to youth's styles—either positively (to the point of imitation) or negatively. This would earn them the respect of the young, prepare them as models, and reduce the polarization within their own age group as well as between young and old.

SUMMARY

Even in a relatively even-tempered social setting not disturbed by rapid social change, the common socialization process is enough to stir up conflict and dissonance between generations. The young do not yet have vested interest in the existing social and economic order and are prone to challenge customs and values. In a rapidly and unevenly changing society, in which each generation experiences a different social climate, intergenerational tensions are bound to open a deep schism.

Major dynamic elements are fermenting in this generational confrontation:

1. Parents suffer from "cultural lag"—from being continuously one step behind the offspring's information exposure—and are pitted against experts who manage the information flow.
2. The young cultivate a "halo effect," generalizing from parental ignorance in scientific and technological details to parental incompetence in general.
3. Parental insistence on authority is frequently interpreted by the young as "irrational" authority they are entitled to oppose.
4. The American way of life embraces a youth cult that exaggerates youth's manipulation of the older generation. It puts youth in a position from which they can bluff under the guise of making valid complaints.
5. The youth cult inflicts an inferiority complex on adults; inexperience and prolonged adolescent conditions impose an inferiority complex on the young. The two complexes reinforce each other and have cumulative effects.
6. Parental and general adult reactions to the dilemma of the generations vary. One reaction consists of permissiveness and acquiescence, whereby adults either passively tolerate the invasion of teen styles or actively seek *rapprochement* by trying to implement equality, communication, and information. A second type of reaction opposes youth's inroads on public life and marshals the forces of traditional adult authority.
7. The prevailing mood of socialization tends to go through cyclic waxing and waning—during one period American society shows greater permissiveness and during the next greater authoritarianism. Apparently, specific national events have only peripheral impact on these fluctuations, although the war in Vietnam polarized the two reactions and widened the generation gap.

CHAPTER 6

THE MODERN FAMILY

Of the various groups to which we belong, the family has the most far-reaching impact on the formation of identity. Quality of family interaction, and its bearing on the way the young grow into adulthood, is significantly affected by the structure of the family. A discussion of the modern family should therefore begin with a look at structural conditions.

Since the discussion focuses on aspects of the family that contribute to the formation of adolescence in American life, it must be selective and may at times appear one-sided or negative. But obviously, *not all aspects* of the modern family promote adolescence and *not all families are the same* in degree and manner of reinforcing adolescence.

As mentioned earlier, such communities as the Amish or Hutterites have succeeded in immunizing their young against adolescence by religious dogma, simple farm life, and isolation from public schools. Other minorities have curbed adolescence sufficiently so that it is different from the typical urban middle-class experience. Hence, the adolescent experience varies according to such background features as ethnicity, race, socioeconomic status, religion, and so forth. It must be added, however, that it is not so much the individual families that may have ameliorating effects on adolescent anomie, but the subcultural community of which the family is a part.

This discussion dwells primarily on historical trends that have intensified the adolescent experience and affected most American families, especially the middle class. We have two concerns: (1) To show similarity rather than diversity among American families; and (2) to identify the new structural conditions that facilitated the rise of modern adolescence.

CHANGING STRUCTURE

Toward the isolated nuclear family. In 1800, more than 90 percent of the population of the United States was classified as rural.[1] This proportion consistently declined, dropping from 85 percent in 1850 to 60 percent in 1900. In 1920, the United States census distinguished between rural population and farm population and found that only 30 percent of the population was farm population. This proportion decreased to 25 percent in 1930, 23 percent in 1940, 15 percent in 1950, 9 percent in 1960, and about 5 percent by 1970.

The traditional rural family often included such close relatives as grandparents, uncles, aunts, and cousins, and the child grew up in close association with them. In addition, occasionally such nonrelatives as maids and farm hands became permanent members of the household. While in 1910 almost every fourth American family included nonrelatives, in 1961 only every twentieth family included such a person.

In the traditional setting, many married children shared the household of their parents. In 1910, for example, 7.7 percent of married couples did not live in an independent household; by the 1960s this proportion had decreased to 2.1 percent. Recent statistics show that the average number of persons per household has decreased from about six in 1800 to 2.9 in the mid 1970s, making it the first time in American history that the average size of households has dropped below three. Statistics indicate a drastic decline in the proportion of families with six or more members. In 1790, slightly more than 50 percent of all American families were large households that included six or more members. At the turn of the century, only 33 percent of the families were that large. By the 1970s, only about 14 percent of all families had six or more members. The small two or three-person family has increased from 20 percent in 1870 to 34 percent in 1900 and to more than 50 percent during the 1970s.

Additional factors that have reduced household size include the divorce rate, which in densely populated West Coast regions has run as high as 70 percent. Nationally, one in every four marriages ends in divorce; this seems to be the main reason why one out of every six children is living in a single-parent family. This is usually not a temporary arrangement, since the remarriage rate, especially for women, is substantially lower than the rate of divorce in families involving children.

---

[1] Most statistics in this discussion are based on *Historical Statistics of the United States; Colonial Times to 1957* (Washington, D.C.: Bureau of the Census, 1970) and volumes 1960–1980 of *Statistical Abstract of the United States* (Washington, D.C.: Bureau of the Census).

A component in the growth of single-parent families is the sharp rise in the number of unwed mothers. Eleven percent of all births are illegitimate, twice the rate of twenty years ago. While more young women are postponing marriage, many decide to have children premaritally. In fact, the number of marriages dropped nearly 3 percent during the mid 1970s, the first significant decline since World War II, and the proportion of women remaining single until they are between twenty and twenty-four years old has climbed by 33 percent since 1960.

Liberalized adoption laws and increased affluence make it possible for single or divorced women to have children and to set up housekeeping without benefit of a husband or integration into families of relatives. Also, each year an estimated half-million teenagers refuse to be part of their families and run away from home.

In sum, the American family has undergone impressive changes, transforming itself from an extended to a nuclear arrangement. However, American society had only an approximation of the classic extended family system that anthropologists describe as existing in other parts of the world.[2] The opportunities of this continent have always incited Americans to move on, to acquire, to seek their own "hearth," and to stake out their own physical and psychological parameters. Youthful activism, material acquisition, and individualism have never fully promoted the true spirit of the classic extended family. Thus, the change in American family structure is more properly described as change from a larger to a smaller nuclear family.

There have also been changes in the relationship between the family and the community—changes that are of equal importance in understanding the nature of the modern family. Due to growth in size of communities, resultant impersonality and anonymity, increase in mobility, and retreat to individualism, the modern nuclear family has lost its integration into the community and has become isolated to a notable degree.

Looser integration into the community is matched by looser internal integration within the family. With today's emphasis on individualism, the family is no longer a coherent and enduring unit. A person's family used to be his or her unalterable fate, but late-twentieth-century Americans view marriage and the family as something arrangeable—just as occupations or homes are. If spouses feel disappointed, they leave; if teenagers are dissatisfied and feel shackled, they may leave, too. The reason is less often related to personal disillusionment with other family members than the simple desire to pursue one's own interests. Theologian Sam Keen encourages modern Americans to face the problem pragmatically, make mobility part of the family, and, through increased flexibility, save it. He likened the family to a gypsy caravan, which serves as a point of stability and yet, simultaneously, keeps on moving. Family members may leave the caravan occasionally and then again catch up with it.[3]

[2] Bernard Farber, *Family and Kinship in Modern Society* (Glenview, Ill.: Scott, Foresman and Co., 1973); Peter Laslett, *Household and Family in Past Time* (New York: Cambridge University Press, 1972), p. 575.

[3] Reported in "American Family: Future Uncertain," *Time*, December 28, 1970, p. 39.

It is doubtful whether this vision will replace that of the family as being supposedly permanent, since the latter belief is a cherished American dream. Nonetheless, the vision may be closer to American reality than the dream; but that is usually neither recognized nor admitted.

Limited adult models. The traditional family was able to provide a number of adults who could serve as significant models. This was possible not only because there were more individuals in the family but also because their work performance was more visible. In addition, the family was integrated into the community and could bring the young in contact with neighbors and relatives whose behavior and occupational pursuits could be observed. This helped the young to learn patterns of problem solving and derive value orientation.

In the isolated nuclear family, learning from available persons is extremely limited. Normally, there is only one adult of each sex present, and if this parent is not readily observable, the young are deprived of models. A current concern of many social scientists is the middle-class boy who frequently suffers identity problems because of father absence.[4]

Even if the male child has the opportunity to associate with his father and observe his actions, one must allow for the possibility that this model, for whatever idiosyncratic reason, may not be acceptable to the child. Rejection of a father can lead to a situation in which the father changes from a model to an object of scorn. A frequent theme underlying cases of father rejection is modern youth's refusal to accept a person as a model whose only qualification is the *position* of father. Regard for institutions and formal positions has changed from the "sacred" to the "secular." Trying to uphold reverence and obedience for a position when it is occupied by a person considered unqualified can result in serious interpersonal disharmony.

Barrington Moore expressed one of the most poignant opinions on this matter. He accused the modern nuclear family of being "obsolete and barbaric" because of the young's "obligation to give affection as a duty to a particular set of persons because of the accident of birth." Moore called attention to "the exploitation of socially sanctioned demands for gratitude when the existing social situation no longer generates any genuine feeling of warmth."[5] Most important, he considered adolescence to be the outgrowth of the modern family's incapability of stabilizing the personalities of its offspring.

While Moore's ideas may have some validity, they are only partial explanations of the variables causing adolescence. Nevertheless, it is true that deprivation of role models may develop in situations where the offspring refuse to acknowledge parental authority. When father-absenteeism is combined with rebellious attitudes, sex-role identification indeed suffers. While such dysfunctional conditions were

---

[4] Michael E. Lamb, "Paternal Influences and the Father's Role," in John Keating, ed., *Social Psychology*, Annual Editions (Guilford, Ct.: Duskhin, 1982), pp. 68–73.

[5] Barrington Moore, "Thoughts on the Future of the Family," in *Identity and Anxiety*, eds. Maurice R. Stein, Arthur J. Vidich, and Daniel M. White (Glencoe, Ill.: The Free Press, 1960), pp. 393–94.

avoided in the larger traditional family, the nuclear family fails to offer children flexibility in choosing models, thereby complicating the transition from childhood to adulthood.

Nonfamilial peers. In the large, traditional family the child usually grew up with peers who were of his or her family group. They were playmates with whom they shared the same sentiments. Charles H. Cooley's concept of primary group found near perfection in this arrangement. Interaction was intimate, face-to-face, and self-perception was in terms of "we" instead of in terms of "I and they."[6] This type of family blended primary and secondary socialization into one process and prevented marginality because integration into the consanguine family group was a lifelong proposition. When the young married, they would most likely remain in the household of the family of orientation, or at least in the same community.

In contrast, most modern nuclear families are isolated from kin and cannot provide playmates who are relatives. Modern youth grow up seeing few, if any, of their relatives; many of them live and grow up with only one parent. Hence, children of nuclear families find their playmates outside of the kin group and commonly transform the school environment into a primary source of friends.

Recreation and leisure have been transferred from the family to commercial agencies. Commercialization aims at individuals, or individuals in certain age groups, but rarely at families as units. This is reflected in movie ratings, music festivals, concerts, and pop musicals.

Parents' prime competitors seem to be their children's nonfamilial peers, who, unlike siblings and cousins growing up in the same family system, frequently have divergent attitudes and fail to share common loyalty to one family. They are a peer group independent of family life. Thus, teenagers enter a marginal status with respect to both the family of orientation and the family of procreation. They are no longer an intrinsic part of the parental home and have not yet formed their own families. They are suspended between two membership groups and compensate by temporarily joining a subculture. James S. Coleman, in his classic *The Adolescent Society*, reported large, complex "teenage societies" among high school youth, organized along lines diametrically opposed to the standards of parents.[7]

Equally powerful is the influence of the mass media, particularly television. Prime targets of the television industry are preadolescents and adolescents. By the time children reach eighteen years of age, they will have watched twice as many hours of television as they spent in the classroom. Although some of the fare is realistic and educational, most of it is violent, unrealistic, and antagonistic to parental values.

Responsibility for youth's peer-family conflict lies partly with parents and partly with the changing structure of the modern community, according to psychol-

---

[6] Charles H. Cooley, *Social Organization* (New York: Scribner's, 1909), p. 23.

[7] James S. Coleman, *The Adolescent Society* (Glencoe, Ill.: The Free Press, 1961).

ogist Urie Bronfenbrenner.[8] Through evaluation of various statistics and their integration into a trend indicator, he predicts increasing isolation of American teenagers from parents and adults. Many factors conspire to isolate the young from the rest of society: (1) decline of the extended family; (2) separation of residential and work areas; (3) impersonal neighborhoods; (4) zoning ordinances; (5) occupational mobility; (6) child labor laws; consolidated schools; (7) television; (8) age-segregated patterns of social and recreational life; (9) working mothers; and (10) delegation of child care, education, and therapy to experts. Bronfenbrenner regards the trend as a manifestation of decreasing opportunity for meaningful contact between generations.

Erosion of cohesiveness of the social network has isolating effects not only on the young but also on the family as a unit. Centrifugal forces generated within the family by its increasingly isolated position have propelled its members into different directions. As parents, especially mothers, dedicate more time to outside careers, children gravitate toward nonfamilial settings, some organized and others informal. For example, the number of children enrolled in daycare centers has more than doubled in recent years, and demand far exceeds supply. The young spend increasing amounts of time in the company of agemates to fill the vacuum created by withdrawal of parents and other adults.

Bronfenbrenner refers to sources showing that today's reliance on the informal peer group, at every age and grade level, has enormously increased, and that this is particularly noticeable among children from homes in which one or both parents are frequently absent. These peer-dependent youth describe parents as less affectionate and less firm in discipline. They also display greater pessimism about the future, rate lower in responsibility and leadership, and are more likely to engage in antisocial behavior.

Social scientists have interpreted these conditions as roots of alienation. Over time, they believe, these conditions will become more prevalent, and greater peer dependency as well as more serious manifestations of alienation will evolve. This, presumably, is the major explanation for rising rates of juvenile homicide, suicide, drug abuse, and other forms of delinquency.

Parents, peers, and autonomy. The contrapuntal peer association *vis-à-vis* the family should not be dismissed as entirely dysfunctional. Excepting certain destructive byproducts, the peer culture can serve a valuable function. Mannheim reminded us that affiliation with peer culture is instrumental in loosening dependence on the family and should not be sweepingly defined as a "social problem."[9] Adolescents' desire to establish distance from their family groups finds implementation through affiliation with nonfamilial peers who, in concerted rebelliousness,

[8] Urie Bronfenbrenner, "Children and Families: 1984?" *Society*, 18 (Jan./Feb. 1981), 38–41; and *The Ecology of Human Development: Experiments by Nature and Design* (Cambridge, Mass.: Harvard University Press, 1979).

[9] Karl Mannheim, *Essays on the Sociology of Culture* (New York: Oxford University Press, 1956).

try out new norms and values and in the process obtain skill in problem solving and develop unique identities. A major function of modern adolescence is renunciation of dependence on the family and substitution of peer groups for the family group. This substitution is thorough and includes fulfillment of emotional needs essential for individual growth, such as stimulation, empathy, loyalty, the opportunity for role playing, identification, and sharing of guilt and anxiety.

It can be said, then, that the peer group facilitates the young individual's autonomy process and emancipation from the family. The end result is an individual who is relatively autonomous in three respects. First, there is *emotional* autonomy as the person relaxes ties to the family and emotionally unfolds to establish bonds of love, support, and confidence elsewhere. Second, there is *behavioral* autonomy as the person acquires skill and courage to do what he or she wants to do. Third, there is *ideational* autonomy as the person thinks and struggles through basic ideas and establishes personal convictions.

There remain unanswered questions concerning youth-parent conflict and the autonomy process. One question is whether conflict with parents is a *sine qua non* of adolescence; that is, whether it is such an important feature that a concept of adolescence would be incomplete without it, or whether it has been exaggerated and there is actually little conflict. Another question deals with just how much and how widespread conflict is. Still another question deals with the focus of conflict; is it the struggle for emancipation from parental rule or are there quite different elements involved, such as envy, jealousy, or competition? Few studies have penetrated to see what lies at the heart of the relationship, what it really is that bothers adolescents when they manifest negativism and antagonism. Hence it is necessary to explore not only how much conflict there is, but what the conflict is about and under what circumstances it is expressed.

Some researchers disagree with the conflict theory and point out that if a contrapuntal subculture does in fact exist, it does not exist to the degree of the peer group advocating different values and engaging in serious conflicts with parents. Psychologist Albert Bandura argues that the "storm and stress" interpretation of adolescence has been exaggerated and that in ordinary middle-class families cooperative and mutually rewarding relationships between parents and teenagers are more in evidence than conflict.[10] Moreover, by the time children become adolescents, they have more or less achieved independence from parents. Actually, establishment of autonomy of the adolescent poses more of a problem for parents than for young individuals, since they have to adjust to the loss of a family member. Having enjoyed a relatively harmonious family relationship, teenagers tend to be discriminative in their choice of reference groups and generally establish peer associations that allow implementation of norms and values they learned in their homes. Hence, Bandura concludes that peer-group membership is usually not in opposition to family values and does not generate intergenerational conflict.

___

[10] Albert Bandura, "The Stormy Decade: Fact or Fiction," in *Issues in Adolescent Psychology*, ed. D. Rogers (New York: Prentice-Hall, 1972).

Bandura tries to explain the discrepancy between his research findings and the traditional theory by pointing out the distortions present in mass-media sensationalism; questioning the validity of generalizations from biased samples (such as data based on deviant adolescents); showing the rigidity of the theoretical approach, which glosses over individual variation; and stating the self-fulfilling prophecy that if adults label adolescents as rebellious, then rebellious they will become.

Eugene Thomas' study of political attitudes between generations supports Bandura's hypothesis,[11] revealing that children of highly politicized parents tend to be like their parents both in political attitudes and political behavior. This supports the conclusion that stratification theory explains political activism much better than generational theory. While the latter presupposes that the young rebel against their parents and therefore resent symbolic authority figures, the former suggests that these attitudes cut across generational lines. Reuben Hill and J. Aldous, Jr., explored attitudes and beliefs of three generations and found that while behavior concerning practical issues (for example, the division of labor in the household) has changed, fundamental values such as religious beliefs have hardly shifted at all.[12]

Additional researchers questioning the validity of the assumption that youth-parent conflict is a primary feature of adolescence are Elizabeth Douvan and her associates, whose data consistently showed a more harmonious youth-parent relationship.[13] Their findings suggest a more peaceful scene than much theory and most social comments would lead us to expect: "'Rebellious youth' and 'the conflict between generations' are phrases that ring; but, so far as we can tell, it is not the ring of truth they carry so much as the beguiling but misleading tone of drama."[14]

However, some of these researchers' data are based on narrow samples. Just as theorists may project generalizations from too broad a base, interviewers may project generalizations from too narrow a base. For example, most of the evidence that led Douvan to make the condemning statement cited above grew out of work dealing mainly with girls, although there was some information on fourteen-to-sixteen-year-old boys. In addition, little elucidation of data was provided to give a fuller picture of developmental changes. It seems, for instance, that seriousness of conflict is progressive; that is, it increases with age within the adolescent span. In one of the few instances where inquiry was directed at age-differentiated conflict and where girls were asked what they most disagreed about with their parents, the results showed three quite distinct peaks: the younger adolescents reported narrow

[11] Eugene Thomas, "Family Correlates of Student Political Activism," *Developmental Psychology*, 4 (March 1971), 206–14.

[12] Reuben Hill and J. Aldous, Jr., "Socialization for Marriage and Parenthood," in *Handbook of Socialization Theory and Research*, ed. D. Goslin (Chicago: Rand McNally, 1969).

[13] Elizabeth Douvan and Joseph Adelson, *The Adolescent Experience* (New York: John Wiley, 1966), and Elizabeth Douvan and H. Gold, "Modal Patterns in American Adolescence," in *Review of Child Development Research*, vol. 2, ed. L. Hoffman and M. Hoffman (New York: Russell Sage Foundation, 1966).

[14] Douvan and Gold, "Modal Patterns in American Adolescence," p. 485.

narcissistic issues; the middle group had interpersonal problems; and the older girls were concerned with broader social issues. Thus, in the under-fourteen group, clothing and make-up were the types of issues over which there was most disagreement; in the fourteen-to-sixteen group, whom, when, and how to date appeared major issues; in the oldest group, most disagreements dealt with basic ideas. Not only do researchers like Douvan and Gold fail to commit themselves to a certain age category when they make generalizations (usually about a harmonious youth-parent relationship), but even more important, they neglect to sufficiently clarify whether boys are equally restrained in their attitudes toward parental rule as girls appear to be. The Douvan studies suffer from the major weakness of comparing a small number of boys at one stage during their adolescent development with a large number of girls throughout the age range. In addition, such studies often fail to discuss their exact methodology, so that it is difficult to tell to what degree the interview approach has influenced the responses.

In any event, the reader is advised to accept either interpretation—the "conflict" as well as the "harmonious" theory—with caution and remain open to further insight that, hopefully, will eventually accrue.

CHANGING FUNCTIONS

The smaller and less stable family has signaled basic changes in how Americans relate to each other. Components of the new family lifestyle are discussed below.

Exit role, enter individual. The traditional family can also be called the "institutional" family because institutional norms and procedures were preferred over personal attitudes and desires. Integrity of the family as a unit used to be safeguarded by the various members playing roles. Deviations were frowned on, punished by informal or formal sanctions, and made difficult by economic dependence on the family unit. Also, the role of spouse or offspring had metaphysical overtones and was commonly considered as a sacred "blueprint" not to be taken lightly. This was familism, the philosophy that the family's goals and purposes have priority over those of the individual.

The modern family, however, places a premium on interpersonal competence rather than on skill in role functioning. The traditional family with its legal rigidity and hierarchical structure has become outdated, and modern Americans seek "self-actualization." Emphasis is now on flexibility, looser integration, and greater individualism. The high divorce rate is a manifestation of these changes, indicating that we are now highly divorce-prone because of the lack of institutional coercion, the easing of economic limitations, and the acceptance of individual volition that is monitored by little other than the rewards of companionship.

This, however, should not be mistaken for abandonment of marriage and the family. On the contrary, Americans adhere to the family as an institution within which they expect fulfillment of emotional needs, which now emphasize individualism and personality functions. These functional changes call for competence in interpersonal relations. Safe but rigid role blueprints are replaced by a highly individualistic style of relating that requires sensitivity, increased communication, and constantly new interpretations of interactional situations.

Demands for interpersonal competence include new emphasis on sexual knowledge and sexual equality, problem-solving skill, sublimating proficiency when frustrated, willingness to resort to professional therapy, and skill in family and couple communication. Interpersonal harmony depends so heavily on improved communication that family sociologists have recommended communication theory be applied to the marital dyad.[15]

Adolescents must learn to replace old, rigid role matrixes with sensitive personal communication. This means giving up the age-old security of knowing *a priori* how to act or react in interpersonal situations, especially in the relationship between the sexes, and accepting the new freedom of being able to style uniquely and creatively every human encounter. Learning to act individualistically takes both courage and experience. While the young may have the former, they may lack the latter. Learning adequate responses to the liberalized style of human interaction constitutes an immensely difficult task—a task requiring the treatment of each social scene as a situation that presents unique problems and requires unique solutions.

Probably the change most vexing to the young is the altered female role. Increasingly, mothers fail to convey an easily predictable role model. Until recently, wives were supplementary to husbands and not expected to express a full range of capabilities. Today, women have much greater expectations—and also frustrations. Nearly 60 percent of American women are now employed; and when a woman is working, she has a new perception of herself, behaves more independently, and refuses to be cast in a cultural matrix. There are difficulties of adjustment to this derigidification process for everyone involved. Girls are thrown back on their personal identities and must become fully conscious of them. Boys, while witnessing the expanding role of the female, are still largely trapped in the rigid role of masculinity and must make concessions. Skillful communication seems to be the basic key for successfully coping with encounters between the sexes, and a family sociologist calls attention to a Family Communication Game that can be used for education and fun by high school students.[16]

Difficulties arising from the modern family situation are not to be construed as having a negative value. New equity and flexibility promise greater opportunity for creativity and identity formation and can lead to deeply rewarding relationships.

From status ascription to status achievement. An individual growing up in the traditional family rarely had to be concerned with the question of social

---

[15] Sherod Miller et al., "Recent Progress in Understanding and Facilitating Marital Communication," *The Family Coordinator*, 24 (April 1975), 143–52.

[16] William Saur, "Family Communication Game," *The Family Coordinator*, 24 (April 1975), 227–29.

mobility, since he or she "inherited" the status of the family. A teenager at the turn of the century was exposed to considerably less intergenerational mobility than his or her counterpart of the mid-twentieth century. Familistic norms and values mitigated the problem of adolescent discontinuity, and a teenager knew his or her "place" in the family as well as in the larger society. Anxieties accompanying contemporary youth's task of determining their place and prestige in the social structure were thereby avoided.

Today, finding one's place is more individualistic. Although family background, especially if the family belongs to either extreme of the socioeconomic spectrum, is still an important influence on status achievement, its influence has diminished and status differences between parents and offspring are common. Many modern families consist of members who differ in social prestige, primarily because they pursue different careers. In short, the criterion for social status in modern society is based more on occupational achievement than on family reputation. Some family sociologists go so far as to conclude that family obligations in modern urban-industrial society tend to detract from single-minded pursuit of highly prized personal success, be the goal scholarly, commercial, or professional.[17]

The shift toward individualism is reflected in such catch phrases as "proliferation of associations," "personality market," "individuation," and "self-actualization." More and more relationships are achieved and are relatively role free, including those cultivated at school, at work, in numerous voluntary associations, and now also in the marital dyad. Achieved relationships are essentially idiosyncratic and potentially boundless. A pessimistic interpretation is that "herein lies their threat to the family, for they, like many other aspects of contemporary life, may readily infringe upon family claims, may alienate members from the family."[18]

The modern family's loss of the placement function, and thus its loss of the status-ascription function, has direct bearing on the problem of adolescence. Teenagers cannot expect much help from home during the process of working out a status by and for themselves. Their parents' statuses do not necessarily have finality in determining their own statuses. While family background is of minimal ascriptive effect, the achievement syndrome is of maximum importance. Absence of status certainty and prospects of an uncharted journey toward some yet undefined and obscure adult status may create feelings that are aptly described by contemporary teenagers when they say that they feel "lost" and are "going nowhere."

Again, it must be pointed out that negative aspects can be balanced by a positive gain: Modern teenagers have an unprecedented *freedom to choose* among different lifestyles. There may be something to be said *for* "being lost" and "going nowhere" for a while, instead of knowing from the beginning where one is going,

[17]Charles W. Hobart, "Commitment, Value Conflict and the Future of the American Family," *Journal of Marriage and the Family*, 25 (November 1963), 405–6.
[18]Ibid., p. 406.

but possibly neither liking the direction nor having the chance to change the course. Factual as well as fictional accounts of a past era are replete with the tragic stories of young individuals who had to pursue a course in life they had not chosen.

The law and the young: independence, individualism, and isolation. American society appears to look at marital and family affiliations as essentially private relationships outside of the purview of the public's meddling, be this informal interference or legal encroachment. This is not to say that the law is indifferent to what is going on in the family, but rather that serious dysfunctions within the family system are approached as *individual* matters and not as family issues.

This individuation of family members includes the adolescent. If the adolescent exhibits disturbed or delinquent behavior, he or she is approached as an isolated individual and not as a representative of a primary group the disturbances of which he or she is manifesting. The law's pursuit is the individual, and jurisdictional interests proceed regardless of family context. The "hands-off" policy is particularly emphatic in the case of marital dissolution. In a sense, the law concerns itself only with keeping records of who enters and who leaves marriage. During 1974, over 2 million couples obtained divorces. The authorities, and society as a whole, looked on with stolid indifference — because marriage is a "private matter."

This, then, is the individual-centered legal context within which rights and obligations of American children and teenagers must be understood.

A legal landmark in clarifying the young Americans' status was the Twenty-sixth Amendment to the Constitution in 1971 which gave eighteen-year-olds the right to vote and helped them to obtain many other legal privileges. The rights that eighteen-, nineteen-, and twenty-year-olds have gained include the right to own property, make wills, sign binding contracts, sue and be sued, marry without the consent of parents, and undergo medical treatment (including treatment for venereal disease) without parental approval.[19] The majority of states have granted eighteen-year-olds the privileges they formerly had to wait until twenty-one to receive. But some states still refuse to lower the drinking age, and a few states will not grant across-the-board freedom to eighteen-year-olds, still requiring parental consent up to nineteen, twenty, or twenty-one in such matters as abortion, pregnancy care, and birth-control prescriptions. For example, Hawaii and Missouri require individuals to be twenty and twenty-one, respectively, to obtain contraception prescriptions without consent of parents; Wyoming and Nebraska determine nineteen to be the minimum age for pregnancy-related health services, including abortion, without consent of parents. Apart from such exceptions, the states recognize eighteen as being adult age.

In fact, the states are now extending "without consent" medical rights (including pregnancy care, birth-control prescriptions, abortion, treatment for

[19] "Kids, Sex, and Doctors," *Time*, November 25, 1974, pp. 91–93, and Lavelle E. Saunders, "Ignorance of the Law Among Teenagers: A Barrier to the Exertion of Their Rights as Citizens?" Paper presented at the Annual Meeting of the Pacific Sociological Association, Victoria, British Columbia, April 1975.

venereal disease, drug addiction, and psychiatric problems) to youths under eighteen. In all states (except Wisconsin) younger teenagers have the right to get treatment for venereal disease without consulting their parents. California's emancipated youth laws extend this right to anyone over twelve years old. New Jersey allows minors of any age to obtain pregnancy care and abortion without parental consent but, ironically, requires parental consent for contraceptive prescriptions up to age eighteen. Oregon has dropped the age of medical consent to fifteen, and Alabama to fourteen.

The age group most conspicuously affected by the new laws are college students, who have been freed from *in loco parentis* authority. Colleges may no longer require students to live in campus dormitories; out-of-state students may find it easier to establish legal residence within a state and thus pay lower tuition fees for state-supported institutions; parents may no longer get a chance to see the grades of their adult children or be informed of any trouble they have gotten into, unless their son or daughter specifically gives the college permission; students from higher-income families, previously barred from most financial aid in college, may now claim they are independent of parents, account for only their own income, and receive financial aid; and students can sue and be sued, which enables colleges to take students to court in cases of vandalism, disruption, or cheating without involving the parents, and, likewise, students can file legal complaints.

Many parents, educators, and administrators feel that their authority is being undermined. They perceive an exaggerated, if not perverted, emphasis on individualism that results in too much independence for the young and thus creates an atmosphere of isolation. This isolation is becoming ingrained by moving liberalized and individual-centered legislation to the forefront of human interaction. As legalistic consciousness grows, the informal cooperation and personal trust that used to be a natural part of family life is being diminished. Nonetheless, the new laws are rapidly becoming our new tradition. It may be years before we know the full social and psychological effects of adulthood at age eighteen.

The rise of the personality function. Industrialization has prompted the transferral of one traditional family function after another to specialized institutional settings. The economic and production function has been relegated to the factory and office; the educational function has been entirely absorbed by schools; the religious function has been formalized and is now the exclusive domain of the church or synagogue; the recreational function has been commercialized and is dominated by profit-seeking institutions like movie theaters and sports stadiums; the medical function has been transferred to the doctor's office and the hospital. Family members usually go to these places individually, not as a family unit.

The family is left to provide affection for its members, but little else. In short, the trend of increasing specialization in American society has affected the family and made it a specialist. It now specializes in gratifying psychological needs. The question of whether the modern family can meet basic personality needs, in particular such needs as the feeling of belonging and security, is important for youth's physical as well as mental health. Experience of structural discontinuity between statuses of child and adult is difficult and confusing under normal and secure circumstances. If, in addition, there is lack of psychological security, youth faces an extremely difficult time.

Many sociologists have attempted to answer the question of whether the modern family is able to offer this vital security, and two main theories have emerged. Interpretations of the changes in family life have led one group to answer "no" and the other "yes" to the question of the family's psychological functionality. Besides Barrington Moore, a well-known spokesperson for the "no" group, there is Carl C. Zimmerman, whose work offers an extensive historical study of the family, draws conclusions from previous societies, applies them to the contemporary scene, and predicts the doom of the modern family.[20] The hypothesis is supported by historical data suggesting that the modern family has lost too many functions to be of further importance.

Opposing interpretation is offered by Talcott Parsons, who presents a more optimistic point of view.[21] Changes are interpreted as processes reforming the family into an agency specializing in the "personality function." This specialization is the American response to the need to derive from the family psychological security to a degree heretofore unknown.

These acute psychological demands appear to be symptomatic of the problem of identity, which can be considered the prominent mental problem of the modern era. It is within the confines of the family that Americans hope to find the answer to the basic question, Who am I? This burdens the family with an immense responsibility. If people fail to find the coveted identity and feeling of security in a particular marriage or family, they are apt to terminate membership and try anew with different partners. According to Parsons, this insistence on "self-fulfillment" explains the high divorce rate in modern America. The rate, as alarming as it may seem, does not necessarily indicate the doom of the family institution but rather the need of contemporaries to succeed in gratifying psychological needs. If the need is not met with one particular partner, the partner is changed; but the same conventional institution, marriage and the family, is used, reused, and upheld.[22]

Without necessarily endorsing Zimmerman's negative outlook, we nonetheless must acknowledge that the nuclear family is beset with difficulties that limit the success of the personality function. The detracting conditions include (1) high divorce rate; (2) high mobility, both social and geographic; (3) insufficient family communication; (4) increasing numbers of mothers directing their attention to out-

---

[20] Carl C. Zimmerman, *Family and Civilization* (New York: Harper and Row, 1947).

[21] Talcott Parsons and Robert F. Bales, *Family, Socialization and Interaction Process* (Chicago: The Free Press of Glencoe, 1955).

[22] There is a significant difference between a particular *family group* and the *institution of the family*. The two should never be confused. The former refers to a specific group of people, in this case a primary group within which the members engage in an intimate face-to-face interaction. The concept of institution is more abstract, referring to norms, values, and customs with which society regulates family life.

side careers; and (5) continuing remoteness of fathers from the socialization process. These conditions cause many adolescents to be inadequately involved in family communication—without a definite sense of being accepted and understood, and without a basic trust in the stability of the family group.

Some of these detracting conditions must be singled out as particularly important. For example, communication is a skill not automatically earned by merit of being a parent but must be acquired by practice. How many children grow up doubting whether they are loved and accepted by their parents, consequently suffer under these doubts, and later in life reproach a reticent parent for not having communicated love and care? As mentioned earlier, proficiency in communication is imperative for success in the modern family, where role playing is no longer the predictable form of communication. To implement the modern personality function, the communication process must be improved by greater sensitivity and by spending more time on it.

But modern parents' time schedule has not always taken the need for more communication into account. Modern fathers are known as notorious shirkers of the responsibility to equitably share in socializing the young, and excuse themselves as being absorbed by their jobs. Admittedly, this aspect of modern family life seems to be undergoing modification thanks to the protests of the women's liberation movement. But the progress made in this direction tends to be neutralized by the mothers' newly acquired taste for career pursuits. While this may connote progress to many creative mothers who heretofore were cloistered in the kitchen and nursery, it may be an obstacle to the increased communication needed by the child in order to feel secure and understood.

Communication does not merely mean "talking to each other," it means *doing things together*, using the media of common projects, work, and recreational activities. These media can be used to express thoughts and feelings to each other, to get to know each other, and to feel a belonging to each other that can rarely be established by way of abstract verbalizations. Actions speak more convincingly than words, and the young can benefit immensely by shared feeling, touch, and motion —ingredients that will generate common emotions, which form the foundation for conveying the sense of belonging and security.

Another obstacle to the personality function is mobility. Spatial mobility of Americans is truly remarkable: every five years about one-half the U.S. population moves. In the process, they increase the variety of readjustments they must make, lose the immediate support of neighborhood and friendships they had enjoyed, and decrease informal discouragement against separation or divorce they had (or could have) derived from integration into the community.

Mobility plays a prominent role in the lives of businessmen, white-collar workers, and young executives who are constantly on relocation call for the corporation and have been called "corporate nomads." The price of promotion includes a willingness to be geographically mobile. A typical example is the mobility record of a newly promoted assistant secretary at Humble Oil and Refining Co., who at the age of thirty-three had moved six times in eleven years. His nine-year-old son had never finished a single grade in the same school. Within ten months, a young aspiring executive of Johnson Wax was moved from Wisconsin to New York and then to Chicago to become regional office manager, with his son going through kindergarten in three different schools.[23]

Young people need consistency in life patterns, including physical and social arrangements, to achieve stable reference points. Informal associations like the peer group, neighborhood, and friendships, and formal associations like school, church, and clubs, constitute social-control mechanisms, and youth's integration into them has a stabilizing influence — provided that it is consistent and continuous.

Although one could say a few things in defense of the functionality of high mobility, for example that exposure to a wide variety of stimuli can contribute to a more sophisticated outlook on life and that job contingencies require knowledge of a variety of human interactions, they seem to be neutralized by such dysfunctions as exposing the young to too many stimuli (and possibly inconsistent ones) and to more people than can be meaningfully integrated in the understanding of the young — a typical consequence of overstimulation and overexposure. Although the relationships may turn out to be expedient and efficient, they tend to remain shallow. In other words, quality of human interaction is replaced by quantity. Relationships of deep understanding and genuine loyalty require time to grow — time many mobile parents fail to provide for their children. The sense of impermanence of these relationships intensifies the need for *some* relationship that is durable. And it is, given the impersonality of the larger social system, almost invariably the family that is sought out for this important function.

But now we have arrived at a circular irony. The family seems to promise personality security, commonly fails to live up to its promise, and Americans nevertheless keep trying to make marriage and the family work. It is like Sisyphus attempting to roll a boulder uphill, and the whole situation smacks of overdependence on a limited structural arrangement.

Whether these changes will eventually bring about the downfall of the family system as we know it today are speculations that cannot be put to an empirical test at this time. In any case, the functional changes of the modern family can be summed up in three points: (1) a number of traditional family functions have been transferred to other institutions; (2) the modern family has become a specialized agency; (3) people turn to the family to derive a sense of total psychological security.

The question of primary group quality.   The socialization experience in the family is so profound that what we conceptualize as "human nature" can be traced back to this primary group. The human organism responds to the slightest variation in style of socialization, and some modes complicate the adolescent process. It appears that a child growing up in a family that fulfills the criteria of a healthy primary group will be better equipped to cope with the contingencies of adoles-

---

[23] "The Job: Corporate Nomads," *Time*, September 29, 1967, p. 56.

cence than a child whose association was either in a disturbed primary group or mostly in secondary groups.

Before pursuing this argument further, the question of what a primary group is must be clarified.[24] A primary group is characterized by intimate face-to-face interaction and spontaneous cooperation. It is primary in the sense that it is instrumental in generating the social nature of the individual. The psychological result of the intimate association is a blending of several individuals into a social entity in which one's self becomes an integral part of the common life and goals of the group. The emergent sentiments involve the sort of mutual identification for which "we" is the most natural expression. The members' identities become anchored in the feeling of belonging to the whole.

This does not necessarily mean that the atmosphere of the group is always one of harmony. There is often self-assertion and passion. But these sentiments are tempered by sympathy and a sense of common fate. While an individual member may show ambition, its chief motivation is the self-esteem he or she derives from the others, and interaction will be governed by allegiance to common standards of loyalty. This is the social-psychological background that explains why a child may come to dispute with teammates his or her place on the team, but will strive toward common glory for the team.

The most compelling examples of such primary associations are the family, peer group, and, decreasingly, the neighborhood or community. Primary involvements are virtually universal and are the basis of what is universal in human nature and fundamental in human sentiments.

The definition of secondary groups consists of elements that contrast with the primary group—impermanence, casualness of contact, fewer ties of deep sentiment among the members, and a lesser degree of derivation of basic values from the group's norms and goals. In reality, groups do not come neatly divided into either primary or secondary types; rather, social reality presents us with a continuum, the poles of which we define as primariness and secondariness of group quality. Groups differ from one another not categorically, but in the *degree* to which the interacting behavior of the participants reflects primariness.[25]

Has the American family shifted along the continuum of primary-secondary group relations? In other words, is the nuclear family less primary than the traditional family? To answer this question, it is helpful to examine specific elements of the criteria of primariness.

An important element of the primary group consists of *common value orientation*. Family sociologists fear that consensus within the family, especially between the generations, has been eroded by modern socialization practices that

---

[24] The statement on the primary group, paraphrased in the following passages, comes from Cooley, *Social Organization*, pp. 23–24.

[25] Definitions like "primary" or "secondary" are ideal-type definitions; that is, they are useful—yet arbitrary—typologies. They are useful for tracing trends, comparing different systems, and facilitating communication. Ideal-type concepts are instrumental in many social analyses and can be called *heuristic* in nature.

promote more nonfamilial exposure of the young to nurseries, day-care centers, peers, schools, and youth subculture than to parents and relatives. Bias for the traditional growth process in the primary group family is reflected by a number of sociologists' negative views of the changes in family functions. They regret, as Hobart put it, that "the shaping of a human life, a human personality, a future of happiness or hell, which is best accomplished in the primary group, is turned over ever earlier and for longer periods to secondary, impersonal, social agencies."[26] But these agencies tend to merely "handle" children in groups, rather than care for them as individuals.

Bronfenbrenner is even more outspoken about parental failure to enforce a value orientation in the children. Reporting about his cross-cultural study of child-rearing practices in America and West Germany, he admitted that he expected German parents to be stricter than American parents. Although the hypothesis was borne out by the findings, it was also found that the German parents were more affectionate and spent more time with the children. This calls into question what exactly is meant by *permissive*; perhaps it means that parents are not paying much attention to their young. American parents have been told by experts to "let children be themselves"; that counsel has been taken to mean "let them grow up by themselves." Bronfenbrenner rejects *laissez-faire* philosophy and believes that the young "should not grow up associating only with other children because they haven't much to give to each other."[27]

Teenagers themselves have complained that parents fail to give them guidance and are too permissive. It seems that they sense a need for more authoritative counsel. A national sample found that teenagers ascribe primary responsibility for excessive teenage drinking and use of "dope" to their parents' failure to wield enough authority.[28] This attitude illustrates teenagers' dissatisfaction with modern home anomie, which allows them a high degree of individual freedom but also creates uncertainty. Anomie is not characteristic of a primary-group setting; rather it offers rules and values of insuperable aid in stabilizing personality.

Common activities, another mark of the primary group, have drastically declined in the modern family. As discussed in previous chapters, the place of work is somewhere else, and children, unless they live on the farm, are not drawn into adult activities. Similarly, leisure activities are usually age segregated because of different interest. If time is spent together, it is usually a passive gathering—watching television, traveling someplace, or being entertained—instead of doing things together.

A core trait of the primary group is that it *forms the social nature of the individual.* To what extent is the modern family still instrumental in carrying out this function? Is it imbuing the young with the same loyalty and empathy as the

---

[26] Hobart, "Commitment, Value Conflict and the Future of the American Family," p. 408.

[27] "The American Family: Future Uncertain," *Time*, December 28, 1970, p. 37.

[28] Leonard Gross, "America's Mood Today," *Look*, June 29, 1965, p. 21.

traditional family? Bronfenbrenner has found that all factors indicating growth, happiness, and effectiveness of the young are declining. Conversely, he discovered increasing isolation and evidence to anticipate impairment rather than improvement in competence and character of the next generation. His pessimistic conclusion was that the system for making human beings human in this society is breaking down and that "the destructive effects of these changes derive from the progressive segregation by age in American society, resulting in isolation of children and those responsible for their care."[29]

As a rule, parents gladly let other agencies take over socializing. Nurseries, kindergartens, schools, churches, and the various media of entertainment encounter little resistance from parents, who willingly surrender a territory that means fatiguing work, time, and often frustration. Television in particular has become a convenient baby-sitting device, changing the family circle to a semicircle.

Finally, the characteristics of the primary group include the *blending of several individuals into a social entity.* But in our age, the young do not defer individual goals to common goals; rather they look at the family as a pragmatic arrangement that can be useful but as only one alternative in learning values. In short, the family has changed from an end in itself to a *means* for individual purposes.

This does not mean that the average family of today is of secondary-group quality. Rather, there has been a *shift on the continuum* toward more secondariness of group qualities, with the family playing a modified role in the process of extending identity. The proliferation of secondary-group affiliations and the impact of the mass media are to some extent replacing the socialization function of the family. It seems that both the family and the secondary influences are not meeting the needs of the young. The paradoxical result is that the young turn to the family for identity and warmth, but are confronted with its ineffectiveness in stabilizing personality and are thus driven back to the conflicting and piecemeal socialization of secondary groups.

MOMISM: INFLICTING
PERPETUAL ADOLESCENCE[30]

The nature and rise of Momism.   Momism has arisen as a peculiar perversion of the personality function in the modern family and focuses on the type of mother who uses her child to gratify her neurotic needs. While the mother, to all outward appearance, does a fine job, her child-rearing practice is geared toward retaining the child and converting him or her into a perennial adolescent.

---

[29] Urie Bronfenbrenner, "The Challenge of Social Change to Public Policy and Developmental Research." Paper presented at the President's Symposium, *Child Development and Public Policy*, Denver, Colorado, April 12, 1975, abstract.

[30] The treatment of Momism in this section focuses on a specific application of the concept – its effects on adolescence. A fuller discussion can be found in Hans Sebald, *Momism – The Silent Disease of America* (Chicago: Nelson-Hall, 1976).

The rationale for treating this clinical issue here is that it deals with an adolescence-producing problem that is increasing in the United States and has regular features in the structure of American society: With amazing frequency, Momism has become a feature of the American middle class.

Early writers to call attention to Momism included Philip Wylie and Sidney C. Howard.[31] They felt that American motherhood was becoming a public danger, inflicting psychological harm on children. They stimulated investigation by social scientists, and the reference to a "Mom" gradually became a relatively objective concept describing the type of mother who retards her child's maturity.[32]

In previous generations, the wife-mother role was more or less the only life task available to women. Although this meant limited freedom, it also meant little anxiety, since women's lifestyle was free from ambiguity. With the advent of women's liberation, the traditional role became only *one* of a spectrum newly available. While this change added freedom to the lives of women, it also added a new worry. It brought restless soul-searching to clarify the question of how the new options could best be used. Liberation from the old-fashioned role introduced the same compulsion toward achievement as has been the psychological torment of the male.

And it is at this juncture that many a half-liberated woman takes an ironic turn: she opts for staying home and becoming an outstanding mother. Motherhood becomes her career, with the output of "perfect" children the tangible evidence of her success. It seems that the visions of liberation did not necessarily match the more slowly changing social structural arrangements that perpetuate the conditions that keep women at home. In other words, psychological emancipation is not fully implemented by structural emancipation. This structural-lag condition inflicts feelings of relative deprivation on the woman who wants but cannot step out into the professional world. Opportunity to compensate for deeply felt deprivation is visualized in a new type of motherhood that establishes evidence of competence. What is overlooked in the haste to preserve self-respect is the fact that the child is not accepted as an end in him- or herself, but only as a means – and a young personality used for the alleviation of a neurosis cannot help but acquire its own.

Focus: the mother-son relationship. Momism usually involves the mother-*son* relationship, since a girl, even if dominated by her mother, can adopt her manners, imitate her, and take on her role. In fact, this is the way many Moms are

---

[31] Philip Wylie, *Generation of Vipers* (New York: Rinehart and Co., 1942), and Sidney C. Howard, *The Silver Cord: A Satire in Three Acts* (New York: Scribner's, 1928).

[32] Edward A. Strecker, *Their Mothers' Sons: The Psychiatrist Examines an American Problem* (New York: Lippincott, 1946); David M. Levy, *Maternal Overprotection* (New York: Columbia University Press, 1943); Erik H. Erikson, *Childhood and Society* (New York: W. W. Norton, Inc., 1963); Martha W. Lear, *The Child-Worshipers* (New York: Crown Publishers, 1963); Margaret Mead, "What Is Happening to the American Family?" *Journal of Social Casework*, 28 (November 1947), 323–30; Arnold W. Green, "The Middle-Class Male Child and Neurosis," *American Sociological Review*, 11 (February 1946), 31–41; and Patricia C. Sexton, *The Feminized Male: Classrooms, White Collars and the Decline of Manliness* (New York: Random House, 1969).

created: a girl patterning her behavior after mother. She is free to do so since both imitator and imitated are of the same sex. This is reflected in the findings of researchers, who found that girls resemble their mothers in terms of personality much more than boys.[33] (The boy's vulnerability to Momism justifies the masculine pronoun when referring to "child" in this discussion.)

Most American fathers are only peripherally involved in socializing their children. This explains why the boy is more vulnerable to Momism than the girl; he lacks a close and daily visible male model. In fact, Momism can occur only if the father fails to enact his part in child-rearing.[34]

The core technique. The typical Mom tries to achieve her "success" goal by manipulating the child's behavior by extending or withdrawing love, or by promising to do so. It is powerful "love"-oriented sanction that is responsible for impairing personality growth in the child and establishing a mother-dependency that does not go away when he reaches adolescence; it should be replaced with personal autonomy. Since love is experienced as something *conditional* — contingent on how he behaves and not as something he deserves on the basis of his innate worth — the slightest disapproval of mother (and later of any outside authority) will cause him anxiety. His feeling of acceptability depends on constant approval by others. A mind so conditioned has little reprieve from anxiety.

An important element of this conditioning process is the boy's belief that he *needs* that love. "Not the need for parent love, but the constant threat of its withdrawal *after the child has been conditioned to the need*, lies at the root of the most characteristic modern neurosis."[35] Empirical evidence suggests that maternal achievement pressures are more effective than paternal pressures because of mother's use of the "love"-oriented sanctions.[36]

A tentative profile of the Mom has emerged by now. She (1) is most likely middle class; (2) has a good education, has been steeped in "scientific child-rearing," and has been affected by the promises of the feminist movement; (3) has turned to mothering as a method of producing evidence of competence and "success"; (4) has a husband who is peripherally involved in the socialization of the child; (5) has a son, usually an only child, she uses for alleviating feelings of relative deprivation; and (6) uses the "love"-oriented conditioning.

[33] Ruth E. Hartley, "Children's Concepts of Male and Female Roles," *Merrill-Palmer Quarterly*, 6 (January 1960), 83–91; Lionel M. Lasowick, "On the Nature of Identification," *Journal of Abnormal and Social Psychology*, 51 (September 1955), 175-83; and David B. Lynn, "The Process of Learning Parental and Sex-Role Identification," *Journal of Marriage and the Family*, 28 (November 1966), 466-70; and *The Father: His Role in Child Development* (Belmont, Calif.: Wadsworth, 1976).

[34] Fitzhugh Dodson, *How to Father* (Bergenfield, N.J.: New American Library, 1975); Michael E. Lamb, "Paternal Influences and the Father's Role," in John Keating, ed., *Social Psychology 82/83* (Guilford, Ct.: Dushkin, 1982), pp. 68–73.

[35] Green, "The Middle-class Male Child and Neurosis," p. 39. (Italics added.)

[36] R. R. Sears, E. E. Maccoby, and H. Levin, *Patterns of Child-Rearing* (Evanston, Ill.: Row & Peterson, 1957); and Garven Hudgins, "Cheating: Grave Pressures," *AP Education Service*, February 1969.

No two Moms are exactly alike, and their styles of manipulation differ widely, are remarkably colorful, and could fill a museum of psychopathology. While some may meet the above profile only partly, they all seem to have one thing in common: to manipulate the child in such a way that he remains dependent. The "love"-oriented sanction system is patently suited to serve that goal.

Although essentially retaining this core technique, some Moms become specialists in the style in which they apply the leverage. Major types include the overindulgent, overprotective, permissive, domineering, child-worshipping, "star," absolute authority, and "martyr" Moms.[37]

Consequences: from "true believer" to suicide. Common elements can be observed among the affected males: (1) the inability to make decisions; (2) feelings of inferiority; (3) a particular brand of anxiety; (4) patterns of irresponsible behavior; and (5) emotional parasitism; that is, insufficiently controlled narcissism and egocentrism.

These consequences do not always become obvious. The Momistically impaired person tends to gravitate toward a "normal" situation, such as a marriage where he locks into complementary interaction. In most instances he marries a Mom type who substitutes for his erstwhile Mom. This constitutes the "silent majority" of which no one takes much notice.

There are also the sensational types: the sexual deviate, drug addict, psychopath, schizophrenic, and suicide. For example, a team of New York City social workers trying to discover why they were unsuccessful in helping young addicts found the latter's mothers employing various stealthy techniques to keep the sons addicted and thereby Mom-dependent. One mother was the "martyr" Mom; another bailed her boy out of jail while he was waiting to be admitted to a hospital for addicts.[38] Some mothers encouraged the drug habit by giving their sons ten dollars every day "for a haircut," or fifteen dollars "for a shirt." Similarly, the Family Institute of Chicago, studying heroin and barbiturate addicts, discovered that the stars of the drama were the inefficient father, the domineering-but-protective Mom, and the helplessly dependent son.[39]

An extreme case concerned a thirty-seven-year-old Wisconsin man whose mother took him everywhere in a wheel cart, allegedly because he suffered from polio. Welfare officials finally prevailed and had him examined – he was found capable of walking. It was his *mother*, not polio, who had disabled him. When the son had been temporarily removed from the mother at age fifteen to attend school, he curled up in a fetal position and remained in this position for twenty-two years,

---

[37] These types are discussed in detail in Hans Sebald, *Momism: The Silent Disease of America.*

[38] "Mom is the Villain," *Time*, May 21, 1965, p. 83.

[39] John Schwartzman, "The Addict, Abstinence, and the Family," *American Journal of Psychiatry*, 132 (February 1975), 154–57.

spoon-fed, diapered, and wheeled around by his mother who insisted that "I like him just the way he is."[40]

A common and yet often undetected outcome of Momism is the individual who has always relied on his mother for decisionmaking and who later adheres to a substitute decisionmaking figure. He may become a "true believer," who exhibits a total submission to some supposedly infallible and omnipotent ideology or charismatic leader.[41] It is from people of this temperament that totalitarian movements (be they religious or political) recruit some of their most fanatic followers.

When forced to face an important situation demanding a major decision, a victim of Momism may withdraw from reality to escape pain, guilt, and insecurity. In the process of treating psychoneurotics who were "rejects" from the United States armed forces, psychiatrist Edward A. Strecker diagnosed many of them as suffering from schizophrenia that functioned as a "mom surrogate."[42]

A study in Scandinavian countries discovered correlations between the suicide rate and the style of child rearing.[43] Denmark, with one of the world's highest suicide rates, is characterized by a child-rearing style that creates highly guilt-conscious and dependent personalities. Norway, with one of the lowest suicide rates, is much like Denmark in most variables, *except* in child-rearing procedures.

The consequences of Momism should be understood with the following points in mind:

1. The effects usually overlap and form combinations.
2. Mother influence can be detected in the lives of entirely healthy males, and a pathological connotation should not be attached to all symptoms.
3. Momism should therefore be defined as exceeding normal influence to the point of crippling the personality.
4. Duration of symptoms of Momistic impairment differs from victim to victim, in some cases lasting a lifetime and in other cases disappearing soon after the offspring leaves home.
5. Only a proportion of males suffering from such problems as drug addiction, homosexuality, and suicidal tendencies can be traced to a Momistic experience.
6. Momism often ensues because the father defaults in helping with child rearing.
7. Diagnosis of a disturbance as an outcome of Momism is often difficult and should be attempted only after careful investigation.

[40] "Rehabilitation: Return From the Womb," *Time*, May 17, 1963, p. 93.

[41] This concept was first coined by Eric Hoffer, *The True Believer* (New York: Mentor Books, 1951).

[42] Strecker, *Their Mothers' Sons*, pp. 1112–21.

[43] Herbert Hendin, *Suicide and Scandinavia* (New York: Grune and Stratton, 1964).

PARENTHOOD: THE LAST
STAND OF THE AMATEUR

The distress of the modern family has invited critics to blame parents for all the trouble, branding them amateurs in a world of experts. While unqualified accusations merely add insult to injury and overlook the fact that parents themselves are victims of changing times, some critical comments are well taken and should be discussed.

Logic calls for qualifications *before* we encourage, or even allow, parenthood, because little effective remedy can correct defective parenthood after the *fait accompli.* The need for controlling parenthood expresses itself most distressingly at the time of adolescence, when many of the young show evidence of inadequate parental help. Many parents did not know what the socialization process would demand of them; many did not even plan on having children (they came as "accidents"); and many followed gullibly the all-American bandwagon of "parenthood as a natural and beautiful state of existence."

Regulation of, or even mere advice about, the individual's reproductive behavior is considered by most Americans as an encroachment on their "natural right" and flatly rejected. The noncooperative stance has prompted social scientists to suggest radical measures for curbing unqualified parenthood, and some believe that society must restrict the reproductive privilege. Sociologist Kingsley Davis suggested charging high fees for marriage licenses, levying a "child tax," reversing the traditional taxation of singles over persons having children, and legalizing sterilization and abortion.[44]

Anthropologist Margaret Mead recommended that Americans accept what seems to be a naturally evolving dual marriage system. One is the "individual marriage" for young couples not intending to have children; and the other is the "parental marriage" for couples planning on offspring.[45]

Biologist H. Bentley Glass thinks that parenthood should be permitted only after a couple obtains a "child license."[46] The question of enforcement of such an ordinance is understandably pertinent. Glass suggests court-ordered sterilization of parents who violate the license law more than once.

Politicians also recognize the need for laws against irresponsible parenthood. For example, an Illinois state representative sponsored a bill in 1971 that would force Illinois welfare parents who had three children to be sterilized to preclude burdening the public with additional expenses.

[44] Kingsley Davis, "Population Policy: Will Current Programs Succeed?" *Science*, 158 (November 10, 1967), 738. A number of other sociologists have made statements basically in agreement with Davis' concern: Michael Young, Ronald Freeman, Bernard Berelson, Philip Hauser, Orville Brim, Jr., Brewster Smith, Reuben Hill, George M. Foster, Everett Rogers, Nicholas Demerath, and others, in "Meetings: Behavioral Science and Family Planning," *Science*, 158 (November 3, 1967), 677–82.

[45] "Margaret Mead Today," *Time*, March 21, 1969, p. 77.

[46] Los Angeles Times Service (June 24, 1964); AP Report (Atlantic City, N.J., Feb. 13, 1967).

These arguments warn that unchecked parenthood and population growth will reduce living standards and life chances for everyone and that the conventional view of parenthood as an asset to society needs drastic revision. Parenthood has become a *liability*, not only because of all-too-frequent poor parenting, but also because we are endangering our resources through overpopulation.

THE QUEST FOR ALTERNATIVE
STRUCTURES

Widespread disillusionment with the modern family has led to widespread experimentation with alternative primary groups. The vast majority of experimenters consist of adolescents who try new arrangements that they hope will both give them the gratifications of the ideal family and spare them what they see as stifling elements of the nuclear family system.

Many young people fail to recognize, however, that frustration and sacrifice are essentially unavoidable ingredients of the universal experience of growing up and cannot always be explained by the structural contingencies. Not understanding the near universality of emotional distress, they tend to blame the structure in which they find themselves at the time of self-search and during the process of growing up. Frustrating curtailment of desires and painful adjustments are hardly novel aspects of the human condition and cannot justly be blamed on the nuclear family.

This is not to say that the modern family system is faultless and could not be improved. However, it should remind us that there is no structural alternative that will do the soul searching, self-integrating, and growing up *for* the young. Hence, many a search for an alternative family system is really an attempt to run away from basic developmental tasks, an excuse to avoid responsibilities, and a confusion between reality and utopia. At the core of this confusion is a basic misunderstanding of what human nature is. The fact that youthful communes have an extremely short life span and an exasperatingly high turnover of members bespeaks the pseudosolution that these alternatives represent. There is no support for the contention that the alternatives work better than the nuclear family.

Complaints about the modern nuclear family are legion. It has been accused of suffering from isolated structure and from atrophy of vital functions. Bronfenbrenner believes that the modern family is experiencing an unprecedented atrophy and that the all-too-frequent one-parent situation constitutes a highly unreliable structure.[47] Because of its maimed condition, the family no longer provides communion of religious belief, shared work experience, a medium through which to contact others in the community, and a source of convincing norms and values.

[47] "A Look at the Disintegrating World of Childhood," *Psychology Today*, 9 (June 1975), 34.

Additional complaints aim at the larger social system: the emptiness of organized religion, the meaninglessness of the Protestant ethic, the rigidity of Puritanical sexual mores, the anonymity of urban-industrial life, and the agonizing anomie of American culture.

These ills, the young feel, are not cured or alleviated by the current family form, and they are seeking a structure that would correct its failures. They admire the type of integrated environment of such groups as the Amish and Hutterites, the Israeli kibbutz system, and the type of tribal or village life of which they have learned through Margaret Mead's, Oscar Lewis', and Bronislaw Malinowski's anthropological reports. Indeed, the Samoan way of growing up would probably be accepted as ideal. The organization of the Samoan household eliminates most of the seeds that germinate into the dysfunctional emotions and conflicts with which our nuclear-family-raised children seem to be afflicted. The Samoan child's world is composed of male and female adults, all of whom can be depended on and must be deferred to. In cases of disagreement between parent and child, or in cases where it would be useful for a child's learning of a certain skill, the child is free to move into the home of a relative. The child is not falsely protected from the realities of life: sex, pregnancy, childbirth, and death are all familiar occurrences. "Among the factors in the Samoan scheme of life which are influential in producing stable, well-adjusted, robust individuals, the organization of the family and the attitude toward sex are undoubtedly the most important."[48]

Life in the modern American family contrasts sharply with the Samoan vision. The differential fuels the dissatisfaction of modern youth who would like to revert to a type of extended family system that promises fellowship, integration, security, and all the other things they fail to find in the nuclear family.

The closest they have come to that ideal in their experimentation is the *commune.* Communes range from religious economy with sexual exclusiveness to group marriage.[49] Most communes hold property in common, but leave responsibility for other aspects of life to the nuclear units, including the care of children. Other communes are political, espousing revolutionary goals. Still others are non-ideological, the communards' chief concern being "experience"—perhaps with drugs, sex, the occult, or simply "relationships" through which they try to find intimacy and sharing.

While each commune is unique, some common traits can be discerned. To some degree they all share property, minimize competitiveness, and emphasize personal concern and affection over utilitarian and financial relationships. Commune dwellers search for meaning in life and strive toward personal growth, share

[48] Margaret Mead, *Coming of Age in Samoa* (New York: Morrow, 1928), p. 228.

[49] Saul V. Levine et al., "The Urban Commune: Fact or Fad, Promise or Pipedream?" *American Journal of Orthopsychiatry*, 43 (January 1973), 149–63; Bennett Berger et al., "The Communal Family," *The Family Coordinator*, 21 (October 1972), 419–27; Sallie Teselle, ed., *The Family, Communes, and Utopian Societies* (New York: Harper & Row, 1972); James W. Ramey, "Communes, Group Marriage, and the Upper-Middle Class," *Journal of Marriage and the Family*, 34 (November 1972), 647–55; Laurence Veysey, *The Communal Experience* (New York: Harper & Row, 1973).

the work necessary for maintaining property, dwelling, and livelihood, and share a common distaste for the Establishment.

Most experimental communes last only a short time, having an average life of two years. Individual membership lasts about eight months. Joyce Gardener, one of the founders of Cold Mountain Farm, illustrates the condition of rural and urban communes alike: "...empty people who had come to fill themselves, sapping our energies, needing to be taken care of and giving nothing at all —and now there were only between four and six couples and a few single people left....We didn't find a way of sharing our vision...and we didn't have a shared vision to hold us together."[50]

Some communes make compromises with the nuclear family arrangement. An example was Lama, a commune north of Taos in New Mexico, where the members worked together growing and distributing crops, but withdrew to individual nests at nights: a tepee, an A-frame, or a tent, which they shared only with a spouse (or semipermanent companion) and the children. Most couples were married, had children, owned their own homes, maintained middle-class respect for property and work. Although the philosophy of sexual freedom was retained abstractly, it played a minor role in the actual behavior of the communards.[51]

Other communes deviated farther from the lifestyle of the American family and included such groups as the Sandstone Commune in Los Angeles, which kept varying in size between three and twelve members and usually included uneven proportions of men and women. They considered themselves an "intentional family" with sexual freedom, and as one member let it be known: "It's a smorgasbord. It's so much more exciting to have nine different dishes than just one."[52] The group hesitated to have children because it wanted to stabilize its "marriage" first.

The commune movement, then, is a quest for many dreams. It may be a quest for revolutionary restructuring of society, for economic security, for more meaningful relationships than the participants had in their parental homes, or for expanded experiences in respect to sex, drugs, and other interests.

For most, a communard role is short-lived and they fail to find the answers to their questions and the gratification of their needs. In most cases, the communal experiment fails because the members have compounded their problems through interaction with others who suffer from similar troubles of personal anomie. It resembles a situation where one blind person asks another blind person for direction. Sometimes the economic basis of the group is too weak to sustain membership. Sometimes the attempt at a common work project is sincere, but it fails because members lack experience, knowledge, and the actual physical stamina to do the work. Sometimes the animosity of neighbors causes a commune to break up.

[50] Joyce Gardener, "Communal Living: Economic Survival and Family Life," in *Changing Family: Adaptation and Diversity*, ed. Gordon F. Streib (Reading, Mass.: Addison-Wesley, 1973), pp. 117–18.
[51] "The American Family: Future Uncertain," p. 38.
[52] Ibid., p. 36.

And in other cases, the commune gradually fades away because the participants lack the vision to formulate a common goal.

Hence the commune movement of the late 1960s and early 1970s has subsided. But it has not died. While most communes disintegrated, a few proved to have longevity. The idea of the commune is still alive and still attracts numbers of young Americans who hope to find it more rewarding than their nuclear families.

In contrast to the pessimism of Bronfenbrenner, many family sociologists believe that the companionship-type of nuclear family holds out greater promise than any other experimental arrangement, and that in spite of difficulties, it will survive as the preferred lifestyle. David and Vera Mace express this sentiment:

> The companionship marriage, based on intimacy, equity, and flexible interaction, offers a promising new lifestyle which in fact is the preferred choice of the great majority of men and women in our culture today. The other new lifestyles which have been given such prominence are by comparison of minor significance, and are best viewed as pioneering social experiments which as yet have come up with nothing that could remotely offer a viable substitute for traditional marriage.[53]

SUMMARY

Family dynamics penetrate into the individual's personality and have a decisive influence on how he or she weathers the crisis of adolescence. Family processes are complicated today because of rapid changes. The following points sum up major changes affecting the modern family and, in turn, the lives of adolescents:

1. Family structure has changed from the large to the small nuclear family, which has relinquished integration into the larger social network and become isolated. The young have become deprived of concrete adult models, visible adult work, and familial peers. This increases the potential of associating with peers opposed to the family culture and stimulates the development of youth subcultures.
2. The modern family has abandoned numerous functions, now taken care of by outside specialization, and has itself become a specialized agency trying to fulfill the "personality function." With increasing isolation and anomie in the industrial environment, the individual has turned to the family to find direction. The identity quest leveled at so fragile a structure appears to be too much of a burden, and the frustration rate is running high.
3. The family has changed from institutional to companionship interaction, minimizing rigid role behavior and maximizing personal uniqueness. The new style calls for an unprecedented degree of communicative skill.

[53] David R. Mace and Vera C. Mace, "Marriage Enrichment—Wave of the Future?" *The Family Coordinator*, 24 (April 1975), 133.

4. Modern young people can no longer rely on the family's placement function, which used to define their standing in the community. Now they must rely on their individualism and personal decisionmaking.

5. Modern legislation has given young people more freedom than any previous generation in America, but has done so without regard to family context. Independence from the family has increased the isolation of the individual.

6. The primary-group quality of the family has decreased. Increasingly, secondary institutions have come to compete with the family. This raises questions about modern socialization's impact on "human nature."

7. Momism has emerged as a modern malaise, stifling personality development in situations where the father shirks his parental responsibilities. It is a "silent disease" because of the traditional taboo of criticizing motherhood and its pathologies. Momistic impairment usually reveals itself during adolescence when the victim fails to make an adequate transition into adulthood.

8. Adolescence is often complicated by parents who lack insight, skill, and even sincere desire to raise children. Restricting such unqualified parenthood has become the preoccupation of a number of educators and scientists.

A final word. While it is true that throughout our discussion certain aspects were selected that promote adolescence and prove to be dysfunctional for literally everyone involved, these adolescence-generating effects do not exhaust all the consequences of family changes. Liberating effects have also been brought about by these changes. These include liberating captive creativity from the bondage of familistic servitude and enriching the personality market with talent, aptitude, and individualism. However, we must not forget that the human condition includes the eternal dilemma of not being able to combine two dreams of humanity: freedom and security. Normally we can enjoy only one at a time, and it seems that modern adolescents, whether they like it or not, are satiated with the former and hunger for the latter.

Chapter 7

The Modern
Educational Experience

TRENDS IN AMERICAN EDUCATION

The American ethos considers the right of every citizen to an education—elementary, secondary, and higher—to be as basic and undisputable as the "pursuit of happiness." For increasing numbers of American students, education beyond high school has become ritualistic, pursued only with minimum motivation in order to comply with the academic expectations.

Education for all was not always the conviction of the American public. Until late in the last century, education was primarily an elementary-school affair. Preparation for higher education was accomplished in private secondary schools and a few public schools. In 1870, for example, teenagers could choose from among only 800 public high schools. Those who attended institutions of secondary education usually had college in mind. Although in 1900 only 11 percent of the high-school-aged youth were in school, two-thirds of the graduates did go on to college —a proportion that has since never been equalled.[1]

The appraisal of high school education in the United States was influenced by the European tradition that considered secondary education in the French *lycée*, the English grammar school, or the German *Gymnasium* as the proper experience for the "educated class." The children of farmers were usually not thought of

[1] James S. Coleman, *Adolescents and the Schools* (New York: Basic Books, 1965), p. 5.

not require young adults in the division of labor, and their entry is delayed as long as possible after high school graduation. This expands adolescence and creates a population of restless youth.

EDUCATION: NONFAMILIAL, LONGER, AND CUSTODIAL

Nonfamilial education. Although in modern societies the institutions of education and the family have always been separate, they have never before been as unrelated as today. Values preached in school and values upheld at home are often either unrelated or even contradictory; the information the child brings home from school is usually irrelevant to actual family life. In short, values and information gleaned from formal education constitute a theoretical manifesto that is more applicable to the outside world than to the family circle.

Some ethnic and religious minorities perceive this duality as a threat to their way of life. An example are the Amish, a Protestant sect living a simple rural life and attempting to survive as a religious enclave within a secular society. They often are at odds with the law, since their views on education differ from legal requirements.[4] Amish elders maintain that "worldly wisdom" taught in public schools undermines their way of life, rural simplicity, and religious values. Confrontations between the law and religious principles have repeatedly occurred in Iowa, Kansas, Ohio, Pennsylvania, and Wisconsin. When Amish farmers were fined for violating Wisconsin's compulsory school-attendance law, the issue snowballed and reached the United States Supreme Court in 1972. The court's decision upheld the Amish's right to religious freedom and restricted the state's compulsory attendance law. This minority was granted the right to maintain its own elementary schools staffed with Amish teachers and was declared exempt from having to send its youth to secular high schools.

State authorities had worried that Amish children who left school before the statutory age of sixteen might become burdens to the public. The record showed such concern to be unfounded: No Amish teenager in Wisconsin had ever been arrested for any crime, no Amish had ever had an illegitimate birth, and none had ever requested public assistance. Additional states complied with the Supreme Court's decision. For example, Iowa exempted Amish children from state education standards and allowed Amish teachers—who usually had only an eighth-grade education—to run their own schools. The Amish are reluctant to employ college-educated and certified teachers who, they fear, might steer their children away from the plain, soil-and-toil-oriented Amish faith. By adhering to this educational policy, the Amish accomplish two main objectives: to retain purity of religious faith and to preserve their young's time and interest for farm work.

[4] Albert N. Keim, *Compulsory Education and the Amish* (Boston: Beacon Press, 1975). "In Pennsylvania: The Amish and the Law," *Time*, April 19, 1982, p. 12.

By contrast, the dynamics of the urban-industrial society create complex educational needs, which are due to at least three major conditions. First, there is rapid social change. American parents cannot mold their children in their own images, since they suffer from chronic cultural lag that may render a portion of their skills, knowledge, and attitudes obsolete. Second, the strong emphasis on individualism prevents parents from determining the occupation of the young by family rule. Rather than relying on familial norms and models for deciding on their future occupation, the young may prefer nonfamilial, formal education. This preference is related to the third condition, the high degree of specialization of modern occupational careers, which calls for vocational preparation outside of the family unit.

The effect of these three conditions has been to shift the responsibility of preparing offspring for their future "specialties" from the family to specialized institutions and to ensconce the young more and more in nonfamilial education.

Longer education.   The most conspicuous feature of American education has been its ever-lengthening duration in the lives of the young. Census Bureau data show that the average American achieved over five more years of education in the 1980s than in the 1940s.[5]   The education gains applied to all regions, men and women, blacks and whites, cities and suburbs. The proportion of Americans who have had four or more years of college has tripled since 1940, going from 4.6 percent to 14 percent today. As a result of these increases, the median educational level reached twelve-and-one-half years by 1980. This means that approximately one-half of all Americans now have finished high school and have spent some time in college. How much longer today's youth spend in educational institutions is illustrated by comparison of the median education level of twenty-to-twenty-six-year olds and the over-sixty-five age group. The former group achieved an average of 12.8 years, the latter only 9.1 years—just over a year of high school.

The typically postindustrial shift of the teenage population from work bench to school desk can be illustrated by statistics from such countries as West Germany. During the 1960s about 20 percent of the thirteen- to fifteen-year-old Germans were in the labor force (usually as apprentices); by the 1970s practically no members of this age group were working. For the boys of the fifteen-to-twenty category the decline was from 81 to 59 percent, for the girls from 78 to 57 percent.[6] This shift is even more clearly demonstrated by German census data showing the proportion of the teenage population in school increasing from 17 to 35 percent between 1960 and 1970, while, conversely, the proportion of apprentices dropped from 19 to 9 percent and the proportion of unskilled teen labor from 13 to 4 percent.[7] These statistics reveal the typical correlation between increasing postindustrialism and increasing years of formal education.

[5] U.S. Department of Health, Education, and Welfare, *Statistical Abstract of the United States* (Washington, D.C.: Government Printing Office, 1980), pp. 148, 149.

[6] "New Work Habits and Life-Styles," *Bulletin*, Press and Information Office of the Federal Republic of Germany, Bonn, December 20, 1971, p. 350.

[7] "Jugend," *Kulturbrief*, Internationes, Bonn, Vol. 5, December 1975, p. 26.

The United States has been prototypical in setting this trend—a trend continuing unabated in the 1980s when school enrollments dropped and caused closing of elementary schools and concern among high school and college administrators. Dropping enrollment is not indicative of shortening the educational experience but rather of declining *numbers* in age groups; the *proportions* of age groups enrolled have increased. Census figures concerning eighteen-year-old Americans show that in 1950 56 percent, in 1960 72 percent, and during the 1970s 75 percent graduated from high school.[8] It has been estimated that the percentage will increase to approximately 77 percent during the 1980s. In conclusion, most American youths are involved in long years of education during which they are suspended between childhood and adulthood.

Custodial education. The assumption that the protracted sojourn in the educational institution is primarily motivated by desire to absorb knowledge and learn skills has long since been revealed as illusory. School has assumed a custodial function and tries to stem the potential flood of over-sixteen-year-olds that could inundate the labor market. Such inundation would create job scarcity and bring about a disastrous swelling of the ranks of the unemployed. Postindustrial automation simply has no use for this excess of young workers. So they end up completing high school, entering college, and establishing their ghettos and subcultures.

Since youth's stay in high school (and often in college) is not entirely motivated by free will and enthusiasm about education per se, disharmony with authorities can evolve. In its overt manifestation the discord can degenerate into vandalism and other school-related delinquency. In its more covert manifestation the problem consists of a type of psychological warfare in which the Establishment tries to impose "colonial treatment" on the young, and where the young counter by collectively rejecting the moral and intellectual expectations of the authorities. It is this resentment that has fueled not only the teen subculture but also the more militant counterculture.

A number of writers have attempted to illuminate this dark side of our educational system. Many have condemned the custodial function of schools and the isolation of youth from mainstream America. John Holt, for example, suggests that schools relinquish the "jail business" and stop numbing children by overdoses of superfluous authority.[9] He assesses malfunctions of American education in five points:

1. Schools fail to promote the growth of children and substitute the custodial function for the learning function. The young are in school because they are not wanted anywhere else.

---

[8] *Statistical Abstracts of the United States* (Washington, D.C.: Government Printing Office, 1980), p. 165.

[9] John Holt, *Freedom and Beyond* (New York: Dell, 1972) and *Escape from Childhood* (New York: Dutton, 1974).

2. Schools grade, label, and channel the young. This, presumably, is contrary to the true process of education. We cannot expect young people to trust us if they know, as before long almost all of them do, that a major part of modern educators' job is compiling records that will be used to judge them for the rest of their lives.

3. Schools have adopted a missionary zeal to explicitly indoctrinate patriotism, morality (especially sexual morality), competition, the value of the profit system. More subtle indoctrination encompasses the vast field of modern consumerism—implanting the proper consumer attitudes toward grooming norms, dress, cleaning and bath products, cosmetics, and so forth.

4. Schools divide the young into winners and losers and then train them to accept their roles. By this process, the Establishment is assured that the winners will defend the system without guilt and the losers without rancor.

5. The most offensive aspect of modern schooling, which is closely related to the previous point, is its unrelenting attack on the dignity and self-respect of the students, who are cast into simplistic hierarchical roles of winners and losers regardless of their personal uniqueness.

Another critic was Paul Goodman, who considered it meaningless and absurd to grow up in a society that compelled its young to go to school when they cannot profit by it.[10] He accused American schools of ignoring the most important problems of young people, such as job prospects, sexuality, and community processes. Although failure of schools to captivate student interest is usually rationalized by authorities as "failure to communicate" the truth probably is that the message has been communicated clearly but is unacceptable to the young.

Problems of school are symptomatic of the pathologies of society. Goodman felt that youth resents what American society fails to provide:

1. Opportunities and worthwhile goals.
2. Enough and visible work positions.
3. Honest public speech.
4. People who are to be taken seriously and can serve as models to youth.
5. Opportunities for imaginative minds.[11]

Another critic of American education is Edgar Z. Friedenberg, who disapproves of compulsory school attendance, believing that such compulsion strips victims of personal autonomy and civil rights. He thinks that coercion does not serve a truly intellectual function but bows to economic pressures of a society wanting to delay youth's entry into the labor market. "A people have no right to cling to economic arrangements that can be made halfway workable only by imposing an infantile and unproductive status on adolescents and indoctrinating them with a need for trashy goods and shallow meretricious relationships that they know to be degrading."[12]

[10] Paul Goodman, *Growing Up Absurd* (New York: Random House, 1960).

[11] Ibid., p. 12.

[12] Edgar Z. Friedenberg, *Coming of Age in America* (New York: Random House, 1965), p. 249.

The list of critics could be extended. Although some criticisms are well taken, many are less than pragmatic; they are romantic, if not utopian. For example, George B. Leonard believes education could be ecstasy—pure joy, involvement, and growth for both student and teacher—but that competition and bureaucratic regimens turn off the student's mind.[13] To overcome such obstacles in school, Leonard recommends that we "learn delight, not aggression; sharing, not eager acquisition; uniqueness, not narrow competition."[14] In the absence of an effective plan for restructuring our educational framework and changing our cultural premises, such suggestions fall more in the category of poetry than science.

Modification of the rule of custody. *In loco parentis* authority used to greatly enhance the power of custody wielded by the educational institution. But a significant legal decision curbed this abstract parental power: in 1971 the United States Supreme Court granted eighteen-year-olds adult privileges. Virtually overnight, most *in loco parentis* impositions became antiquated. This particularly affected college students who had been subject to rules of curfew, housing, and specific concepts of morality. The law also curbed such parental prerogatives as examining their eighteen-year-old offspring's school records, or making their marriage and contract decisions contingent on parents' approval. Loosening custodial authority has shifted responsibility from the institution to the young individuals, in the process promoting a sharper transition from adolescence to adulthood. In fact, most colleges have made it standard procedure to give students a voice in administrative decisionmaking. This innovation in part resulted from the demands of the counterculture to give youth a say in administering their schools.

The case against college. Some critics of American education have taken a radical view and actually suggest that a noncollege education might be preferable for large numbers of American youth. Sociologist James S. Coleman argues that the focus of American schools is too limited, too competitive, and fails to develop in students the ability to manage their own lives in a responsible fashion.[15] Schools not only fail to promote these qualities, they so monopolize young people's time and energy to prevent them from acquiring these skills elsewhere. Until a few generations ago, children learned adult qualities from family models. However, segregated by age, modern youth is saturated with information but deprived of experience. Coleman suggests an alternation between study and work to introduce students to the careers they choose. Prolonged education often renders a distorted view of adult life. Many colleges have tried to correct this by bringing the outside world into the classroom and introducing careers without harnessing students to them too soon.

[13] George B. Leonard, "How School Stunts your Child," in *Children's Liberation*, ed. David Gottlieb (Englewood Cliffs, N.J.: Prentice-Hall, 1973), pp. 145–66.

[14] Ibid., p. 162.

[15] James S. Coleman et al. *Youth: Transition to Adulthood*, Report of the Panel on Youth of the President's Advisory Committee (Chicago: University of Chicago Press, 1974).

The best solution, according to Coleman, would be to graduate the young earlier, at about sixteen, and place them in organizations like businesses, hospitals, factories, and symphony orchestras. These establishments could make use of the youths' contribution, while training them and supervising further part-time schooling. This would be a fundamental shift from the customary American view of education as a means of secular salvation to the old way of socializing through apprenticeship. Coleman's design would provide all sixteen-year-olds with vouchers worth four years of college tuition; the vouchers could, however, also be used to join an apprenticeship program or for enrolling in a vocational school.

Implementation of Coleman's plan might diminish adolescence and its collective expression. Young people would usefully integrate themselves into society, build self-respect through meaningful work, and avoid being segregated. Integration would reduce unrealistic segregation from adult responsibilities and limit the breeding of subcultural lifestyles.

Another argument against coercion to attend college was raised by Caroline Bird, who believes that the majority of college students are not in college because they like it or because they want to learn. She estimates that hardly one-fourth of the students enjoy academic work and that the rest, at best, experience college as a social center and at worst as a detention center preventing them from entering adult life for several more years.[16] During these years students feel unwanted and useless. Postindustrial efficiency, with its labor-saving automation, renders them superfluous. To get them temporarily out of the way, we send them to college — where only a few of them are intellectually motivated and prepared to enjoy studying. According to Bird, many college students describe their time in college as if it were a sentence to be served — and yet, as unpleasant as it is, preferable to the drudgery of a boring job or to the possibility of being unemployed.[17]

THE HIGH SCHOOL DROPOUT

No other issue tells us more about the nature of education in postindustrial society than the dropout problem. The revelatory nature of the problem prompts us to explore the reasons for its existence which has become distressing to many parents, educators, administrators, and politicians.

The extent of the problem.   The term "dropout" is applied to everyone who leaves high school without a diploma. Dropping out is usually interpreted as an indication of a youngster's unwillingness or inability to learn. The reason authorities and the general public consider the act of dropping out with as much dismay as they currently do emerges from the fact that outside high school there is no

---

[16] Caroline Bird, "College is a Waste of Time and Money," *Psychology Today*, 8 (May 1975), 28.

[17] Ibid., p. 32.

appropriate place for the high-school-aged youngster. Crudely and yet fittingly, quitting school prematurely messes up the social structure. The failure to provide an alternative status to that of a high school student is as much a function of the general value orientation of the culture as it is of modern economic conditions that pattern social structure.

Some statistics documenting the scope of the problem are misleading. It is true that the number of dropouts has increased over the past decades. The *rate* of dropouts, however, has not increased, and has, in fact, decreased. If there are *more* dropouts today than previously, it is because there are many more teenagers to start with. It has been estimated, for example, that approximately 7½ million teenagers were dropouts during the decade 1960-70 — a figure unprecedented during any previous decade. On the other hand, the dropout rate was around 30 percent, which constituted a notable decrease from the rate of 50 percent during the 1950s.[18] The public concern about the dropout problem is thus due to the increase in the sheer number of dropouts.

In general, it appears that the dropout rate will change less dramatically than during previous decades. The small changes that will take place will further reduce the rate — probably to about 20 percent during the 1980s.

The dropout incidence is not evenly distributed throughout the high school population, but differs among communities, socioeconomic classes, and ethnic and racial minorities. The highest dropout rate occurs in urban high schools that draw their students from neighborhoods composed predominantly of lower socioeconomic classes and minority groups. The prevailing value orientation as well as the trying economic conditions among slum or semislum dwellers are not conducive to a high valuation of education. Youngsters from such neighborhoods are known for their chronic truancy and tendency to drop out of school as soon as they reach age sixteen. Little serious official effort is made to persuade them to remain in school, because they usually have established a record of being problematic, if not delinquent, and are considered a "bad influence" on peers, who otherwise might successfully complete secondary education.

Rural environments also present a temptation to leave high school prematurely. Youngsters may prefer, or actually be asked by parents, to join the family's agricultural enterprise. Unlike in an urban slum setting, a job is waiting for them, and success in the agricultural vocation does not, in their or their parents' opinion, depend on schooling beyond the eighth grade. Although most farm families see to it that the children fulfill their legal requirement and stay in school up to sixteen years of age, they may consent to, or even suggest, withdrawal after that age. The farm people's rejection of schooling beyond the three basic "Rs" was strikingly illustrated by the Amish refusal to send their children to high school.

Probably the lowest incidence of premature termination of high school is found in the middle-class suburb. Value orientation as well as long-range profes-

---

[18] U.S. Senate, 89th Congress, 2nd session, *Profile on Youth*, Senate Document No. 124, Part I (Washington, D.C.: Government Printing Office, August 1966), 2, 30.

sional plans keep the youngsters in high school until graduation. For a sizable proportion of the youth of suburbia, high school is preparation for college. In fact, a number of upper- and middle-class youngsters prefer to attend a special prep school rather than the general high school in their own community.

Who are the dropouts? Major characteristics of dropouts are embedded in scoioeconomic conditions, family interaction, peer association, and school life. In addition, idiosyncratic problems play an important role in the decision of the adolescent to remain in school or to drop out. The conditions overlap, and characteristics of dropouts found in one sector are probably correlated with characteristics in other sectors, thus forming a syndrome rather than isolated features.

Socioeconomic status. Dropouts coming from lower socioeconomic strata constitute a significantly higher proportion of the dropouts than those from middle and upper classes—the respective percentages being 65 percent, 24 percent, and 13 percent.[19] Sociological research, as early as August B. Hollingshead's study of high school youth in *Elmtown's Youth*, has consistently indicated correlation between socioeconomic background and academic achievement. For example, Hollingshead found that, regardless of intelligence, one-third of the lower-class pupils as opposed to only 5 percent of the combined middle- and lower-class pupils received failing grades.[20] The social-class position of the teenager's family is of great influence in patterning the youth's orientation to education, and the middle-class student has advantages over lower-class peers. Home conditions of middle-class students conducive to academic success include the following:

1. Their parents are usually better educated and hence can help and tutor the offspring.
2. The parents' language facility is more proficient and enables the child to read, comprehend, and respond faster.
3. The parents instill motivation for learning in their children by being able to point to careers that can be achieved through academic effort. Homework, otherwise devoid of practical projection, takes on purpose; and exercises in English composition, arithmetic, and social studies make sense to the child.
4. The child's educational trajectory includes college education, possibly as a family tradition that gives the child an academic identity and the psychological assurance that he or she is cut out for a career in higher education.
5. There is usually a coordinated pressure of parents, relatives, friends, and neighbors that reinforces the child's academic self-view and sustains motivation to work toward scholastic success.

The vast majority of lower-class children do not enjoy the benefit of such conditions. Their value orientation shuns the academic way of life and focuses on

[19] Alvin L. Bertrand, "School Attendance and Attainment: Functions and Dysfunctions of School and Family Social Systems," *Social Forces*, 40 (March 1962), 231.

[20] August B. Hollingshead, *Elmtown's Youth* (New York: John Wiley, 1949), p. 173.

issues tied up with everyday life in the inner-city or working-class neighborhood. Anthropologist Walter B. Miller has perceptively identified the typical lower-class preoccupations by the concepts of trouble, toughness, smartness, excitement, fate, and authoritarianism—all of which have an anti-intellectual tenor.[21]

The negative correlation between social class and dropout rate has been confirmed by sociologists Starke R. Hathaway and Elio D. Monachesi, who used more than 15,000 Minnesota high school students in a study spanning several high school generations. They found that among day-laborer families, 38 percent of the boys and 32 percent of the girls dropped out of school, whereas among professional families only 5 percent of the boys and girls left school prematurely.[22]

An early 1970s study by the U.S. Department of Health, Education, and Welfare found that nearly 5 percent of America's school children aged twelve to seventeen cannot read at a fourth-grade level, and hence are defined as illiterate.[23] This segment amounted to about one million children, who came mostly from lower-class families. The study found that in families with less than $3000 annual income, 10 percent of white youths and 22 percent of black youths were illiterate. If parents had little or no formal education, 22 percent of the whites and over 30 percent of the blacks could not pass the literacy test.

Racial and ethnic minorities. Overlapping the above lower-class characteristics, black and Spanish-speaking youth make up a disproportionately high segment of the dropout population.

A much larger percentage of Spanish-speaking persons than either whites or blacks have dropped out before graduation from high school. During the early 1970s, the proportion of the youth population of Chicanos and Puerto Ricans who had dropped out was more than twice that of whites: 34 percent compared to 14 percent; for the black population it was 21 percent.[24]

The high rate for the Spanish-speaking minority reflects two handicaps: lower socioeconomic class and language barrier. Parents of many of these youths are immigrants to the United States and in their native countries had limited educational opportunities. They were unskilled labor, and their young often have to drop out of school to help support the family. The young of these families also face a language problem that automatically puts them behind Anglo children in scholastic competition and discourages many from completing school.

It is the language barrier that distinguishes the Spanish-speaking minority from the blacks who, otherwise, resemble them in socioeconomic conditions. The black inner-city youth, deprived as he or she may otherwise be, and despite the use

[21] Walter B. Miller, "Lower-Class Culture as a Generating Milieu of Gang Delinquency," *Journal of Social Issues*, 14 (1958), 5–19.

[22] Starke R. Hathaway and Elio D. Monachesi, *Adolescent Personality and Behavior* (Minneapolis: The University of Minnesota Press, 1963).

[23] Associated Press Report, May 4, 1974.

[24] Anne M. Young, "The High School Class of 1972: More at Work, Fewer in College," *Monthly Labor Review*, 96 (1973), 26–32.

of a nonstandard English dialect, has no such drastic drawback as having been brought up speaking a foreign tongue. Though figures for Spanish speakers were not included, a study for the U.S. Department of Health, Education, and Welfare revealed the consequences of the black-white socioeconomic differential in terms of literacy. Of the twelve-through-seventeen age group, 5 percent of the white males and 2 percent of the white females were found to be illiterate, compared with 20½ percent of black males and 10 percent of black females.[25] There was a double effect when the lower-income variable was added to the racial variable.

The "pushouts."   The definition of the dropout as unwilling or intellectually incapable must be modified in the face of poverty and cultural deprivation. Some writers have used the phrase "pushouts" to designate academic failures who quit high school not necessarily because they were dissatisfied or inept, but because of poverty.

The 1975 Children's Defense Fund report indicated how short the United States falls of implementing the promise of universal education and equal opportunity.[26] The report charges that the U.S. census figures of nonenrolled children underestimates the real numbers and fails to note that the burden of exclusion from school falls heavily on the poor, the blacks, the non-English-speaking—in short, those who are "different" and do not fit the white, middle-class mold. In a large number of cases, the reasons for nonenrollment are simply a matter of economics: the inability to pay for books, fees, lunch, transportation, and adequate clothing.

In other cases, nonenrollment was due to specific learning disabilities that were either not discovered by school officials or were disregarded by them. Again, the children involved were not dropouts in the sense of not wanting to be in school, but were *pushed out* because of a range of handicaps: from poverty to special mental, emotional, or physical needs for which adequate provisions were not available.

Family interaction.   Quality of interaction in the adolescent's family has definite influence on school behavior. A typical study found that dropouts expressed less rewarding relationships with their fathers, suffered from lower acceptance by their fathers, and consistently tried to avoid their parents more than in-school youths did.[27] Another study has shown that the degree of intrafamily consensus is significantly related to the school success of the sons. Boys who were well-adjusted in school came from families with high consensus, boys consistently

[25] Associated Press Report, May 4, 1974.

[26] *Children Out of School in America* (Cambridge, Mass.: Children's Defense Fund, 1975).

[27] M. S. Tseng, "Comparison of Selected Familial, Personality, and Vocational Variables of High School Students and Dropouts," *Journal of Educational Research*, 65 (July 1972), 462–66.

underachieving in school came from families with lower consensus, and boys known for aggressiveness came from homes with the least family consensus.[28]

Parents' education is frequently reflected in their children's school accomplishment: the higher the education of the parents, the lower the dropout rate of the children. Typical findings come from a Maryland study showing that 70 percent of the mothers and 80 percent of the fathers of the dropouts had never finished high school.[29]

A definite relationship was discovered between family size and achievement motivation, and thus school attendance. Children of larger families consistently exhibited lower motivation to achieve than did children of smaller families. This finding might have been expected, for larger families are typical of lower classes, and studies have shown that lower classes have a low valuation of educational achievement. But even *within* the same social stratum large families tend to produce lower achievement motivation in their children.[30]

The broken home is strongly associated with dropping out of school. Children whose parents are divorced or separated are likely to drop out at roughly twice the rate of their peers from intact families. These dropouts amount to more than one-third of all the teenagers from broken families.[31]

Particularly strong dropout-proneness was found related to those teenagers who suffered abuse at the hands of family members. A Minneapolis study conducted by Linda H. Harris discovered that 67 percent of the students flunking or dropping out of high school (but only 27 percent of the control group) had been victims of severe beating, sexual assault, and/or incest. One-third of the dropout-prone girls (vs. 9 percent of the other girls) acknowledged having been forced into incestuous relations with a father, stepfather, uncle, or grandfather. Besides being dropout-prone, the abused teenagers manifest symptoms of delinquency and/or mental distress, such as running away, drug use, self-mutilation, and suicidal tendencies (30 percent of the abused teenagers vs. only 1 percent of the control group had attempted suicide).[32]

The power of the home environment in forming academic attitudes and determining the scholastic success of the young seems strong enough for some researchers to conclude that the quality of the school has little to do with how well students learn. Harvard sociologist Christopher Jencks, basing his conclusion on a survey of 4000 public schools, including 645,000 students, believes that the quality of a school's output depends largely on a single input: the quality of the entering

[28] Barbara G. Myerhoff and William R. Larson, "Primary and Formal Aspects of Family Organization: Group Consensus, Problem Perception, and Adolescent School Success," *Journal of Marriage and the Family*, 27 (May 1965), 213–17.

[29] Percy Williams, "School Drop-Outs," *NEA Journal*, 52 (February 1963), 10–12.

[30] Bernard C. Rosen, "Family Structure and Achievement Motivation," *American Sociological Review*, 26 (August 1961), 574–85.

[31] Hathaway and Monachesi, *Adolescent Personality and Behavior*, pp. 93, 94, 181.

[32] Linda H. Harris' paper was presented at the 1980 convention of the American Association of Psychiatric Services for Children and summed up under "Adolescence," *Psychology Today*, December 1980, p. 102.

children.[33] Everything else—the school budget, its policies, the teachers—were found to be either secondary or entirely irrelevant. Schools seem to serve primarily as selection and certification agencies, whose task is to measure and label individuals, and only secondarily as socialization agencies, whose capacity is to change and mold individuals. The most important factors in the lives of the young, heredity and home environment, cannot be controlled by schools.

Jencks' findings constitute a poignant rebuttal to the cliché blaming schools for failing to socialize, change, and educate the young. According to his study, the school is merely a limited receptacle of youth whose prime socialization takes place elsewhere.

Peer involvement and delinquency.   Some sociologists have found that the peer group has such a strong influence on the teenager that in many situations it can override the advice of parents and teachers.[34] Sometimes, the pressure of the peer group and the contagion of collective behavior are strong enough to introduce a teenager to delinquent activities. What about the dropouts? To what degree is he or she enmeshed in peer relations?

There is reason to believe that if a dropout is deeply involved in peer activities, they are most probably delinquent activities. The bulk of dropouts are lower-class youths who have probably severed most ties with formal adult institutions. Unless this teenager has a job, he or she is almost totally absorbed in activities revolving around the gang. What the high school and the clique are to in-school youth, the gang is to the jobless dropout, i.e., a bridge device to span the gap between childhood and adulthood. The gang commands the dropout's loyalty and he or she, in return, obtains security, belonging, and adventure. Most middle- and upper-class youth do not form gangs, since they have adequate transitional institutions, such as advanced education and family-social-class sponsorship in jobs. On the other hand, even before they drop out, lower-class youngsters tend not to become members of cliques. The nature of cliques and gangs is class-selective.

The delinquency-proneness of the dropout is supported by a Minnesota study employing the Minnesota Multiphasic Personality Inventory (MMPI) to assess the dropout's characteristics.[35] The findings revealed considerable overlap between the students who dropped out and those who were delinquent. In fact, 39 percent of the boys and 31 percent of the girls who dropped out had a delinquency rating. The delinquency rate for the male dropout was only 1.62 times the base rate for all males, but for the female dropout it was 2.98 times the base rate for all females. This indicates that dropping out and delinquency are more closely related for girls than for boys. It was also noticed that delinquent teenagers tend to drop out most

---

[33] Christopher Jencks, *Inequality: A Reassessment of the Effects of Family and Schooling in America* (New York: Basic Books, 1973).

[34] Examples: Hans Sebald and Becky White, "Teenagers' Divided Reference Groups: Uneven Alignment with Parents and Peers," *Adolescence*, 15 (Winter 1980), 979–984; James S. Coleman, *The Adolescent Society* (New York: Free Press, 1963).

[35] Hathaway and Monachesi, *Adolescent Personality and Behavior.*

frequently during the early years of high school, suggesting that their causes for dropping out reach peak intensity in the eighth grade or earlier. Thus, remedial measures should be initiated at early school levels.

Further support for the assumption that a significant correlation exists between dropping out and delinquency comes from a study of working-class youth in six metropolitan areas. This study attempted to clarify whether the youth culture in the United States is independent of or dependent on parental control, i.e., whether youth choose parent or age-mate influences.[36] The findings discovered a decided cleavage between responses of dropouts and the matched high school graduates. The dropouts operate within an independent subculture. This is reflected in their responses to questionnaires concerning intergenerational mutual understanding and in their attitudes toward their parents' disapproval of their choice of friends. On the other hand, the graduates' attitudes and value orientations indicate that their subculture is characterized by harmony with parental values and integration into adult society. These findings challenge those who maintain that an independent *general* youth subculture exists. Examples of this assumption were discussed in earlier chapters, when reference was made to such sociologists as Talcott Parsons and James S. Coleman.

Whether an independent or a dependent teenage subculture exists remains controversial and awaits conclusive testing. One may be certain at this time, however, that in the case of dropouts an independent subculture does exist, that they are involved in delinquent activities to a larger extent than their in-school peers, and that they are cut off from adult institutions and reject parental advice.

School violence and vandalism.   The nation has been appalled by the extent of crime, delinquency, and destruction committed by students in their school facilities. There has been no letup of such behavior. On the contrary, it has increased and, most significantly, it has spread from inner-city schools to suburban and affluent school systems.

The relationship between the potential dropout and school crime is sparsely researched. But it seems safe to conclude that those who become dropouts carry the major responsibility for the destruction and violence. The major problem is that compulsory school attendance laws force young people to be in school whether they like it or not. Most states set the age ceiling at sixteen, but some states have expanded it to eighteen. One of these states, Ohio, has suffered from increasing numbers of hostile and aggressive youths who during recent years have committed more serious acts of violence than in the past seventy-five years.[37] A major cause of this increase is seen in Ohio's having extended mandatory school attendance to age eighteen (although provisions are made for some students to leave school at sixteen if they have a job). This necessitates the presence in the school system of

[36] Lucius F. Cervantes, *American Youth Culture: Independent or Dependent?* (a mimeographed paper read at the Annual Convention of the American Sociological Association, Chicago, 1965).

[37] UPI Report, June 19, 1975.

young people who, unable to achieve and not receiving any preparation for future employment, are continual behavior problems. Ultimately, violent and destructive students tend to quit high school before graduation, but before their demise they demonstrate unwillingness to be in school by destruction and violence that cost the taxpayer too much for the small gain of retaining the dropout just a little longer.

Learning disabilities. Closely overlapping with violence and vandalism and perhaps partly explaining them, is the problem of learning disability. Often school officials define disruptive or truant behavior as delinquent, unaware that the underlying reasons may be physiological, including such conditions as auditory and visual defects, memory impairment, and aphasic symptoms. Victims of such disorders often become "pushouts." Their true problems are not recognized. While not all children with such disabilities become juvenile delinquents, they meet with constant failure in school, and as a means of establishing a minimum of self-assertion they often resort to delinquent or deviant behavior.

Chester D. Poremba, chief psychologist at Denver's Children's Hospital, estimated that 70 percent of juvenile delinquents committed to institutions suffer from learning disabilities.[38] Paul Broder and Noel Dunivant at the National Center for State Courts classified 37 percent of the delinquent boys as learning disabled whereas only 19 percent of the nondelinquent boys were so classified. The proportions remained the same even when age, social class, and ethnic background were taken into account. A new insight of the study was that the delinquency of learning disabled youth is often defined on the basis of a peculiar linguistic inability to describe simple events — a disability all too often interpreted by judges and attorneys as recalcitrance or acting "smart."[39]

If victims of learning impairments indeed make up such a high proportion of delinquents, courts and the entire correctional system are wasted on many offenders. What is needed are medical and physical therapy, not legal correction. Dr. Poremba warns that although it costs $3000 a year to educate a learning-disabled child it costs several times that much to deal with such a child if he or she turns criminal. He estimated that it costs about $24,000 to educate a learning-disabled child from kindergarten through twelfth grade. The average criminal, however, costs the taxpayer $40,000 a year; it costs about $7000 to incarcerate a juvenile for the first year, and this figure increases to $10,000 in the fourth year.

Learning disability is tied up with the whole gamut of physical and mental health. Such problems are difficult to recognize and frequently characterized by unwillingness to learn, adjustment problems, and a variety of neurotic expressions, including depression, agitation, inability to concentrate, withdrawal from social contacts, and inability to communicate. Often there is confusion in distinguishing

[38] Chester D. Poremba, "Disability is Linked to Delinquency," *Arizona Republic*, March 8, 1975, p. 28.

[39] Paul Broder and Noel Dunivant, "Problems in Learning Breed Problems in Court," *Psychology Today*, June 1981, p. 92.

between emotionally troubled students and delinquent students; the two types of expression are not necessarily identical and one does not automatically lead to the other. In fact, the earlier-mentioned MMPI study discovered that neurotic, socially introverted, and schizoid adolescents are more likely to drop out of school than become delinquent.[40]

Academic performance and attitude. Probably the most conspicuous feature of dropouts is their lack of interest in school work. Of the dropouts in the Minnesota study, one boy in three and one girl in five cited disinterest as reason for dropping out.[41] It is true that both the delinquent and the dropout are unhappy with school activities and discipline, but often have different motivations. The dropout's dissatisfaction stems not so much from appeal of alternative activities but from a rejection of school activities. Delinquents, on the other hand, possibly conflict with school discipline because they prefer what they think are more adventurous and exciting activities. This distinction is obviously only applicable when the dropout is nondelinquent.

The usual grade distribution of *all* youth in school runs as follows: 45 percent have Bs or above, 51 percent have Cs, and 8 percent have Ds or lower. Dropouts deviate significantly: 15 percent have Bs or above, 46 percent have Cs, and 39 percent have Ds or lower.[42] The same study found that of the in-school youths, 83 percent did not have to repeat any grades and 16 percent had to repeat two or more grades. In contrast, among dropouts only 35 percent did not have to repeat any grades, 39 percent had to repeat one grade, and 26 percent had to repeat two or more grades.[43]

The decision to promote or not promote a pupil to the next grade is most vexing to American teachers. On one side beckons the democratic ethos of keeping all educational avenues open and giving the student every conceivable opportunity to advance. On the other side, no one profits from promoting a youth who simply cannot or does not do the work. American public schools, almost without exception, refrain from forcing students to languish year after year in the same grade, even though they may be extremely poor readers and may almost qualify as illiterate. Except in rare cases, students are held back no more than once in elementary and once in junior high school. Those who repeatedly fail to meet eighth- and ninth-grade standards will nonetheless eventually be admitted to high school.

Many school systems try to solve the dilemma by spending extraordinary amounts on individually prescribed programs based on the students' deficiencies and needs. Noble as such attempts are, they usually have an ironic ending when slow or unwilling students decide to drop out of school anyway. Funds, extra

[40] Hathaway and Monachesi, *Adolescent Personality and Behavior*, p. 93.
[41] Ibid.
[42] Bertrand, "School Attendance and Attainment," p. 231.
[43] Ibid.

classrooms, and skilled teachers are often wasted on a dropout. Some skeptical educators feel that such costs and extra provisions could be more fruitfully applied to the school in general and to the better students in specific.

More often, however, school authorities' response to poor performance is to acquiesce and even lower the academic expectations. A New York panel investigating declining test scores made discoveries exemplifying this pattern. Homework assignments had been cut nearly in half during the period from 1968 to 1977. Students often simply refused to do them. Uncooperative students' attitudes were usually blamed on overexposure to TV, which reduces attention span, and on such demoralizing events as Watergate, the Vietnam War and the "Me" culture.[44]

IQ scores show that the average dropout is by no means uneducable. Although, on the average, he or she tends to score lower than his or her in-school peers, a nationwide study by the U.S. Department of Labor discovered that 70 percent of the dropouts in the sample had IQ scores above 90. A six-year study in New York disclosed that 13 percent of the dropouts had IQ scores above 110.[45] In a Maryland study, almost 50 percent of the dropouts had average or above-average intelligence.[46] Thus, for the majority, the decisive factor in dropping out is primarily attitude.

The attitude responsible in many cases is rebelliousness. Of the many forms that adolescent rebellion can take, underachievement is probably the most subtle. It is rarely recognized for what it is either by the student or by parents and teachers. Thus, consistent underachievement of an otherwise bright youngster may seem inexplicable. By the time the rebellious undercurrent is recognized, it may be too late to salvage a career. What is commonly termed laziness, lack of will power, or poor attitude is at heart often a resentfulness expressed by refusal to do anything demanded by authority.

Gender differences. Although the dropout population is divided almost equally between the sexes, some of the reasons for dropping out differ between them. Boys who drop out frequently list military service or a job as reasons; a survey showed that one in four had dropped out for military service, one in seven to work. Few boys quit school because of marriage. On the other hand, the majority of females quitting school do so because of marriage or illegitimate pregnancy.[47]

Personality characteristics. Comparison of a group of dropouts with a group of high school graduates, matching individuals of both groups with one another on as many important demographic variables as possible, used the TAT projective

[44] "Help! Teacher Can't Teach!" *Time*, June 16, 1980, p. 59.
[45] Daniel Schreiber, "School Drop-Out," *NEA Journal*, 51 (May 1962), 51.
[46] Williams, "School Drop-outs," p. 11.
[47] Hathaway and Monachesi, *Adolescent Personality and Behavior*, p. 94.

technique to identify a number of personality attributes typical of the dropout. The following sums up the major points.[48]

The dropout can be characterized as an individual feeling relatively helpless in mastering or coping with the environment. Such persons are preoccupied with basic physical and security needs rather than with self-improvement or achievement, and focus on immediate contingencies rather than on aspirations and abstractions. Their value orientation is loose and unstructured, with few principles to guide their behavior other than those momentarily dictated by the environment itself. Their thought processes follow stereotyped matrixes rather than original ideas.

In personal relationships, dropouts are more peer- than family-oriented and relatively unresponsive to authority, parental or otherwise. Their attitudes are self-centered and narcissistic and possibly derived from alienation from the family. They lack warm, affectionate bonds. It is thus understandable that they withdraw into themselves and become preoccupied with gratification of immediate and more physical needs.

The analysis found also personality parallels between the delinquent and the dropout. This is not to say that the dropout will become a delinquent, but rather that the two groups share common features—especially the inadequate family relationships. In both groups the background of a weak or absent father figure is prevalent, and in either case the children, especially males, have difficulty establishing adequate sex-role identifications and clear self-concepts. Such boys tend to develop hypermasculine symptoms, most likely to overcome uncertainty in the area of male identification.

Thus, on a statistical level, the personality of the dropout and the graduate differ significantly, the differences manifesting themselves particularly in the former's poorer capacity to adapt successfully to the social demands of his or her environment. The study lends support to the assumption that the academic dropout is a product of the social milieu—that the underachiever is made, not born.

AFTER SCHOOL—THE WORLD OF WORK

When they leave high school, both the graduate and the dropout face the awesome question: What now?

When dropouts abandon school, they face a labor market in which they command little bargaining power. One of the first facts they will have to learn is that unemployment among youth is of epidemic proportions. The unemployment rate of young Americans is roughly twice the general rate. Dropouts will also have to realize that they contribute disproportionately to the ranks of unemployed youths because they are undereducated and generally fall into the unskilled-worker cate-

---

[48] A. Barclay and Lucius F. Cervantes, "The TAT as an Index of Personality Attributes of the Adolescent Dropout," *Adolescence*, 4 (Winter 1969), 525–40.

gory. This category is characterized by an unemployment rate twice as high as the rates of all other job categories.

Graduates are equipped with a wider range of options: they can enter college *or*, like the dropouts, search for a job. One out of three decides to go on to college; the other two try to settle in the labor force. While they are provided with better prospects to obtain a job than their dropout peers, it is well known that unemployment of the young—all young—is notoriously common; the 1982 percentage of unemployment of the U.S. teen population was 22 percent; for black teenagers the rate reached 50 percent.

The correlation between increasing industrialization and the increasing unemployability of youth can also be noted in other parts of the world. Youth unemployment in the industrialized nations of the West and in Japan has steadily risen during the 1980s. Italy is hit hardest, with 30 percent of the fourteen–twenty-four age group unemployed. In West Germany youth unemployment grew from 3.7 percent in 1979 to about 10 percent in 1982. Similar conditions are reported from England and France. Limited demand for the largely unskilled young workforce is also becoming a problem in developing nations, where we witness an alarming growth in unemployment of recent high school graduates and a simultaneous scarcity of skilled laborers.[49]

Dropouts will usually begin, and in most cases stay, at the bottom of the job pile. They will experience surges of unemployment whenever there are declines in business activities, in the labor demand, or in general economic conditions. As a consequence, they tend to become members of the hardcore jobless, among those last hired and first fired. At least two-thirds of the jobless have less than a high school education.

Dropouts will find it increasingly difficult to obtain jobs, because the kinds of positions they can suitably fill are becoming more and more obsolete. Also, many of the factors which have influenced young persons to leave school, such as poor academic skills, discontent with programs offered, health problems, trouble with authorities, or unwillingness to concentrate on work, are also likely to be a hindrance to employment. Add to these factors the dropout's relative youth and inexperience—most are sixteen or seventeen—and employment prospects grow ever dimmer.

Years of education and income are directly correlated. Those dropouts holding jobs earn an income substantially lower than high school graduates. The high school graduate at peak earning power makes at least 25 percent more than the person who dropped out of school. During the mid 1970s the mean income of individuals twenty-five years and over with less than eight years of schooling was only $5235; with eight years of schooling, $6756; with nine to eleven years of schooling, $8449; with twelve years of schooling, $10,433; with thirteen to fifteen years, $11,867; with sixteen years, $15,256; and with seventeen or more years, $17,346.[50]

[49] "Unemployed Youth," *World Press Review*, May 1982, p. 54.
[50] *Standard Education Almanac 1975–76*, p. 265.

To find a satisfactory job—or any job at all—more education and longer training are required. On the average, the professional or technical workers of today have more than four years of college; clerical workers have training and education in excess of their high school diploma. These academic requirements and specialized training programs will increase in importance in the future. Automation, mechanization, and other scientific advances are responsible for the decreasing number of unskilled jobs. The school dropout of the future may well become a dropout from the usable labor force.

But this does not mean that the high school graduate garners particular usability in the labor market. Both are poorly prepared for a vocational career. And this brings into focus America's public high school dilemma: the dual attempt to prepare some students for higher education and at the same time and within the same curriculum to prepare others for the immediate entry into the labor market. The dilemma deals with making the American high school truly comprehensive (universal), offering programs geared to the diverse needs of *all* students in secondary education. This formidable question has not yet been solved—indeed, may not be solvable given the structure of American education.

In the meantime, the other question, what to do with the dropout?, has not fared much better, though numerous salient efforts at remedy have been made. A common approach is to see what can be done to ease the dropout into the labor force. One way is thought to be via returning them to high school, having them complete the degree, and *then* integrating them into the labor market. However, a return to regular high-school life, even if the dropout were willing, is usually not advisable because of the lapse of time and the consequent age difference. More adequate means appear to be night courses, adult education programs, or correspondence courses. Nonetheless, some cases are exceptional. For example, high school girls who get pregnant are invited back to school as soon as possible. Even during pregnancy, some schools set up special classes that enable expectant mothers—wed or unwed—to continue their education without interruption. Some high schools in Phoenix, Arizona, arranged for the pregnant girls to withdraw from regular classes before their conditions become apparent and to attend separate, accredited classes.

Alternative ways of completing secondary education are limited, take longer, and are available in only a few localities. Sometimes dropouts may complete the requirements for a high school diploma while in the armed forces, and a comprehensive standard examination after adequate study may belatedly furnish a high school degree. Another institution enabling completion of high school was established by the Encyclopaedia Britannica Company in Chicago, offering evening high school primarily for dropouts and applying advanced techniques of teaching. Generally speaking, the once rebellious adolescents showed excellent performance results.

Regardless of these attempts, the principal solution of the dropout problem lies in absorbing the dropout into the labor force. Thus, remedial action calls for expanding job possibilities for these out-of-school adolescents. This is a complex and trying enterprise, for placement possibilities are narrowed by the dropouts' lack of marketable skills, their underdeveloped academic ability and social immaturity. There are a number of possible methods, however, to reduce the oversupply of untrained dropouts.

First, existing job opportunities for which dropouts qualify must be made known to them. New channels of publicizing such positions must be initiated. The typical dropout from the lower class lacks occupational contacts and role models within his or her immediate environment. In contrast, the middle-class teenager's father knows a manager or other high-placed worker, who can give advance information about job openings. Considering that only a small fraction of jobs are obtained through such formal channels as employment agencies and newspaper ads, it becomes clear that the lower-class lack of occupational "connections" is a formidable barrier to employment. Role models, which are the natural bridge to adult careers, are largely absent in the lives of youth from deprived inner-city areas.

The need to promote a more intimate acquaintance between the world of the lower-class child and the world of vocations and professions is echoed in many research findings. A typical study revealed that lower-class children and dropouts had minimal knowledge of occupations and their differential prestige.[51] Such deficiencies in information may partly account for the dropouts' high degree of uncertainty about future occupations and their low motivation to achieve.

A second remedial program consists of selectively stimulating the rate of new job creations, thus increasing the demand in those sectors of the labor market where there is oversupply. This approach is obviously severely limited by the natural growth of the modern economy, which simply does not call for as many unskilled workers as are available.

A third possible remedial approach would involve expanding existing job training programs and moving the dropouts from areas of heavy oversupply of labor to areas with moderate supply, thus giving the youngsters greater assurance of lasting employment and, while the period of training lasts, keeping them out of the saturated labor force. Programs such as the Job Corps and the Urban Youth Service Corps are promising. These living-training-working arrangements have a number of useful functions: (1) they prepare dropouts for jobs they could otherwise never obtain; (2) they enable completion of interrupted education and open up opportunities for further, higher education; (3) they teach adolescents how to carry out work responsibly, developing in them the ability to enter a successful career in the labor force; and (4) they relieve the labor market of the oversupply of unskilled youth.

Carefully planned job training programs might correct situations in which a number of job positions go begging in the face of high unemployment. This is an old problem in the United States. In the 1960s, New York City suffered from 75 percent youth unemployment in the slum areas while there were only five qualified persons for every seven skilled positions, with serious shortages in auto mechanics,

---

[51] M. S. Tseng, "Comparison of Selected Familial, Personality, and Vocational Variables."

stenography, and nursing.[52] The 1980s reflect similar incongruities. Figures released by the Department of Labor show at least two dozen occupations with wide open employability. Filling them would depend on training persons for certain skills. In some cases only minimal skills are needed, skills that could be acquired in work training programs. (See Table 7-1.) Selective training of high school graduates as well as dropouts and their adequate placement into the labor force would go a long way toward reducing unemployment and hardship among underprivileged adolescents as well as improve the overall economic structure of the nation.

TABLE 7-1   Occupations with Openings and Growth Rates during the 1980s

JOB TITLES	ANNUAL AVERAGE OPENINGS	PERCENT GROWTH IN TOTAL JOBS, 1978-1990
Industrial assemblers	77,000	43
Blue-collar-worker supervisors	69,000	16
Bookkeeping workers	96,000	12
Cashiers	119,000	50
Receptionists	41,000	28
Secretaries and Stenographers	305,000	45
Bank clerks	45,000	50
Typists	59,000	19
Building custodians	176,000	20
Cooks and chefs	86,000	32
Waiters and Waitresses	70,000	18
Licensed practical nurses	60,000	67
Registered nurses	85,000	50
Nursing aides, orderlies, attendants	94,000	52
Local truck drivers	64,000	18
Retail-trade sales workers	226,000	33
Wholesale-trade sales workers	40,000	14
Soil conservationists	46,500	27
Industrial-machinery repairers	58,000	66

Source: U.S. Dept. of Labor, 1980.

AMERICAN EDUCATION
IN PERSPECTIVE

The attacks on American education are legion. And they usually come from within and not from without the nation, being part of the syndrome of American self-consciousness. No other nation indulges in such merciless self-criticism.

One cannot help but wonder how much of the criticism is based on romantic expectations and utopian fancy instead of on realistic assessment. For example, such critics of the American school system as Edgar Z. Friedenberg, Paul Goodman,

[52] *A Proposal for the Prevention and Control of Delinquency by Expanding Opportunities*, 2nd ed. (New York: Mobilization for Youth, Inc., August 1962), pp. 95-96.

John Holt, George Leonard, and David Gottlieb have complained that schools require adolescents to surrender and/or suppress their creativity, individuality, and identity to the demands of the skill- and information-oriented curriculum in order to qualify for "success." Schools have been accused of causing foreclosure of creative and individualistic potential for the sake of making children acceptable to postindustrial society in general and the school authorities in specific. The price is too high, these critics claim, and the diminishing of unique individuality and the obscuring of personal identity is a defeat not justified by the educational accomplishments gleaned from American schools. Most of all, these critics feel that the true happiness of the young is foreclosed.

Part of the argument, as in most issues in life, is correct. It is undoubtedly true that the socialization process, be it couched in formal educational terms or in informal familial terms, necessitates some degree of abrogation of individuality and establishes some degree of conformity. How could it be otherwise? The young everywhere must be socialized, and individuality can be tolerated only within certain limits. This individuality, in fact, is a product of the socialization process as it is uniquely experienced by the young individual, and not of some mysterious, innate quality of humans.

Perusal of the writings of these romanticist critics creates the impression of a Rousseauan presupposition: the myth of the innocent child of nature, the innate goodness and fairmindedness of the young, and the destruction of these natural impulses by our corrupt urban-industrial society. From a sociological perspective, there is not a shred of evidence to support such wishful thinking. In fact, one could cite research showing that those young individuals who have made adjustments to school and society, thus falling in the category of the supposedly foreclosed subjects, were more comfortable than those fighting foreclosure. They were more comfortable in school and held more positive attitudes toward their educational experience, whereas the uncommitted and searching (those taking unbridled advantage of the adolescent moratorium) evaluated their educational experiences negatively.[53]

Of course, this finding could be turned around and used in favor of the romanticist critics, presumably showing the placidness of the suppressed individuals. But any style of socialization, including the formal educational process, will create problems and leave many wishes unfulfilled because of the very definition of socialization, which implies involuntary submission to the indoctrination of a culture. The American system must be viewed with these universal limitations in mind.

From a cross-cultural perspective, the American educational structure is a far greater success than many guilt-racked Americans would allow. In spite of certain limitations, it does function as an equalizer between racial, ethnic, and socioeconomic groups. If it has not shone with particular brilliance in this respect, the fault does not lie with the structure of the American school system, which probably has

[53] A. S. Waterman and C. K. Waterman, "The Relationship between Ego Identity, Status and Satisfaction with College," *Journal of Educational Research*, 64 (1970), 165–68.

the soundest potential of any school system in the world. Many European systems do not offer this potential. Their educational structure is a parallel system whereby most children go through nine (it used to be eight) years of elementary education plus two years of part-time school and are then irrevocably finished, while a minority—often motivated because of upper socioeconomic background—switches in the fourth grade to a radically different system that eventually allows them entry into the university. These parallel structures divide the young into elite and proletariat, into intelligentsia and passive masses. Quite differently, the American system pursues a sequential structure that allows the individual to continue in educational endeavor, to continue where he or she left off. It is a democratic system and the structure bears it out, permitting everyone to progress, drop out, and reenter without having experienced a prohibitory bypassing of certain mandatory and absolute switching points.

Another oversight of the critics deals with the assumption that the school is not only the central instrument of education (which it certainly is), but also nearly the only one, which it certainly is not. When it is argued that the home and the mass media have more to do with the success or failure of education than do the schools themselves, such observations are received as a sort of treason against the august function of education.

But the facts indicate that the educational structure is paralleled by so many other socialization influences that shape the attitudes of the young that their success or nonsuccess in the educational structure can no longer be blamed on this structure alone. Take alone the fact that the average American child spends more hours in front of the TV screen than in the classroom, and that his or her affiliations with formal and informal organizations, clubs, and groups have proliferated to the extent that school is just one of them.

Perhaps we ask too much of school. In the past we expected our schools to accomplish what in the Old World the family, the church, apprenticeship, and the guilds accomplished in concert. Today we ask that the school render the services of what their modern equivalents, plus a hundred voluntary organizations, fail or refuse to do. In short, modern American schools have become the scapegoat for the failures and shortcomings of a multiphasic and anomic society.

What parents, particularly middle-class parents, expect school to give to their offspring amounts to virtually *everything*: loving attention, advanced babysitting, academic brilliance, effective preparation for a profession, character building, skill in getting along with others, a sense of creativity as well as a sense of conformity, athletic excellence, and, most pronouncedly, psychological health (whatever that may mean). The dropout is seen as the patent failure of the school in conferring these qualities to children. With a peculiar zest for guilt feelings, many Americans, including what appear to be masochistic educators, actually believe in a simple cause-effect relationship—the cause for dropping out is the failure of the school. Notwithstanding the enormous difficulties and the staggering demands levelled at the American educational structure, American education renders an amazingly successful service.

Probably the greatest dilemma of the American high school lies in doing justice to a divergent population of students: to those preparing for entry into the labor market and those preparing for college. The American democratic ethos tries to safeguard the privileges of both groups, and in the process perpetuates the dilemma and makes it practically unsolvable.

This makes high school the weak link in the American educational system. But what are the alternatives? A European system that favors some sort of elite and sorts out, at a preposterously young age, the "lower" from the "higher" educational material? Most likely this would result in unspeakable, even though unintentional, hardship for masses of young people who recognize their interests and their educational potential at a later age—an age when they find themselves excluded from the trajectory of higher education.

The Europeans, incidentally, have learned from the tragedies of this arbitrary and parallel system and are trying to correct it. In the process of modifying their archaic structure, they are working out a "middle way" that presumably gives young people a second chance at higher education once they have bypassed the significant switching point at age ten. But the overall structure has become only more cumbersome and complex. Worst of all, it has failed to eliminate the socioeconomic bias of the old system: West German official reports in 1982 admit that the elite/proletariat pattern is still recognizable, with only 14 percent of all university students coming from working-class families. This statistic becomes more glaring when one considers that working-class youngsters are the largest group in the student age population of West Germany.[54] Many European educators wish they had inherited a sequential system like the American one with its democratic simplicity rather than a structure that divides the young into two categories alienated from each other by different unbridgeable educational careers.

SUMMARY

Education in postindustrial society is nonfamilial, longer, custodial, and has a ghetto atmosphere that age-segregates the population and promotes the formation of a subculture. It is typical of modern society to shift the teen population from work bench to school desk. High school education has become not only a "basic right," but also a coercion. This reflects not merely an abstract value of the American society, but also the necessity of keeping the nation's youth from entering the labor force at an age when they are unprepared for the labor market, and when the labor market is unprepared for them.

It is primarily economic factors that have changed dropping out from being a private decision to being a public problem. The number of the nation's dropouts have increased over the past decades, but this increase is primarily a function of the increased number of teenagers in the population. The actual percent of dropouts

[54] "Bildungspolitik," *Mitteilungen* des DAAD, 5, May 1982, p. 7.

has decreased. Dropping out is significantly related to a number of variables: socioeconomic background, racial and ethnic minority belonging, learning disabilities, family health and stability, peer involvement and delinquency, school violence and vandalism, attitudes toward academic work, and a number of personality traits, especially self-concept.

Both the graduate and the dropout face formidable decisions after they leave school, with the graduates having more options to choose from, including entering college. The job market is notoriously inhospitable to the young, leaving out in the cold at least 13 percent of the graduates and at least twice that rate of the dropouts.

Efforts to improve the life conditions of youth who have dropped out are not well developed. Potential remedial approaches include (1) encouraging completion of education by correspondence, extension, or other special arrangement; (2) increasing employment opportunities; (3) making existing job opportunities more visible; and (4) improving employability by work-study projects.

Critics accuse the American school system of squelching the development of individuality and creativity, and some go as far as hinting that the dropout is one who tries to preserve these qualities. Much of such criticism is based on romantic visions of what some kind of hypothetical human being might be — "if the school would only give him or her a chance." The myopia of the criticism overlooks that (1) postindustrial society has spawned so many other influential media and affiliations that the blame for failing to successfully socialize the young can no longer be justifiedly laid at the doorsteps of the school; (2) socialization is not a liberating process but by definition has to some degree a suppressive function; and (3) the sequential nature of the American school system is of greater democratic value than the European system, which is based on an elite/proletariat dichotomy.

Chapter 8

The Role of Television and Other Mass Media

Human beings have the capacity to think in symbolic terms and need not rely on the actual presence of persons or objects to form views of themselves and the world. Humans are also inventive and have created mass media to expose vast audiences to a constant barrage of stimuli that bear significantly on personality development.

SCOPE OF EXPOSURE

Of the various media, television reaches nearly all people in this country; it is notoriously popular, easily accessible, and commands the largest share of time Americans spend on any of the mass media. Television has absorbed some of the functions of the press, radio, and movie industry. Movies, for example, have become almost synonymous with television, and it is only a matter of time before the latest productions can be seen at home. Television is probably the most influential source of common experience in the lives of American children, and, along with home and school, has come to function as a major socializing agent for the young. Through mass media, the actual live person or group can be bypassed, and personal interaction can be replaced by the spectator-mass-media relationship, allowing an almost unlimited range of vicarious identifications.

One should not conclude that the personal significant other and the concrete group have been replaced entirely. The feeling of security that a child derives from association with caring parents is still of paramount importance for personality development. But needing parents and wanting to be like them are two different processes. The first deals with the need for security and the second with the absorption of ideas, impressions, and behavior styles. Parental care is a universal imperative for survival that has rarely been successfully replaced, while identification is a process allowing alternative objects of identification. Mass media offer a vast number of such alternatives. Modern children, although depending on their parents physically, can select ego images from the characters presented by ubiquitous mass media. Through screen, radio, and print, characters of many different types are presented to youth, who cannot escape from the incessant flow of stimuli and cannot avoid incorporating some aspects of these "types" into their behavior patterns and identities.

The effects that the mass media have on the personality of the young are not yet well known. It may safely be assumed, however, that the effects are not superficial, when one considers that at least 99 percent of American homes have a minimum of one television set and that among American children time spent viewing television ranks second only to sleeping.[1] By the time the American teenager reaches eighteen years of age, he or she will have watched an average of about 22,000 hours (that is approximately 2½ years) of television compared with 11,000 hours spent in the class room. The average American, both child and adult, views over six hours of television daily. By the age of fourteen, the typical viewer will have witnessed 11,000 TV murders; by the age of eighteen he or she will have been exposed to 350,000 commercials.[2]

Television viewing starts early in America, and it soon starts to reflect the symptoms of addiction. A study at Michigan State University discovered that when four- and five-year-olds are offered a hypothetical choice between giving up television or their father, one-third would rather part with father.[3] Children get up early in the morning to watch television before leaving for school, and millions of children under the age of twelve watch television as late as 10 P.M. on week nights. The peak of television viewing is reached somewhere between the sixth and the eighth grades, just before entering the adolescent years, and then decreases slowly until around the twelfth grade, when the adolescent is reaching a plateau of about two and one-half hours of television viewing a day.[4]

The main reason for the heaviest period of viewing occurring between the sixth and the eighth grades and then dropping off can be found in the new freedom that this age group experiences in staying up later in the evening. The gradual

[1] Robert M. Liebert et al., *The Early Window. Effects of Television on Children and Youth* (Elmsford, N.Y.: Pergamon, 1982), p. xv.

[2] Joan A. Wilkins, *Breaking the TV Habit* (New York: Scribners, 1982), pp. 10, 13, 32.

[3] "Getting Unplugged," *Time*, October 11, 1982, p. 99.

[4] Wilbur Schramm, Jack Lyle, and Edwin B. Parker, *Television in the Lives of Our Children* (Stanford, Calif.: Stanford University Press, 1961).

decrease after this age is no doubt largely due to the social involvements of the adolescent. The television set is at home, and home is not where most adolescents want to spend their time. Their process of autonomy and their increasing interest in the peer group and in members of the opposite sex mean less time for television.

Americans most likely hold the world record in television viewing; but other countries are not far behind. Statistics show that West German children rate television their favorite pastime, spending approximately one and one-half hours daily watching it, and list as their favorite shows (1) comics, (2) wild-life shows, (3) children's programs, and (4) Wild West movies.[5] Concern about TV's family-destructive potential has been expressed on the highest government level. For example, in 1982 West German Chancellor Helmut Schmidt called on his nation to observe a family night at least once a week—*with TV off.*

Nonetheless, television as an internationally ubiquitous medium is on the rise. Its growing magnitude in technologically advanced societies illustrates the emphasis that postindustrial systems place on the service function, including entertainment, communication, and advertisement.

PROMINENT INGREDIENTS:
VIOLENCE AND UNREALISM

Television portrays a variety of values that cannot fail to have impact on the young. A number of the dominant values conflict with those that most parents would like to instill in their children:[6]

1. Violence. It is virtually impossible to watch television without seeing humans killed, tortured, or maimed, and it has been estimated that by fourteen, the average child has seen eighteen thousand humans killed on television.
2. Unreality. Television exposes the young to a world of unreality that not only invites escapism from real life—a function of fantasy that is often useful—but seriously distorts reality. Fantasy is more honest: it openly admits that it is not reality but simply a flight of fancy.
3. Sex. Sexuality is usually presented in movies and television on a physical level, both visually and verbally, but disguised as "love."
4. Idealization of immaturity. Idols and heroes are often immature and teenage-like and seem to have achieved wealth and fame with minimal talent.
5. Materialism. Many programs imply that happiness comes with success, and success means houses, cars, vacations, and so forth.
6. Instant achievement and solution. This theme glorifies the power of technology and promises instant solutions to life's problems. Many commercials peddle chemicals assuring immediate success in problems that range from

---

[5] "Fernsehen," *Kulturbrief Inter-Nations*, 2 (August 1972), 22.

[6] Most points are based on a discussion by E. E. Le Masters, *Parents in Modern America* (Homewood, Ill.: Dorsey Press, 1974), pp. 159–61.

romance to insomnia. During a two-hour television period, forty-two such claims were presented in the form of commercials.[7]

In addition to these themes, there are, of course, more positive values presented, and they will be discussed later in the chapter. For the moment, we are concerned with two dimensions: unreality and violence.

Unreality, as mentioned above, is a generic concept that can be divided into *fantasy* and *deception*. Fantasy identifies itself as such and is youth's favorite in the form of cartoons, fairy tales, ghost stories, comedies, and science fiction. Although the interest in the fantastic is not new in history, the recent preoccupation with it is of more than literary significance. For the first time in history, it is now possible to intensively expose children to such themes every day. Interpretations of this preoccupation have described it as symptomatic of the present anomic age — as wishful thinking, as searching for solutions, as another version of longing for magic that can solve problems, and, finally, as escape from a world that looms confusing and perilous.

Rarely, however, does fantasy lead to confusion between real and unreal, and there is speculation that television fantasy, and the vicariousness with which the young experience it, has therapeutic effects by providing an outlet for frustration and a reprieve from anxieties.[8] Fantasy may even stimulate creative thought and the ability to solve problems.[9]

However, researchers have found that exposure to television — a prolific source of fantasy — does not significantly improve the child's school performance. Studies of two samples of children, one group with and the other without a television set at home, revealed that the group exposed to television entered school with larger vocabularies — an advantage that was of short duration. After a period of school attendance, the language proficiency of the two groups became comparable. Also, there was little difference between them in respect to interest in class work, completion of assignments, and test performance.[10]

Exposure to fantasy may lose its beneficial effects through overexposure. A child may become "addicted" to mass media fantasy, try to substitute the "safer" world of make-believe for the real world, and actually find it difficult to separate the real from the unreal. A chid or teenager watching television more than four hours a day has to do an extraordinary amount of switching back and forth between the two worlds. This oscillating existence does not contribute to his or her ability to concentrate on real problems and tasks.

[7] Henry L. Lennard et al., *Mystification and Drug Misuse* (San Francisco: Jossey-Bass, 1971), and Hans Sebald, "The Pursuit of Instantness in Technocratic Society and Youth's Psychedelic Drug Use," *Adolescence*, 7 (Fall 1972), 343–50.

[8] For details on the function of fantasy, see Eleanor E. Maccoby, "Why Do Children Watch TV?" *Public Opinion Quarterly*, 18 (Fall 1954), 239–44.

[9] Alfred R. Lindesmith et al., *Social Psychology* (New York: Holt-Dryden, 1977), p. 154.

[10] Eleanor E. Maccoby, "The Effects of TV on Children," in *The Science of Human Communication*, ed. Wilbur Schramm (New York: Basic Books, 1963), pp. 116–27.

A chronically disturbed youth is particularly prone to experience detrimental effects from prolonged exposure to fantasy, since fantasy can reinforce escapism to the point where a youth loses touch with reality and refuses to be bound by the rules of the social environment. Maybe the greatest danger is the possibility that the young use certain mass media images and models to formulate identities that become harmful not only to themselves but to others. Many of the television crimebusters invite emulation, although imitation of their techniques would be disastrous in real life. The world of fantasy has different rules and protects the foolhardy hero, who is pictured as invincible. If children act as though they were protected by the rules of fantasy and withdraw too often from the real world into the euphoria of make-believe, they are then headed for serious adjustment problems. George Gerbner, one of the nation's foremost TV-fare analysts, concludes in his recent research that young persons may come to view themselves in the light of fantasy and acquire a pseudoidentity that would have to be changed for everyday life.[11]

It might well have been of television's fantasy and its overexposed "addict" that the poet Gibran spoke when he said, "...that stealthy thing that enters the house as a guest, and then becomes a host and then a master."[12]

Another aspect of unreality concerns pretension about the real world. No genre of the mass media is immune from portraying reality deceptively: comedy, drama, adventure, detective stories, love stories, and the news—all have their own slant. It is this type of misrepresentation that generally is more harmful than pure fantasy. While fantasy may prove to be relatively ineffectual in respect to identification and personality formation because the average youngster *knows* that it is make-believe, the pseudoreal programs seriously tempt the young to identify and select models for emulation. Movies are a frequent source of such identifiable images and models. The heroes are part of plots that range from "real-life" detective thrillers and Wild West epics to the "wholesome" swim-ski-and-surf type stories.

Grant Noble speaks of the danger of projecting mass media personalities into real life:

> These characters serve as something akin to a screen community with whom the viewer regularly talks and interacts. Viewers who feel they know these characters well may indeed compare new people they meet in real life with such characters in order to predict how these new people are likely to behave later.[13]

[11] Reported in "Life According to TV," *Newsweek,* December 6, 1982, p. 136.

[12] Kahlil Gibran, *The Prophet,* copyright © 1961, p. 32. Reprinted by permission of Alfred A. Knopf, Inc.

[13] Grant Noble, *Children in Front of the Small Screen* (Beverly Hills: Sage, 1975), p. 164.

It is this type of projection that the study by Gerbner and Gross found more noticeable among respondents under thirty years of age, the first TV generation. They are more likely to accept media descriptions as reality.[14]

Books are another medium through which unreality or violence is conveyed. Interestingly enough, the invasion of the home by television does not seem to have had a noteworthy effect on the amount of reading done by children. In fact, research has found that television stories often encourage children to read the book that was the basis for a given show.[15] Books therefore continue to be an important influence on the formation of attitudes and behavior patterns of the young. One of the most typical conveyors of unreality is the Gothic novel, which presents a plot in which all the heroine need do is be beautiful as she travels through mysterious adventures and ultimately finds fame, fortune, and the man of her dreams.

These plots, whether occurring in books or on television, purport to depict real life but actually select only certain aspects of life. They convey situations, achievements, and human relationships that have little or no validity in the real world. The heroes as well as the villains of these stories display superior strength, imagination, and achievements, making the parents seem pale and unimaginative in comparison.

Violence, the other major theme, is heavily laced with unreality—both in quantity and quality. The vast majority of all types of violence in real life takes place between persons who are friends or family members. In only about 10 percent of all homicides are the assailant and the victim strangers. In the television world, the majority of violent acts occurs between strangers. Similarly, crooks make up 17 percent of all TV characters vs. 1 percent or less in real life.[16] Gunslingers, psychopaths, and sadists have leading roles in a significant portion of television entertainment, and their behavior is shown to millions every day. A content analysis of one hundred television hours of the so-called children's hours, 4:00 p.m. to 9:00 p.m., Monday through Friday, produced an impressive list of nonhumorous (as distinct from cartoons and comedies) acts of violence:

12 murders

16 major gunfights

21 persons shot (apparently not fatally)

21 other violent incidents with guns

37 hand-to-hand fights (15 fist fights, 15 incidents in which one person slugged another, an attempted murder with a pitchfork, 2 stranglings, a fight in the water, a case in which a woman was gagged and tied to a bed, and so forth)

1 stabbing in the back with a butcher knife

4 attempted suicides, three successful

[14] George Gerbner and Larry Gross, "The Scary World of TV's Heavy Viewers," *Psychology Today*, April 1976, 41ff.

[15] Maccoby, "The Effects of TV."

[16] "Learning to Live with TV," *Time*, May 28, 1979, p. 49.

4 people pushed over cliffs
2 cars running over cliffs
2 attempts made in automobiles to run over persons
A psychotic raving in a flying airliner
2 mob scenes, in one the mob hangs the wrong man
A horse grinding a man under its hooves
A great deal of miscellaneous violence, including a plane fight, a hired killer stalking his prey, 2 robberies, a pickpocket working, a woman killed by falling from a train, a tidal wave, an earthquake, and a guillotining.[17]

It has been estimated that the television audience is subject to an average of five acts of violence per hour.[18] If this is correct, it means that an eighteen-year-old American, who on the average has watched 22,000 hours of television, has witnessed over 100,000 acts of violence.

QUESTIONS OF IMITATION AND OTHER EFFECTS

Such staggering figures raise the question as to how violence influences the audience, especially the malleable young.

The controversy. Representatives of the broadcasting industry claim that television has no harmful effects on the viewer. Mental health officials, social workers, teachers and the general public are divided over the question, some believing that exposure to violence breeds violence, and others assuming that exposure has a cathartic and pacifying effect, allowing children to identify with the aggressor and in this way rid themselves of pent-up hostile emotions.

The divergence of interpretations is typically exemplified by the dispute between sociologist Paul Hirsch and communication researcher George Gerbner. Hirsch, using National Opinion Research Center data, compared heaviest and lightest viewers and concluded that heavy watchers show no negative signs. On the contrary, he thinks, TV is probably more of a solution to their problems than a cause. Gerbner rebuts by pointing to Hirsch's biased sample, which was only 6 percent of those polled by NORC, including housewives and retired folks whose TVs are almost constant companions against loneliness and not agitators intent on imitation. Hirsch's study is not representative of teenage viewers, who may watch less but more violent fare and may be affected quite differently.[19]

The classic lab experiments. More reliable insight into the nature of media violence influence is derived from the classic Bandura experiments at the Stanford University psychological laboratories, which evaluated the impact of televised

---

[17]Schramm et al., *Television in the Lives of Our Children*, p. 139–40.
[18] "Five Acts of Violence per Hour," *Saturday Review*, March 14, 1970, p. 104.
[19] "Are TV Addicts Healthy?" *Time*, October 20, 1980, p. 81.

aggression on preschool children. Experiments tested the extent to which children copy aggressive behavior when such behavior is demonstrated by models in three different situations: in real life, on film (television), or as cartoon characters on film. The experiment divided the children into four groups. While three groups witnessed violent behavior under the different conditions mentioned above, the control group was not shown any violence. After the children of the three groups had watched the acts of violence, they and the control-group children were individually placed in an observation room under conditions that mildly irritated them. The observation room contained a variety of toys, including a three-foot Bobo doll that could be used as an object of aggression. Each child spent twenty minutes in the room, and his or her behavior was rated by psychologists observing through a one-way mirror. The results left little doubt that exposure to violence stimulated aggressive tendencies. Children who had viewed the aggressive adult demonstrated approximately twice as much aggression as those in the control group. The researchers concluded: (1) exposure tends to reduce inhibition to act in a violent manner, (2) exposure tends to shape the form of aggressive behavior. While most of the children from the first three groups sat on the Bobo doll and punched its nose, beat it on the head with a mallet, tossed it in the air, and kicked it (the exact kinds of attack they had observed), the children of the control groups rarely acted that way. (3) Display of violence on film is almost as influential as a display in real life. The child exhibits a high degree of imitation in both situations. However, the children were slow to imitate cartoon characters.[20]

Reports and studies.   Periodic upsurges in public concern over possible negative consequences of violence-filled TV programs have prompted a number of official inquiries. The first major inquiry was the 1972 study by the Surgeon General's Scientific Advisory Committee on TV and Social Behavior, yielding five volumes of findings. Generally, the findings linked violence on TV with aggressive behavior in young people. Here are two representative studies.[21]

Monroe M. Lefkowitz studied 900 third-graders, observing them over a ten-year period. He found that children unpopular as third-graders stayed unpopular ten years later. The child unpopular in the third grade watched TV more as he or she grew older and continued to be unpopular. There was a direct correlation between degree of violent program preferred and aggressive behavior, both in the third grade and ten years later. While the researchers conclude that this phenomenon illustrates the impact of TV violence on personal aggressiveness as well as its cumulative effects, the study as such does not prove its contention but merely points out a correlation.

---

[20] Albert Bandura, Dorothea Ross, and Sheila A. Ross, "Imitation of Film-Mediated Aggressive Models," *Journal of Abnormal and Social Psychology*, 66 (January 1963), 3–11.

[21] Surgeon General's Scientific Advisory Committee on TV and Social Behavior, *TV and Adolescent Aggressiveness*, vol. 3 (Washington, D.C.: Government Printing Office, 1972).

A similar study by John Robinson and Gerald Bachman completed a longitudinal study of 2200 tenth-graders throughout the United States between 1966 and 1970. Among the boys who initially were found to be most aggressive, preference for violent TV shows was linked to their behavior. More instances of violent fights occurred among heavy viewers of TV violence than among those who had no violent shows among their favorites. Again, it is not clear whether this finding is a correlation or a causal relationship. Is TV viewing a causal factor of violent behavior, or do violent individuals simply prefer violent fare? Most studies fail to explain this.

Predictably, the television networks reacted defensively and, reminiscent of the parallel rationalizations by the tobacco industry, tried to capitalize on the technicality that though a *correlation* was established, there was no proof of a *causal* relationship between TV violence and aggressive behavior.

The matter was more or less laid to rest until 1982 when the National Institute for Mental Health published another notable report. *Television and Behavior: Ten Years of Scientific Progress and Implications for the Eighties* derived from a two-year review of hundreds of research studies and reached an unambiguous conclusion: Television is a "violent form of entertainment" that clearly leads to aggressive behavior by children and teenagers. The findings include data showing that the percentage of programs containing violence has remained about the same since the 1960s, although the number of violent acts per program has increased. Children's shows are violent in a cyclical way, up one year and down the next.

Again, network reaction to the report was quick and predictable. All three networks rejected the report. NBC felt certain that many of the report's conclusions would be challenged by social scientists conducting independent research. It also announced that it would publish its own report at a later time, showing that the NIMH conclusions about the effect of viewing TV violence are not supportable. The networks' basic argument was that, based on high ratings, the programs are giving the public exactly what it desires and the networks are therefore serving the public interest.[22]

In addition to these comprehensive reports, which integrate masses of research data, there are numerous specific studies that contribute valuable insights. For example, one study's focus dealt with gender-differentiated responses to media violence. Up to about 1970, researchers had regularly found girls to be less influenced by media violence; either they did not watch TV violence in the first place or did not respond aggressively to such violence. Boys, on the other hand, were more interested in violent shows, viewed more of them, and reacted aggressively. This gender difference has changed. Psychologist Leonard Eron's latest study shows that such gender-differentiated responses to media violence has been erased.[23] His explanation: TV's violent female role models have dramatically proliferated and

---

[22] "Warning from Washington," *Time*, May 17, 1982, p. 77; also AP report, Washington, May 9, 1982.
[23] "Learning to live with TV," 49.

star in such regular shows as *Bionic Woman*, *Wonder Woman*, *Charlie's Angels*, and *Policewoman*.

In spite of what appears overwhelming evidence for negative influence, some social scientists continue to remain aloof from the imitation theory. They are convinced that television is a secondary cause of real-life violence and that other factors, such as the individual's background and personality, are much more causative. Some feel that television violence may actually make viewers *less* violent by allowing them to cathart their pent-up hostility. Among those who deemphasize the imitative role of media violence are Seymour Feshbach and Robert D. Singer, who experimented with several groups of boys aged nine to fifteen and varied their exposure to media violence under controlled conditions.[24] Some groups watched aggressive programs, such as *The FBI*, *Gunsmoke*, and *The Untouchables*; other groups watched milder ones. The experimenters kept track of the changes in aggressive attitudes and values as well as in the number of aggressive acts in which the boys engaged during their exposure to the different fare. The findings failed to support the traditional theory. The group that watched the milder programs engaged in more than twice as many fist fights as the group that watched the rougher shows; as for angry arguments, the "nonviolent" group had 859 arguments, compared with the "violent" group's 407. Criticizing or insulting others amounted to 973 versus 456 instances, respectively, manifestations of jealousy compared 254 to 87 instances, and instances of destruction of property were equal.

The researchers arrived at the conclusion that *no* group became more aggressive as a result of viewing aggressive television programs and that some subgroups actually became *less* aggressive. Astonishingly, they found that youngsters who watched the nonaggressive television programs became *more* aggressive in their behavior. In short, they concluded, the vicarious aggressive experience is therapeutic and calming.

Another reason mentioned by social scientists for nonimitation of violence is viewers' ability to discern between fiction and fact. Robert P. Snow found children capable of interpreting acts of violence on television as taking place in a "play" setting; they were rarely tempted to reenact them.[25] If seen in this light, the experiments by Bandura lose some of their significance insofar as the children may have realized that a Bobo doll is not a real person, and beating it is therefore not to be equated with any degree of violence against another human being. In other words, the children knew that the whole thing was a play.

Examples of Imitation. The argument that media violence breeds imitation in real life can be more effectively supported by reports that clearly show its existence. Some examples (from the author's "imitation" file) include:

---

[24] Seymour Feshbach and Robert D. Singer, *Television and Aggression: An Experimental Field Study* (San Francisco: Jossey-Bass, 1971).

[25] Robert P. Snow, "How Children Interpret TV Violence in Play Context," *Journalism Quarterly*, 51 (Spring 1974), 13–21.

(1)   Teenage girls gang-rape a San Francisco girl in imitation of a scene from the 1974 TV movie *Born Innocent* in which Linda Blair played the victim of sadistic teenage girls.

(2)   An inmate escapes by helicopter from a Michigan prison; the escape planned after seeing the movie *Breakout*.

(3)   Teenagers commit several inventive Chicago murders, following in vivid detail the killings depicted in the TV detective series *Shaft*.

(4)   Teenagers immolate a woman in a Boston street forcing her to douse herself with gasoline, in imitation of a scene in the TV police story *Fuzz* presented two nights earlier. Later that year the scene was reenacted in Miami where a derelict, as in the movie, was set on fire; three young teenagers were charged with murder.

(5)   A seventeen-year-old boy stabs to death a young woman, imitating a scene from the Emmy-Award-winning TV movie, *The Marcus-Nelson Murders*. The boy had memorized the movie down to the last detail and arranged the crime scene to look exactly like it did in the movie.

(6)   A sixteen-year-old boy kicks to death an old man after he had seen it done by the "hero" in *A Clockwork Orange* and tells the police that he remembered his act "like a scene from the film."

(7)   Two fourteen-year-old boys commit suicide when they imitate the mock hanging they had seen performed on TV by rock music star Alice Cooper.

(8)   A young man extorts $500,000 from Quantas Airlines in a pressure-bomb hoax modeled after Rod Sterling's *The Doomsday Flight*, which had just been shown on Australian TV. When the movie was shown on American TV, bomb threats against airlines went up 80 percent within a week.

(9)   A fifteen-year-old boy shoots to death an eighty-three-year-old woman and is defended in court as a victim of "involuntary TV intoxication" and his parents in 1978 filed (unsuccessfully) a $25 million damage suit against the three major TV networks.

(10) Two California youths rob a bank in imitation of an *Adam 12* story and hold twenty-four hostages against a $1 million ransom.

(11) A sixteen-year-old girl sprays a crowded San Diego elementary school with rifle fire in 1979, killing and wounding several persons. The sniper told police later that she had always fantasized about being a sniper and derived idea and technique from watching *SWAT* on TV.

(12) In the movie *Taxi Driver* a disturbed cabbie, played by Robert De Niro, sets out to shoot a presidential candidate in an attempt to impress a child prostitute played by Jodie Foster. John Hinckley, after seeing the movie 15 times, so identified with the film's hero that he bought an Army fatigue jacket, took to drinking peach brandy, and sent emotional messages to Foster, as did De Niro's character. Then, in 1981, he shot President Reagan.

(13) Three youths, aged fifteen, nineteen, and twenty-one, sadistically murder a Florida talk-show celebrity in 1982 by reenacting a bizarre ritual patterned after the movie *The Shining* (involving ice to suffocate or freeze a person to death and the word "redrum" — murder spelled backwards). The movie had been shown on television during the week of the slaying.

Besides such spectacular imitations, making national if not international headlines, most imitations remain local news. A sampling includes numerous TV-inspired burglaries. Among them were an eleven-year-old boy and his seven-year-old accomplice, who imitated detailed techniques of breaking into homes. A Washington youth committed burglaries by skillfully forcing skylights, a method he had observed on TV. An *Ironside* script had Jackie Cooper playing a scientist who was locked in an explosive belt by a criminal. Ten days later a young man was arrested when he tried the same method to kidnap a Hartford businessman's daughter. A four-year-old Brooklyn boy died in 1979 when he fell seven stories from a building ledge while imitating Superman. Inmates of the Florida State Hospital in 1980 armed themselves with sharp metal objects and makeshift clubs for a three-hour rebellion minutes after they had watched the TV movie *Attica*, which depicted a similar situation. Teenagers affected by the 1979 movie *The Warriors* went on a rampage and caused several thousand dollars worth of damage at a Scottsdale, Arizona elementary school.

Imitation of media violence has crossed national borders and shaken the public in other countries. For instance, a fourteen-year-old London boy committed self-immolation in 1979 in exactly the same manner as he had seen on TV the night before; the diary he left behind attested to his carefully planned imitation. This case, and others, dramatically illustrate the findings by William A. Belson, sociologist at the London School of Economics' Survey Research Center, whose six-year study of nearly 1,600 London teenage boys disclosed that long exposure to TV steeply increased their acts of violence (smashing cars, damaging phone booths, setting fires, etc.)[26]

"Disturbance" theory.   Many researchers warn, however, against overgeneralizing the extent of television violence. They think that such imitation occurs only under certain circumstances, as in cases where "disturbed" adolescents are exposed to violent fare. While this assumption has the ring of plausibility, it raises questions of definition. What is "disturbed;" what is "normal"? These definitions are not yet clear and differ among researchers. For example, if we equate what Freud called "moral anxiety" — the entirely normal control emotions that accompany the conscience and without which a person would be a sociopath — with being "disturbed," then normal would mean being occasionally anxious and disturbed. Most research concentrates on imitators and, indeed, finds many of them disturbed to some degree. But it would be difficult to prove that all nonimitating viewers then must be "normal." It is possible that the amount of violence imitated by viewers definable as "disturbed" is not significantly larger than that imitated by viewers definable as "nondisturbed." We don't really know how these amounts compare. At this time, equating "disturbance" with receptiveness to violence imitation remains a hypothesis.

---

[26] William A. Belson, *Television Violence and the Adolescent Boy* (Lexington, Ma.: Heath, 1978).

Desensitization. Another possible effect of exposure to media violence is desensitization toward violence. Habitual viewing of violence may lead to the viewer thinking and feeling that violence is a normal, everyday phenomenon. Such interpretation may ultimately induce endorsement of violence as an acceptable, tolerable, and perhaps unavoidable way of solving problems – and studies have indeed borne out that this attitude has been engendered in children.[27] Desensitization has also been measured through physiological indicators. Comparison of boys with different histories of exposure to media violence showed that autonomous nervous system responses (blood pressure and galvanic skin response) to violent scenes were significantly stronger in the low-exposure boys than in their TV-tempered peers.[28] This simply means that boys who were overexposed to media violence were no longer upset by it.

Inconclusiveness. In spite of the prolific research done on the subject, there seems to be little consensus about the effects of television violence on the young. Some of the reasons for the uncertainty include:

1. The complexity of the developmental processes in childhood and adolescence and the variations from one individual to another make it extremely difficult to predict the effects of a single stimulus, let alone the multitude of stimuli coming from television.
2. Interpretation of television fare depends heavily on the family environment and the control parents impose. Imitation is "screened" by the youth's primary group.
3. It is difficult to design studies that isolate the variable of television violence without making the experiment artificial and removed from real life.
4. Researchers suffer from lack of consensus with respect to definitions and research techniques that would allow verification and comparison of findings.
5. Political interests enter the picture and limit funds and accessibility to the subject matter. The media industry has vested interests and is powerful enough to guard its interests.

Although the debate about the effects of television violence continues, there is little doubt that some individuals, old and young, do imitate the crimes seen on television. While they remain a tiny minority of the viewing audience, their acts of mimicry can destroy human lives and happiness.

---

[27] Joseph Dominick and Bradley Greenberg, "Attitudes Toward Violence: Interaction of TV Exposure, Family Attitudes, and Social Class," in *TV and Adolescent Aggressiveness*, vol. 3 (Washington, D.C.: Government Printing Office, 1972).

[28] Victor B. Cline et al., "Desensitization of Children to TV Violence," *Journal of Personality and Social Psychology*, 27 (September 1973), 360–66.

CONTROL ASPECTS

Most research suggests that televised models are important sources of social behavior and can no longer be ignored as influences on personality formation. However, one must distinguish between learning and acting out. Although children readily learn patterns of social behavior, including violent acts, from television programs, their imitative behavior may be limited by at least three factors:

1. Children ordinarily do not have access to the weapons necessary for duplicating what they have observed. If, however, they had switchblades, blackjacks, brass knuckles, and six-shooters, it is safe to predict that the incidence of harmful imitative aggression, patterned according to television stories, would rise sharply.
2. Normally, parents suppress any learning that conflicts with what they consider "proper" conduct. Often such television-produced conflicts are merely on the verbal level, and parents have no particular difficulty in correcting them. The influence of television is ordinarily checked by the standards of parents and other adults, and the full impact of television can be measured precisely only when parental supervision is removed and the children are given the instruments they need to reproduce the aggressive behavior.
3. It is often assumed that an ethical ending to a story, in which the villain is punished, will serve to extinguish what a child has learned from exposure to antisocial models and therefore keep him or her from imitating the violent behavior.

What can be said in response to these control expectations?

First, the nonavailability of instruments is a weak argument, since consumption-oriented postindustrial society provides just about any instrument, including guns and knives, that a young American desires. The public debate about curbing the sale of handguns, especially the so-called Saturday-night specials, is testimony to the concern of many citizens about the easy availability of deadly instruments.

Second, with rising employment of mothers, children increasingly associate with peers who do not necessarily endorse parental standards. It is interesting to note the paucity of concrete suggestions in the professional literature telling parents how they can curb excessive television exposure, neutralize its negative effects, and, if necessary, substitute more creative activities. One of the best methods might be to encourage the young to take up a constructive hobby rather than spend all their time in front of the television set. But for such suggestions to be effective, parents would have to apply more than verbalization: they would have to guide and join the offspring in such projects—something they usually find too time-consuming. The majority of parents find it more convenient to turn their children over to the babysitting function of television and even leave the program selection up to them. Research found that 53 percent of six hundred parents studied who had eleven-year-old children did not prohibit their offspring from watching any program.[29]

[29] P. Musgrave, "How Children Use TV," *New Society*, 13 (1969), 277-78.

Third, research seems to indicate that the "ethical ending" (or the "happy ending") is a weak safeguard against imitation.

This point can be illustrated by some of Bandura's experiments. A group of nursery school children watched a television movie in which Rocky, the villain, took all of Johnny's toys. Clearly, the story showed that aggression pays off. Another group of children saw the same program with a different ending: as Rocky tried to seize the toys, Johnny overpowered him and gave him a sound beating. The two groups of children were then tested. As might have been expected, children in the first group, who witnessed that Rocky's aggression was rewarded, readily imitated his physical violence and his hostile remarks, while children in the second group, who saw him punished, showed little imitative aggression. Further inquiry, however, presented the researchers with a surprise: all the children were highly critical of the way Rocky behaved and called his action "mean" and children who imitated him did so because his aggression "paid off" or "worked."[30]

Another experiment testing this question found that when a fantasy sequence in a comic strip pictured a villain as relatively successful, children were more likely to identify with him or her and wanted "to be like him or her," while they were reluctant to identify with a weak hero. The children tended to admire and copy "what works" and preferred to be like the character who was successful, regardless of the method used.[31]

These studies suggest that when children see an individual punished, they are not likely to spontaneously imitate his or her behavior. However, they seem to retain information concerning the method of aggression, regardless of the punishment of the villain. There is no denying the possibility that they may put this knowledge into practice on future occasions if they are provoked, obtain access to the necessary weapons, or anticipate a sufficiently attractive reward. The ethical ending of a story functions merely as a *suppressor* of violence, but not as an *extinguisher.*

Despite ominous correlations between TV and violence, the influence of television is obviously somehow limited. The majority of adolescents grow up without ever engaging in violence, let alone the type of violence they have viewed for so many years. Perhaps elements of the American ethos proclaiming fair play, kindness, and cooperation somehow percolated through to their personalities.

When television suggests values and models inconsistent with principles parents have demonstrated, there is no evidence that the influence of television is paramount. When children have internalized values on a given subject and are not suffering from anomic blanks, television models seem to have relatively little effect.[32] "It is in the area of the unfamiliar, where parents have not yet made clear

[30] Bandura et al., "Imitation of Film-Mediated Aggressive Models," pp. 3-11.

[31] Robert Zajonc, "Some Effects of the 'Space' Serials," *Public Opinion Quarterly*, 18 (November 1954), 367-74.

their own point of view and where the child has little real-life experience to use as a guideline, that TV influences beliefs and attitudes."[33]

Additional conditions significantly limit the persuasiveness of mass media. Reactions to persuasion attempts are determined by what is said, who says it, and the personal characteristics of the individual to whom it is said. There are a number of personal characteristics that seem to influence responsiveness to persuasion attempts.

Youths who remain relatively uninfluenced by any form of persuasion attempt can be categorized into two types: (1) they tend to display overt hostility toward people he or she encounters in daily life; (2) they show definite symptoms of withdrawal from social involvement, stay aloof, maintain weak and unreliable emotional attachments to love objects, marked preference for seclusive activities, and few affiliations with formal or informal groups.

On the other side, youths relatively responsive to persuasion attempts were found to be among the following three types: (1) they use rich imagery and exhibit strong emphatic responses to symbolic representations; (2) they have low self-esteem, as manifested by feelings of personal inadequacy, social inhibitions, and habitual depressions; (3) they are "other-directed" and prefer group conformity.[34]

It must be stated in all fairness that not all television material thrives on violence and unreality, and that many programs convey other images and values. In fact, some of the other ingredients may help to control or balance violence and unreality. We now turn to a discussion of such additional fare and its functions.

OTHER FARE AND FUNCTIONS

The mass media have the potential of adding to the emotional and intellectual growth of children. Selective exposure to television constitutes a liberal education: available are samplings of history, music, the arts, political science, anthropology, the behavioral sciences, and various physical and biological sciences. This encounter with the world of knowledge stimulates curiosity, communication, and verbal skills. Probably the main reason why such positive effects have not been sufficiently researched is their nonproblematic nature. Positive effects are relatively inconspicuous because they are acceptable and do not arouse public concern.

---

[32] The relative ineffectualness of television in trying to change a person's perception once definite images have been established was illustrated by a study with college students on election day in 1960. It was found that students with a definite image of and preference for a presidential candidate were hardly affected by the so-called Great Debate, the public television confrontation of the candidates. See Hans Sebald, "Limitations of Communication: Mechanisms of Image Maintenance in Form of Selective Perception, Selective Memory, and Selective Distortion," *Journal of Communication*, 12 (September 1962), 347–51.

[33] Maccoby, "The Effects of TV on Children," p. 125.

[34] Irving L. Janis, "Personality as a Factor in Susceptibility to Persuasion," in *The Science of Human Communication*, ed. Schramm.

The information function of television for children should not be under-estimated. While children, like adults, watch television primarily for entertainment rather than for education and edification, they absorb much "incidental" informa tion about society and the world. They become electronic cosmopolites and acquire a plethora of detailed knowledge, albeit not integrated in a meaningful manner. For example, the young television pundit may know the finer points of docking in outer space, can distinguish Picasso from Michelangelo, can become a connoisseur of styles and fashions, may understand the principle of biofeedback, and may know the latest in the world of sports. In addition, these stationary tourists become storehouses of such miscellany and trivia as the facts that whales' backs get sun-burned and peel, you do not tip the stewardess on an airplane, Japan is the size of California and has a population of over 100 million, and no one knows the cause or cure of arthritis.

One of the classic learning programs, *Sesame Street*, has had a particularly valuable function for children who are relatively isolated or culturally deprived.[35] Its entertaining format achieved success in learning complex cognitive processes as well as verbalizing them. The product of collaboration among educators, psychologists, writers, and artists, *Sesame Street* became a fast-paced variety show with humor, intelligence, and artistry. It became an international hit, winning youthful audiences the world over.

Through television, children learn about our society's division of labor and various types of occupations. The medium's "homogenization effect" breaks down complex occupational responsibilities into images children can understand. Sociologists Melvin and Lois DeFleur warn, however, that in the process of homogenization the world of work becomes stereotyped and oversimplified with superficial and even misleading cues.[36]

Television also functions as a force for social change, since it makes social events so vivid and immediate that it creates a sense of involvement not experienced with other media. It can bring the Mideast conflict, the energy crisis, ecological disasters, and racial injustices into the living room as no other medium can. This tangible immediacy of current problems has contributed to the rise and perpetuation of youthful activism. While it has made American youth keenly aware of social issues, television has underplayed the tedious and time-consuming inner workings of the democratic process and, instead, presented the "show business" side of the political apparatus. This reinforces the youthful activist's tendency to embark on political projects by direct intervention, demonstrations, and a variety of "the-voice-of-the-people" proclamations. Simplistic as this approach may appear, it has rendered useful functions by speeding the completion of long-overdue work on the part of legislators and politicians. The popularity of direct confrontation with the

[35] Gerald S. Lesser, *Children and Television: Lessons from Sesame Street* (New York: Random House, 1974).

[36] Melvin L. DeFleur and Lois B. DeFleur, "The Relative Contribution of TV as a Learning Source for Children's Occupational Knowledge," *American Sociological Review*, 32 (October 1967), 777–89.

Establishment is reinforced by constant television exposure to shows of action and emotion, not words. Such conditioning leads more to action than logic or abstract negotiation.

Some social scientists are certain that the generation gap is in part perpetuated by the nature of television fare. Margaret Mead believed that television, more than anything else, brought about the confrontation between the generations by bringing actuality into the home and destroying many myths and half-truths adhered to by parents and teachers.[37] She assumed that television's unedited reporting of reality gives youth a glimpse of the world and an orientation very different from that of the parents, whose thinking is grounded in the edited views of writers and moviemakers. Marshall McLuhan added his imaginative theory that the generation gap is inevitable because television-raised and -oriented adolescents seek tactile depth experience and immediate involvement, while their "print-oriented" parents have a linear surface approach and a compulsive future orientation.[38]

Television fare can also serve as a medium for identification. While this has obvious psychological risks and can lead to aberrations of personal identity, it can also be of temporary comfort until concrete and more suitable models are found. This may be of special aid to children whose parents fail to function as adequate models. A primary task of adolescence is to consolidate one's identity and substantially answer the question "Who am I?" In order to accomplish this, the adolescent must learn something about the adult world and the appropriate roles in that world. He or she often turns to television for help.

One of the dangers of selecting models from television fare is that they are culturally stereotyped. Women on Words and Images, a special interest group of the women's liberation movement, completed a content analysis of 1974 prime-time television and found a surfeit of men among the major characters: in situation comedies, 55 percent of the characters were male; in adventure shows, men played 85 percent of the parts.[39] The diversity of male occupations portrayed was nearly twice that of females'. While men were more often depicted as confident, independent, worldly, and decisive—in short, competent—women were more than twice as likely as men to be incompetent, bungling opportunities, and making serious mistakes. In fact, approximately 20 percent of women's behavior consisted of such incompetent acts.

The study included the analysis of over two hundred commercials during these shows. The stereotypes conveyed showed men working more, playing more, eating more, and getting sick more often. Women were shown to be primarily concerned with their appearance; after that, they did housework, shopped, cooked, and cared for others—including their sick males.

---

[37] Margaret Mead, "Our Leaders Do Not Understand TV," *TV Guide*, December 6, 1969, pp. 10–15.

[38] Marshall McLuhan, *Understanding Media* (New York: McGraw-Hill, 1964).

[39] Women on Words and Images, *Channeling Children: Sex Stereotyping in Prime-Time TV* (Princeton, N.J., 1975).

Another imposition of TV on the female image deals with influencing the viewers' perception of physical attractiveness. Most actresses starring in movies and shows exhibit a physical beauty that—because of a highly selective process, the help of modern make-up, and skillful photographic techniques—can rarely be matched in everyday life and hence carry an element of unrealism. How do teenagers respond to this type of unrealistic beauty? For example, can the boys' normal, everyday girlfriends live up to these images? Do these images become expectations in the minds of the teenagers? Do the images inflict inferiority feelings on the girls? To some extent, of course, the reverse questions could be asked, focusing on unrealistically attractive male images. But, it seems, in American culture the burden to be beautiful weighs heavier on the female.

Psychologists at Arizona State University examined some of these questions by conducting experiments in which males were asked to rate a picture of a moderately attractive female as to dating desirability and attractiveness. Two groups of college men, depending whether or not they were watching *Charlie's Angels*, were selected in their dorms. The perceptions of the two groups were compared and it was found that the males viewing the highly attractive females on the *Charlie's Angels* series rated the photo of the moderately attractive female significantly less attractive than those who were not watching the program. This "contrast effect" persisted even when the experimental conditions were altered in a number of ways. For example, one series of experiments included female subjects, who, it was found, reacted similarly and also demonstrated the "contrast effect."

In today's world where media exposure is at an all-time high, it seems possible that the "contrast effect," even with a limited span of effectiveness, could pose a serious social problem. It becomes a real possibility that an individual might reject or be less satisfied with a normally acceptable date or mate if the relationship is influenced by media exposure that conveys unrealistic levels of physical attractiveness—and possibly makes such levels the norm for everyone. This would be particularly crucial for adolescents, who are forming criteria for date and mate selection; they might confuse artificial media images with reality, seeking the former and rejecting the latter.[40]

Similarly unrealistic are the standards of living depicted on the screen. Usually they are unrealistically high (or unrealistically low to provide contrast), and myriads of commercials are trying to engrain this as a fact in the child's perception. The basic question of "Who am I?" becomes tied to ephemeral and superficial commercialism that guarantees the viewer a front seat in the social-status circus if he or she just uses the right deodorant, mouthwash, toothpaste, flashy clothes, and stylish car. Any serious attempt to gain prestige and sincere recognition by peers on the basis of such commercial goading would most likely end in mental and social disasters of the person gullible enough to try. Fortunately, most adolescents have

[40] Douglas T. Kenrick and S. E. Gutierres, "Contrast Effect and Judgments of Physical Attractiveness: When Beauty becomes a Social Problem," *Journal of Personality and Social Psychology*, 38 (1980):131–140. Also see Kathleen J. Goren, *Media's Influence on Judgment of Physical Attractiveness*, Unpublished Research Paper, Arizona State University, 1982.

the ability to discern fake from fact. Nevertheless, as mentioned earlier, disappointments, inferiority complexes, and the constant effort of sorting out reality from fiction keep the young busy, while they could be spending their time more creatively.

A good deal of television fare is couched in stereotypes that suggest formulas to be emulated. This is particularly true of commercials, which advise youngsters to equate sugar with health and snacks with happiness, ignoring the lack of nutrition in most of these edibles. The television viewer is persuaded to consider him- or herself primarily as a consumer and is promised such rewards as being or looking like the glamorous, sexy female or popular he-man who uses the product in the ads. But stereotypes presented on television lack empirical referents or are unavailable to the vast majority of viewers. While idealization can serve as a temporary comfort and an object of identification, in the long run there is the danger of frustration, especially for the adolescent who is generally hypersensitive about his or her appearance.

One particularly insidious stereotype reinforced by television is the equation of "good looks" with "good personality." It is simple to figure out who's who in the movies and on television at one glance. The good guys are handsome, while the bad guys range from plain to ugly, and the same holds true for female counterparts. Unfortunately, the habit does not stop with the mass media—there is evidence that people tend to make the same judgments in real life. Studies by psychologist Karen K. Dion reveal that attractive children were judged less likely to commit offenses, or if they had, to repeat them in the future, and less likely to have antisocial dispositions.[41] Unattractive children, however, were regarded as more dishonest and unpleasant than their good-looking counterparts in similar circumstances. Transgressions committed by attractive children were considered less undesirable than *the same acts* committed by unattractive children. This prejudiced association has serious implications. First, good-looking children get away with more than plain-looking children; there is a tendency to punish and reprimand unequally. Second, reinforced stereotypes may become self-fulfilling prophecies, with the children assuming the roles ascribed to them. Evaluation by others ultimately tends to become self-evaluation: The unattractive child may grow up with an antisocial disposition simply because adults expect it.

Functions of television not yet clearly understood deal with intellectual stimulation and creativity. Generally, the functionality in these two overlapping areas seems to be at a minimum, although television may be of some benefit to the culturally deprived child for whom it is a window to the outside world. In general, however, television is better at stimulating interests and contributing to existing interests than in stimulating intellectual activity and creativity. It is interesting to note that the upper-third IQ children in a study by Wilbur Schramm spent over an

[41] Karen K. Dion, "Physical Attractiveness and Evaluation of Children's Transgressions," *Journal of Personality and Social Psychology*, 24 (November 1972), 207–13.

hour per day less watching television than the lower-third group.[42] Interviews with the more intelligent children disclosed that by the time they entered high school, television had ceased being a challenge to them and they therefore appropriated less time to viewing. Whether bright children are bright because they do not watch television, or whether they do not watch television because they are bright, is, of course, an open question. At this time, it is simply stated as a correlation.

Several researchers are convinced that television viewing suppresses creativity. When persons become habituated to looking at a medium that is as anti-intellectual as television largely is, they develop a noncritical attitude and a disposition to "look without seeing."[43] Stanley Stern completed experiments with 250 intellectually gifted grade schoolers, dividing them into seven groups, and exposing six of them for several weeks to cartoons, educational television, sports, comedies, and dramas.[44] The seventh group was not exposed to television. The children took a battery of creativity tests before and after the experimental periods. Only the seventh group registered consistent improvement, while the other six showed a notable decline in all areas of creativity except verbal skill. Cartoons had the worst effect, but even educational programs decreased creativity scores.

One of the concerns voiced by a few social scientists is not so much what television does to the young but what the young are *not* doing while viewing. Semanticist S. I. Hayakawa pointed out that the average eighteen-year-old American has lost 22,000 hours of potential interaction with other human beings, and that, for all the value television may have, it cannot teach human interaction.[45] The loss may be reflected by lack of skill in social interaction later in life when many of them "express their thoughts in form of tantrums." There simply is no substitute for human interaction, which includes misunderstandings, expressing and solving problems, and getting to know people. Excessive television viewing detracts from this experience, precludes this experience. Vigo A. Demant supported this notion, saying that a group watching television "can no more be called a social interaction than a number of monologues in the same room is a conversation."[46] Additional views and studies demonstrate that television seriously inhibits family communication. An interesting study of Australian adolescents by W. J. Campbell found that they spent less time entertaining, dancing, visiting, playing, and talking to friends three years after television was introduced into their homes compared to before they had television.[47] The interpretation here again expresses concern that teenagers misappropriate time and miss out on interaction with family and peers.

---

[42] Schramm et al., *Television in the Lives of Our Children.*

[43] Vigo A. Demant, *"The Unintentional Influences of TV," Cross Currents*, 5 (1955), 220–25.

[44] Stanley Stern, "Creativity and TV – A Depressing Picture," *Psychology Today*, 7 (November 1973), 14–16.

[45] S. I. Hayakawa, "Image and Reality," *The Bulletin of the National Association of Secondary School Principals*, 53 (May 1969), 35–48.

[46] Demant, "The Unintentional Influences of TV," p. 223.

[47] W. J. Campbell, *TV and the Australian Adolescent* (Sydney: Angus and Robertson, 1966).

Other researchers, however, disagree with the negative interpretation and believe that teenagers learn appropriate ways of social interaction by viewing television. Self-reports by teenagers indicate that they feel they learned appropriate behavior modes from watching dating, playing football, and family stories.[48] Whether the images accepted as adequate and realistic will turn out as real and dependable in life is, of course, a question that still has to be answered.

SUMMARY

Exposure of American children and adolescents to television is enormous. Among the themes and values projected by the medium, two are prominent: violence and unreality. Unreality can be divided into straightforward fantasy and deceptive description of reality. Most experts believe that fantasy is not harmful and, on the contrary, can be beneficial by stimulating creative thought. Pseudoreality, however, is apt to lead the young in the wrong direction in their search for realistic models.

Opinions on what the effects of violence might be are sharply divided between those who believe that violence serves a cathartic function and those who believe that it leads to imitation. Both camps present logical thought and empirical findings in defense of their interpretations. A point accepted by both is the susceptibility to imitative violence on the part of the disturbed child or adolescent. Also, high-exposure children lose sensitivity to violence and show no or greatly reduced physiological reactions when viewing it.

Most parents fail to control viewing habits of their offspring. The fact that the vast majority of American adolescents, in spite of growing up with violence-laced television, fail to engage in any violence indicates that some kind of control mechanisms do operate. They may include nonavailability of necessary instruments of violence, parental indoctrination, fear of an unsuccessful ending, and effects of the general American ethos of decency and fair play. Yet, there is evidence that children are tempted to imitate the villain if they profit from it and "get away with it."

Television serves a variety of functions. Among them are general information, stimulation of social activism, fueling the generation gap, selection of models for identification, reinforcement of cultural stereotypes, promotion of commercial motives, decline of creativity, learning appropriate behavior for a number of situations, and transferring time from human interaction to television.

The complexity of the phenomenon is aggravated (or reflected) by widespread disagreements among the experts, contradictory research findings, and many unanswered and unexplored questions.

[48] Schramm et al., *Television in the Lives of Our Children.*

Chapter 9

Etiology and Dimensions of Subculture

Beginning with this chapter we now shift from the individual adolescent to the adolescent collectivity, thereby leaving the psychological domain and moving deeper into sociological territory.

The collective stirring of modern youth is largely a consequence of the adolescent crisis in postindustrial society; and the formation of youth collectivities compensates for this crisis and provides a temporary collective identity. The need for an identity is at the core of the teen subculture as well as the youth movements.

We can divide the collective developments into the general teen subculture, mainly including high school age youth and the younger portion of the college population, and youth movements like the counterculture, including older, activistic, and politically sophisticated youth. However, the boundaries between the collectivities are not rigid and there is considerable membership overlap.

This chapter is a general and theoretical treatment of the question of how subcultures evolve and are sustained. The dimensions that are suggested as generic to the rise of a subculture can be applied to the general subculture as well as to specific youth movements. To start, we present a theoretical exploration of the development and dimensions of subculture. The following two chapters supply illustrations and descriptions: Chapter 10 describes the general teen subculture and Chapter 11 discusses the counterculture and a number of specific youth movements.

DEFINITION AND DIMENSIONS

At the present time, the conceptualization of subculture is beset with at least two major problems. First, sociologists do not agree on the specific dimensions that characterize a subculture. Although the sociological literature reflects some suggestions concerning some specific subcultural elements, the notions are not followed up by a concerted effort to integrate, systematize, and apply them consistently. The second problem deals with the frustrating fact that the definitions that succeed in eliciting some agreement are immensely general and lack operationability. An example is the definition stating that subculture "refers to norms that set a group apart from, not those that integrate a group with, the total society."[1] This definition is so general that, while it cannot fail to be theoretically correct, it is practically unusable in research. Another example is the proposal to combine a number of factors, such as "ethnic group, social class, region, occupation, religion, and urban and rural residence."[2] Unfortunately, these factors lack generic dimensionality and have no operational specifications. Finally, to epitomize the sociological disregard for the concept, Fairchild's *Dictionary of Sociology* did not even have the word *subculture* as a listing.[3]

Since *culture* refers to a blueprint of behavior for an entire society, the largest human grouping, *subculture* refers to the blueprint for behavior of a smaller group within the society. This subsidiary blueprint is frequently formed without the encouragement, acceptability, or full cognizance of the "parent culture." It is a special blueprint that accommodates a number of people whose needs and desires are not provided for by the main blueprint of society. Thus, there are subcultures for narcotic addicts, longshoremen, inmates in prison, Texas oilmen, those in the world of fashion, jazz musicians—and adolescents.

A subculture can be defined by its *functions*. As noted above, the general function of the subculture is to compensate for the failure of the main culture to provide a definite status, a feeling of acceptance, and need-satisfactions unique to a certain group of people. To accomplish these functions and to make the subculture a viable process, a number of prerequisites must be met.

Eight dimensions are proposed as basic elements of subculture: (1) Relatively unique (or uniquely accentuated) values and norms. (2) In-group lingo not shared with the larger society. (3) Distinct channels of (mass) communication not shared with or dependent on "outsiders." (4) Unique styles and fads (including grooming, dress, gesture, and other behavioral patterns) often resulting in subcultural ritual. (5) A sense of solidarity and *esprit de corps* manifested by thinking in terms of "we" instead of "me and them" (or simply the cogency of ingroup versus outgroup

---

[1] Milton J. Yinger, "Contraculture and Subculture," *American Sociological Review*, 25 (October 1960), 628.

[2] Milton M. Gordon, "The Concept of the Subculture and its Application," *Social Forces*, 25 (October 1947), 41.

[3] H. P. Fairchild, ed., *Dictionary of Sociology* (Totowa, N.J.: Littlefield, Adams & Co., 1968).

sentiments). (6) Status criteria in terms of cognizing them and adhering to them in actual peer relationships. In other words, existence of a working order of social positions—at a minimum, clarifying what makes for prestige, leadership, and follower. (7) Influence and power of leaders enhancing the identity and *esprit de corps* of the collectivity. This is the dimension of *charisma*. (8) Gratification of specific needs that the larger social structure fails to provide. The significance of this item is the subcultural institutionalization of need fulfillment.

A methodological paradigm has been proposed for consistent use of the eight dimensions in examining collectivities concerning their degree of subcultureness.[4] This design provides a tool that, if consistently applied, would promote comparability of different research findings, greater reliability in following the fluctuations of a subculture over its lifetime, and, most important, a measurement in terms of *degree of subcultural quality*. This latter point brings up the simplistic fashion in which the definition of subculture has traditionally been handled. It was customary to dichotomously answer the question whether a certain collectivity is a subculture with either "yes" or "no"—a method totally inconsistent with reality and with most procedures in other matters of sociological endeavor. Qualities always exist in terms of degree, and methods of analysis must be responsive to this fact. Therefore, a paradigm measuring collectivities as to their degree of subcultural quality is eminently necessary.

The above mentioned definitional dimensions, enumerating major functions of the subculture, must be checked against the youth subculture to see whether there is enough empirical evidence to bear out some degree of subcultural salience:

1. Young people have derived from their interaction a peculiar set of *norms and values* that no longer consists of child standards nor is part of the adult world.
2. They speak an *argot* that is not shared with adults. In fact, it is only partially understood by outsiders and is often unacceptable to the Establishment.
3. Youth's channels of *mass communication* consist of mingling in youth "ghettos" (the high schools), various "underground" media (youth newspapers), and their own programs via general mass media (radio, television, etc.)
4. Young Americans cultivate their own independent *styles and fads*, and are not willing to share them with adults. For example, teenage grooming and hair styles led to vehement confrontations during the late 1960s and early 1970s. The young tend to change a style as soon as adults imitate it.
5. Adolescents acquire a *primary-group belonging* in which they are accepted as total individuals. Peer involvement functions as a partial substitute for the teenagers' families, which they leave gradually to establish personal autonomy. The adolescent peer group helps young individuals in their emancipation from parental control.

[4] The technical aspects of the subcultural paradigm are discussed in Hans Sebald, "Subculture: Problems of Definition and Measurement," *International Review of Modern Sociology*, 5 (Spring 1975):82–89.

6. Youths derive *status relationships* that make them predictable in peer inter-
    action. Status criteria help to ameliorate the lack of social status during the
    transition from child to adult. The peer group also provides criteria and
    models that allow emulation during a time when such models in the adult
    society are either lacking or too frightening.

7. They are receptive to *charismatic leadership.* The world of the American teen-
    ager includes outstanding and famous personalities who, if not precisely
    leaders, function as heroes. The charismatic aura of such heroes is entirely a
    function of teenage hero worship.

8. Adolescents have needs, problems, and anxieties for which the adult social
    structure makes only partial allowance. Hence, young Americans have come to
    work out their own substructures over the years. This *institutionalization of
    patterns of need-fulfillment* is probably the most powerful indicator of how
    far a given collectivity has matured into a subculture — or even a counter-
    culture. (Here we approach the study of social movements and of social
    change.) The highly subculturized — or counterculturized — activities of
    American youth during the tumultuous late 1960s and early 1970s can serve
    as an example. The collective behavior of youth during that period — and to
    some extent still today — indicates a high degree of social structure. Among
    the behavior patterns — patterns consistent and recurring enough to justify the
    application of the concept of subcultural institutionalization — are how food is
    supplied and distributed, legal aid, entertainment, psychiatric first aid,
    business, education, and literature.

The most salient of the dimensions deals with the establishment of social
institutions within a collectivity markedly separate from the main society. I call
these internal structures — dedicated to specific need fulfillment — *subcultural
institutionalization.* It is this enmeshing of persons in their own segregated social
structure that is of utmost importance to sociology, since structural arrangements
result in regular patterns of human behavior and relationships.

It should be added that subcultural institutionalization usually arises only
when a sense of solidarity prevails. Conversely, a latent function of the new specialized substructure that fulfills needs is a reinforcement of the *esprit de corps.*
Subinstitutionalization often allows for behavior that would not be permitted
within the structure of the larger society. In so doing, subinstitutionalization
enables relatively new forms of behavior, of which drug use is an example. Some
subinstitutionalizations, however, merely establish counterparts to already available
avenues in the larger society. Many forms of dating, entertainment, and recreational
activities are examples. In general, the desire for exclusivity, freedom from adult
supervision, and unique styling determines the contours of subinstitutionalization.

THE QUESTION OF ETIOLOGY

What are the conditions and processes that make for the emergence of a subculture?
It seems that the *necessary condition* for the emergence of a subculture is the
existence of a *number of persons* in society who seek solutions to common problems and who *effectively interact* with one another.

It might be added that every collective segment of society has its own problems. Certain social categories, determined, for example, by age, sex, race, ethnicity, or occupation, exhibit unique problems. "The structure of society generates, at each position within the system, characteristic combinations of personality and situation and therefore characteristic problems of adjustment."[5]

The early formative stage of subculture, before the in-group structure and the norms and values become firmly established, includes a process of "exploratory gestures." This process consists of mutual explorations and joint elaborations of possible solutions, often accompanied by mass-communicative and/or physical (crowds, mobs) interchanges during which a set of common sentiments is specified and subsequently reinforced. Once a subculture is established, interaction moves in calmer and more routine channels.

The *sufficient conditions* for the establishment of a subculture lie in the acceptance of common norms and values specifying the "proper" way of doing things. When a sufficiently elaborate corollary of symbols has become the unique property of the persons involved, a collective identity has been born. One can then speak of a subcultural or a new cultural form "because each actor's participation in this system is influenced by his perception of the same norms in fellow actors."[6]

Membership in such a group or category ordinarily functions not merely as a problem-solving device in a narrow and technical sense, but also as a source of values, which ultimately has formative influence on the individual's self-perception. The price for gaining a clearly defined frame of reference is conformity to the norms of the group. In return, the member has access to ready-made conclusions, solutions, and peer-approved actions that help to solve a number of conflicts and ambiguities. There are compelling incentives not to deviate from the established ways of the group: fear of disapproval or even ostracism by the peers and fear of an inhospitable larger culture combine to keep the member within the confines of the subculture.

A collectivity of individuals becomes subcultural only when its system of norms and values is significantly different from the main culture. The solutions to the problems of the given collectivity are embodied in the larger society neither in terms of structural provision nor, frequently, in terms of cultural acceptability. The new solutions may conflict with society's traditions and may result in the collectivity being labeled deviant, thereby generating antagonism and mistrust between the larger and the smaller social systems. From the subcultural point of view, the so-called deviant-solution approach may more effectively ameliorate needs and problems than the existing solutions institutionalized in the larger society. In addition, members of the subculture frequently do not feel that their activities could harm individuals inside or outside of their group and thus see no reason to change their patterns. As a result, they tend to perceive their activities not only as effective but also as justified.

[5] Albert K. Cohen, *Delinquent Boys: The Culture of the Gang* (New York: Free Press, 1955), p. 55.
[6] Ibid., p. 65.

It seems to be the rule rather than the exception that repression of subcultural norms results in strengthening rather than in destroying them. History is replete with examples. Probably the most outstanding instance in Western civilization was the attempt to suppress the early Christians, who eventually were victorious, and, no longer a rejected minority, turned into a powerful majority that rose to dominate most of Western culture.

New solution approaches and the symbols of subcultural membership may, from the outsider's point of view, be perceived as relatively haphazard and undefined behavior. For the in-group members, however, it is structured and well defined. This misconception on the part of outside observers arises because of a tendency to judge unfamiliar behavior in terms of one's own values, not realizing that the seemingly nonconformist behavior actually conforms to subcultural expectations.

One of the aspects most often ignored by observers is the subculture's different criteria for ascribing prestige. Frequently the members of the subculture, prior to their joining, have encountered serious obstacles in the path of achieving status in the larger society – a condition certainly true of adolescents. Within the confines of the subculture there are opportunities for achieving status and respect. The solution for teenagers who share this predicament of unclear status in the adult world is, therefore, to gravitate toward one another and jointly establish new criteria of status that describe as meritorious those characteristics they *do* possess and the kinds of activities of which they *are* capable. This, quite obviously, is a group approach to an individual problem. If an individual adolescent tried to establish such criteria alone, he or she would probably not only fail to achieve status in the larger society, but also would suffer alienation from peers.

The usual side effect of joining a new status system that encourages behavior frowned on by the larger social system is an inverse correlation: the more the individual gains status in the new group, the move he or she will lose status outside the group.

Belonging to and depending on a subculture usually has far-reaching effects on the personality of its follower. The influence may be strong enough to provide the basic character of one's identity. Indeed, the decision to join a subculture is normally indicative of the person's need for a clear identity. The subculture, then, comes to function as an important psychological refuge.

A chapter on the development of subcultures is not complete unless it describes, at least briefly, pertinent etiological theories. Among the models purporting to explain the origin of subcultures are the psychogenic, culture-transmission, and behavioristic. Familiarity with these theoretical frameworks aids in understanding specific elements in the complex process of subcultural development. Although they represent different ways of looking at the empirical phenomenon, they are not incompatible but rather complementary, emphasizing different aspects of the process.

The psychogenic model. The basic assumption of this theory is that a sub-culture evolves from problems of adjustment that are common to a large number of persons. Emphasis is on the independence with which individuals contrive solutions. The individual is depicted as a creative innovator. Although the role of the social milieu as the genesis of the problem is recognized, its role in determining the solution is minimized. New cultural forms emerge as a *parallel* development of individual solutions, which, more or less unaccountably, merge into a collective entity. The aspect of the subcultural development that is unaccounted for in this framework is the process of social interaction as a necessary condition during the incipient phase of a subculture.

The psychogenic approach views teenage behavior as an effort to solve the problems characteristic of the frustrating and confusing sojourn in adolescence. The adolescent, standing between child and adult statuses and being devoid of a clearly structured social position, may frequently ponder the agonizing question of who he or she really is and come face to face with the issue of identity. Erik Erikson, Gordon Bronson, Margaret Mead,[7] and others maintain that the major task facing the adolescent is the search for meaningful identity. This task is obviously more difficult in the modern urban-industrial setting than in smaller folk or tribal socie-ties. The rapid pace of social change, exposure to a confusing variety of secular and religious value systems, and revolutionary technological innovations of the twentieth century make the world appear too relativistic and unpredictable to provide the teenager with a stable frame of reference. Youth of previous generations experi-enced a more practical introduction to adult responsibilities, a sort of apprentice-ship during which they could acquire an identity.

Modern teenagers receive a much less practical and more abstract introduc-tion to life, which results in the perception of the world as complex and ambiguous. They have difficulties in seeing just where and how they fit in. Their escape attempts lead them to other teenagers. In concerted action they establish a sub-stitute for the identity that is denied them in the adult world and develop peer-group symbols to reinforce a subcultural identity. In the process of maintaining this identity, special clothes, language, and attitudes toward the world play an important role. In the past, this manner of symbolizing an identity was characteris-tic almost exclusively of deprived and/or delinquent groups that did not have a respected place in society. Examples would be transvestites, members of delinquent gangs, beggars, and narcotic addicts. In short, the need for the peer culture with its peculiar symbolizations is symptomatic of the search for identity.

[7] Erik H. Erikson, *Childhood and Society* (New York: W. W. Norton & Co., 1963); Gordon W. Bronson, "Identity Diffusion in Late Adolescence," *Journal of Abnormal and Social Psychology*, 59 (November 1959), 414–17; and Margaret Mead, "The Young Adult," in *Values and Ideals of American Youth*, ed. E. Ginzberg (New York: Columbia University Press, 1961), pp. 37–51.

The psychogenic model appears to accurately reflect empirical processes. However, it is limited in its explanatory *range*, unable to give an explanation of the exact nature of the *formative* process of the collectivity. One of the more unexplored areas in sociology remains the analysis of the bridging process that leads from discrete individual problems to the actual beginnings of subculture.

The culture-transmission model. This theory is concerned with the perpetuation of an already established subculture by transmission of its values and unique behavior patterns from one generation to the next. This approach is interested more in understanding the *learning process* whereby, for example, the younger teenagers acquire their older peers' modes of thought and actions than in understanding the *prime* origin of these subcultural patterns. The limited scope of this approach often excludes from consideration those crucial problems that render each new generation susceptible to the established subcultural form. At the most, this theory suggests a number of plausible mechanisms of subcultural transmission, such as the learning of rules that lend orientation and direction to the life of the teenager and the role of the mass media in disseminating these rules and ideas.

Mass media, especially television and teen magazines,[8] are probably the most effective mechanisms for transmitting and perpetuating the teenage subculture. Mass media offer ready-made solutions to teenagers and promise to save them the effort of searching for new forms. David L. Altheide makes this point forcefully: "Youth culture is both a product and a target of the media...The development of youth as an idea was a by-product of media culture and the discovery that young people could consume."[9]

A specific example of this process was the rise of rock music. It actually *changed* American youth, helped to create a self-conscious teen generation, and perpetuated this self-consciousness from generation to generation of teenagers. Before the 1950s there was no music, or any other medium, that enveloped so powerfully the feelings and behavior of young Americans. Rock music spoke clearly to the interests and needs of adolescents. "It defined the correct behavior...and noted the irrelevance of school routines as compared with the realities of fast cars, surfing, and the exhilaration of dancing. Throughout rock lyrics there were pointed contrasts between the teen way of life and the behavioral norms imposed by adults."[10]

The idea that rock music was a significant carrier of youth culture is further developed by Bernice Martin. Rock music evolved into what became probably the most truculent vehicle, telling, as it were, the epic story of American adolescence.

---

[8] Charles H. Brown, "Self-Portrait: The Teen-Type Magazine," *Annals of the American Academy of Political and Social Sciences*, 338 (November 1961), 20.

[9] David L. Altheide, "Mass Media and Youth Culture," *Urban Education*, 2 (July 1979): 224.

[10] R. A. Peterson and D. G. Berger, "Three Eras in the Manufacture of Popular Music Lyrics," in Denisoff and Peterson, eds., *The Sounds of Social Change* (Chicago: Rand McNally, 1972), p. 296.

Rock music became a sacrament; it interpreted agonies, joys, the holy and the unholy in the lives of teenagers. Martin visualized the role of rock music as symbolizing the "sacred" in youth culture, not unlike the need to symbolize the "sacred" in primitive tribal society. The feeling of *Communitas*, belonging together, is expressed by "ritualized symbols of group identity particularly in the beat of music, in common fashions and through the star performer who acts as sacred 'totem.'"[11]

In summary, the media facilitate connections between adolescents, and perpetuate certain themes. These themes dwell on solving problems of loneliness, confusion, and alienation from adult society. They are embodied in songs, the beat of rock music, TV programs, movies, teen magazines (particularly those with "Letter" departments), and the actual physical mingling of teenagers in their ghettos – the school campuses, gangs, dance places, and rock concerts. These lyrics, rhythms, programs, stories, statements, and places are the media for communicating and transmitting subcultural thought and behavior. These media are not limited to one generation of teenagers, but span generations of teenagers, helping them to learn anew the ways of older peers. Needless to say, these media are powerful conditioners, often commercially exploiting the need of teenagers to communicate with other teenagers and derive a feeling of belonging to the peer culture.

The behavioristic model. Although behaviorism has neglected to apply its framework to the question of subcultural formation and to formulate a precise etiological theory, it is capable of pointing out significant steps in the process of converting children into members of teenage subcultures. It would be presumptuous to attempt to present a complete picture of the behavioristic approach in this limited context; a few remarks must suffice.

Application of behavioristic principles to explain the rise of subcultures has resemblance to using the psychogenic model. The point of departure is again the frustrations that youths experience during adolescence. If tensions and frustrations are equated with pain, one finds American teenagers frequently exposed to it when interacting with adults who technically would be called *aversive stimuli*. To carry the process to its logical conclusion, it follows that teenagers try to avoid this type of stimulus and hence tend to withdraw from the adult world. This type of behavior is defined as "escape behavior"[12] and is illustrated by escape attempts from tensions of the youth-adult confrontation. This reaction is common to most adolescents since the same hedonistic principle applies to all. Graphically speaking, on the escape route the adolescent meets other adolescents who have similar problems. The result is a grouping together that again can be explained by behavioristic principles. Through interaction among themselves, adolescents discover that they are free of stringent adult expectations, which they have found difficult to meet

[11] Bernice Martin, "The Sacralization of Disorder: Symbolism in Rock Music," *Sociological Analysis*, 40, 2 (1979):87.

[12] See, for technical treatment and definition, Arthur W. Staats and Carolyn K. Staats, *Complex Human Behavior: A Systematic Extension of Learning Principles* (New York: Holt, Rinehart & Winston, 1964), p. 44.

and accept. As a result, they experience a lessening of tension and frustration. Interaction among peers consists of stimuli that are largely gratifying to teenagers and that form patterns of subcultural behavior. These stimuli can be called positive reinforcers, which are usually more powerful than negative reinforcers because the natural enjoyment of common activities and interests is a collectivizing force. Thus, independently from adolescent problems, normal gregarious activities help to sustain the peer culture.

In the final analysis, these two types of reinforcers, the negative (escape from pain) and the positive (finding security and the gratification of fellowship), effectively establish and perpetuate the subcultural milieu.

There is still another aspect of the adolescent phenomenon that can effectively be explained by behavioristic principles. It deals with the consequences of consistent and inconsistent conditioning. Teenagers are exposed to a variety of inconsistent stimuli. In one instance they are told to be responsible and independent, while in another instance they may be prevented from showing responsibility. In many cases, American teenagers are expected to show responsibility and independence concerning vocational preparation, but must obtain their parents' advice or permission in questions of finances, dating, and marriage.

Such inconsistent stimuli are also definable as inconsistent and ambivalent role expectations, as mixing relatively indiscriminately a number of elements from the adult and the child roles.

Inconsistent stimuli due to such unclear role expectations have a tendency to produce ambivalent behavior—sometimes defined as neurosis.[13] The initial reactions to such ambivalent conditioning include frustration and tension. Eventually, this frustration makes the adolescent choose the less frustrating conditioning system of the peer culture with its simpler and more consistent adjustment processes.

DISAGREEMENTS ON THE EXISTENCE OF THE TEENAGE SUBCULTURE

Although this book relies on the assumption that the teenage subculture is a fact, dissident voices should at least receive a hearing. As has been pointed out in the discussion on peer-parent conflict and the autonomy process (chapter on the family), opinions of experts range from affirmative to negative.

Clarity of the argument is impaired by lack of a consensual definition of *subculture*, thereby graphically illustrating the dilemma mentioned in the first section of this chapter, where we deplored the simplistic "yes-or-no" determination

---

[13] Behavioristically inclined psychologists have demonstrated the effect of ambivalent conditioning in laboratory situations using animals as their subjects. They found that inconsistent conditioning can result in neurotic disturbances, possibly to the extent of a so-called nervous breakdown. See, for example, Jules H. Masserman, *Behavior and Neurosis* (Chicago: University of Chicago Press, 1943).

of what a subculture is and the lack of specific dimensions. Generally, however, the criterial dimension on which both sides of the argument focus deals with "unique norms and values." It is this single dimension that has become the bone of contention between the two camps, one maintaining that the dimension does in fact differentiate the young from the adult culture, the other denying any significant difference between the generations.

The argument of the *proponents* can be summed up by three related assumptions:

1. The typical adolescent is characterized by symptoms that can be described as socially caused "storm and stress." These expressions stem primarily from the adolescent's uncertain position in the social structure. Some of the confusions and insecurities typical of the American adolescent arise from uncertainty of occupational choice, difficulties in identifying with adult models, inconsistencies in authority relationships, conflicts between generations, sexual frustrations because of conflict between physiological maturation and social prohibitions, and discontinuity in socialization patterns.

2. A teenage subculture exists and is powerful and widespread. The youth subculture is a social reaction to the young individuals' uncertain statuses in the adult world and eases the transition from childhood to adulthood. The subculture is particularly dominant in metropolitan areas, exerting far-reaching demands on its followers, creating a feeling of belonging and a status system that judges behavior by subcultural standards. James S. Coleman's large-scale surveys concluded that the American adolescent is progressively becoming more ensconced in secondary institutions, from nursery school through college:

> He is "cut off" from the rest of society, forced inward toward his own age group, made to carry out his whole social life with others his own age. With his fellows, he comes to constitute a small society, one that has most of its important interactions *within* itself, and maintains only a few threads of connection with the outside adult society. In our modern world of mass communication and rapid diffusion of ideas and knowledge, it is hard to realize that subcultures can exist right under the very noses of adults — subcultures with languages all their own, with special symbols, and, most important, with value systems that may differ from adults.[14]

Talcott Parsons thinks that the characteristics of the adolescent subculture include three main aspects: (1) the rebelliousness of youth against adult expectations and authority; (2) the tendency toward peer conformity, guarded by considerable in-group intolerance of differences; and (3) a romantic adherence to emotionally significant objects.[15] Robin M. Williams, Jr., contends that the social distance between generations is sometimes so great that parents and children confront each

[14] James S. Coleman, *The Adolescent Society* (New York: Free Press, 1963), p. 3.

[15] Talcott Parsons, "Psychoanalysis and the Social Structure," *Psychoanalytic Quarterly*, 19 (July 1950), 378–79.

other as members of vastly different subcultures.[16] Arnold W. Green believes in the existence of a teenage subculture and calls it a "world of irresponsibility, specialized lingo, dating, athleticism, and the like, which rather sharply cuts off adolescent experience from that of the child and from that of the adult."[17]

3. The concluding assumption suggests a causal relationship between "storm and stress" and the teenage subculture, implying that affiliation with peers provides a structured social environment and personal identity. The subcultural arrangement is reinforced and its survival guaranteed by the satisfaction the teenagers derive from having found status among peers.

Most of the opponents of the subculture theory have completed various and sundry studies—mostly small in scale—and concluded that the difference in values between adolescents and adults is not large enough to call the young's attitudes a value system. In fact, these researchers conclude that parental values are socially inherited by the offspring and manifested in the youngsters' choices of peer affiliation and value orientation. They concede, however, that there may be differences in norms, the rules and the means of doing things and achieving certain goals (goals that are synonymous with values and presumably coincide with those of the parents). The young, hence, may sometimes resort to deviant means to achieve such basic goals as status, success, and material gains. While it is an essential purpose of the socialization process to teach the young the proper means, some researchers feel that the basic goals are "naturally" learned and imitated.

There is the possibility that these researchers mistakenly equate basic human needs and propensities, such as seeking security, acceptance, expression, and new experience within the peer environment, with the cultural values of American society. In other words, the equation of seeking acceptance among peers (by cooperation and sporting material accessories) with the cultural values of cooperation and materialism of the adult world is spurious. The young's seeming imitation of cultural goals is really nothing more than their way of coping with a peer situation.

Also, much of the research findings meant to deflate the subculture theory are based on highly specific and nongeneralizable samples. For example, Frederich Elkin and William A. Westley's mid-1950s study resulted in a widely publicized and often quoted dissent from the subculture theory, since they found the teenagers of a Montreal suburb more integrated in the adult society, its customs, norms and values, than was generally thought.[18] Family ties were close, and the degree of family consensus was high. The adolescents acknowledged their parents' right to guide them and set rules concerning dating practices, discussed their choice of school courses and vacation plans with parents, and often engaged in joint parent-child activities, such as parties, dances, and community sports events. Parents

---

[16] Robin M. Williams, Jr., *American Society: A Sociological Interpretation* (New York: Knopf, 1960), p. 80.

[17] Arnold W. Green, *Sociology* (New York: McGraw-Hill, 1968), p. 113.

[18] Frederick Elkin and William A. Westley, "The Myth of Adolescent Culture," *American Sociological Review*, 20 (December 1955), 680–84.

expressed few complaints about socialization problems or peer group activities of their teenage children, and the continuities of socialization were more striking than the discontinuities. In short, the patterns of the adolescents' social lives were not significantly different from those of the older generation, and adolescents demonstrated "responsible" and "adult" perspectives.

Despite the highly specific character of the study the findings were widely generalized, disregarding the fact that the data were derived from interviews of a sample of only twenty adolescents and their parents and from life-history material of another twenty teenagers. This selection is by no means an adequate sample from which to safely draw conclusions about American teenagers in general—especially when the researchers themselves admitted that the sample may not have been completely representative of the community from which it was taken. Also, allowance should be made for possible differences between Canadian and American teenagers. Montreal, heavily influenced by English and French traditions, may have a different type of teenager than most cities in the United States. Moreover, the locale of the research was a well-to-do suburb, classified by the authors as upper-middle-class, where "typically, when a girl gives a party, she sends out formal invitations, and her guest list includes those she *should* invite as well as those she wants to invite. The girls take great pains to play their hostess roles properly, and the boys strongly recognize their escort responsibilities."[19]

The formal manner of social interaction in this suburb seems to be more typical of the United States upper class than of the broad middle class. Since the present focus is more on adolescents of the broad American middle class, Elkin and Westley's study has only minimal relevance.

Other advocates of nondifferentiated youth-adult culture include psychologist Albert Bandura, who has argued that the "storm and stress" of adolescents has been exaggerated and that parents and teenagers are more in agreement than in conflict.[20] L. Eugene Thomas revealed that children of highly politicized parents tend to be like their parents both in political attitude and political behavior.[21] Elizabeth Douvan and her coworkers consistently discovered harmonious youth-parent relationships.[22] Reuben Hill and J. Aldous, Jr. found that religious beliefs remain relatively stable between generations.[23] Daniel Offer, Eric Ostrov, and Kenneth Howard try to explain adults' concern about a teen subculture as a mis-

---

[19] Ibid., p. 682.

[20] Albert Bandura, "The Stormy Decade: Fact or Fiction," in *Issues in Adolescent Psychology*, ed. D. Rogers (New York: Prentice–Hall, 1972).

[21] L. Eugene Thomas, "Family Correlates of Student Political Activism," *Developmental Psychology*, 4 (March 1971), 206–14.

[22] Elizabeth Douvan and Joseph Adelson, *The Adolescent Experience* (New York: John Wiley, 1966), and Elizabeth Douvan and H. Gold, "Modal Patterns in American Adolescence," in *Review of Child Development Research*, vol. 2, ed. L. Hoffman and M. Hoffman (New York: Russell Sage Foundation, 1966).

[23] Reuben Hill and J. Aldous, Jr., "Socialization for Marriage and Parenthood," in *Handbook of Socialization Theory and Research*, ed. D. Goslin (Chicago: Rand McNally, 1969).

conceived view of their offspring's growth of independence. That is, parents over-emphasize the influence of the peer group and "use the peer group as an external-ized object and influence that provides a reference group for expressions of dissatisfaction with their offspring."[24]

What the latter authors are trying to say is, more plainly, that parents have invented a teen subculture to use it as a scapegoat for the complaints they have about their kids. This is a surprising psychoanalytic exercise for writers who, throughout their work, vehemently dispute the validity of any psychoanalytic notion. The Offer team ostensibly relies directly on the responses they have col-lected from their surveys and claims that "data collected directly from normal adolescents are often significantly different from what many adults assume teen-agers feel about themselves."[25] That may well be so, but what the data mean becomes a matter of *interpretation*. The Offer team submits an interpretation that tolerates no differing view. But, perhaps because of taking teenagers' statements verbatim, they actually fail to make an interpretation at all. What teenagers say may not adequately reveal what they really feel and experience. It would be naive to expect most teenagers to be able to articulate their adolescent experiences, which may well be turbulent. To conclude that if teenagers don't verbalize turmoil (and the subcultural compensation for it), then such a phenomenon simply does not exist is less than insightful. In sum, it appears, the Offer team holds an a priori bias according to which there simply is no subculture. They interpret their data accord-ingly and add a bit of psychoanalytic magic to explain why most adults differ from their view. By discrediting critics via psychoanalytic means, they hope to keep their theory intact.

I have no quarrel with the studies *in and by themselves*. They are probably correct and truthful in themselves, but their generalization to the American teen population is unwarranted. As has already been discussed in the family chapter, the samples are either nonrepresentative and too specific or the data derived from them were inadequately interpreted.

THE DIVERSITY OF TEENAGE SUBCULTURES

One of the more justified criticisms of the portrayal of the youth subculture deals not so much with the basic question of whether it does or does not exist, but how diversified it is. This criticism calls attention to the fact that there is no uniform subculture for all teenagers, but a number of significantly different versions. Many sociologists deplore the blanket application of the concept "teenage subculture" because it implies a monolithic membership group for all teenagers. They remind us

---

[24] Daniel Offer, Eric Ostrov, and Kenneth I. Howard, *The Adolescent: A Psychological Self-Portrait* (New York: Basic Books, 1981), p. 122.

[25] Ibid., p. 121.

of important differences in peer culture based on such variables as socioeconomic class, age, race, ethnicity, and rural or urban residence. For example, a black inner-city teenager living in the slums exhibits different values, has a different outlook on life, and belongs to a different type of peer culture than a white middle-class teenager growing up in suburbia.

For the purpose of communication, subcultural diversity must be simplified by some arbitrary guidelines: when the unqualified terms *youth subculture* or *teenage peer culture* or a synonymous phrase appears, reference is made to the nondelinquent middle class, reaching over into the upper-lower socioeconomic stratum. The teenage groups, cliques, campus crowds, etc., of this socioeconomic range are characterized by their independence from and usually nonviolent rejection of many adult standards, their conformity to peer-group patterns, their observance of teenage fads and fashions, their romanticism, and their participation in hedonistic activities. Specific expressions may include distinct ways of dressing, grooming, and talking. Their argot, representing a relatively exclusive communication system, is not shared with adults. In the case of lower-class youth, subculture often connotes delinquent behavior forms.

The upper socioeconomic class of the American population can hardly be said to have a youth subculture. In that social stratum one would most likely encounter the type of nonadolescent youth who is integrated in his or her family and special community and who suffers little status uncertainty—often to the point where there is no need for a compensating teenage subculture.

On the other side, lower-class youths live a subcultural life that has its own ethos. Anthropologist Walter B. Miller suggested a culturistic etiology of delinquency and tried to explain youthful offenses by a particular lower-class set of values and problems that increase the probability of law violations.[26] Over years of observing and analyzing lower-class street-corner groups, Miller discovered a number of "focal concerns" of lower-class culture that set it distinctly apart from other positions in the social order. These focal concerns include "trouble," "toughness," "smartness," "excitement," "fate," and "autonomy." They should not be understood as being in opposition to the law, but rather as helping to bring about the circumstances that invite criminal behavior. For example, the search for excitement may lead to auto theft, and the stress on toughness may encourage not only verbal insult, but physical violence as a retribution for it.

Other criminologists feel, however, that a youngster's membership in a delinquent subculture is better explained by "differential opportunities." Richard A. Cloward and Lloyd E. Ohlin, for example, think that there is more than one delinquent subculture among working-class youth and that a main goal of research should be to detect how selections of delinquency adaptations are made.[27]

---

[26] Walter B. Miller, "Lower-Class Culture As a Generating Milieu of Gang Delinquency," *Journal of Social Issues*, 14 (1958), 5–19.

[27] Richard A. Cloward and Lloyd E. Ohlin, *Delinquency and Opportunity: A Theory of Delinquent Gangs* (Glencoe, Ill.: The Free Press, 1960).

According to the theory, these selections depend more on characteristics of community organization than on psychological differences among delinquents. In other words, types of delinquency depend on types of illegitimate *opportunities* which, in turn, are primarily dependent on organizational features of the community. Cloward and Ohlin specified three major types of delinquent subculture adaptations and called them *criminal-oriented, conflict-oriented*, and *retreatist-oriented*. These types differ from each other in activity patterns as well as in etiological conditions. In terms of behavior, the criminalistic form concentrates on systematic theft as a basic way of life and a major avenue for upward social mobility into the world of organized crime. The conflict form is the result of disorganized communities in which traditional agencies and institutions of control have been rendered ineffective by high population mobility and diversity. The retreatist form provides isolation from conventional values and persons, and focuses on "kicks" through drugs, alcohol, and sex. In this form, steady work is eschewed in preference to "getting by," and the art of being "cool" is practiced—in short, this may be a lower-class version of the stereotypical hippie.

A special type of delinquency has become notorious over the past few decades: youth-ghetto delinquency in the form of school vandalism. A 1975 U.S. Senate subcommittee on juvenile delinquency reported that the mid-1970s annual crime index in our public schools included over 100 student murders, 70,000 serious physical assaults on teachers, hundreds of thousands of student victims of assaults, and about $500 million in repair of school vandalism (approximately the total amount spent on textbooks per year).[28] Another 1975 subcommittee hearing revealed that between 1970 and 1973, homicides in schools have increased 18.5 percent, rapes and attempted rapes 40 percent, robberies 37 percent, assaults between students 85 percent, and assaults on teachers 77 percent.[29]

The situation has not improved since this information was gathered. A 1980 report shows that 110,000 teachers, 5 percent of the U.S. total, were assaulted by students, an increase of more than 50 percent over the annual rate of the late 1970s. For example, school muggings, lawsuits, thefts, and vandalism in 1980 cost Los Angeles schools over $100 million while city and school officials were stymied over jurisdictional problems.[30]

The diversity of juvenile subcultures has been summed up:[31]

The "parent" male subculture. This is the small gang, described as nonutilitarian, malicious, negativistic, versatile, and characterized by short-run hedon-

---

[28] "Violence in Evanston," *Time*, June 2, 1975, p. 39.

[29] UPI Report, June 19, 1975.

[30] "Help! Teacher Can't Teach!" *Time*, June 16, 1980, p. 63.

[31] Albert K. Cohen and James F. Short, Jr., "Research in Delinquent Subcultures," *Journal of Social Issues*, 14 (1958), 20–37.

ism. It is referred to as "parent" subculture because it is the most common and generic collective delinquency form.

The conflict-oriented subculture. This is usually a highly developed form of collective delinquency, exhibited in large gangs, the membership of which may run into the hundreds. They have an elaborate organization that often includes such roles as president, vice-president, war-chief, and armorer. They have a territorial base, a name, a strong sense of corporate identity, and a public personality or "rep" in the gang world.

The drug-addict subculture. There is usually a correlation between drug addiction and delinquency. In most cases, the addicts were already delinquent before grouping themselves into subcultures. Their delinquency is almost always of the nonviolent and income-producing type that makes their drug habit possible.

Semiprofessional theft. This is a loosely integrated forerunner of the subculture of professional adult thieves proficient in ordinarily nonviolent thievery. In a sense, it is a stage in the life history, a specialized delinquency before ascending to the elite thievery of the adult professionals.

The middle-class delinquent subculture. Cohen and Short anticipate empirical exploration of a phenomenon not yet clearly developed. The traditional form of middle-class delinquency is usually of the "parent" type, but it may evolve into other forms. For example, the above-mentioned youth-ghetto delinquency (school violence and vandalism) could possibly be placed into this category. Generally, however, the middle-class delinquent subculture may not be clearly defined simply because it largely lacks empirical representation.

The female delinquent subcultures. A female's status is largely dependent on the status of the males with whom she is identified. There are some exceptions, however, for example, when girls organize in gangs for sexual pursuits (usually prostitution), drug addiction, or as counterparts of the male hoodlum gang. Though research literature on female delinquency is sparse, there are indications that the traditional double standard has also declined in respect to delinquent activities and that girls are catching up with boys in the arena of law violations.

But, of course, not all teenage subcultures are of a delinquent nature. Many of them rally around relatively harmless and recreational fads and styles, such as the subcultures of the surfers, bikers, backpackers, athletes, punkers, religious groups, cults, and movements. Delinquent subcultures have been dwelled on primarily because they are clearly discernible as subcultures and illustrate some of the principles of the three explanatory models of subculture etiology, particularly those of the psychogenic approach in which common problems become shared problems for which the conspirators invent a delinquent solution.

ADOLESCENT NONSTATUS
AND TEENAGE STATUS: A PARADOX?

Classification of certain adolescent activities as subcultural behavior introduces a theoretical problem: How can the portrayal of teenagers as confused and uncertain adolescents be reconciled with their portrayal as members of the teenage subculture, within which they have found role security and certainty? This seeming paradox is not easily resolved, since teenagers are actually characterized by *both*. The decision as to which of the two characterizations is more applicable depends entirely on the *specific teenager-other* relationship that is to be analyzed. When examining the teenager's relationship with adults, a multitude of problems are detectable that in their sum total substantiate the claim of the existence of adolescent uncertainty. Problems intrinsic to this *teenage-adult* relationship include confused communication, unclear authority definitions, generalist-specialist discontinuity, incongruous standards, and many other problems that have been discussed in previous chapters.

However, the *teenager-teenager* relationship is characterized by few, if any, such confusions and uncertainties. Among themselves, teenagers have created a relatively stable, though temporary, social structure. They know that they belong together and observe norms and values not necessarily consistent with the adult world's folkways and mores. In other words, there is a subcultural arrangement that compensates for the experience of adolescence in those situations of interaction that include the adult world. In their peer culture they find status, and, consequently, the *role of teenager*.

One can formulate still another relationship: the *teenage-collectivity-adult* relationship. The definition of collectivity that is involved in this relationship is susceptible to subjective interpretation; it depends either on the adults' acknowledgment of teenagers as a subculture with relatively closed ranks, common problems, and common compensations, or on their perception of teenagers as a mere accumulation of young individuals with more or less discrete problems and noncollective actions. Many adults, sociologically untrained as they may be, recognize that adolescents have found a way to collectively share the problems of their interim position and *en masse* compensate for them in a subcultural framework. If adults acknowledge that teenagers occupy a position and perform a role within their peer culture, the characterization of adolescence as a subcultural phenomenon is largely endorsed.

In summary, the seeming paradox must be understood as a problem of *differential analysis*. Most modern teenagers are *both* typically confused adolescents in the adult world and relatively self-assured and status-conscious members of their peer groups — depending on the interaction being analyzed.

A final word of modification should be added. Allowance must be made for the fact that not *all* teenagers are adolescents and members of teenage subcultures. It is possible to be an adolescent and not a member of some discernible peer culture. This would be the case of a youth who is socially isolated from peers and suffers from adolescent symptoms without recourse to an age-mate subculture. Such a youth might lack opportunity to communicate with peers and become aware of the commonality of adolescent problems. However, such a socially isolated adolescent would be a rarity, because almost any degree of social interaction would provide enough opportunities to communicate, meet, and share problems with peers. In general, for American teenagers the adolescent condition constitutes an ever-present latent force whose gravitational pull aids the formation of a compensating subculture.

It is also possible to be a member of the teenage subculture and suffer minimally from adolescent tension and confusion. This relatively conflict-free situation may be due to either one or both of two circumstances. First, the teenager may be so deeply involved in the peer subculture, may carry out peer commitments and follow peer standards to such a degree that he or she derives a sense of total belonging from the subculture. Adult standards affect him or her only minimally, and he or she suffers little or no ambiguity and confusion as to where to place loyalty. Second, a teenager may be a member of the peer culture not because of basic psychological needs but rather because of proximity or coincidental acquaintances, such as neighborhood friends and school environment. This nonadolescent may be integrated in the family, have clear perceptions of a future occupation, satisfactory access to adult models that he or she emulates, and may freely adhere to the value orientations of adults. Participation in the teenage subculture is therefore merely perfunctory and of superficial significance to personality development. This type of youth is in the minority. It is safe to assume that the majority of American teenagers are both adolescents and members of peer cultures.

SUMMARY

Many social scientists agree on the existence of the teenage subculture as an empirical reality. Numerous studies and a multitude of daily manifestations seem to support the assumption.

Care must be taken in defining subculture to specify *which* type of teenage subculture is to be discussed. Generally speaking, the present discussion refers to the teenage culture within the broad American middle class.

The seeming paradox that a teenager can be both an adolescent and a status-ascertained member of the peer culture can be resolved by *differential analysis*, by focusing, respectively, on the adolescent-adult or the teenager-teenager interaction.

The functions of the teenage subculture that meet the needs of the participants and enable the subculture to become a continuous semi-institution include a number of "services": (1) common norms and values; (2) a subcultural argot; (3) channels of communication not shared with "outsiders"; (4) unique styles and fads; (5) a sense of solidarity; (6) a status structure; (7) the charisma of leaders or heroes; (8) gratification of specific needs through subcultural institutionalization.

Three etiological theories complement each other in explaining subcultural formation. The *psychogenic* and *behavioristic* models focus on the prime origin of subcultural evolvement and start with the problems characteristic of a number of persons. *Behaviorism*, with its premise of human nature as hedonistic, explains the attraction of teenagers to their peer culture as escape from painful confrontation with the adult culture and as gravitation toward common interests. The *culture-transmission* model deals with learning and communicating. Television, movies, radio, and magazines perpetuate subcultural ways of thinking and acting.

It must be emphasized that motivation to join and maintain a normally non-delinquent teenage subculture does not stem entirely from the need to alleviate adolescent frustration and confusion. Motivation also stems from gregariousness and the enjoyment of fellowship. Teenagers enjoy engaging in activities (for example, dating) and in sharing interests that are neither entirely child nor adult. This enjoyment of peer companionship positively reinforces the subculture and operates in conjunction with the more negatively reinforcing influence of adolescent insecurity. In fact, even for teenagers relatively unaffected by adolescent disturbances, the gregarious enjoyment alone is a sufficiently powerful positive reinforcer to attract them to the subculture of their peers.

Chapter 10

Inside
the Teen Subculture

While the preceding chapter was theory oriented, this chapter is more graphic and draws from popular as well as professional sources. The inclusion of popular material illustrates actual behavior and events in the teen subculture and adds a descriptive element to the abstract, sociological interpretation.

The material is ordered into eight dimensions that are elemental to subculture. No claim is made as to the completeness of illustrating the dimensions, since some are not readily expressed by the members of the collectivity and others are not easily observable by outsiders like social scientists. On the other hand, some of the dimensions can be abundantly illustrated since there is a surplus of data for them; for example, crowd behavior, hero worship, and styles.

This chapter is oriented toward the general American teenage collectivity, high school students and the younger college students, rather than the older or more activistic segment of American youth. In spite of some overlap of these collectivities, the distinction may prove helpful in ordering the immense amount of material available from the overall youth scene. The next chapter will grapple with the question of the youth movements, the conglomerate of young intelligentsia, radical political groups, liberation phalanxes, cults, and other factions of the youth population.

226

NORMS AND VALUES

The first section examines the norms and values governing in-group concerns; the second examines youth's basic attitudes toward the Establishment; and the final section discusses value commitments, i.e., how young people behaviorally implement values they hold.

In-group norms and values. Any group of individuals interacting over a period of time will sooner or later come to agree on a blueprint that creates predictable behavior patterns. These patterns include norms, rules concerning *how* to achieve certain values and do certain things, and values, the goals and basic attitudes concerning *what* is important.

Teen groups hold norms and values that, though not always entirely different from those of the adult community, at least reflect a unique accent. We will now explore some teen in-group standards, such as popularity, prestige, friendship, and sex.

Researchers have repeatedly noted that popularity is the most emphasized value among teenagers. The dynamics of popularity are complex and involve such features as admiration and recognition by peers. The data of the National Norms for Entering College Freshmen show that "obtaining recognition from peers" is essential to about 40 percent of beginning college students and that this proportion varies little from year to year.[1]

James S. Coleman, in his famous survey of American high schools, likewise found a strong desire to be popular. Interestingly, the desire is more intense among girls than boys.[2] The Purdue Opinion Panel supported this and showed that 60 percent of the teenage girls answered affirmatively to "want people to like me more," while 47 percent of the boys answered in the affirmative. Of the girls, 47 percent affirmed "wish I were more popular," while 36 percent of the boys did.[3] Still another study corroborated the sex-differentiated emphasis and found that girls with middle-class background showed persistent preoccupation with popularity and social success.[4]

The most pronounced emphasis on popularity was found among girls whose fathers occupied managerial, business, and professional positions commonly referred to as upper middle class. These girls daydreamed of popularity and often cited it as a source of worry. They indicated that they would like to have more social skill, be more popular, and be more accepted by peers. This preoccupation

[1] National Norms for Entering College Freshmen, annual reports for 1966, 1967, 1968, 1969, 1970, 1971, 1972 (Washington, D.C.: Office of Research, American Council on Education).

[2] James S. Coleman, *The Adolescent Society* (New York: Free Press, 1963), p. 30.

[3] H. H. Remmers and D. H. Radler, *The American Teenager* (New York: Bobbs-Merrill, 1962), p. 85.

[4] Elizabeth Douvan and Joseph Adelson, *The Adolescent Experience* (New York: John Wiley, 1966), p. 406.

was not exclusively a result of the standards of the high school crowd, but was reinforced by the middle-class parents. Lower-class girls and boys, regardless of specific family circumstances, were markedly less concerned about popularity.

A longitudinal study specifically prepared for this book shows that the importance attached to being popular in the high school crowd has only changed slightly over the past years.[5] Samples taken from the same suburban high school in the Phoenix metropolitan area were surveyed in 1976 and in 1982. The 1976 responses to the question "How important is it to be liked and accepted by other teenagers?" showed that 47 percent felt it to be of "very great importance," 37 percent of "great importance," 14 percent of "some importance," and 2 percent of "no importance." The 1982 distribution was, respectively, 17, 37, 41, and 4 percent (1 percent no response). The 1982 proportions show a marked increase of the "some-importance" category. However, the "no-importance" category changed little, showing an increase of only 2 percent. When combining all categories that report "importance," comparison between 1976 and 1982 shows an insignificant decrease from 98 to 95 percent.

Likewise, the respondents in both surveys chose very similar *criteria* of popularity. Both distributions of answers to the question "What is expected of a teenager by his or her friends in order to be popular with them?" ranked the conformity principle first (doing, speaking, thinking, dressing, etc., "our way"). Second was what could be summed up as "good personality" (being friendly, cheerful, getting along with others, etc.). Third was "being yourself" or a similar reference to individualism. Fourth was taking an interest in others and helping them. And fifth was being honest and trustworthy. The rank order of these major categories did not change between 1976 and 1982.

There were, however, some changes in the gender-differentiated responses. The 1980s responses showed a diminishing of the girls' previously extremely high emphasis on conformity and now approached the proportion of the boys (roughly a third) who felt conformity was a criterion of popularity. Shifts of gender-differentiated responses were also noticeable in some of the minor categories: While anti-Establishment behavior as a criterion of popularity elicited 2 percent of the boys' and none of the girls' responses in 1976, the responses were reversed in 1982. A shift in the same direction occurred in regard to "having money:" The 1970s responses showed 4 percent of the boys and none of the girls considering it a means to be popular. The 1980s responses showed 3 percent of the boys and 2 percent of the girls considering it so. "Helping and caring," previously an almost exclusive female response, attracted 8 percent of the boys and only 4 percent of the girls. Several of these changes seem to suggest a shift away from the traditional feminine role.

Nonetheless, conformity still seems to be the main price of popularity for both sexes. Other studies have corroborated this and discovered a consistent age

[5] Hans Sebald and Karen Krauss, *A Longitudinal Study of Popularity among Adolescents*, unpublished survey study, Dept. of Sociology, Arizona State University, 1982.

correlation: While conformity is not particularly characteristic of children below seven to nine years of age, it increases thereafter, reaches a peak during early adolescence (around thirteen), and then declines. Young teenagers are therefore more vulnerable to the influence of peers than older adolescents.[6]

What qualities do teenagers seek in a friend? The Douvan and Adelson research found that boys and girls have somewhat different expectations, with the former seeking someone who is first "amiable and nice" and secondly "supporting in trouble," and the latter seeking a friend who first of all is "not a gossip," secondly is "amiable and nice," and thirdly is "supporting in trouble."[7]

Sometimes a teenager's prestige determines desirability as a friend; for a minority, it is a primary criterion for choosing a friend. It is more common, however, that such choices are made on the basis of a combination, such as desirable personality traits and prestige in the group.

The prestige of a friend can cause complications—especially among girls. There is frequent rivalry among girls for popularity with boys. A girl-girl friendship must recognize the problem of differential popularity—that is, popularity sought among boys and popularity sought among girls—and make protective adjustments. This problem has generated an interesting value orientation among girls in general. In order to avoid hostility and envy from her female peer group, the girl who is popular must learn to accept her good fortune modestly. In fact, the adolescent girl ordinarily is far more concerned about her acceptance by other girls and often uses her popularity with boys for its effect on her appraisal by her own sex-peer group.

The definition of friendship has not remained unaffected by the vagaries of sociocultural change. Friendship has become a value of considerable inclusivity among modern teenagers and is now applied to relationships that formerly would have been perceived as romances. A significant portion of heterosexual cohabitations and communal living arrangements, frequently with sexual freedom, are now defined more on the basis of being symbiotic friendships than committed and exclusive love relationships. As a result, sexual relations are no longer considered as extraneous to a friendship as they were during preceding generations and have moved somewhat closer to rational assessment. However, the aura of sexual romanticism is timelessly attractive and never entirely out of reach. Even in a liberated and sexually pragmatic age it is patiently waiting in the wings to be called on to infuse a relationship with the traditional romantic hue.

Nonetheless, sexuality is now more openly admitted, and American teenagers demand not only information but even contraceptive means. Over recent years, many American campuses have dealt with the student demand that college health facilities provide "the pill." The pragmatic attitude toward sexuality is one of the most striking bones of contention between the younger and older generations.

---

[6] Jane E. Brownstone and Richard H. Willis, "Conformity in Early and Late Adolescence," *Developmental Psychology*, 4 (May 1971), 334–37.

[7] Douvan and Adelson, *The Adolescent Experience*, p. 406.

While social scientists are not certain whether the *actual* sexual activities of previous generations have really been drastically different from those of the present one, the outspokenness and matter-of-factness of current sexual expressions are largely unpalatable to the parental generation.

Surveys comparing teenagers' attitudes toward premarital sex indeed found a sharp decline in the opinion of "wrongness" of such behavior between 1950 and 1970. On a scale of 1 to 10 (with 10 being "most wrong") boys in the 1950s averaged a value of 5.1 to the statement "Having sexual relations while unmarried," and boys in the 1970s averaged merely 2.8. Girls in the 1950s averaged 8.2, and in the 1970s only 3.1. Even the statement "Having illicit sexual relations after marriage" yielded a noticeable reduction in "wrongness" between the samples: girls decreased from 9.4 to 7.5, and boys from 8.3 to 6.5.[8]

This liberated attitude can be further illustrated by a study asking adults if they believed sexual intercourse to be acceptable if a couple were engaged: only 20 percent of the adult males and 17 percent adult females said "yes." In a student group, 52 percent of the males and 66 percent of the females answered the same question affirmatively. Another question asked mothers and their daughters to respond to the question, "How important do you think it is that a girl be a virgin when she marries?" Of the mothers, 88 percent answered "very important," 12 percent "somewhat important," and none answered "not important." Of the daughters, 55 percent answered "very important," 34 percent "somewhat important," and 13 percent "not important."[9]

It would be misleading to assume that teenagers look exclusively to their peer group for value orientation. There is no such uniform reference group. In some areas of decisionmaking they align their values with peer standards and in other areas with the views and advice of adults, particularly parents. The Arizona study (Table 10-1) indicates that adolescents are selective in their conformity and in some matters are guided by the opinions of the peer group and in other matters by their parents. In still other matters they listen to both sides, and in some sectors of life they seem uncertain, lacking a definite reference group. For example, in matters of money, choosing courses at school, deciding on future careers and plans to go to college, they tend to consult their parents more than their peers. However, in matters of dating, clothing, hobbies, attending social affairs, choice of magazines, and joining clubs, they follow the opinion and advice of their peers.[10]

The teenagers express uncertainty (or, as some specified, self-reliance) in certain areas. Roughly half of both girls and boys are uncertain whose advice they would follow when it comes to reading books other than school texts (maybe the explanation is the majority's failure to read outside books in the first place), buying magazines, selecting a spouse, going steady, how intimate to be on a date,

---

[8] Ted Goertzel, "Changes in the Values of College Students 1958 to 1970/71," *Pacific Sociological Review*, 15 (April 1972), 235–44.

[9] Ira Reiss, "The Sexual Renaissance: A Survey and Analysis," *Journal of Social Issues*, 22 (April 1966), 123–37.

[10] Sebald and Krauss, 1982.

TABLE 10-1　1982 percent distribution of boys' and girls' responses to the question: If you had to decide between your friends' and your parents' opinion and feeling in the following situations, whose opinion would you consider more important?

	FRIENDS'*		UNCERTAIN**		PARENTS'*	
	BOYS	GIRLS	BOYS	GIRLS	BOYS	GIRLS
1. On what you spend your money	19	2	27	38	54	60
2. Whom to date	41	47	46	40	14	13
3. The clubs you join	54	60	38	33	8	7
4. Advice on personal problems	27	53	24	29	49	18
5. How to dress	43	53	46	44	11	2
6. Which courses to take in school	8	16	35	20	57	64
7. Which hobbies to take up	46	36	41	56	14	9
8. In choosing your future occupation	0	2	35	42	65	56
9. Which social events you attend	65	60	27	29	8	11
10. Whether you go to college or not	0	0	35	36	65	64
11. What books other than those requested by school you read	38	40	49	53	14	7
12. What magazines you buy	46	51	46	47	8	2
13. How often you date	35	24	51	49	14	27
14. Whether you participate in drinking parties	46	40	35	42	19	18
15. In choosing your future spouse	8	9	57	67	35	24
16. Whether you go steady or not	30	29	57	56	14	16
17. How intimate you are on a date	35	24	54	67	11	9
18. To whom you go for information about sex	30	44	32	16	38	40

Source:　Hans Sebald and Karen Krauss, survey data specifically collected for this book, metropolitan area of Phoenix, Arizona, 1982.

*Categories include responses of "definitely" and "probably" friends or parents, respectively.

**24% of the boys and 35% of the girls modified the label of this category by writing in "myself," "own opinion," or something to that effect.

TABLE 10-2 Comparison of 1976 survey with 1982 survey in terms of percent distributions of boys' and girls' responses to the question: If you had to decide between your friends' and your parents' opinion and feeling in the following situations, whose opinion would you consider more important?

SURVEY QUESTIONS	'76:FRIENDS' BOYS	'76:FRIENDS' GIRLS	'82:FRIENDS' BOYS	'82:FRIENDS' GIRLS	'76:UNCERTAIN* BOYS	'76:UNCERTAIN* GIRLS	'82:UNCERTAIN** BOYS	'82:UNCERTAIN** GIRLS	'76:PARENTS' BOYS	'76:PARENTS' GIRLS	'82:PARENTS' BOYS	'82:PARENTS' GIRLS
1. On what you spend your money	45	22	19	2	24	23	27	38	31	55	54	30
2. Whom to date	64	54	41	47	32	29	46	40	4	17	14	13
3. Clubs you join	71	66	54	60	23	25	38	2	6	7	8	7
4. Advice on personal problems	40	60	27	53	23	5	24	29	37	35	49	18
5. How to dress	63	62	43	53	31	29	46	44	6	9	11	2
6. Courses you tak school	42	22	8	16	26	34	35	20	33	44	57	64
7. Hobbies to take	66	54	46	36	28	36	41	56	6	10	14	9
8. Choosing your future occupation	10	4	0	2	47	31	35	42	43	64	65	56
9. Social events you attend	76	77	65	60	20	13	27	29	4	10	8	11

10. College or not	11	7	0	0	38	23	35	36	51	70	65	64
11. Books you read other than those requested by school	52	50	38	40	41	42	49	53	8	8	14	7
12. Magazines you buy	62	54	46	51	34	40	46	47	4	6	8	2
13. How often you date	62	19	35	24	26	24	51	49	12	57	14	27
14. Whether you participate in drinking parties	62	54	46	40	20	20	35	42	18	26	19	18
15. Choosing future spouse	27	9	8	9	47	49	57	67	27	42	35	24
16. Going steady or not	54	21	30	29	32	47	57	56	14	32	14	16
17. Intimacy on a date	53	33	35	24	39	50	54	67	8	17	11	9
18. Whom to go for info about sex	46	34	30	44	30	23	32	16	24	43	38	40

Source: Hans Sebald and Karen Krauss, survey data collected for this book, metropolitan area of Phoenix, Arizona, 1976, 1982.

*17% of the boys and 16% of the girls amended this category by writing in "myself" or "own opinion."

**24% of the boys and 33% of the girls amended this category by writing in "myself" or "own opinion."

and how often to date. Uncertainties in exactly these areas prevailed among the high schoolers of six years earlier. (See Table 10-2.) But a serendipitous finding revealed that one thing had changed: In 1976 17 percent of the boys and 16 percent of the girls had amended their "uncertain" responses by saying that he or she was guided by "myself" or "own opinion." The proportions of "uncertain" responses increased in 1982 to 24 percent of the boys and an astounding 33 percent of the girls. This was purely the initiative of the respondents, since this option had not been listed on the questionnaire.

Such a response possibly signals increasing individualism and, conversely, decreasing familism of teenagers of the 1980s. It may specifically signal increasing female liberation, since many more girls than boys shifted from parent orientation to "uncertain" or self-reliant. While the 1976 girls sought significantly more parental advice than boys in seventeen out of the eighteen areas, the 1982 girls sought more parental advice in only six out of the eighteen areas. On the other side, the 1976 girls were more "uncertain" than boys in eight of the eighteen areas, while in 1982 they were more "uncertain" (or self-reliant) in eleven of the eighteen areas. (See Table 10-2.)

Sex-differentiated responses are clearly visible in a number of items. In the 1976 as well as in the 1982 survey, boys significantly more often than girls turn to friends' opinions in regard to how to spend money, whereas girls more often listen to their parents in this respect. "Advice on personal problems" has always elicited a more peer-oriented response from girls. This might be explained by the possibility that girls understand "personal problems" to include matters of feminine hygiene, a realm where girls tend to consult girl friends more often than parents. This tendency may also be reflected by the 44 percent of girls vs. 30 percent of the boys who go to friends for information about sex. Generally, however, the 1982 survey suggests a far less gender-differentiated picture than the earlier survey.

The identical eighteen questions were asked in a 1960 survey in a suburban high school of Columbus, Ohio, a school socioeconomically (largely middle class), religiously, and ethnically (largely Protestant and white) comparable to the Phoenix metropolitan school.[11] Adding data from that survey to the longitudinal view introduced above enables us to compare the responses of 1960, 1976, and 1982. Scrutiny of the responses reveals that certain changes have occurred over this period and that these changes indicate how the role of parents in the lives of teenagers has fluctuated. We can generalize that 1960 was characterized by conservative, parent-oriented attitudes, 1976 by powerful peer orientation, and 1982 by a balancing of the peer and parental reference groups.

Comparing 1960 and 1976 reveals a loss of parental influence and shows a sweeping shift toward peer orientation in *all* areas. Some of the more radical shifts (amounting to at least 20 percent) away from parent orientation affected the areas

---

[11] Hans Sebald, *The Crisis of Adolescent Discontinuity*, mimeographed research report. The Ohio State University, Columbus, Ohio, 1960.

of how to spend money, whom and how often to date, going steady, clothes, which courses to take at school, which social events to attend, and participation at drinking parties. However, other decreases are just as significant, especially when considering that the time-honored tradition of consulting parents in matters of personal problems and troubles declined by 15 percent. There were also declines in following parental advice in career plans, going to parents for sex information, and seeking parental advice about mate selection. (See details in Table 10-3).

Comparing 1976 and 1982 reveals that by the 1980s parents had partly recovered the territory they had lost during the 1960s and 1970s to peer influence or to the "uncertain/self-reliant" attitude. Perhaps the pressure of the economic slump of the early 1980s prompted increases in reliance on parents: 15 percent in money spending, 23 percent in course selections, 7 percent in career questions, 5 percent in college decision, and 2 percent in book purchases. In most areas the increases were minor, and in seven areas the changes were negative, though not as drastic as in 1976. Most of the decreases took place in the social realm, including how to dress, whom and how often to date, and in the private realm, such as advice in personal or sexual problems.

From the vantage point of the 1980s, reliance on parental advice has not recovered its 1960 standing. With the sole exception of consulting parents on college plans (only 2 percent increase over 1960), all eighteen areas have experienced decreases in parental consultation. The sharpest decreases exist in social and personal affairs, with decisions about dating, dressing, and partying now being more "uncertain" or dependent on the teenager's own taste and opinion.

The generalizations of the Ohio-Arizona surveys could be refined by controlling a number of variables, among them, for example, dropout-proneness and graduation-orientation. Identifying respondents by one of the two categories might result in a polarized picture, showing the former type of student more aligned with the peer culture and the latter with parental values. Lucius F. Cervantes' study found a sharp cleavage between the two types, establishing that dropout-prone students indeed have their own peer culture.[12] This finding deserves to be verified in future studies. In the meantime we accept the Ohio-Arizona findings as showing that teenagers in general cultivate divided reference groups, selectively looking to peers and parents for advice and guidance.

The demand of the parents to be taken seriously as a reference group is not always obeyed. Gallup Polls found that teenager-parent arguments erupt over a number of issues. Asking parents of teenage children "What do you argue about most with your teenager(s)?," the poll found a number of major clashes: 18 percent about chores/housework, 15 percent about freedom/responsibilities, 12 percent about evening curfew, 9 percent about homework, 8 percent about money, 6 percent about where the teenagers go, and 5 percent about choice of friends and

---

[12] Lucius F. Cervantes, *American Youth Culture: Independent or Dependent?* Paper read at the Annual Convention of the American Sociological Association, Chicago, 1965.

TABLE 10-3 Changes of proportions of teenagers seeking parental advice in 18 areas between 1960, 1976, and 1982. (Boys and girls combined.)

AREAS	PERCENT OF TEENAGERS SEEKING PARENTAL ADVICE			PERCENT CHANGE		
	1960	1976	1982	1960-1976	1976-1982	1960-1982
1. On what to spend money	62	42	57	−20	+15	− 5
2. Whom to date	31	10	13	−21	+ 3	−18
3. The clubs you join	23	6	7	−17	+ 1	−16
4. Advice on personal problems	51	36	32	−15	− 4	−19
5. How to dress	35	7	6	−28	− 1	−29
6. Which courses to take at school	69	38	61	−31	+23	− 8
7. Which hobbies you take up	14	8	11	− 6	+ 3	− 3
8. In choosing your future occupation	64	53	60	−11	+ 7	− 4
9. Which social events you attend	30	6	10	−24	+ 4	−20
10. Whether you go to college or not	63	60	65	− 3	+ 5	+ 2
11. What books other than those requested by school you read	20	8	10	−12	+ 2	−10
12 What magazines you buy	21	5	5	−16	none	−16
13. How often you date	58	33	21	−25	−12	−37
14. Whether you participate in drinking parties	64	23	18	−41	− 5	−46
15. In choosing your future spouse	39	34	29	− 5	− 5	−10
16. Whether you go steady or not	41	21	15	−20	− 6	−26
17. How intimate you are on a date	23	12	10	−11	− 2	−13
18. To whom you go for information about sex	48	32	39	−16	+ 7	− 9

Source: Hans Sebald, *The Crisis of Adolescent Discontinuity*, mimeographed research report, The Ohio State University, Columbus, Ohio, 1960; and Hans Sebald and Karen Krauss, survey data collected for this book, metropolitan area of Phoenix, Arizona, 1976, 1982.

dates.[13] In general, 30 percent of the parents felt that they were not strict enough with their teenage offspring, 11 percent felt they were too strict, 54 percent thought they were just about right, and the rest qualified their responses or had no opinion.[14]

Important attitudes held by teenagers concern their sexual activities. Over the past ten years there has been talk about a New Sexuality, evidently characterized by liberated attitudes and equally unrestrained behavior. Statistics showing evidence of increased and ever younger sexual involvement has been cited earlier in the text and thus here we will only summarize youth's attitudes correlated with or underlying the New Sexuality:

Noncommittal sexuality. Sex is accepted as pleasure, and the fulfillment of it is not seen as requiring a commitment stipulating exclusivity, loyalty, or continuous personal care and concern. The New Sexuality implies the intention of the young to preserve as much independence and individualism as possible—and yet to enjoy sexual intimacy. This endeavor can already be observed in dating patterns. Many parents have been surprised and baffled to notice that their offspring are increasingly abandoning old-fashioned couple-only dating, preferring group dating where a number of friends of both sexes get together for common activities such as partying, going to movies, riding around, or attending social events. The decision to join in the evening's events is usually made independently by each participant without being contingent upon a specific invitation by a member of the opposite sex. When it is time to go home, pairing-off decisions may be made. It is then that more intimate dyads evolve, with couples engaging in sexual play or intercourse based on a minimum of strain toward commitment, obligations, or repeat performances.

It would be exaggerated, however, to say that this new pattern has replaced the dating dyad; it is more correct to see the new development as a modification of older dating habits or as an additional option.

An extension of noncommittal sex can take the form of cohabitation. This, however, involves usually more than just mere license for sex. It is an arrangement among older teenagers and young adults, and, most significantly, is a form of subcultural institutionalization that will be discussed later in the chapter.

Tolerance or acceptance of varying sexuality. Sexual liberation includes many of the sexual expressions previously considered deviant. It is largely to the credit of the vocal counterculture and the women's movement that homosexuality and lesbianism are now looked upon as relatively acceptable alternatives and no longer as pathological aberrations. Many homosexuals now openly admit their orientation and insist on being respected as such. The avant-garde of sexual liberation is found among college and university students, who cultivate a tolerance (at

---

[13] *Gallup Opinion Index 1978*, #156, pp. 22-23.
[14] Ibid., p. 24.

least in theory) that is not necessarily shared with other segments of the population. The academic institution has a history of combining tolerance and intellectualism to promote the cause of the deviant and the underdog.

Female sexual liberation.   As spelled out earlier (especially in Chapters 2 and 5), the most important aspect of the New Sexuality is the changing role of women. Young women have become more aware of their own sexuality and seek equal satisfaction. Young males increasingly view the female as an active partner in the world of sex.

Attitude changes between phases in the life span.   Liberalized experimentation often fails to yield the expected results. On the basis of books, movies, talks, rumors, and pseudoacademic promises, adolescents are faced with sexually superhuman promises that sooner or later must lead to frustration and disappointment. From the author's counseling experiences with college students, it appears that many young persons are disappointed by their initial sexual experience. The failure of sex to be as glamorous as expected tends to downgrade the value of sexuality. This disillusionment becomes crucial when it is combined with the failure to establish a secure human relationship. Inexperienced teenage lovers may be left deeply disillusioned with sex as a cure for alienation and loneliness.

Such experiences have manifold results. Those who have been hurt may seek other routes of escape from isolation and may turn to drugs, suicide, creative sublimation, or a new Victorianism. The last reaction rejects the New Sexuality and turns toward a New Asceticism which is expected to heal disappointment, solve confusion, and supply missing psychological security.

This reversal pattern may actually be a *generational* experience in which most young people go through the liberated, disappointed, and finally puritanical stages, ultimately becoming relatively conservative adults. Such a pattern may well explain in large part why there always exists a mass of conservative adults who just a few years prior were rebellious youngsters. It may also explain why each adult generation continues to view premarital sex as deviant behavior.

The realism/romanticism seesaw.   The New Sexuality is inimical to a sense of romanticism. Sexual realism deprived the young of the mystery of sexuality that used to include the reverent ritual, passion-amplifying delay, pulse-raising awe, ideal-inspiring imagination, and every sort of sublimation. The New Sexuality has branded these mental gyrations as dishonest and fallacious. Shooting down romantic pathos also killed the mystique of sex, and the survivors found themselves with banal physical lovemaking that soon conveyed a feeling of relative deprivation.

Combined with the heady sense of freedom was a sometimes uneasy feeling of pressure to take advantage of the new freedom. As Dustin Hoffman said in *The Graduate:* "I'm starting to feel the same way about getting laid as I did about getting into college."

This upswing in educational participation by America's young modified the functions of secondary education. No longer were high school graduates destined only for college, but instead primarily for business and industry. Concomitant with the growth of the proportion of teenagers attending high school was a decline in the proportion of graduates enrolling in college. The college-entering proportion dropped from two-thirds in 1900 to about half in 1920 and finally to about one-third in 1940, indicating that the majority of teenagers preferred to go directly into jobs after graduation. This preference stimulated significant changes in secondary school curricula. Preparation became centered on immediate vocational fields rather than on extended higher education. This new emphasis gave rise, indeed often priority, to such short-range and "practical" goals as typing, bookkeeping, industrial arts, shop, and mechanics.

The change in the function of the high school, coupled with the coercive nature of attendance, has produced an essentially new atmosphere in the secondary school system. Academic preparation is no longer the prime objective; rather, general "life preparation" has moved to the forefront. An NEA committee attested to the new orientation in 1918 by issuing seven basic principles of secondary education: health, command of fundamental mental processes, mature home-membership, vocational preparation, civic education, constructive use of leisure time, and ethical character. More than academic endeavor, the pursuit of these principles constitutes a general program for "life adjustment." The responsibilities of high school teachers now include not only transmission of knowledge, but also character formation, the instillment of motivation, and the counseling of personal problems. In essence, by taking over character-forming functions from the family, secondary education became more a place of general socialization than of information service. Furthermore, this socialization experience was not optional; teenagers had to submit to it, and teachers were burdened with the extra task of convincing them that school was worthwhile.

This is not the end of the story of modern education in the United States, however. Industrialization and automation have progressed to the point where the lack of demand for youth's labor continues after high school. College education has developed into another means of preventing youth from swamping the labor market, while at the same time trying to prepare them for the ever-increasing number of white-collar and other sophisticated positions. As a consequence, the steady decline of the proportion of high school graduates enrolling in college from 1900 to the 1940s is being reversed. Since 1950, there has been a 10 percent average annual increase in students entering college for the first time to work toward a degree. However, during the 1980s there has been a slowdown, with the number of those entering college increasing by only 2 percent in 1982. Starting in 1984, a steady decline is forecast. The decline will be due to decreasing numbers of eighteen-to-twenty-four-year-olds in the population, not to a decreasing proportion of youth enrolling in college.

In any case, the American public is now almost as concerned about the college dropout as it is about the high school dropout. Postindustrial conditions do as members of this class, and before or directly after the eighth grade they generally left school to work with the agricultural family unit. Similarly, workers' sons left school to become apprenticed for a trade.

The adulation of secondary and higher education is thus relatively new. It would be a misconception, however, to interpret this development as the exclusive result of adherence to a value *in abstracto*. Pragmatic reasons underlie this valuation. One involves the fruits of education and vocational training, which have increased the amenities of life. Another reason, currently most pressing, is the need to keep teenagers out of the labor force. This necessity has developed with industrialization, automation, antichild-labor legislation, and the rural-urban migration. At the same time, automation has arrested the increase of blue-collar jobs while expanding the number of white-collar positions that require high school training—clerks, accountants, salespeople, and office workers. In effect, the division of labor no longer needs—or even allows—the labor of children. Barred from the labor force as well as from free-roaming idleness, America's teenagers were "institutionalized" and delivered into the care of high schools. The institution of secondary education not only kept them out of the way, but even succeeded in preparing some of them for the new white-collar jobs. High school education ceased to be a voluntary matter chosen by the few who prepared for higher education and became an involuntary mandate for all. Statistics illustrate the trend: in 1900, 11 percent of the high-school-aged youngsters attended school; in 1920, 32 percent; in 1930, 51 percent; in 1940, 73 percent; and in the 1960s the percentage achieved a level of over 90 percent, at which it has remained ever since.[2]

The expanding role of high school in the lives of the young is also illustrated by the percentage of young adults (twenty-five to thirty-four years old) who *completed* four years of high school. The proportion of white males was 36 percent in 1940, 51 percent in 1950, 59 percent in 1966, 77 percent in 1970, and 82 percent in the mid 1970s. For white females, the proportion was 41 percent in 1940, 55 percent in 1950, 63 percent in 1960, 75 percent in 1970, and 81 percent in the mid 1970s. For black males, the proportion was 10 percent in 1940, 18 percent in 1950, 30 percent in 1960, 49 percent in 1970, and 67 percent in the mid 1970s. For black females, the proportion was 12 percent in 1940, 22 percent in 1950, 36 percent in 1960, 57 percent in 1970, and 64 percent in the mid 1970s.[3]

These figures show that over approximately the past thirty-five years the white males' high school graduation rate has increased by 46 percent and the white females' by 41 percent; the black males' by 57 percent, and the black females' by 51 percent. These data reveal that the blacks' increase was about 10 percent higher, diminishing the 1940 black-white differential of 27 percent for the males to 15 percent by the mid 1970s, and that of females from 29 percent to 17 percent.

² Ibid.

³ *Standard Education Almanac 1975-76*, 8th ed. (Chicago: Marquis Academic Media, 1975), p. 63.

When circumstances are created that are so realistic that they allow complete insight into the everyday life of the other sex, romantic feelings go out the window. Surveys found that men and women sharing coed dorms prefer to bring in sex partners from outside.

The desire for romanticism is strong. Our Western civilization is permeated with romantic attitudes and promises waiting to be called upon to embellish human relationships that otherwise appear too sober and unexciting. Whether the New Sexuality can maintain itself in the face of such historical force must be ascertained in the future.

Conflicting emotions and desires. Though the New Sexuality has fulfilled some heretofore frustrated needs and desires, new needs and problems have arisen. Although, for example, sexual tension is released and a source of fun and pleasure tapped, the lack of personal commitment may endanger psychological security and lead to anxiety. The prevalent emotional repercussion to adolescent sexuality during the era of repressive mores was feelings of guilt and shame; the new emotional response is anxiety and a vague feeling of meaninglessness. This anomic version of the sexual relationship seems to weigh heavily on the minds of the young. Humans display a natural need for norms and predictability—especially when it comes to sexual relationships—and a phase of liberal excursion is usually followed by a phase of reconsideration and conservatism.

There are indications that casual sexuality is being gradually replaced by older monogamous rules. As a college woman put it: "It's all right to live with your boy-friend, but to sleep around isn't all right." There is a lessening of the endorsement, if there ever was one, of promiscuity. Apparently, noncommittal sex makes gratifying intimacy difficult. Young people want more than sexual relief; they want human relatedness that is difficult to derive from ephemeral episodes, and they even seem to be willing to sacrifice some of their sacred independence to regain some of the benefits of the old-fashioned twosome.

Attitudes vs. behavior. Many people are tempted to equate a verbal statement about behavior with behavior as such. The New Sexuality consists to a large degree only of the New Verbiage—a greater outspokenness, a greater willingness to express and look at the fact of human sexuality. Symptomatic of this new expressiveness are pornography, four-letter expletives, and coed dorms.

But, alas, the actual implementation of the verbal liberality may be slightly different. Though change in attitudes is quick and seemingly radical, behavior neither follows at the same pace nor to the same extent. Insofar as it concerns *attitudes*, the New Sexuality represents indeed a new and somewhat radical change, but actual sexual behavior still has a way to go before matching the verbal openness.

The emotional lag. The old sexual mores are by no means forgotten. They still exist and work their now-muted webs. The liberation has not totally obscured the old "rights and wrongs," and though many young Americans speak—and perhaps even act—as if liberated from them, they still respond to them on an emotional, albeit unconscious level. Though it may be true that the more prevalent modern reaction to premarital sex is anxiety (the typical reaction to normlessness), there are many who suffer guilt and shame as a consequence of the old proscriptive standards.

Diversity of standards. Though it is probably true that sexuality is now more acknowledged and accepted, it does not follow that young people choose no restrictions at all. Those growing up with a religious commitment tend to disassociate themselves from the New Sexuality. Religious commitment is still the strongest foe of the New Sexuality. Another obstacle to sexual liberality is the traditionally greater sexual conservatism of girls, which still is not entirely abolished. Although girls may now be more liberal with their boyfriends and fiancés, most still frown on casual sex.

The academic fabrication of the New Sexuality. There is exaggeration in the accounts of social scientists when they indulge in the grand forecasting of changing sexual behavior. For example, Herbert H. Otto, chairperson of the National Center for the Exploration of Human Potential, forecast in 1971 that "there are 12,000 communes in the U.S. and I foresee that within five years, 20 percent of American families will be involved in them."[15] Such misextrapolation gives the impression that modern marriage, family, and sexual patterns are changing radically.

Another example of possible misinterpretation is the high premarital pregnancy rate, which is attributed to a higher premarital coitus rate. While this may be so, this rate is not an accurate indicator since it may merely be a function of fewer young people feeling obliged to marry because of the pressure that such pregnancy exerts.

Tenuous interpretations have led some social scientists to predict and even recommend changes in lifestyles. For example, well-known humanistic psychologists have suggested exploring the many dimensions of monogamy, reinventing marriage by "engaging in serial polygamy" (Sidney Jourard), and trying out an "intimate network of families" for collective problem solving (Frederick Stoller).[16]

Sexologist Albert Ellis interprets cohabitation as an intelligent decision to learn whom not to marry. It is not a "copping out" of human responsibilities. Ellis' opinion is that "anybody who marries without living with someone for at least six months is copping out."[17] He also foresees a change in the family structure that

[15] "Marriage and Family," *Arizona Republic*, December, 1971, p. 47.

[16] Herbert A. Otto, "Has Monogamy Failed?" *Saturday Review*, April 26, 1970, pp. 25, 62.

[17] "Noted Psychologist Is Seminar Speaker," *Arizona Republic*, June 24, 1972, p. 51.

allows "legalized adultery," i.e., two people will marry mostly for each other but will have casual sexual experiences with others. Lawrence Casler, in *Is Marriage Necessary?*, proposes a similar restructuring of traditional marriage, allowing for "permissive matrimony."[18] The list of academic supporters of the New Sexuality could be expanded.

Though many academic suggestions are based on valid insight, some are unduly generalized and give an exaggerated picture of changed social and sexual mores. Social scientists are heavily influenced in their opinions by their immediate social environment, which is relatively isolated in academia. Their students live in an artificial hothouse climate that is significantly different from the world of working people. Their attitudes and behavior patterns tend to influence the interpretations of sociology and psychology professors, whose research more often than not samples this population, leading them to believe that what their students say and do is what *American youth* says and does.

For example, the mostly theoretical tolerance of sexual practices previously defined as deviant is not only not shared by nonacademic Americans but is often abandoned by college graduates when they enter the world of employment and family life. Much of their professed tolerance adds up to verbiage merely deemed sophisticated and liberated among college peers.

The academic factor has been discussed in order to warn of the intrusion of bias into the formulation of the New Sexuality. To some extent its formulation has been inspired by academicians who are overimpressed by the immediacy and vociferousness of students.

In sum, these are qualifications that must be added in order to understand more clearly the complexity and instability of the New Sexuality. Some of the forces of modification deserve close attention, for they may work toward a Newer Sexuality.

Another teenage in-group attitude deals with anti-intellectualism. Learnedness has always been the nemesis of popularity and friendship, and it usually is laid down on the altar of peer acceptance as the sacrificial offering for "belonging." Nothing has changed in this respect, and various studies have borne this out—from the early Purdue Opinion Panel (60 percent disdained intellectualism and preferred to be popular rather than brilliant) to the Goertzel survey that showed an even further increase in anti-intellectualism.[19] What are the social psychological dynamics behind this almost invariable pattern?

The young teenager must be understood in terms of *subcultural* involvement. The individual reaches adolescence conditioned in the skills of group membership, having learned how to get along with peers and to do the accepted things. Naturally other-directed and with little self-consciousness, he or she is attuned to behave in concert with others. As an adolescent, he or she enters a life phase that increasingly

[18] Lawrence Casler, *Is Marriage Necessary?* (New York: Human Sciences Press, 1974).
[19] Ted Goertzel, "Changes in the Values of College Students 1958 to 1970/71," *Pacific Sociological Review*, 15 (April 1972), 235–244.

calls for independence. But at the same time he or she becomes even more sensitive to the security he or she has enjoyed among peers. It is now that he or she relies on the subculture most heavily—and this subculture demands conformity. Deviation from group norms would incur alienation—a dreadful punishment for any youngster. For the most part, idiosyncratic qualities among members are suppressed. Intellectual pursuits constitute such idiosyncrasies and are immediately suspect. Researchers have shown that this attitude runs through the core of secondary schooling and that "friendliness, popularity, and mediocrity" are more highly regarded than being a "good student."

Modern education often employs the self-defeating *individual* approach when learning problems arise, overlooking the fact that the teenager is essentially other-directed and marches to the drumbeat of peers. Learning problems are frequently not individual problems but are *social* problems with the intellectually negating power structure of the adolescent peer group being the hostile background. Some sociologists have suggested that we seriously explore ways of moving adolescent peer groups collectively toward intellectual interests, rather than continue the futile piecemeal attempts to correct individual students in the hope of diverting them from identifying with their peers.

Attitudes toward the Establishment.   American youth, and probably Western youth generally, in the early 1980s reflected somewhat different attitudes toward the Establishment than their peers of the stormy '60s and '70s. Anti-Establishment outbursts had become muted and the young had turned from protest rallies to school work. There was also some renewal of concern for the future of the country and a longing for the traditions that proved to be of comfort in the past. Although the values were no longer the militant ones of the '60s and '70s, they were still far from having reverted to the conventions of precountercultural years. No single label—conservative or liberal, conventional or radical, "turned off" or "turned on"—fit the young of the early '80s. They were reaching adulthood under conditions of greater complexity and more vexing conflict than previous generations. It is therefore not surprising to discover similar complexity and conflict reflected in the views and values of the young of the '80s.

Moral attitudes.   In respect to human relationships there are incongruent—some might say hypocritical—attitudes. On one hand, there is the young's reluctance to embrace traditional standards of exclusivity, loyalty, and dedication in their dating and mating habits. On the other hand they are critical of family and marriage problems in the adult world. As one teenager complained, "I know only one family among my friends where the parents aren't divorced. It's awful!"

In respect to the ethics of voluntary social service, youthful volunteerism has not yet regained the levels of the '50s and '60s. The Offer-Ostrov-Howard surveys, stretching over nearly twenty years, found that the 1960s subjects had the highest ethics score, suggesting that they had somewhat more stable and well-structured ethical standards than the young of the 1970s. The latter seemed to have turned more inward, and reflected a greater concern for themselves than for others.[20]

Political attitudes. Compared with the generation of the counterculture, the young of the '80s are quieter, less conspicuous in dress and manners, and less prone to exhibit radical views or actions. The reasons for being subdued include ending of the Viet Nam War, the abating of racial problems, and improvement in the area of civil rights. These problems, at their glaring heights, presented clear targets against which the young could vent their anger. The problems of the '80s are less clear and much more complex, the villains and heroes are less definable, and it is difficult to build up a sense of moral outrage. Add to this the economic difficulties of the early 1980s, and you have a generation that is more concerned with personal advancement and economic security than with lofty causes.

The calmer political climate is reflected in the Carnegie Council on Policy Studies in Higher Education, in which college students calling themselves "left to liberal" dropped from 44 to 35 percent between 1969 and 1975.[21] While the Yankelovich surveys of the early '70s indicated widespread unhappiness of the young with the American system (nearly two-thirds felt the nation was democratic in name only), the mood lifted by the end of the decade and approximately two-thirds opined that "the United States system of government is the best in the world."[22]

Yet the lesson of the demoralizing Viet Nam War was not lost on the young, and few national issues have continued to be as controversial as the military draft. Some of the outbursts disturbing the youthful calm of the early '80s were directed against conscription. Nonetheless, there is fear of war and worry about the nation's readiness. The peculiar combination of unwillingness to serve in the military and the concern about the war has created confusion and a lack of luster in the nation's youth.

In this connection, a 1982 survey prepared for this book tried to assess college students' attitudes toward nuclear armament and war. Asked to check one item on an escalating scale, the respondents' attitudes toward nuclear armament and war against the Soviet Union became apparent. The sample consisted of 144 Arizona State University undergraduates, 58 percent women and 42 percent men, scattered throughout most majors, with the main categories being business 21 percent, sociology 15 percent, social work 13 percent, criminal justice 9 percent, and psychology 8 percent. The majority fell into the eighteen-to-twenty-two age category and were a nearly nationally representative cross-section in terms of socio-economic backgrounds. The possible responses ranged from "The U.S. should

[20] Daniel Offer, Eric Ostrov, and Kenneth I. Howard, *The Adolescent: A Psychological Self-Portrait* (New York: Basic Books, 1981), pp. 56–57.

[21] "Today's Students: More Conservative, But Not Much," *Psychology Today*, June 1977, p. 94.

[22] "Youth on the Move," *U.S. News and World Report*, January 5, 1981, p. 72.

unilaterally disarm, regardless of whether the Soviet Union disarms or not" to "We should attack the Soviet Union now, and not wait and see what they might do or not do." Over half of the subjects preferred bilateral disarmament, i.e., only if the Soviets agreed to disarm simultaneously. It is interesting that not one of the respondents opted for the radical "attack now!" choice. Women seem to be more polarized on the issue, choosing twice as frequently as men the categories of "unilateral disarmament" and "never disarmament." (See details in Table 10-4.)

TABLE 10-4   Distribution of a sample of college students' attitudes toward nuclear armament and war against the Soviet Union.

ATTITUDE CATEGORIES	RESPONDENTS					
	MALE N = 61	100%	FEMALE N = 83	100%	TOTAL N = 144	100%
1. The United States should unilaterally disarm, regardless of whether the Soviets disarm or not.	5	8	15	18	20	14
2. The U.S. should bilaterally disarm; i.e., only if the Soviets agree to disarm at the same time.	37	61	37	46	74	51
3. The U.S. should disarm only if the Soviets disarm first.	4	7	2	2	6	4
4. The U.S. should never disarm, regardless of what the Soviets do.	7	10	17	20	24	17
5. We should attack the Soviet Union *now*, and not wait and see what they might do or not do.	0	0	0	0	0	0
6. I don't know what to do.	8	14	12	14	20	14

Source: Hans Sebald, survey prepared for this text, Arizona State University, 1982.

Another study examined the question of whether knowledge about a certain subject matter is related to attitudes about the same matter, and it used the issue of the war in Vietnam as a test. Hans Sebald and Rudolfo Gallegos quizzed over 400 college students on their knowledge of Southeast Asia and the war and on their attitudes toward American involvement.[23] The sample was divided into 110 antiwar demonstrators, 50 prowar partisans, and 276 students whose noncommittal attitude

[23] Hans Sebald and Rudolfo N. Gallegos, "Voices of War and Peace – What do They Know? Attitudes and Knowledge About the War in Southeast Asia," *Pacific Sociological Review*, 14 (October 1971), 487–510.

put them within the purview of the so-called silent majority. All of the students were given identical sets of questions relating to political, geographic, military, and historical conditions of Vietnam and adjacent areas. The "doves" did best, getting 55 percent correct; the "hawks" scored 47 percent, and the silent majority only 45 percent. Higher scores among the activists had been expected since they were the ones who had to defend their dissent, but all scores were surprisingly low. Also, the differences between the groups were not significant.

The lack of knowledge of a vital national as well as international issue was astounding: 25 percent of the students could not identify North and South Vietnam on an unmarked map; 33 percent were unable to name a single ally fighting with the United States; less than 10 percent could name a single North Vietnamese leader; and 25 percent could not even name Saigon as the capital of South Vietnam. This was at the height of the war (1970), when over forty thousand young American men had lost their lives!

The conclusion is that there is hardly a correlation between knowledge and attitude, and that emotionality, expressiveness, and vociferousness about a given issue are relatively *independent* of knowledge about the issue. It seems that the genesis of an attitude does not lie at the root of knowledge or ignorance, but at the root of emotional predisposition and basic orientation–a condition to be remembered when we look at the variously expressed attitudes of youth.

Economic attitudes.   For generations, Americans have modeled their ideas of success after the Protestant ethic, with occupational status, money, investment, and possessions as focal points. The new generation seems to have shifted its preoccupation to various forms of self-fulfillment, moving psychological demands to the forefront. The new emphasis has effected corresponding changes in their sense of obligation to friends, family, employer, and community. Materialistic-competitive attitudes of old have given way to a privatism that cultivates social and political isolationism and aims at the satisfaction of personal psychological needs. The genesis of this attitude must be sought not merely in temporary reactions to political events, but in postindustrial conditions that encourage and allow exactly this type of self-service.

The nadir of the work ethic was reached during the late '60s and early '70s, when only about half of young Americans believed that "hard work always pays off."[24] In the meantime, with economic hardship providing motivation, the work ethic has made a modest comeback.

Nevertheless, it is surprising that young Americans remain relatively unimpressed by the economic crisis and somehow seem to assume that some satisfactory economic security will materialize for them. This is not so much personal optimism as it is a new *philosophy of entitlement* anchored in the burgeoning American welfare state. With the counterculture evolved a curious conversion of wants and

[24] Daniel Yankelovich, *The New Morality: A Profile of American Youth in the '70s* (New York: McGraw–Hill, 1974), p. 26.

desires into presumed "rights." This evolution of "social rights" feelings manifests itself in such attitudes as students assuming that they are entitled to codetermine how to run a university. The desire "I'd like a creative and enjoyable career" becomes the righteous demand that "I am entitled to a creative and enjoyable career." The desire "I'd like a secure income" becomes "I am entitled to a secure income." While the tendency to feel righteous about one's desires is natural and has been with us for a long time, the equation of desire with right has grown significantly in the current generation. Whether the equation can be solved is of course another question.

Notwithstanding the new philosophy of entitlement, careerism is as strong as ever. Concentrating on a career is a natural function of privatism, which is typical of modern youth. Careerism is particularly evident among modern young women. Increasing numbers of them put the career first and having a family second; while wanting both, they want them in this sequence.[25]

Religious attitudes. While many American teenagers have declined in traditional religiosity with and since the counterculture, a new religiosity has evolved over the past fifteen to twenty years. The new form is a synthesis of Oriental and Western beliefs. From an historical perspective, the extent to which it has reached masses of young people in virtually all Western societies is an unprecedented development. Theodore Roszak, the chronicler of the counterculture, emphasizes in his book, *The Making of a Counter Culture*, that the infusion of Oriental philosophy was the unique benchmark of the 20th-century counterculture.

One of the bizarre outcomes of the new religious-mystic synthesis is that teenagers who think of themselves as Christians now innocuously add the belief in reincarnation to their personal belief system—notwithstanding the lack of logic or compatibility. Survey data collected and currently analyzed by this author shows that up to 20 percent of college students classifying themselves as Catholics, Protestants, or nonspecific "Christians" believe in reincarnation, karma, and other Oriental or occult notions. The most interesting aspect of this development is that the young synthetic believers, given the historical ignorance of most of them, fail to be aware of the disparate cultural origins of the components of their beliefs and, in the process of trying to integrate the components, create a religious credo that is neither Christian nor Oriental. The making of this religious synthesis was an integral part of the counterculture and thus is better discussed further in the next chapter.

These, then, constitute some aspects of the new cultural values as they are emerging with the young generation. One of the most noteworthy discoveries of the nationwide surveys was the involvement of working noncollege youth in the new cultural trends. In many instances, the traditional and almost customary distinction in attitudes and values between noncollege and college youth has been erased. This is a new development!

[25] "Youth on the Move," p. 76.

While this lack of division may bespeak a keener awareness of life's conditions and chances, it may also herald new frustrations and confusions for this segment of the youth population. This large group (seven out of ten American youths are not college educated) may experience intensified feelings of relative deprivation. Having absorbed the new cultural values of self-fulfillment, enjoyable careers, and the liberated work ethic, they may experience difficulties implementing them in their work life. Their comparatively less interesting and independent work life will offer fewer psychological rewards than that of college-educated people and is bound to exacerbate feelings of inferiority and deprivation. This, indeed, may lead to a split within the youth population that may be more severe and may prove to be more dangerous to American society than the split between generations. American society may soon be confronted with racial demands on the part of young non-college-educated workers for the same enjoyment and privileges as the college-educated workers, and the demands may aim at earlier retirement, shorter work weeks, more generous vacations, greater participation in industrial planning and management, and other methods of reducing the traditional monotony and power-lessness of the industrial worker. The future will most likely bring clashes between the new cultural attitudes and the built-in rigidities and limitations of the industrial work place.

It is interesting that most of the new values had their genesis in the counter-culture of the late 1960s, traveled the customary route through the student population, and have now reached working-class youth. The legacy of the counterculture is now becoming visible in the form of pervasive new cultural attitudes and feelings that affect nearly all segments of the young generation.

Value commitment. A portion of the teenage population manifests values that are harmonious with adult standards. These values are not indigenous to the teen subculture but are expressions of motivation transcending the circle of peers. Justification for discussion of nonsubcultural behavior is twofold: (1) to render a more complete picture of youth in contemporary America and (2) to provide a contrast to subcultural behavior.

Student volunteerism manifests itself in civic concern, political interests, and various social services all across the nation. The commitments include a wide range of voluntary public service programs: tutoring disadvantaged children, assisting the poor with tax returns, entertaining and nursing patients in hospitals, clearing slums, cleaning up ecological disasters, and offering health care for the underprivileged.

Many volunteers work through such organizations as Candy Stripers, 4-H Clubs, Boys' Clubs of America, Tri-Hi-Y, Scout and Camp Fire groups, student governments, and various school clubs. Also, many of the service programs of the religious communities have been supported by young people, including Catholic, Protestant, Jewish, LDS, and other religious organizations. Additional examples of value commitment include teams of medical, dental, and special-education students who go into impoverished Appalachia, giving and teaching badly needed health care; architecture students in many states who design playgrounds and summer camps for underprivileged children; law students in several states who give advice to consumers and teach ghetto children to use the law rather than to fear or despise it; language students at New York high schools who tutor Spanish-speaking people; and young people in many cities who help to maintain "hot line" telephones.

Federal organizations have attracted thousands of young Americans who seek fellowship and the experience to serve others. Thousands of young Americans have served as Peace Corps volunteers in many parts of the world to bring about technological innovations, and at the same time have respected the customs and mores of the natives. The success of the Peace Corps can be attributed to volunteers who (1) put into practice the American value of helpfulness; (2) feel enthusiastic about performing vital tasks; and (3) want to learn more about others and themselves.

Participation in VISTA (Volunteers in Service to America) has been widespread and constructive. A study by sociologist David Gottlieb showed that more than 50 percent of the participating youths felt VISTA had changed their career decisions, and 76 percent said their experience had increased their commitment to solve the nation's problems.[26]

Another federal organization is the Youth Conservation Corps, which pays young Americans a minimum salary and teaches them conservation techniques, often pitching them against forest fires and other disasters. Again, the participants accrue tremendous personal benefits, learn to get along with coworkers of varying ethnic, racial, and socioeconomic backgrounds, and often develop a lasting interest in a conservation career (forestry, fish and game administration, construction, and reclamation work).

The California Conservation Corps is a successful example. Its twenty-five work centers are sworn to the work ethic and are home to nearly 2000 men and women between the ages of eighteen and twenty-three. The CCC members work all day and then, if their literacy is poor, take classes at night—35 percent do because they cannot read beyond a third-grade level. There are no alcohol, drugs, violence, or refusals to work. A member breaking the rules is discharged immediately. For respecting the rules corps members receive $580 a month (minimum wage), but must return $135 for room and board. The skills they learn include sandbagging hillsides to stem floods, smashing boulders to repair High Sierra trails, building recreational facilities, battling forest fires, erecting solar panels, and planting trees. In the early '80s the CCC had a nine-month backlog of requests from all over California to do work that cities and counties could not afford. According to a study, for every dollar invested in the CCC, the state benefited $1.20. As a result, several other states are considering initiating similar projects of their own.[27]

The American Red Cross attracted four million unpaid youth volunteers during the early 1980s. Young people were found to work longer hours, had more energy, and were willing to take physical risks for helping people in need.[28]

---

[26] New York Times Service (May 24, 1971).
[27] "The CCC," *National Wildlife*, 20 (Feb./March 1982), 17–18.
[28] "Youth on the Move," p. 76.

Tornado-devastated Grand Island, Nebraska, benefitted from youth volunteers, some of whom put in 90 hours a week. A 1980 Washington, D.C., fire left 140 people homeless, and youth volunteers helped set up shelter with food, blankets, and other needs. Blood-donor centers, hospitals, homes for the elderly, and recreation centers are regular recipients of youth volunteer help.

It would burst the frame of this chapter to try and enumerate all the service projects that young people make possible all over the nation. The above examples, showing American high school and college youth lending more than a token hand in many vital services, must suffice as illustrations.

Every experience has a variety of consequences. Some of the results may simply be the achievement of material goals that projects set out to accomplish; but there are also unanticipated consequences, which involve psychological byproducts. In the case of youth volunteerism, these byproducts include:

Integration into society. Service work is an integral part of society and provides a status rooted in the Establishment. This bonds youth to society and alleviates youth's feelings of alienation, showing them a side of society with which they can identify.

Self-testing. The service experience is an example of the welcome respite that Erik Erikson called a psychosocial moratorium. Not only is the youths' delay in choosing a vocation socially accepted while they are serving in voluntary agencies, but there is a simultaneous opportunity to assess one's own resources, capabilities, and interests, and thereby apply a valid test to one's identity.

Independence. Meaningful service is a constructive expression of independence from parents and provides a sound resolution of the adolescent conflict. Peace Corps returnees reported that they appreciated the high degree of responsibility given and the extent to which they could exercise their own initiative. It seems that volunteer service helps young individuals achieve social maturity, which otherwise might be delayed or not achieved at all.

Solidification of values. Joining volunteer service is often a symptom of experimentation with alternative values. While many choose to pursue more competitive and materialistic values, those who focus on humanitarian values are able to test their chosen values through service projects. The outcome of the test often reinforces these values, and the person achieves greater certainty and self-assurance. This last point has been supported by a survey of returning Peace Corps volunteers who overwhelmingly (75 percent of the men and nearly 90 percent of the women) reported great satisfaction with their experience. While both sexes thought they had gained in self-assurance and outgoingness, the young women were especially convinced of having gained in the areas of self-determination, greater curiosity in life, and effectiveness.[29]

[29] Norma Haan, "Changes in Young Adults After Peace Corps Experiences," *Journal of Youth and Adolescence*, 3 (1974), 177–93.

The reasons American youth participate in service in the adult world involve a complex mixture of motivations. While the desire for service probably is a prevalent motive, healthy self-seeking, curiosity, interest in travel and other people, and a patriotic desire to improve the image of the United States are other elements.

ARGOT

Argot is a "special language" reflecting the idiom of a particular group or social class. It is used by persons who interact over a considerable period and share special circumstances. One example of an argot is the language of the law. In the course of their professional associations, lawyers employ a language markedly different from ordinary speech. Other examples are the ecclesiastical language, the argot of thieves, the military establishment, miners, and medical doctors.

These sublanguages are adaptations to particular circumstances; most people speak only a few of them well and have little knowledge of others. The common characteristic is the function of adapting communication to the particular needs and interests of the group. Medical students have to learn a medical vocabulary; students of this textbook must be familiar with some sociological and psychological terminology.

Acquisition of an argot means more than just learning a new vocabulary. It signifies membership in the subculture to which the lingo is indigenous. It promotes group cohesiveness and insures privacy. It also stands for new knowledge and insights, both cognitive and affective.

Teen lingo is a special language. An adult listening to typical teenagers talk is aware of being a stranger to their ways of thinking. Iona and Peter Opie, in their study of several thousand English schoolchildren and their lingo *outside of the school*, discovered a lore and terminology of the children's argot that was largely unknown to the adult population.[30] Adults in England or the United States are not familiar with many of the terms and idioms of teenagers, and consequently not capable of cognizing and reacting in the same way. Usually, the only way to acquire the meaning is to join teenagers and participate in their activities—provided they accept the adult. Of course, many adults recall their own teenage days and may be able to roughly equate terms of today's argot with similar terms they used themselves, since many of the experiences, conditions, and circumstances of the adolescent phase have remained similar throughout recent generations.

The reason why teenage argots evolve and are tenaciously maintained must be sought in their functions. At least six major functions can be discerned:

Shorthand device. Many of the terms of teenage argot are designed to save time when referring to complex processes in which teens are involved. For example, to spell out the fine details and connotations of what is meant when referring to a

---

[30] Iona Opie and Peter Opie, *The Lore and Language of School Children* (Oxford: The Clarendon Press, 1959).

person or an event as "cool" would take considerable time and unduly hamper expedient communication. The word evokes a clear concept for teenagers, saves time and effort, preserves their unique style of in-group communication, and prompts them toward expected subcultural emotions and actions.

Precise reference. In conjunction with the exposure to unique adolescent circumstances and conditions, the teenager finds that adult standard language does not include a sufficient reservoir of expressions to describe many of the ensuing experiences. Teenagers meet their need by modifying the general language with a battery of subcultural words that, in effect, lead to an argot. As a result, teenagers use words that are literally untranslatable into adult language because the empirical referents are unknown in the normal adult environment. In essence, then, having different experiences and perceiving human relations from a different angle, as teenagers do, calls for a correspondingly different set of words.

Teenage lingo can be vivid and clever. It can be sly enough to fool the uninitiated, occasionally describing the diminutive without bothering to use the diminutive grammatical form. Many teenagers play their lingo like virtuosos, skillfully hitting just the right nuance of pronunciation and accompanying it with studied body language.

Not all experts credit teenage slang with discriminatory acuity. The dissenting opinion apparently fails to take seriously the claim that teenage talk is profoundly discriminatory between nuances of meaning. For example, Cleveland Amory in one of his classic columns in *Saturday Review* dissected a number of frequently, if not ubiquitously, used teenage expressions. He concluded that they were practically interchangeable since their meanings hardly differed. What differed was merely the sound between the phrases as "with it," "far out," and "right on."[31]

Status criterion. Ardent and masterly use of argot functions as a prestige gauge among peers. The symbolic bluffs that can be played out by clever use of argot are sufficient to determine leader and follower statuses. Not unlike other species, it is not necessarily the physically strongest of the group (or pride, flock, covey, or herd) who assumes the leadership position, but the one who impresses most. This may be the lion in a pride who consistently roars loudest and most ferociously, or the teenager who uses subcultural lingo most cleverly. In both instances, no physical test of strength is necessary; status differentiation is accomplished through the use of signs or symbols.

Group solidarity. When teenagers use or hear their "own" words, they are strongly reminded of their peer membership. Hence the use of lingo functions as a phonetic banner proclaiming association with the peer group.

[31] Cleveland Amory, "Curmudgeon-at-Large," *Saturday Review*, October 2, 1976, p. 51.

Value statement. Argot reflects what is important to members of the sub-culture. The index of argot is such a sensitive indicator of peer values that it can be used to determine the type of association of a given individual. Research found that although argot, peer values, self-reports, and police contacts measure different refer-ents, they are so highly correlated that measuring argot by itself is sufficient to determine the nature (delinquent or nondelinquent) of a teenager's peer involve-ment.[32] The high correlation is due to the unity of argot, values, and behavior.

Cultural linguists discovered that the significance to a group or a society of a given thing is indicated by the number of words they use to refer to it. The classic example is Benjamin Whorf's oft-cited observation that Eskimos have various terms referring to snow, while standard English has only one.[33]

Linguistic conditioner. Once firmly entrenched, value-laden argot greatly influences (if not determines) the way members of a group perceive their social environment and, most significantly, therefrom pattern their behavior.[34] It is through this linguistic process that habitual and distinctive ways of thinking and behaving of the typical teenager can be explained to a significant extent.

Teenage argot, as based on the above six major elements, does not consist of a uniform body of linguistic expression for the American teen population. Rather, it is divided into sublingos, bearing out the principle that different environ-ments and different needs call for different vocabularies. It is therefore no surprise to hear the teenage surfers of the West Coast use a set of words and expressions of their own. The psychedelic drug users have developed their own lofty vocabulary. So have the Jesus Freaks. Inner-city and black youths cultivate another version of argot that is closely related to racial and ethnic lingos. And the lingo of the athletes illuminates still another side of the youth scene. These vocabularies, of course, overlap and are probably understood, although not spoken, by most teenagers; they are like slightly different dialects of one language.

Research discovered that familiarity with subcultural phrases also varied according to age and sex.[35] Frequency of argot use increases during childhood and reaches a peak during adolescence. Some topics prompt greater increases than others, with relatively small increases used in referring to money, cigarettes and smoking, and clothes and styles. These, apparently, are issues that do not change much in significance between the years of childhood and adolescence; thus no significant changes in style of references take place. However, there were large increases for topics concerning alcohol and drinking, popularity, and (particularly

[32] Paul Lerman, "Argot, Symbolic Deviance and Subcultural Delinquency," *American Sociological Review*, 32 (April 1967), 209–24.

[33] Benjamin Whorf, *Language, Thought, and Reality* (New York: John Wiley, 1956).

[34] Gary Schwartz and Don Merten, "The Language of Adolescence: An Anthropological Approach to the Youth Culture," *American Journal of Sociology*, 72 (March 1967), 453–68.

[35] Edward A. Nelsen and Edward Rosenbaum, "Language Patterns Within the Youth Subculture: Development of Slang Vocabularies," *Merrill-Palmer Quarterly of Behavior and Development*, 18 (July 1972), 273–84.

among males) for cars, motorbikes, and girls. Girls tended to use more argot references concerning clothes, styles, appearance, and being popular or unpopular. As seems plausible, boys and girls linguistically accentuate those aspects of their lives in which they are more involved and interested.

Although every generation of teenagers seems to adhere to an argot, its specific content, such as particular words and expressions, changes from one generation to the next. What was "keen" twenty years ago changed to "tough," "boss," or "dapper," and finally back to "keen"—all referring to roughly the same phenomenon. It would therefore be futile to present a glossary of current teenage lingo, since it would rapidly become outdated. The linguist Jacques Barzun reminds us of the ephemeral lifespan of argot and slang expressions: "Only 50 years ago, in a representative novel of college life called *The Plastic Age*, the young men and women say: isn't it the darb!, that's the bean!, pike along, pash, razz, bughouse, simp, smack for him, and other mysterious remarks. The very word *plastic* in the title of that book has almost lost its original meaning thanks to the chemical industry."[36]

How do certain teenage expressions spread and become part of the argot of the national teenage subculture? Often it is the entertainment media that are responsible for the transmission. The argot of the "valley girls" of Los Angeles' San Fernando Valley suburbs went national when, in 1982, parody-rocker Frank Zappa and his fourteen-year-old daughter created a record with "Val-speak."[37] Teen slang, up to that time not heard in any other part of the country, suddenly was imitated by teenagers everywhere.

On a more local scene, teen expressions spread as a result of imitating the talk of a teen hero. Ghoulardi, a Cleveland television semicomedian of the mid-1960s, invented the word *Knif* (fink spelled backward) and began offering Knif buttons. The teenage television audience immediately accepted his neologism, spread the vogue, and bought thousands of buttons. In one show, Ghoulardi coined the expression "All the world's a purple Knif." The idiom spread throughout the region and became a popular saying of the teenagers. Similarly, he named a pet crow Oxnard, and subsequently Cleveland's teenagers called each other Oxnard.[38]

A deliberate experiment to generate argot was attempted by students in a Phoenix high school communications class to study the process of word acceptance. The students invented a number of new words (*thacka, verk, greazums, shigbig,* and *bahamas*) and spread them around their school in personal conversations and in announcements on popular teenage radio stations. After two months, the experimenters visited more than fifty English classes to assess the results of the experiment. They discovered that *bahamas* (meaning "underwear") was the most widely

[36] Jacques Barzun, *Simple and Direct; A Rhetoric for Writers* (New York, Harper & Row, 1975), p. 38. See also two witty essays on this topic: Sam Hinton, "Moribund Metaphors Rise Again," *Verbatim*, 5 (February 1978), pp. 3–4; Lance Morrow, "If Slang is not Sin," *Time*, November 8, 1982, pp. 91–92.

[37] "It's Like Tubular!" *Newsweek*, August 2, 1982, p. 61.

[38] "What Catches the Teen-Age Mind?" *Time*, September 27, 1963, p. 55.

accepted. *Verk* ("punk"), *greazums* ("French fries") and *thacka* ("turn on") followed second, third, and fourth in acceptance. The reactions of the students to the invented terms were varied, but several remarked that the words were "dumb and weird." The linguistic innovations did not get a firm foothold in the community, and within two months the use of the words died out.[39]

There is notable lack of research in the genesis of argot vocabulary, and the question of etiology awaits more exploration.

CHANNELS OF MASS COMMUNICATION

The role of mass communication in transmitting, even creating, the youth subculture has been discussed in the section on "culture transmission model" in the preceding chapter and in Chapter 8, The Role of TV and Other Mass Media. A brief review is offered here.

Subcultures need channels of communication to maintain a sense of solidarity. Communication can proceed through various media, the simplest being direct person-to-person communication and general milling on America's high school and college campuses. Some of the communication in such situations does not need to be verbal; mere appearance is sufficient to convey a sense of belonging.

However, direct interaction within these ghettos is not sufficient to sustain the type of nationwide subculture that American teenagers form today. Various mass media must come into play to accomplish that. It is no empty slogan to say that the media become the message: TV, radio, magazines, and the lyrics of music bombard the teen population with ideas and values that become singularly adolescent property. The media as well as their contents become the world of the teenage subculture.

The role of TV is most likely primary in encouraging the disseminating ideas and styles. It could hardly be otherwise, since its influence can be felt in virtually every living room.

Equally tangible is the medium of the record industry, which conveys lyrics, the ideas of teen heroes, subcultural values, and common joy and pain. Whether heard on the radio or on the stereo at home, records constitute a form of mass communication. The power of this medium is illustrated by over ninety record companies who release more than nine thousand pop records, including a total of fifty-two thousand songs, each year.[40] Closely related are the music festivals and rock concerts where many musical heroes appear in person.

A medium of considerable communicative importance to teens is magazines. Influential teen magazines are available at newsstands and drugstores. They try to attract attention by "teen"-connoting titles like *Teen World, Modern Teen, Teen Time, Teens Today, Teen Parade, Seventeen*, and, simply, *Teen*. Other magazines

[39] "Students Buy, Soon Forget Slang Words," *Arizona Republic*, January 1, 1968, p. 35.
[40] R. Serge Denisoff, *Solid Gold* (New Brunswick, N.J.: Transaction Books, 1975).

have taken their titles from slang vocabulary and have assumed that such terms as *Dig* and *Flip* would appeal to teenagers. A survey in the 1960s revealed that most of these magazines seem to have limited circulations. Typical examples are *Dig*, founded in 1955, with approximately 171,000 purchasers, *Teen*, with about 245,000, and *Modern Teen*, with about 221,000. One reason for limited circulation is the fact that these magazines are aimed at specific readership within the teenage population. Some of them are for young teenagers, some for girls only, some for middle teenagers, others for older teenagers including college students. Still others have a certain socioeconomic slant, as for example *Seventeen*, which caters to upper-middle-class girls. One of the variables that distinguish one category from another is the degree of sophistication, usually reflected in the style of humor. While publications for younger teenagers appear intense and humorless, a more relaxed style emerges for older readers.

The diversity of youth publications can be illustrated by juxtaposing *Kids*, "The Magazine by Kids for Kids," and *Rolling Stone*, a newsmagazine with some political sophistication. The former addresses teenagers younger than fifteen, and in 1975 prided itself on being the "only national magazine written and illustrated totally by kids for kids." Its objective is to give children and teenagers a medium through which they can learn from each other and about each other, and at the same time enjoy working on a common communication project.

The biweekly *Rolling Stone*, however, which addresses the eighteen-to-twenty-five-year-old category, emphasizes modern music, offers views on a lifestyle that is a combination of counterculture and rock world, and publishes "personal ads" reminiscent of the style of the underground press. It is a heavily politicized publication that used to be part of the "youth revolution."

These publications are probably at opposite ends of the spectrum of youth magazines. In between lies a colorful array of printed matter, all vying for a segment of the youth population.

The factor that remains constant throughout all youth publications, and that is of foremost sociological importance, is the magazine's function of conveying a sense of collective identity. This unity function can be illustrated by the large volume of "Letters to the Editor," in which young people describe themselves, talk about their problems, and give and ask advice.

In addition, the magazines driving at younger teenagers have fan club and pen pal departments. The close communication within the world of peers is strikingly illustrated by the exchange of personal views and problems.

FADS AND STYLES

Some media through which peer-group belonging can be signified include clothing, grooming, music, dancing, and lingo. While these media are timeless, the specific content can be quite ephemeral. And this is where the definition of fad enters the picture. Ray Gold defines *fad* as "markedly novel, trivial, and ephemeral behavior which spreads rapidly through whatever portions of society choose to adopt it. Fad behavior may involve crowd-like imitation directed toward momentary circumvention of folkways and mores; it may also provide substitute ways of expressing normatively thwarted emotions, such as status yearning and sexual drives."[41]

The major elements of the definition include ephemerality, novelty, triviality, creation of status criteria, identification with the in-group, compensation (for powerlessness, alienation, and sexual frustrations), and the security of "sameness."

The elements can be recognized in the fads of American youth and can be paraphrased:

1. Almost all youth vogues are *short lived*, one displacing the next in rapid sequence. It is difficult to determine the average duration of a youth fad; it may range from a few months to several years.

2. For a behavior style to qualify as a fad, it must introduce a relatively *new* way of doing, speaking, grooming, or dressing. It must draw attention and be clearly distinguishable from both the preceding habit in the given behavior area and the customary folkway in the adult world.

3. The significance of the fad is usually *trivial* compared with the mores of society. This implies that fads are "odd" forms of existing folkways, normally within the range of the permissible and not violating the mores. However, one can find instances where society has reacted with a severity toward teen fads that ordinarily is reserved for punishment of infractions of the mores. For example, the vogue of shoulder-length hair for boys during the late 1960s was judged so negatively by some school administrators that suspension from school was threatened or actually enforced.

4. Teenagers use fads as *status measurements*. Fads allow them to achieve prestige in the eyes of their peers by conforming and excelling in observance of the vogue.

5. Teen fads are meant for teens only. This exclusivity is both crescive and deliberate; that is, fads spring up more or less spontaneously and are imitated by teenagers without particular scrutiny of their purpose. However, once established, a fad is jealously guarded and deliberately kept from adults. In fact, it has been observed that as soon as adults accept and imitate a teen faddist style, teenagers reject it. The fad is part of the *identification function* of the subculture, using the uniform appearance or habit as a boundary-maintaining device.

6. Fads serve as *outlets for thwarted creativity* and as compensations for various frustrations. An example would be rechanneling of sexual aggressiveness into harmless, "safe," and culturally tolerated behavior forms (for example, teenage dancing). Also, compensatory fads may harness hostility into tolerable forms of rebelliousness.

7. There is psychological, and maybe even physical, *security* in uniformity of looks and behavior patterns. The young can feel safely ensconced in a peer group, are not only accepted but also protected by sameness, and do not suffer feelings of standing out and being vulnerable to outside forces. Apparently fad adherence serves the same universal function as the uniform: submergence of the individual into a protective body of collective sameness.

[41] Ray L. Gold, "Fad," in *A Dictionary of the Social Sciences*, ed. Julius Gould and William L. Kolb (New York: Free Press, 1964), pp. 256–57.

With these theoretical background remarks in mind, specific areas of youth fads and styles are now examined.

Clothing. Clothing is a visual means of communication. Teenagers are able to identify in-group members by their appearance. Once clothing has given a teenager an idea of the social identity of a person, he or she is able to pattern his or her behavior and responses accordingly. If a teenager looks like a teenager, he or she is likely to be treated as a teenager, just as a schoolteacher who looks like a schoolteacher is likely to be treated as a schoolteacher. It can therefore be concluded that clothing influences the type of social interaction a person experiences.[42]

Clothing fads serve three additional functions beside the main functions of identification and protective "sameness." First, they serve as a medium of rebellion against the adult world; second, they often afford utilitarian comfort; and third, they allow for aesthetic expression.

Of these functions the one signaling rebellion is of primary interest here. Rebelliousness of youth has varied roots. Partly it is the age-old hedonistic resistance to being reined in by cultural dicta. Such rebelliousness becomes particularly accentuated, virtually provoked, if the culture is low in self-confidence and proceeds with diffident permissiveness in socializing its young. This condition seems to prevail, unlike in simpler societies, in most postindustrial countries. Additional roots of rebelliousness are found in the many adolescence-creating conditions that age segregate, frighten and confuse teenagers vis-à-vis a complex Establishment.

Many writers specify another malaise as a significant root of rebelliousness: adult hypocrisy. Most teenagers, they believe, suffer dismay on discovering that their parents and other adults are fallible individuals beset with inconsistencies. They see adults preaching one thing for teenagers and doing different things themselves. Children's dreams of adult loyalty, honesty, and virtue are shattered when they discover that promises are frequently broken, as, for example, in divorce, or when smoking and drinking are condemned for children and teenagers as "bad and unhealthy" while parents indulge in them. The result is that the adult world may take on a phony appearance. Not wanting to surrender to this hypocrisy, teenagers avoid becoming integrated into the adult social structure; many openly reject conventional adult society and seek "truth and reality" in their own experience. As one facet of the rejection syndrome, the young rebels have a tendency to reject even the conventional garments of adults and so determine their own fashions.

It appears that the hippie movement, emerging in the mid 1960s, was originally based on just such a rejection. What took form was not a mere faddist mood, but

---

[42] Social-psychological functions of clothes have been examined by such writers as John Brooks, *Showing off in America: From Conspicuous Consumption to Parody Display* (New York: Little, Brown, 1981); Hilda M. Buckley and Mary E. Roach, "Clothing as a Nonverbal Communication of Social and Political Attitudes," *Home Economics Research Journal*, 3 (December 1974), 94–102; Mary S. Ryan, *Clothing: A Study in Human Behavior* (New York: Holt, Rinehart, and Winston, 1966).

a social movement; it rejected not only conventional clothing but also middle-class art, philosophy, and values.

It would be a mistake to label the persistent wearing of some common garment a fad. If a certain period is exceeded, and certain clothes become customary for one or more generations, they can no longer be defined as faddish. Wearables such as blue jeans, for example, are not sufficiently novel, ephemeral, and different from adult clothes to warrant the label of fad.

Occasionally, a leading member of some teenage subgroup asserts his or her ideas, or the ideas of the group, by adding special adornments to his or her clothing. Examples were (and still are) T-shirts that sported slogans and/or pictures on the front and/or the back. It was a medium through which the wearer could express serious or not-so-serious whims, concerns, complaints, political and philosophical views, and anything else he or she wanted to proclaim ("Don't Bother Me, I Can't Cope," "Fly Me, I'm Henry," "Cocaine, The Real Thing"). Major department stores, as well as thousands of small T-shirt shops across the country, have been (and still are) cashing in on the craze that has consumed millions of decorated T-shirts.

One of the more esoteric clothing styles was implemented by the hippies of the late 1960s and early 1970s. While not as limited and specific as some other styles, the hippies conveyed a studiedly worn and bedraggled image, usually including regulation denim, regulation ornamentation (medallions and the popular Indian beads), and regulation hiking boots.

Vestiges of many if not all fads are still found. Perhaps no fad ever dies completely; it only slumbers to be reawakened, and often goes through fascinating metamorphoses to reappear in a slightly altered form. If this is true, fads leave us with a richer repertoire of choices for dress, grooming, and appearance. They may well be among the more colorful caprices that help young Americans make their existence in urban-industrial society more palatable.

Music. Unlike clothing fads, music styles have proved of longer duration. Popular music, once primarily an adult-oriented entertainment, underwent radical changes in the mid 1950s and emerged at the end of that decade as the almost exclusive property of youth. The driving force behind this development was a combination of musical styles that fused the sounds of country and western music and rhythm and blues into rock 'n' roll. This original musical hybrid sired a number of offshoots, such as rock, soul, psychedelic, bubblegum, and even punk music. Compared with the music of the Roaring Twenties, which lasted only about ten years, the rock 'n' roll tradition has endured much longer.

Adult reactions to youth-oriented popular music were severe and swift in coming. Frank Sinatra condemned it as a "rancid-smelling aphrodisiac"; Samuel Cardinal Stritch compared it to "tribal rhythms"; Pablo Casals publicly called rock "poison put to sound"; a group of psychologists, mindful of the teenagers' frenzied response to Elvis Presley, called it a "medieval type of spontaneous lunacy"; and a

United States Senate subcommittee started investigations of possible connection between rock and juvenile delinquency.[43]

Part of the reason for the virulent reaction had to do with the personality cult, the riots by fans, and the sexual innuendos associated with the new music. Elvis Presley is indelibly associated with the early history of rock 'n' roll, having helped introduce the new style to the teen world. The initiation was ecstatic and often unruly, causing numerous fan riots—not only in this country but around the world. The authorities took a dim view of this novel lack of inhibition and restraint. This was also the time when scientists started to voice concern about the physiological effects of the onslaught of the up-to-then unheard-of-decibels characteristic of the new style; they exceeded one hundred decibels in front of a rock band— equal to the noise level of a moon rocket blastoff.

Chubby Checker introduced the twist in 1960. For the first time since the decline of the jitterbug, American teenagers had their own dance. But about two or three years later the twist became obsolete and taboo for connoisseurs, and such free-style versions as the "Watusi," "hitchhiker," "frug," "jerk," and the "monkey" appeared.

These versions of rock 'n' roll spread and became an international fad. Some English musicians, for example, were particularly influenced by American rock 'n' roll and began to refertilize the American mainland with their own versions. In 1964 the Beatles appeared on the Ed Sullivan Show before a television audience of almost 70 million, received one of television's biggest publicity coverages, and embarked on one of the most successful show business careers in history. With the Beatles began the actual rock revolution that subsequently defined an emerging segment of the American population, literally financed a counterculture, spawned a $2 billion industry, and gave young Americans a common means of expression— a common music, a common language, and even a common dramaturgy with roles of heroes and martyrs.[44]

Rock style has not remained uniform over the years. The folk rock of Bob Dylan was different from the more sentimental eloquence of the Beatles at the height of their career; the acid rock of the Rolling Stones became more sophisticated over the years; the mid 1970s brought a gentler variety of rock sounds with soothing melodies and reconciliatory lyrics; and the early '80s saw the spread of the cacaphonous, nihilistic Punk and New Wave spinoff.

One can only theorize about the reasons for these changes. The fading of the ear-numbing, acid rock may be a rejection or the decline of the fervor of the youth revolution that stirred emotions as well as drums during the late 1960s and early 1970s. It may symptomize a general exhaustion of youth activism and the new trend toward introversion, privatism, and greater sensitivity toward self. This trend may also be reinforced by the new freedom experienced by young talents

[43] "The Sound of the Sixties," *Time*, May 21, 1965, p. 85; and *New York Times*, February 23, 1957.

[44] Bernice Martin, "The Sacralization of Disorder: Symbolism in Rock Music," *Sociological Analysis*, 40 (1979):87–124.

fiom the past conformity-coercing youth era, enabling them to create and perform more as individuals rather than as "representatives" of a youth sub- or counter-culture.

It may be this flexibility that made rock the viable musical form it turned out to be and that allowed it the retention of certain basic characteristics since the 1950s.

Rock did not remain the sole domain of the teenagers—it captured a large adult following, adults who fervently, and in a sense uninvitedly, imitated the youngsters, forming an adult fan club that was unwanted and embarrassing to the teenagers. More than 40 percent of the "teen beat" records sold in the United States at one time were bought by persons over twenty years old. Teenagers complained about adult intrusion and felt that their "sacred" domain was invaded by uninvited parents.[45]

Dancing.   Obviously, this type of music was inseparable from dancing. The simple beat seemed monotonous to the musicologist and too loud for the sensitive, but it had a kinetic effect on dancers that proved compelling to teenagers and adults alike. As a result, the discotheques, places of sustained rock 'n' roll rhythm and performing go-go girls, multiplied throughout the nation.

The dancing itself was a private choreography, enabling the dancer to be creative in steps, gestures, and motions. A partner was not really necessary since no bodily coordination between partners was needed. In essence, the partners danced by and for themselves, most of the time paying little attention to each other. Some observers called it a kind of "fertility rite," intended to alleviate the sterility of urban-industrial life.[46] However, it was "fertility rite" minus sexual contact—a paradox. On one hand, modern dance openly displays a degree of sexual suggestiveness that no other Western dance forms have dared before; on the other hand, it cooly refrains from any bodily contact with the partner—in fact, it studiously ignores the partner altogether. It sounds like a contradiction. Why do young Americans in an age of sexual permissiveness choose to dance in isolation?

Several explanations are possible and probably make a stronger point in combination. One is that our age of liberation is also reflected in dancing behavior. Each dancer is "doing his or her thing," expressing rhythms and improvisations without having either to lead or follow a partner. This development may have been supported, on an unconscious level, of course, by the female's general surge toward emancipation over the past decade or so. It may be part of her general revolt against having to follow the male lead. A second reason may deal with American youth's increasing presumption that instantness in all things is possible, including dancing skill. The old-fashioned dance forms required learning and effort. Dancing apart from one another required none of the initially tedious synchronization of steps and movements. Modern dancing could be achieved instantly! A third

[45] "The Sound of the Sixties."
[46] Samuel Grafton, "The Twisted Age," *Look*, December 15, 1964, pp. 37-38.

reason might presume that dancing that lacks rules—none of the participants know "proper" steps and movements, in fact, none care about rules—represents a miniature model of present-day society, characterized by anomie and alienation. Dancing, then, consists of an isolated, gyrating body unaccompanied by an identity. Still another encouragement for this dance style comes from the awkwardness and inexperience that many adolescents bring to a situation where they have to intimately interact with the other sex. Rock dancing largely eliminates the embarrassment of sweaty hands, missing a beat, stepping on the partner's toes, and not knowing what to say. Dancing in isolation to music usually too loud for conversation lets the adolescent off the hook.

Given these "safety" factors, inhibitions all but disappear and highly sensual nuances can be observed, the anatomical gyrations of the dancers sometimes frankly suggesting copulatory motions. The judgments and opinions concerning the sexual expression of rock 'n' roll dancing vary widely. Some parents condemn it completely; others think that some of the dances are acceptable. Analytical observers conclude that this type of dancing is "safe sex" for teenagers. Harvard psychiatrist Philip Solomon sees these dances as healthy outlets for youthful restlessness and as sublimated sexual desires.[47]

Studies have revealed that the predominant feelings experienced by young dancers are *release* and *abandon*, sensations that social scientists explain by the dancers' temporary retreat from the tensions and frustrations of being status-deprived adolescents. It was also found that teenagers considered adults at a discotheque to be trespassers and intruders.[48]

It seems, then, that rock 'n' roll music meets a number of the teenagers' needs—their desire to express themselves bodily without limiting coordination to another moving body, without the need to converse, and without the fear of getting out of step. Moreover, erotic expressions pass with impunity and are rendered relatively inoffensive because of the dancers' abstention from physical contact.

Explained on the basis of these various functions, the longevity of rock 'n' roll is not surprising.

Hair style. The youth style fomenting extremely hostile reactions on the part of adults and frequently jolting authorities into severe countermeasures was young males' infatuation with long hair. Of all the fads and styles of the past decades, long hair seemed to offend the mores and the aesthetic sensibilities of the Establishment most profoundly. The new hairstyle was not perceived as a fad but as a perversion.

It is not ascertainable how and why the fad of long hair for boys developed. Coincidentally or causatively, the style started around 1964, when the Beatles exhibited their trademark, long hairdos, in the United States.

---

[47] "The Sound of the Sixties," p. 88.

[48] Lucille H. Blum, "The Discotheque and the Phenomenon of Alone-Togetherness," *Adolescence*, 1 (Winter 1966), 351–66.

Tho controversy over long hair applied exclusively to boys. Girls, it seems, enjoy almost unlimited license to fashion their hair in any way they wish, whether short or long, bleached or colored, ribboned or loose. To be sure, feminine hairdos go through fashions too; but since, by societal consensus, *all* of their styles pass as acceptable, deviant or "odd" fads are rarely ascribed to them. The difference between male and female hair styles is that the former are described as fads or deviations and the latter as fashions. Fashion, by definition, is a style approved or at least tolerated by the larger society and should therefore not be equated with fad.

In their own defense, boys point out that long hair has been a symbol of virility ever since biblical days and confess that they often grow luxuriant tops because their girlfriends admire them. They complain that a more liberal policy on hair styling is necessary to provide them with an opportunity to create more individualistic appearances to compete with girls, who traditionally are allowed more styling alternatives concerning not only hair but also dress, colors, shoes, hats, scarfs, make-up, and jewelry. Finally, some youngsters added that they wear long hair simply because they *want to* and because they want to look *different* from others, especially adults.

As the opposition grew, so did the hair—and with a fascinating display of obstinacy, the style spread, persisted, and even eventually influenced adult hairstyles to some degree.

The path of the new style abounded with innumerable clashes—many comical, others sordid, and some outright tragic. Examples from the earlier period include the action by the dean of Cardinal Hayes High School in the Bronx, who met students returning for the fall semester with a pair of scissors and shortened the locks of several boys; the refusal of the Kenosha, Wisconsin, high school to admit nearly two hundred boys because of their long hair; the order by Federal Judge Richard Duncan of Kansas City that a young delinquent get a haircut because "I refuse to sentence anyone I can't see"; and hundreds of teachers who apparently agreed with the judge and refused to teach students whose visibility was obstructed by a surplus of hirsute resources.[49]

Some extreme outcomes include the cases of a California father, who, after a longstanding feud over his son's long hair, shot the boy to death in anger;[50] two Texas brothers, thirteen and sixteen, who fatally shot their father, an Air Force officer, when he was asleep because he objected to their long hair and refused to buy motorbikes for them;[51] and a fifteen-year-old Rolling Stones fan who threw himself to his death under a train after he had been forced to have his long hair cut.[52]

[49] Reported by Hal Cooper in an AP report (New York, December 3, 1965), and by "The Unkindest Cut for Student Moptops," *Life*, August 24, 1965, p. 4.

[50] UPI Report (April 24, 1971).

[51] UPI Report (November 10, 1972).

[52] AP Report (January 19, 1966).

The controversy was still alive in the mid 1970s, raging between students and school administrators, employers and employees, and especially between parents and offspring. But by the late '70s two convergent trends resolved the controversy and calmed the emotions: At a time when the public turned more accepting, teenagers' insistence on long hair dissipated, possibly because adults had gradually imitated it to some extent. So ended one of the most vehemently embattled youth fads.

Besides fad formation in the areas discussed above, there have been many additional youth fads that were minor, regional, or very short-lived. They range from the '60s wave of wearing Nazi medals to the '70s "streaking" (a craze perhaps short-lived but hardly minor) to the mock violence of Punk style in the '80s. The examples mentioned in the above discussions are just that—examples. They are not intended to catalog the innumerable fads that have delighted, dismayed, or left this nation indifferent over the past decades.

SENSE OF SOLIDARITY

The youthful sense of solidarity emanates from all the dimensions discussed so far. There is really no separate dimension by which this *esprit de corps* can be measured; it is conveyed through teenagers' attitudes, values, lingo, music, dancing, fads, styles, hero worship, status criteria, and subcultural institutionalization.

Their attempts to exclude adults from their activities and styles is one of the surest indications of youth's solidarity. This exclusion is frequently manifested by discontinuing a fad or style as soon as adults begin to accept and imitate it. The habitual reference to the impersonal third-person "they" (the adults, the Establishment) as distinct from the first-person "we" and "us" is a constant reminder of modern youth's practice of setting itself apart from the larger society.

Teen lingo in general is a good measure of how much an in-group awareness prevails and reinforces a separate identity. A sense of solidarity almost invariably results in a distinct lingo. Worshiping common heroes is another indication of solidarity. Such individuals serve as focal points for youth's need to consolidate feelings and values. Heroes are often defined as such because they represent alternative or even deviant values from the larger society and thus function as exponents of the youth collective's sense of solidarity.

Certain drugs, especially marijuana, serve as a means of cultivating a sense of separateness, which is a cornerstone of the sense of solidarity. Engaging in a deviant or illicit practice is a powerful means of generating a feeling of being a distinct collectivity, a community of the "persecuted," "rejected," or "victimized." Some social scientists have likened the typical setting of marijuana smoking and the stereotypical demeanor displayed at such times (the ritualistic passing of the "joint" around the circle of the initiated) to the passing of the Holy Eucharist among the believers to merge the participants into a common body. Such illicit, deviant, or at least unique, rituals play a powerful role in substantiating a feeling of belonging to the in-group and accentuating a feeling of alienation from the out-group.

An unfailing sign of the youthful sense of solidarity is the fervent cultivation of the generation gap by word and deed. The frustrations growing out of the socialization process find their consolidating and consoling culmination in solidarity, using adults as scapegoats. The sense of solidarity is greatly enhanced if the in-group can identify a common adversary or "enemy," since it enables the followers to focus their dissatisfaction away from the in-group interaction and directs frustration and hostility to an out-group target. This habit also clarifies group boundaries, an important condition for maintaining cohesiveness.

Sociologists have not been particularly successful in clarifying the construct of solidarity and, for this reason, have not developed useful instruments for measuring the concept. A significant step was made by James A. Cramer and Dean J. Champion, who believed that solidarity refers specifically to the *affective content* of group relations and is made up of the positive emotional elements prevailing among the members of a group, resulting in sentiments of "we-ness."[53] The researchers completed a factor analysis of a list of logical items (based on previous efforts to measure group cohesiveness and family solidarity) and determined a number of items that are best suited for measurement of solidarity. These items included such statements as "Troubles and discouragements just draw us closer," "When we have a job to do, everybody pitches in," "Members are close knit, stick together through thick and thin," and "Spend lots of time together because we prefer each other's company." On the basis of factor analysis, the researchers recommend a distinction between cohesiveness and solidarity, since the former might mean different things in different situations. One group's cohesive bond may be strongly attached to the function or goal of that group, while another's bond may be generated by affective bonds of love and solidarity. Differentiation between these two elements would enable future researchers to scan the nuances of group dynamics.

STATUS CRITERIA

Just as in the case of the sense of solidarity, status criteria must be deduced from various dimensions of behavior. What is counted as status and prestige is directly correlated with success in such behavior as fads, drug use, dating, use of teen argot, and material acquisitions that reflect and enhance subcultural belonging.

Hence, a pair of faded jeans is not just clothing, it is a symbol of belonging and status; having a date with a member of the opposite sex is frequently not a human encounter based on personal attraction but on prestige derived from being seen with a popular girl or guy; flaunting possession of the latest popular hits does

[53] James A. Cramer and Dean J. Champion, "Toward the Clarification of Solidarity," *Pacific Sociological Review*, 18 (July 1975), 292–309.

not necessarily mean enjoying them as personally meaningful, but means letting others know that you are up on the latest productions; participating in marijuana smoking frequently has nothing to do with the enjoyment of the elusive "high" (that is actually as often faked as it is honestly experienced), but has something to do with the recognition by peers that you are "cool"; fads are often not enjoyed because they gratify the youth's need for creativity and colorfulness, but are embraced to achieve the necessary "look alike" and to be accepted as "one of the gang"; speaking the argot is not so much preference as coercion to live up to peer expectations (many teenagers are dimly aware that they engage in a contrived and affected style that contains many superficial elements); and joining in the worship of certain heroes is not always an expression of liking or respecting that individual, but an attempt to impress peers and to appear knowledgeable as to who is "great" and who is not, what is "in" and what is not, and in general to convey an air of appreciating the presumed spokespersons of their generation.

All of these behavior forms are part of the fine art of followership and correlated prestige. Beyond a certain point of following, the skill of leading emerges; that is, the teenager with the biggest achievement in these behavior patterns earns the highest prestige and qualifies for leadership status. However, to achieve true leadership requires additional personality features.

The desire for status among peers often seems to influence the choice of friends among teenagers. Boys and girls sometimes choose, or are chosen, "friends" on the basis of prestige. It appears that the prestige of a teenager carries over to his or her associates and, thus, a "friend" actually functions as a status criterion. In most cases, however, a modified process operates whereby teenagers look as much at personality features as the prestige potential of a friend to be.

Status criteria differ from peer group to peer group and depend heavily on the teenager's orientation. Hence, behavior that would be prestigious among delinquent youths would be rejected by nondelinquent youths. Significant items of prestige among middle-class youths might be different from those of working-class youngsters and, of course, the racial and minority groups imbue their young with still other status criteria.

However, certain items are used throughout most, if not all, groups to assess a teenager's standing. One of them is clothing and appearance. Research found that urban high school girls used these aspects in deciding whether new girls qualified as personal friends and as group members. However, when they discussed old friends, the question of appearance receded and personality, friendliness, and similar interests and involvements became more important. It followed, then, that once the appearance of a newcomer was assessed and a decision to pursue or not pursue a friendship was made, appearance was more or less taken for granted.[54]

[54] Joanne B. Eicher et al., *A Longitudinal Study of High School Girls' Friendship Patterns, Social Class, and Clothing* (East Lansing, Mich.: Michigan State University Agricultural Experiment Station, 1974), p. 20.

The study also discovered that girls are able to infer socioeconomic background by the way a female peer dresses. Girls in lower socioeconomic classes were found to be "improperly" dressed by more affluent girls and not accepted into certain groups. In most instances, the rejected girls were well aware of the ostracism but maintained their own ideas about clothing and appearance. They eventually formed their own groups, cultivated their own clothing styles, and thus avoided isolation.

The consequences that follow from this status behavior are of considerable significance to educators and social workers. The status criteria of clothing and appearance separated the high school girls to the disadvantage of students in lower socioeconomic classes. "The situation in the school was almost a case of 'never the twain shall meet,' so that girls were denied opportunities to learn ways different from those they had grown up with."[55] This implies that such youthful status behavior reinforces and perpetuates the *status quo*. It is suspected that such labeling behavior contributes more to the isolation and eventual dropping out of lower-class youth than difficulties that are purely academic.

Being rejected by peers must be one of the most tragic experiences for a young person. That this occurs on the basis of "first impression" is particularly unfortunate because it means the decision of accepting or rejecting another person is not being made on grounds of more rational and important factors. The moral of the story is that if teenagers from different social backgrounds want to be accepted by one another, they must learn to understand each other's views regarding dress.

There were some age differences, however, in the approach of choosing a friend. Ninth-graders considered personality as the most important basis on which a given girl would be judged. But twelfth-graders put personality in second place and considered "looks and appearance" as the first standard. These older teenagers relied more heavily on "first impression" and believed it gives them a realistic assessment of lasting reliability.

It is interesting that the opinions of teenagers concerning the criteria of popularity and what is sought in a friend have hardly changed over the past decade. The 1974 Eicher study (mentioned above) and the 1982 Sebald survey (see section on Norms and Values) have come up with basically the same rank order of criteria.

Researchers have noted that determined status-seeking girls sometimes use sex as a means to enhance their prestige. They try to attract high-status boys for dates, and to do so they occasionally engaged in rather intense petting without endangering their "reputation." The interaction consisted of a precarious game of providing just so much sexual favor for so much prestige by association. On the other hand, boys' status behavior was found to primarily consist of drinking and dating practices through which "manhood" was tested and proved. In conjunction with the drinking behavior, a sort of daredevil approach to the problem of the purchase of beer or liquor developed, and accomplishing the illicit purchase was considered

---

[55] Ibid.

an act of cleverness and "having guts" that added to the status among peers. Such a purchase (with faked IDs or lying about one's age) was a battleground reserved for the courageous only, and the risk to the boys' self-esteem was great. If a boy revealed that he was afraid of showing a false ID or otherwise bluffing his way through demands to prove his age, he lost face within his peer group. This was the acid test of "keeping your cool." Any boy who failed to rise to the occasion had his claims to "coolness" ruthlessly deflated by his peers.[56]

Status expectations differ among groups. There is no *one* system with perfectly hierarchically arranged status positions for all. Studies seem to indicate that young people perceive of status as a set of ranked, slightly ambiguous prestige categories that are internally differentiated. This can be explained by pointing first to a horizontal dimension that is an array of different lifestyles heavily influenced by the teenagers' socioeconomic background. Each lifestyle differs somewhat in dress, speech, interpersonal demeanor, and prestige in the community (boys in a lower-class neighborhood, girls in a predominantly middle-class high school, college coeds, and rock 'n' roll groupies). Second, a vertical dimension can be visualized within each group according to which the members are assessed and status-ranked. While the horizontal dimension is qualitative, dividing teenagers into distinct categories that might be judged delinquent or nondelinquent, lower or upper class, the vertical dimension is a quantitative measure ascribing more or less popularity to a member of the group.

The process of status attribution is complex. Status does not simply derive from objective talents and characteristics, such as a boy's athletic ability or a girl's physical attractiveness. Teenagers acquire esteem in a variety of contexts and obtain subcultural validation by adherence to their group's standards. An element that seems to run through all modern peer groups is the presentation of oneself as "cool." To the extent that "coolness" becomes a part of a teenager's behavioral routine, peer acceptance and admiration will rise—and that, after all, is what status among teenagers is all about.

HERO WORSHIP

Most identifiable subcultures come equipped with leaders. Yet, when we look at the teen subculture in America on the national level, we find leadership conspicuously absent. Instead, heroes abound who are idols of the masses, passive figures of the world of entertainment, whose ability to lead is negligible and whose vision is myopic. With rare exceptions, they are profiteers cashing in on fads and styles that they have not created. Many of them become millionaires not because they are particularly talented or have something to say but because they were lucky enough

[56]Schwartz and Merten, "The Language of Adolescence," *American Journal of Sociology*, 72 (March 1967), 453–468.

to get into the limelight of the world of entertainment. This individual becomes the target of the teenagers' emotional accolades and their need for heroes. The result is hero worship—which is not to be confused with following a leader.

There are, however, certain segments of the youth population that have, or had, leaders. Among them were the spokespersons of the counterculture, the political activists and radicals (Joan Baez, David Harris, Jerry Rubin, Pete Seeger, Bob Dylan, Jane Fonda, and others) who stood up against the Establishment and in some cases became martyrs for their causes. There are also the leaders of the local teenage scene: the leaders of cliques, gangs, and crowds who rally their followers in the community, neighborhood, or school.

The present discussion focuses on the general, nationwide teen subculture and, because of the peculiar hero-orientation of the American teenagers, deals more with heroes from the entertainment world than leaders in the real sense of the word.

Hero worship is a timeless indulgence. It appears to be such a deep-seated need that if no real heroes are available, supernatural ones tend to be invented. This need is observable in both adults and teenagers. Depending on the cultural milieu, the hero may be a military figure, a political personality, an outstanding athlete, or a popular entertainer. Commensurate with the American ethos, which cherishes popularity more than Spartan values, teenagers in the United States exhibit special admiration for entertainers, singers, actors, and musicians. The worship of these popular heroes often proceeds in overt demonstrations. At concerts, cheering crowds manifest their loyalty; in teenagers' bedrooms, pictures on the wall silently testify admiration; in record stores, sales reveal listeners' adoration; and dress and hair styles often imitate popular idols.

The attractiveness that heroes have for the masses is composed of a number of complex elements. Some of them have been verified by research, and some have been assumed by theory. Major gratifications American teenagers derive from hero worship include:

Romanticism. Romanticism refers to emotions and attitudes that usually are insufficiently based on facts. The appeal of romantic emotions lies in the heroic, remote, mysterious, and idealized. This emotional disposition can be related to a number of areas in life, but it is most frequently observed in connection with attitudes toward love relationships. Teenagers are particularly prone to adhere to romantic perceptions of the male-female relationship because they lack the experience of the older generation and are reluctant to accept adult standards. As a result, teen heroes can easily capitalize on the romance hunger of their followers, reinforce unrealistic perceptions, and become tangible foci of romantic identifications.

Teenagers see in their heroes the incarnation of many of their fondest dreams and desires. Since the unrealistic nature of the dreams makes implementation in the life of the individual teenager impossible, they are transferred to a person whose popularity seems to attest to their success in materializing such dreams. Popularity is perceived by the teenage followers as the *carte blanche* of all dreams and hopes.

Sex and Fetishism. Expressions of hero worship have frequently been interpreted as substitution and sublimation of sexual tension whereby some material aspect of the popular hero, such as his or her clothing or hair, becomes a fetish. In other words, a fetish is a tangible substitute for the coveted person that can provide a certain degree of erotic gratification. A mild, usually socially acceptable and widespread fetishistic practice is collecting and/or pinning up pictures of heroes. Expressions of this romantic adulation can be gleaned from almost all teen magazines, which provide fan departments, print pin-ups, and advertise "real photos of rock stars."

American teenagers have established by now an impressive history of fetishistic pursuits (often exploited by business). Frankie Avalon, an earlier rock 'n' roll balladeer, was attacked by his fans numerous times. Once, teenage girls pulled the shoes off his feet; another time, a crowd of excited teenagers trampled him and sprained his back in an effort to touch him and tear off pieces of his clothing.[57] On their 1966 return to the United States, the Beatles were beleaguered at their hotels by hundreds of shrieking girls. A teenager who let it be known that she had a lock from the head of one of the Beatles was mobbed by the other girls who wanted to touch and kiss it. At numerous performances, the Beatles' music and lyrics were completely drowned out by the screaming teenage audiences, who were more interested in seeing than hearing their idols. Several hotels at which the Beatles slept turned the teenagers' fetishistic desires into lucrative business by cutting up and selling square inches ($1.00 a piece) of the bed sheets used by the heroes.[58] A similar fate awaited the sheets used by the Rolling Stones at a 1973 stopover in New Zealand, where businessmen purchased them to make them into souvenir handkerchiefs and shirt panels.[59]

Some sexual expressions are less substitutional and more direct. Groupies constitute a special institution of teen subculture and are female hero worshipers who, according to the simple definition of Frank Zappa (leader of the rock group called the Mothers of Invention) are "girls who go to bed with members of rock 'n' roll bands."[60] These girls, also known as "rock geishas," fulfill their erotic fantasies by engaging in sexual activities with rock stars and their immediate entourages. Groupies cultivate numerous relationships, and it is not uncommon for them to extend sexual favors to several members of a group within one night. An internal status system has developed among the groupies that largely depends on which famous bands they can list as their "friends." Many of them travel with bands, staying with one for a week, then changing to another. These girls are a small minority. For the rest of the masses of teenagers, their heroes remain more distant, romantic figures with whom they stay in touch by various fetishistic practices.

[57] Thomas B. Morgan, "Teen-Age Heroes: Mirror of a Muddled Youth," *Esquire*, March 1960, pp. 65–73.

[58] UPI Report (Chicago, August 13, 1966).

[59] AP Report (Auckland, New Zealand, March 22, 1973).

[60] "Manners and Morals," *Time*, February 28, 1969, p. 48.

Crowd ecstasy.   Heroes often serve as catalysts for the type of mass behavior that allows "abandon" and "release." Youthful rambunctiousness and excitement find an outlet when heroes perform in front of large teen audiences. Concert settings give the young an opportunity to physically express exuberance by screaming, touching, and moving rhythmically. Being in a mass of peers is a visceral experience to the teenager, not unlike dancing, and offers an outlet for frustration and tension. The behavior at teen concerts is governed by completely different rules (and maybe needs) than that at adult concerts. While the heroes perform, the audience is not expected to remain silent and motionless; band members are not usually disturbed by the noise their appreciative audience makes.

A good part of the behavior at such rallies is not intended as listening but as a testimony of *belonging.* A number of physical expressions of "worshiping," such as screaming, jumping, and even "fainting," have a mutually reinforcing effect in a crowd situation. The reinforcement is due to the rewards derived from the prestige assigned to such peer-approved and peer-encouraged actions. It is interesting that many vociferous teenagers are not looking at their heroes on such occasions, but at each other, apparently to make sure that they are seen screaming. Back rows usually do not scream, but merely applaud conventionally, since they are outside of the field of observation.

An interesting example of crowd-reinforced imitation comes from the early days of the rock 'n' roll era. Frankie Avalon's presence and singing would always induce some girls to faint—or to pretend to. It became the thing to do. During a Milwaukee presentation by Avalon, twenty-one girls ostentatiously fainted. At another performance on television, when Avalon sang "Boy Without a Girl," the camera showed a number of sobbing teenagers. *From then on*, this behavior became a routine and was imitated whenever Avalon appeared and sang that particular song.[61] Avalon's record was broken in 1975 when 250 young girls fainted ritualistically at a concert given by a Scottish group, the Bay City Rollers.

The fascination with the bizarre and the absurd.   Humans of any age category can be made into a captive audience by the bizarre and the absurd. The heroes of modern American teenagers cultivate this fascination by a freak style that during previous epochs was confined to the semiunderground adult theatres à la Marquis de Sade. Today's teenage version is the Punk rock hall where teenagers act out the macabre and ghoulish. For those preferring to celebrate the freakish from the vantage point of a safer and more comfortable seat in a movie house, the Rocky Horror Picture Show has been offering a suitable fare for youthful crowds for many years.

Such mid 1970s freak heroes as Alice Cooper, Mick Jagger, and Elton John devised freak gimmicks to win teen attention that included transvestitic, surrealistic, sado-masochistic, and macabre appearance and performance. As mentioned earlier, among the most notable acts was Cooper's ritualistic suicide fake in front of

---

[61] Morgan, "Teen-Age Heroes," p. 65.

shrieking teenage audiences with the tragic consequence of a number of imitations that proved fatal to teen fans.

Many teen aficionados are attracted to the freak shows because they find them "scary," "weird," and they make their skin "tingle" with excitement. Is the type of teenager attracted to the freak style an exceptional youth, characterized by deviant tendencies, or the quite normal youth who simply responds to the unusual, the bizarre, and the grotesque? This may be a forced question, and the best one could do at this time is to reiterate that attraction to the bizarre is a phenomenon universal to all humans regardless of personality tendencies. However, one might hypothesize that persons with serious personality problems may go a step further than merely enjoying the "weird and tingling" sensation that the vision of such fare induces and try to imitate the grotesque in their personal lives.

Generally, however, the '80s initiated a more subdued entertainment style, excepting Punk. Even rock 'n' roll for general teenage consumption has taken on a bland sound and calm look. In a sense, teenage music and entertainment of the '80s is recycled past. While youngsters of the rock generation found an identity in it, their youngsters have yet to find a sound of their own. The same goes for the heroes; teenagers of the '80s to a remarkable extent still feed on the heroes of preceding teen generations.

Identification.   A hero is a ready model for identification and imitation. He or she provides the "worshipers" with an image to which they can aspire. It must be noted that the first-class teen hero is a recording star and not a politician, business-man, or intellectual. Compared with the entertainer, even the top athlete is only moderately admired. It has been suggested that the reasons for this preference are the similarity in age and ability of many entertainers to the crowd-oriented teen-agers. It seems easier for teenagers to identify with someone who is crowd-oriented like themselves, and is mediocre, "humble," and nonserious. Teenagers, due to the adolescent experience, need collective protection within which they feel safe from and invisible to adults. They are afraid of exposing themselves individually to evaluation and criticism, and they project this negative feeling onto personalities who are outstanding. Their aversion is aimed at the politician for his or her *principles*, the businessperson for his or her *enterprise and success*, and the intellec-tual for devotion to the *hard truths* — all representing values that tend to separate the individual from the crowd, expose him or her, possibly make him or her unpopular and therefore insecure. Teenagers try to escape exposure and seek the security of the crowd. They prefer virtues of conformity, mediocrity, and sincerity. Through their heroes, songs, and dances they can express themselves without leaving the secure environment of the group.

The Beatles, for example, were admired for their simplicity and sincerity. When asked whether they liked being idolized, they answered "we just like the money." Another important element that made the Beatles loved and admired heroes was the fact that they conveyed a nonserious image. By doing so, they enabled their fans to relax and meet them as equals. The Beatles admitted publicly that they did not think much of their own music but that they had "fun" entertaining and getting paid for it.

Another condition that induces identification with many of the teenage heroes is based on the subtle rivalry that girls introduce between the idols and their boyfriends. Directly or indirectly, boyfriends are frequently urged to look and act like the teenage heroes, and they are rewarded, if they are successful in a certain degree of imitation, with some of the type of admiration that is ordinarily reserved for the popular idols.

Heroes as "messengers."   Heroes are significant others who have influence on teenagers' thinking and value-orientation. However, of all the functions American teen heroes perform, extending values is probably the least effective. The need to express and release emotional dispositions and the use of the hero as a catalyst for that purpose by far supersede the need for more rational formulations and value-orientations.

Nevertheless, one could classify some of the "folk rock" heroes of the 1960s as advocates of certain values of adolescents—probably of the *older* and more intellectual adolescents. One of the best known was Bob Dylan, a young poet-songwriter who achieved popularity with such songs as "Tambourine Man," "Subterranean Homesick Blues," and "Like a Rolling Stone." His songs criticized social conditions and focused on civil rights, the threat of nuclear war, and the war in Vietnam. Although his singing made him a millionaire, he maintained an image that teenagers found acceptable and imitable. To his fans, the scruffy hair, wrinkled shirt, and faded jeans meant that he was one of them.

Others like Joan Baez, Judy Collins, Joni Mitchell, and Peter, Paul and Mary, followed the lead of Dylan, expounded social commentary and showed talent in distilling the moods of their time. The recurrent themes in their creations were justice for all, peace, brotherhood, love, sensitivity and the condemnation of urban-industrial conditions. Their collages pieced together images of tension between the generations, the loneliness of the young in an anomic society, the bittersweets of young love, the search for a stable and secure reality, and the fear of the fleeting and blurred meanings of our age.

While the charisma achieved by these heroes made their message credible to many, the majority of young teen fans approached the message more from the visceral, musical, and hero-worship angle, and the folk rock following was never as broad as the rock 'n' roll enthusiasts in general. The political and philosophical messages of the protest heroes, however, made an impression on the older and more serious young population and contributed to countercultural development.

The 1980s finds the teen scene devoid of almost any type of hero. Young people have become somewhat more individualistic, not exhibiting the need to flock around idols as much as the young of the '60s and '70s. The recycled sound of rock has lost its cutting edge, counterculture figures have become history, and most rock bands are faceless groups failing to send teenagers into ecstasy. There still are outstanding groups such as the *Rolling Stones*, which, at the beginning of the '80s, was the most glamorous rock band, earning $50 million in 1981.

But what once was inspiration and ecstasy to teenagers has become entertainment. Even the *Rolling Stones* descended to the general interest level, which is a tacit admission that rock music is no longer the unifying force of a generation. While the creations of the Beatles mirrored the restless questing of a generation in revolt, the musicians and entertainers of the '80s merely ride the ebbing waves of the rock generation.

SUBCULTURAL INSTITUTIONALIZATION

It is a sociological commonplace that all societies institutionalize the functions deemed necessary for taking care of basic needs. This means that behavior aimed at satisfying such important needs as sex, reproduction, training of the young, trading, protection, order, and leadership is not permitted to occur at random or by idiosyncratic preference, but is prescribed by the cultural blueprint. The institutions for the above mentioned needs are therefore, respectively, marriage, family, education, business, police or the military, and government. An institution, or institutional behavior, implies the dictum to follow the functional norms as implemented by specific structures, such as the monogamous relationship, the family group, the organization of public schools, and so forth.

If the main culture fails to provide an institutional framework for the gratification of a certain need, subcultural institutionalization may develop to facilitate fulfillment of the need. This is particularly applicable to collectivities which feel that their needs are not fulfilled by the institutions set up by the Establishment. In fact, subinstitutionalization is probably the most telling indicator of how far a collectivity has matured into a subculture. These new structures may or may not be in conflict with the larger society, may or may not totally replace the Establishment's procedure, and may be seen as deviant or as merely supplemental.

American adolescents have begun to develop several institutions of their own. By doing so, they manifest, more convincingly than by any other means, their attempt to be independent of the adult world. The manifestations can be recognized by regularities in behavior that indicate a surprising degree of organized social structure within the youth collectivity. It is the enmeshing of young people in their own segregated social structure that is of utmost sociological pertinence, because a structural proviso makes for regular patterns of social behavior.

Some subinstitutionalizations have already been mentioned. The whole area of youthful entertainment, including music, songs, dancing, and festivals, can be called institutions of the young. Of similar nature are teen magazines that promote hero worship and, most importantly, serve as channels of mass communication. A few more subinstitutions are:

Dating. Dating is an example of a supplemental institution that is not necessarily in conflict with adult norms and institutions but rather defines the culturally accepted meeting ground between boys and girls and patterns their interaction. To a large extent, however, the specific norms and expectations are defined by the young people themselves, and certain aspects of the subinstitutional behavior border on the "forbidden," such as heavy petting and premarital sexual intercourse. Such behavior adjuncts exemplify the need fulfillment of young people who cannot find a legitimate outlet for sexual desires within the institutions of the Establishment, since such participation is reserved for adults and presumably limited to the institutions of marriage and the family.

Cohabitation. On the more involved level there are "open relationships" in which the dyad holds a considerable degree of primacy, but does not rule out the individual's freedom for additional episodes and extra sexual explorations. The prototype of the open relationship is the institution of cohabitation, in which some degree of responsibility and mutual accountability is introduced—but far short of a definite, legal commitment. Perhaps a major reason for this reluctance toward making total commitments is the perennial witnessing of marital breakups, often involving the parents of one or the other cohabitating party, and the fear of having to go through the same legal morass, financial obligations, and emotional pain. But the most compelling reason seems to be the young's fear of losing their independence and having to assume responsibilities. Such a loss would be out of line with the preponderant fun-morality that generally governs sexual activities. To many, whether they admit it or not, cohabitation is primarily a convenient sexual relationship that lasts as long as there is "fun" in it. The old monogamous rules would limit such license—a license that disguises itself as "self-actualization."

This is not to deny the benefits of a premarital moratorium that young people can use to get to know each other and to eventually base a more committal decision on such knowledge. The subinstitution of cohabitation can be used or abused as can any other institution; its most dismal abuse stands out when partners enter it with different motivations and objectives, so that sooner or later one or the other party gets hurt.

Social scientists who have foreseen the modern trend and the need for a halfway institution have suggested the usefulness of an arrangement that provides the secure framework of a dyad without the presumedly absolute commitment of a marriage. Margaret Mead, for example, long ago proposed two different types of marriages, one for people who want to enjoy each other's company without children and the other for people who want children and plan the conventional marriage-family.[62] Under the "individual marriage," young people could enter and leave the unions relatively freely with a minimum of obligations to each other. In a sense, the modern cohabitational arrangement represents this idea (except that Mead had some contractual and legal agreements in mind) and provides sexual gratification, companionship, and, assuming the woman is employed, two contributors to the household expenses.

---

[62] Margaret Mead, "Marriage in Two Steps," in *The Family In Search of a Future*, ed. Herbert A. Otto (New York: Prentice–Hall, 1970), pp. 75–84.

Commune. The New Sexuality is also visible, if not implemented, in the popular commune movement where, again, commitment is at a minimum, with no legal pressure to enter or stay. The commune is a subinstitution ideally suited to accommodate young people who prefer a moratorium on marital and familial commitments and yet desire some of the benefits of the equivalent adult institution such as: (1) the experience of human intimacy; (2) a feeling of belonging; (3) a feeling of security, physical as well as psychological; (4) a chance to satisfy curiosity about other people; and, most prominently, (5) sexual gratification on a regular basis.

In summary, the subinstitutions of dating, cohabitating, and communal living meet the needs of modern youth who shy away from total self-surrender and hesitate to enter into the symbiotic fusion found in traditional marriage. Many apparently are no longer willing to give themselves completely to one person and no longer expect to get all of the emotional satisfaction they need from a single lifelong partner.

Business. Ever since the counterculture, young Americans have been trying their hands at their own business ventures. They are establishments run by youth for youth; some are legal and others illegal. The former include stores dealing in clothes, jewelry, candles, records and tapes, posters, and antiques. In the vicinity of college campuses can be seen book exchanges, small boutiques, food co-ops, vegetarian restaurants, and often small workshops manufacturing furniture, leather goods, glassware, ceramics, and art work of all sorts.

Hovering between legality and illegality are shops that sell drug paraphernalia. The early '80s witnessed an onslaught of legislative bills which, if passed, would outlaw the sale of articles ostensibly meant to accompany or facilitate the use of illegal drugs.

Clearly illegal is the subinstitution that procures and often grows or manufactures illicit drugs, including marijuana, LSD, heroin, cocaine, and so forth. An intricate subterranean network, with well defined roles at various levels of procurement (including the roles of producing, smuggling, transporting, and retailing), caters to the desires of young and not so young Americans — desires not covered by the legitimate institutions of society.

The automobile. The role of the automobile in the lives of American teenagers has been cited by some writers as another example of subinstitutionalization. While having or needing a car is of course not an exclusive youth syndrome — on the contrary, it is typically an adult pattern — the *purpose* for which teenagers use and desire "wheels" defines it as subinstitutionalized behavior. Teenagers use the car not so much as a utilitarian appliance but to promote status, as compensation for the feeling of powerlessness, and to make dating possible.

The role of the car can be best understood in terms of its functions for the teenager. Besides providing transportation to school and work, the car usually serves one or several of four additional functions:

1. Owning or having regular access to a car is *prestigious* in the eyes of peers. The newer or more customized the car, the higher the prestige. A teenager may spend all savings on customizing and maintaining a car according to what his or her peers consider admirable.

2. The car is of great *instrumental* importance for dating and related activities. For the teenage boy, having a car is not only prestigious but usually imperative when asking a girl for a date. It allows for mobility and privacy, providing American teenagers with the most frequent setting for sexual experimentation.

3. For some boys a car is a *hobby*. In fact, researchers discovered that the most frequent hobby of high school boys was "working on their cars."[63]

4. Finally, driving an automobile can provide a *sense of power*. Since the adolescent experience includes a feeling of restriction and powerlessness, some teenagers use the car as a symbol of freedom and escape from adult control. Psychiatrist J. M. Murray hypothesized that driving a powerful automobile allows teenagers to express frustration and hostility with a minimum of risk of punishment and often with complete anonymity.[64]

There are a number of additional behavior patterns among young Americans that can be defined as subinstitutionalized behavior, but they tend to prevail among older youths who have achieved some degree of political and philosophical sophistication and countercultural stature. Such advanced youth or countercultural institutions include legal aid, "hot line" telephone centers, underground press, free schools, psychiatric "first aid," and many others.

SUMMARY

This chapter illustrated eight dimensions of subculture. No claim of completeness is made, since there are more variables and aspects in the vast teen world of the United States than would fit into one chapter or even one book. The illustrations were usually interpreted in a functional perspective to introduce the reader to the often hidden meanings of a behavior form.

(1) Teenagers' values and attitudes can be divided into three categories: in-group values are preoccupied with the issue of being popular and having status. Attitudes toward the out-group, that is, the Establishment, reflect caution and distrust. Of particular noteworthiness is the decline of the work ethic, the search for "self-actualizing" careers, the new psychology of entitlement, the sensitivity toward the question of war and peace, and the weakening of sex-role stereotypes. Value commitment to the American civilization may be a minority phenomenon, but it is nevertheless alive with thousands of young Americans choosing volunteerism as an expression of their philosophy and curiosity.

[63] Coleman, *The Adolescent Society*, p. 12.

[64] J. M. Murray, "Emotional Problems in Relation to Driving," *Action Achievement Report*, 8th Annual Massachusetts Governor's Highway Safety Conference, Boston, May 25, 1954.

(2) Teen argot is as puzzling to adults as it is functional to teenagers. Its functions include phonetic ease, relevance to the adolescent experience, maintenance of a sense of solidarity, provision of a status criterion, reflection of values, and a system of linguistic conditioning.

(3) Subcultures depend on channels of communication for survival. The simplest and most direct communication centers are the high school and college campuses, where young people have ample opportunity to share ideas and attitudes. Other media include television, radio, teen magazines, the record industry, and rock festivals.

(4) Teen fads and styles come and go. Their intentional as well as unintentional functions include status measurement, group identification, compensation for thwarted creativity, a relatively harmless expression of rebelliousness, security in uniformity of looks and behavior, and communication of belonging.

(5) A sense of solidarity is reflected in almost all forms of teenage behavior. It becomes most conspicuous in teenagers' effort to retain exclusivity of style and behavior forms, to preserve group authority and cohesiveness, and thereby maintain boundaries that clearly indicate the in- and the out-group. Solidarity is greatly enhanced by the identification of a common adversary and the common modes of defense and attack.

(6) Status criteria must be deduced from various behavior forms within the peer group. Group members learn early what makes for prestige. Prestige depends on the type of friend a teenager has, the type of clothes (especially for girls) a teenager wears, the show of bravado (particularly for boys), the popularity of one's date, the degree of adherence to peer style and argot, and the degree of convincing demeanor of "coolness" in everyday life.

(7) The American teenager is more oriented toward entertainment heroes and passive idols than toward true leaders. The functions of hero worship include the fueling of romanticism, various sex-substitutions (including fetishism), cathartic crowd behavior, attraction to the bizarre, identification with successful and yet "humble" youthful heroes, and the need for values.

(8) Teenagers have devised structures for gratifying needs and desires not sanctioned by the Establishment. Subinstitutionalization centers on desires for sexual expression, drug use, the use of the automobile, and the world of entertainment. Subculturally institutionalized behavior is probably most indicative of the strength of a subculture. It is also a useful approach to understanding a counterculture or social movement.

We now move to just such a discussion, and the next chapter will examine the more serious, goal- and action-oriented youth movements.

Chapter 11

Activism and Radicalism: The Making of Movements and Countercultures

Most of this chapter is history. The lessons taught by history must not be forgotten —whether they are contained in the history of the nation or in the youth scene. Examination of these lessons may prepare us to anticipate and better cope with recurrences of similar conditions and events.

DIFFERENCES BETWEEN SUBCULTURE AND COUNTERCULTURE

The general teen and pop subculture is to goal-oriented youth movements as a cops-and-robbers game is to a military battle. Differences between the teen sub-culture and the counterculture can be illustrated by a number of contrasts: static quality vs. dynamic quality; faddist-orientation vs. goal-orientation; entertainment vs. action; coexistence vs. intolerance; not intent on changing others vs. intent on proselytizing.

While this juxtaposition gives the impression of two radically different phenomena, the differences should be understood as differences in degree, with the typical subculture and counterculture occupying opposite poles, thus allowing for modified versions. For example, it is quite possible for a relatively passive subculture to undergo significant changes over time and to emerge as a militant counter-culture (or vice versa). It seems helpful, therefore, to look at the definitions of these two types of collectivities in the Weberian tradition of *ideal types*, of heuristic constructs that facilitate communication and research. This kind of definition has been encouraged by other students of collective behavior, such as Milton J. Yinger, who placed subculture and "contraculture" on a continuum and related them in a number of ways.[1]

It is possible to operationally implement the idea of a continuum by applying the eight dimensions discussed in the two preceding chapters and gauging the salience of the major dimensions to determine whether a degree of "cause" and solidarity has been achieved which would make the definition of movement or counterculture plausible. A counterculture would reflect sharper goals, clearer sub-institutional (or counterinstitutional) structures, and a keener sense of solidarity.

Another problem in sorting out the countercultural lifestyle from that of the subculture is that there are not concrete contours of belonging within the amorphous and unorganized mass of American youth, only blurred, overlapping, and interwoven shadows. Because there is no sharp boundary between the subculture and the counterculture, the *ideal-type* construct is again a helpful point of departure. In reality, the teen subculture absorbed many countercultural characteristics, and vice versa; for many practical purposes, the two collectivities largely coincided in sentiment and preference. Yet the true bearers of the counterculture were those called "youth" by Kenneth Keniston: the older-than-eighteen adolescents who made a serious attempt to change the American social system. These young adults were concentrated in the colleges and universities, claimed to be the youthful intelligentsia of the country, were politically radicalized, and came from the ranks of the psychedelic movement and other nonconformist groups. They coalesced into the "melting pot" of the counterculture.

ADOLESCENCE AND ALIENATION

The incentive to participate in social movements may spring from a variety of sources. Sociologists have suggested such major reasons are *relative deprivation*,[2] *the mass society*,[3] *social class aspiration*,[4] *personal pathologies*,[5] *the search for*

---

[1] Milton J. Yinger, *Countercultures* (Riverside, N.J.: Free Press, 1982).

[2] C. Y. Glock, "The Role of Deprivation in the Origin and Evolution of Religious Groups," in *Religion and Social Conflict*, ed. Robert Lee and Martin Marty (New York: Oxford University Press, 1964).

[3] William Kornhauser, *The Politics of Mass Society* (New York: Free Press, 1959).

[4] D. E. Morrison and A. D. Steeves, "Deprivation, Discontent, and Social Movement Participation: Evidence on a Contemporary Farmers' Movement," *Rural Sociology*, 32 (1967), 414–34.

[5] Hans Sebald, *Momism: The Silent Disease of America* (Chicago: Nelson-Hall, 1976); Bruno Bettelheim, "Obsolete Youth," *Encounter*, 23 (1969), 29–42.

meaning,[6] *and alienation.*[7] In life, many of these factors overlap and combine. For example, an exaggerated need to depend upon and be approved by an outside authority may combine with the attempt to satisfy the search for meaning; or the frustration suffered from relative deprivation may intensify the sense of alienation. The success of a movement in attracting followers depends therefore on the problems and sentiments of people and on how a movement's objectives relate to them.

American adolescents form a population that is hyperreceptive to countercultural ideas and radical suggestions because they look for an escape from the alienation that is caused specifically by adolescence and by anomic society in general. Hundreds of thousands of modern American youth struggle to overcome alienation, try to supplant anomie, and search for meaning.

The concept of alienation is probably the most fitting single description of the motivating power that drives modern youth to pursue countercultural objectives or join True Believer movements. A cause, a sense of destiny, and the accompanying benefits of belonging to a community of peers are strong attractions for the masses of inexperienced youth who desperately seek to alleviate their feelings of alienation and meaninglessness.

Alienation, in degree as well as kind, strikes no two persons the same way; it assumes a multitude of types and hues. It is the favorite playground of sociologists, political scientists, philosophers, and theologians. To simplify things, our discussion focuses on only a few of these types.

1. Probably the most important source of alienation for young persons has to do with the process of *developmental estrangement*; a sense of loss that comes as childhood ways are discontinued and adult ways not yet assumed. From this perspective, adolescence and alienation are inextricably bonded. The young feel rejected by a system that does not give them a productive and egalitarian place and puts them in ghettos for an ever-lengthening period before they are released to enter the labor force. They feel like aliens in the system, fail to establish a sense of belonging, and develop a rejective mood in return.

2. Rapid and uneven social change inflicts alienation through an acute sense of loss of tradition. The rapid chain reactions with which social (as well as technological) innovations succeed each other undermine the feeling of being anchored in acceptable and predictable customs. The supertechnological dynamics of postindustrial society create flux, unpredictability, and a pervasive sensation that something is being lost. This flux-prone lifestyle imposes strain and discomfort on the

[6] Hans Toch, *The Social Psychology of Social Movements* (New York: Bobbs-Merrill, 1965); Orrin E. Klapp, *Currents of Unrest: An Introduction to Collective Behavior* (New York: Holt, Rinehart & Winston, 1972) and *Collective Search for Identity* (New York: Holt, Rinehart & Winston, 1969); Eric Hoffer, *The True Believer* (New York: Mentor Books, 1951); Pitirim A. Sorokin, *The Crisis of Our Age* (New York: Dutton, 1941); Erich Fromm, *Escape from Freedom* (New York: Holt, Rinehart & Winston, 1941).

[7] Karl Marx and Friedrich Engels, *The German Ideology* (New York: International Publishers, 1947).

nervous system, which normally welcomes routine. Institutions, among other functions, serve the purpose of reducing nervous strain through predictable and routine procedures in everyday life.

3. Anomic society provides unwanted freedom. The young have a natural aversion to ideational vacuums and demand orientation and direction. The search for meaning is a powerful desire that often leads to participation in collectivities that promise a definite credo. Eric Hoffer, in *The True Believer*, and Erich Fromm, in *Escape from Freedom*, have called attention to the dangerous susceptibility of anomic populations to the persuasiveness of radical slogans.

4. Alienation of the poor, the jobless, and the victims of racial or ethnic prejudices is nothing new. What is new and has proved difficult for many adults to understand is alienation among segments of our population whose reasons for feeling estranged are obtuse, abstract, and have little to do with poverty, exclusion, oppression, or cultural deprivation of any kind. In fact, the most vocal of the alienated come from socioeconomically advantaged backgrounds. They are a vociferous minority of privileged middle- and upper-class youth who dissent from the established order. Richard Flacks surveyed activist youth and found that the student movement represents the disaffection not of an underprivileged stratum of the student population but of the most advantaged sector of the students, with most of the activists coming from high-income families.[8]

There is no simple reason why this should be so. A major cause probably originates in the affluent and comfortable background that prevents many offspring of well-to-do parents from earning their own livelihoods and working their way through college. The ensuing leisure time can be spent on more abstract activities such as philosophizing about possible reasons why one is bored and cannot find meaning in life. Life has started them out without a struggle — thus, they invent one: the reform or overthrow of a system shot through with injustices and social ills, none of which is personally relevant to them. This is not necessarily a denigration of this type of youth; one could interpret their motivation as either a romantic fancy born out of pampered, unrealistic, and bored lifestyle, or an exquisite vicariousness that, observing the suffering of others, instills compassion and incites activism.

A related insight that came from the same study by Flacks was that activists' parents were decidedly more liberal than the parents of other youth. This held true even when socioeconomic backgrounds were held constant. Only 6 percent of nonactivists' fathers described themselves as "highly liberal" or "socialist," whereas 60 percent of the activists' fathers described themselves in such terms. The implication of this is that activism, at least to some degree, runs in the family and thus is a familial rather than a generational phenomenon.

---

[8] Richard Flacks, "The Liberated Generation: An Explanation of the Roots of Student Protest," *Journal of Social Issues*, 23 (July 1967), 52–75. See corroboration in Hans Sebald, "Die Bewusste Kommune am Heilenden Wasser," *Unter dem Pflaster Liegt der Strand*, 7 (1980):7–28; Mike Brake, *The Sociology of Youth Culture* (Boston: Routledge & Kegan Paul, 1980).

5. For many young Americans, the reason for their alienation was more identifiable: They rejected the protracted war in Vietnam as immoral on the part of their nation and consequently refused to be drafted, preferred to go into exile, or joined antiwar organizations—activities that in turn, as a collectivity, became part of the countercultural movement. Alienation on these grounds cannot easily be ascribed to the adolescent experience, since it seemed to be based on more mature and rational arguments that millions of adults agreed with. Was the alienation of many young Americans truly based on anti-war conviction? This is still an unanswered question, especially in the light of earlier-mentioned research that discovered striking ignorance about the facts, figures, and circumstances of the war, not only among the "hawks" but also among the "doves." The conclusion seemed plausible that alienation is prompted more by basic emotional orientations rather than specific and objective assessment of the circumstances.[9]

The generalization growing out of this discovery suggests that the search for an alternative lifestyle may be based more often on sentiment, bias, and powerful emotion rather than on a rational and cognitive approach.

6. Finally, the process of undergoing socialization in a complex society is enough to cause pain and frustration to the adolescent, creating a rejective and alienated mood toward the Establishment. Only romanticists and a few anthropologists whose explorations never exceeded the horizon of a couple of idyllic islands might venture to suggest that socialization is fun—for the young as well as for the elders. In plain words: most of the time it is not! Given the American ethos of instantness and the technological promises of ease and pleasure in life, it is understandable that America's young find themselves terribly frustrated at having to go through a tedious introduction that includes the learning of a myriad of things which to them appear trivial, trying, and tiring.

Three additional comments should be made concerning youthful alienation in American society.

First, a certain degree of alienation is not to be judged as entirely negative. A society with some youthful alienation can profit from the converted energy and channel it in creative directions. Without any conflict or alienation there would be little motivation to search for improvement, deviate from tradition, and insist on progress. Anthropologists have noted that in societies in which the status of the young is well defined and integrated into the social structure (thus eliminating adolescence), change and innovation tend to be low. On the other hand, in societies in which youth's roles are uncertain and adult responsibilities and privileges are delayed, there is a predisposition to change, innovate, and experiment. The frustration caused by such confusions and delays generates a readiness to respond to new and alien ideas and to try out alternatives to existing institutions.[10] The nature of

[9] Hans Sebald, "Voices of War and Peace—What Do They Know? Attitudes and Knowledge about the War in Southeast Asia," *Pacific Sociological Review*, 14 (October 1971), 487–510.

[10] Frank Musgrove, *Youth and the Social Order* (Bloomington, Ind.: Indiana University Press, 1965), pp. 126–27.

the social structure thus determines at least in part the degree of youth's activism. Karl Mannheim elucidated the functionality of youth as a potentially deviant population when he described them as not committed to the *status quo* and thus free to push for change and innovation.[11] For this function, as we have discussed in an earlier chapter, we must pay the price of intergenerational conflict.

Second, alienation is not a phenomenon that applies uniformly to the youth of a nation. It is usually only a minority that feels alienation keenly enough to express it in the form of agitation and noteworthy opposition to the Establishment. For example, at the height of the counterculture in 1970, most students went along with the system and did not actively work toward abolishing or radically changing it. Harvard sociologist Seymour M. Lipset found in a worldwide study of collegiate political views that despite a season of well-publicized protests both in the U.S. and abroad, the vast majority of university undergraduates were either apolitical or supporters of well-established parties. Lipset claimed that, for example, the leftist, militant Students for a Democratic Society had only 7000 members among the 6.5 million American university students. In contrast, the Young Republicans and the Young Democrats had an enrollment of nearly 250,000. Lipset also believes that during the 1930s far more students were activistic, both on the right as well as the left, than are today.[12]

These moderates were the young who probably distanced themselves from the counterculture and other radical movements, but who nevertheless took part in the general youth subculture with its fads, styles, hero worship, argot, norms, and values. For many young, then, there existed a definite division between the general subculture and the radical counterculture. One might be safe, however, in assuming that countercultural youth most likely were part of or grew out of the subculture, whereas the converse was not necessarily true. This is a good example of the blurring and diffusion that are characteristic of the amorphous youth population.

Third, not all countercultural participation grew out of adolescent alienation — or any alienation, for that matter — but rather out of mature insight, valid information, and loyalty to America as a nation, wanting to influence and deflect the direction of national policies and to contribute constructively to a stronger and saner country. Hence, not out of alienation but out of dedication may a minority have decided to promote the countercultural cause.

It must be realized that the counterculture was not an entirely exclusive youth movement and that many adults were actively involved. In fact, some segments of the movement were pioneered primarily by adults and only later taken over or joined by youthful activists. For example, the psychedelic movement started with adult psychologists and writers (Huxley, Leary, Alpert, Metzner), and the civil rights movement had been borne by adults before youth adopted it.

[11] Karl Mannheim, *Essays on the Sociology of Culture* (New York: Oxford University Press, 1956).

[12] Seymour M. Lipset and Gerald M. Schaflander, *Passion and Politics: Student Activism in America* (Boston: Little, Brown, and Company, 1971).

THE SEARCH FOR ALTERNATIVE
LIFESTYLES

Apart from the exceptional motivations of small splinter groups, alienation seems to be the driving force behind many youth's agitation and search for new lifestyles.

A collective identity search is a symptom of modern society's depriving its young (as well as old) of certain psychological benefits, the lack of which prompts mass groping for activities and symbols in which to anchor a new identity. Young individuals in such situations grope because they are not fully aware of what is wrong and causes them discomfort—especially since they only too obviously cannot blame material or cultural deprivation as the source of their discontent. And yet they feel somehow cheated. When movements become concerned with identity, they develop certain characteristics, such as "style rebellion," self-ornamentation, concern with emotional gestures rather than pragmatic goals, hero worship, and cultism. Such a symbolic and emotional stance indicates that what is sought is not satisfied by ordinary economic and political solutions, but instead, basic questions of meaning and direction.

Youth's sense of being cheated cannot be explained in economic terms because the perception has its roots in our civilization's shortcoming in providing a convincing ideation. It is ideational alienation that is at the heart of modern youth's groping.

There are vast differences in the individual's response to the alienating elements of society. Some youth compensate by sublimation and by making positive contributions to the Establishment. Others see no way to work within the established order and are prone to march down deviant and militant avenues. In the process they generalize their rejection from specific elements and direct their wrath toward the entire social system, seeing justification in wanting to supplant it totally with a new, "just" and "beautiful" society—which, of course, is usually nothing short of utopia.

Utopias have always held a fascination for humans. It is their grand promise to abolish suffering and injustice that attracts humans one generation after another. It is an endearing and comforting thought, enhancing hope and courage, that there might be an ideal solution and that the dim light at the end of the tunnel will reveal itself as a bright and shining light that will safely guide and protect.

Still other youths manifest alienation by withdrawing from society as a whole. Some of them suffer deep and silent despair, apathy, and nihilistic attitude, and find no outlet or compensation for their frustration and confusion. Many of these end up receiving psychiatric care because they turn their pain inside and direct hostility and rejection toward themselves. The masochistic Punk style of the '80s seems to be representative of this type. Others direct hostility outward in such an uncontrolled and vehement form that their actions assume delinquency or criminality of a brutal nature.

An increasing proportion of youth over the past years has tried to alleviate its disappointments and alienation from American society (or Western civilization in general) by engaging in a search for alternative lifestyles. They turn to meditation, Eastern religions, and the occult (if nothing else than an affected dabbling in astrology); or they become ensconced in aesthetic or artistic pursuits, making art, poetry, and music a way of life. They may retreat to the "simple and natural" life of living with "the earth" by plowing the proverbial Idaho soil; or retreat to the symbiosis of communal life. Retreatisms of these various sorts were and are cultivated individually or tribally.

The inclination of American youth to embrace a cultic solution to alienation and the emptiness of anomie has become legendary during and since the counterculture years. Cults that promise to provide a total and absolute meaning for life have multiplied in America (and Western Europe) and are zealously seeking the conversion and allegiance of the young. Conway and Siegelman describe the youthful epidemic of cultic conversions in their book *Snapping*.[13] The twofold motivation of wanting to substantiate a personal identity and wanting to find a romantic (utopian) solution to all personal problems has created a profound vulnerability to the promises of various exotic and esoteric cults. "To snap" means experiencing a sudden personality transformation, being transformed from a seeker to a true believer, becoming totally filled with a new life-orienting meaning, and usually confusing wishful thinking with reality. The unrestrained yearning of youth for an omnipotent and omniscient guru often plays a portentous role in the process of "snapping" and tends to elevate charlatans to charismatic leaders.

The cultic retreat from mainstream society is a particular form of retreatism (the "sacred" type) and its widespread occurrence today is a relatively novel phenomenon in American history. There are and have been more "secular" forms of withdrawal.

Retreatist youth has by now established a tradition in American life. The hip Bohemians of the 1950s were among the colorful founders of the tradition. They constituted a leisure-time and unaffiliated intelligentsia following the European tradition of coffeehouse philosophy, attic art studios, and some peripheral drug experimentation. Two meccas were the San Francisco North Beach[14] and Greenwich Village in New York. These retreatists engaged in relatively coherent and philosophically mature critiques of modern society and had literary flair. However, they soon attracted a "lay" following that infiltrated their ranks and wreaked a metamorphosis of the whole movement. The beatniks evolved in the late 1950s, and were a far less talented and sophisticated circle, though still fairly literate.[15] They, in turn, were the immediate forerunners of the hippies, attracting ever-younger and increasingly unsophisticated followers, including runaways, drug derelicts, and generally very confused teenagers, with Haight-Ashbury becoming the

---

[13] Flo Conway and Jim Siegelman, *Snapping: America's Epidemic of Sudden Pesonality Change* (New York: Lippincott, 1978).

[14] Jerry Kamstra, *The Frisco Kid* (New York: Harper & Row, 1975).

[15] Bruce Cook, *The Beat Generation* (New York: Scribner's, 1971); Jack Kerouac, *On the Road* (New York: The Viking Press, 1955).

epitome of a movement that had no direction and went nowhere.[16] One offshoot of the hippies was the communards who tried a semiretreatist life in the company of the like-minded. A later retreatist development coming in the wake of the debacle of the hippie experiment was the street people, who were relatively indistinguishable from the hippies, except that they seemed to be less gregarious, less prone to affiliate with like-minded peers, and even less sophisticated.

The great upheaval of the counterculture more or less swallowed up these splinter groups, temporarily unified them in a common cause, and later (during the calmer late '70s) regurgitated a metamorphosis: the New Age movement.[17] The New Age people were the true heirs of the counterculture and synthesized into a philosophical core the best of the unique aspects that the counterculture had to offer. These counterculture scions of the '80s had a predilection for communal living, vegetarianism, and a mixture of the occult and Oriental religions. They no longer had the political militancy of their predecessors, but preferred a more philosophical-religious retreat. The economic vision was the Jeffersonian dream, consisting of independent farmers and small craftspersons who would revive the ancient personal bartering system instead of continuing the impersonal industrial lifestyle.

It is among New Age people that we see the clearest evidence of subinstitutionalization. Communes or communities of New Agers specialize in different services, from fruit growing to wilderness survival schools to holistic health centers. A participant-observer study by this author spanned several years during which he saw the rise and fall of a New Age commune settled around paradisal thermal springs in the Arizona desert.[18] The specialty of this commune was to provide alternative healing (as opposed to modern medicine) through exposure to the presumed energy flow from the earth, meditation, a vegetarian diet, and fasting. The central idea of the commune was to be "conscious" of all surrounding life and energy—a canon this group shared with all New Age people. But the specialty, the subinstitution within the movement, was healing. This service was offered to in-group members as well as to outsiders (those from the "straight" society)—to the latter primarily in order to derive an income that would assure continuous existence of the commune. Alas, as appears to be the fate with most, if not all, New Age communes, the "Commune at Healing Water" disintegrated after a few years of attempting to carve out an alternative lifestyle and offering the service of a subinstitution.

[16] Sherri Cavan, *Hippies of the Haight* (St. Louis: New Critics Press, 1972).

[17] Hans Sebald, "New Age Romanticism: The Quest for an Alternative Lifestyle as a Force of Social Change," *Humboldt Journal of Social Relations* (scheduled for publication in 1984).

[18] Hans Sebald, "Die Bewusste Kommune am Heilenden Wasser." (Unpublished English version: *The Conscious Commune at Healing Water: Scions of the Counterculture Celebrate Spirituality at New Sanctuaries*, Dept. of Sociology, Arizona State University, Tempe, Arizona, 1980.)

To be sure, there has been no consistent development or cultivation of a quality that might be judged as the evolutionary core of retreatist youth (such as a consistently ascending political, philosophical, social or altruistic sophistication that would culminate in an historical precedent of significance for youth the world over). Instead, serials of unorganized and largely unremembered trial-and-error experiments go in circles and end up nowhere.

Even the counterculture was somewhat characterized by this tendency. It reached its height about 1969-70 and was sparsely remembered five years later by American youth—though it was better remembered by adults. Obviously, history begins for the masses of American young around eighteen years of age; events and happenings prior to that age recede into a broad blur of relative meaninglessness. Hence, it is almost frightening when a sociology professor addresses current eighteen-to-twenty-two-year-old college students and draws blank stares and questioning looks when referring to counterculture. The current generation of young Americans has already entered a new era, and the counterculture is only known through occasional lectures or reading assigned by compulsive professors. There seems to be truth in the statement that one year's freshmen are likely to be oblivious to the causes, heroism, and battles of last year's seniors.

This is disconcerting insofar as it indicates that learning and the acquisition of social experience and wisdom is an ever-new process among the young, and that the upheavals, sacrifices, and movements of one generation have little pertinence and application to the next. It means that each generation is predisposed not merely to new but to repetitive trials and tribulations. Social maturity is thus not learned in a unidimensionally ascending way, but through repetitive experimenting to come to grips with the contingencies at hand. The best one can say, then, is that besides their follies, humans may also repeat the nobel and the dignified.

Hence, the following discussion of the 1965-72 counterculture as a movement aspiring to an alternative lifestyle is largely an exercise in history.

FROM THE COUNTERCULTURE
TO THE NEW AGE MOVEMENT

The counterculture was a prime example of the search for an alternative lifestyle. It was a collective attempt not only to change certain elements in American society, but the basic tenor of the system as well. Arising in the early 1960s, achieving its peak around 1969-70, and gradually ebbing in the early 1970s, the movement was all but dead by the mid-1970s, and only the last, slight ripples could be felt in 1976. Nevertheless, some discernable impressions, maybe lasting ones, have been left on the shores of the Establishment.

That the counterculture indeed represented a weighty force in social change is convincingly argued by Robert Wuthnow.[19] Derived from Mannheim's

[19] Robert Wuthnow, "Recent Patterns of Secularization: A Problem of Generations?" *American Sociological Review*, Vol. 41, October 1976, pp. 850-67.

theory,[20] the concept of "generation unit" allows Wuthnow to illustrate that a certain age group can be far more than merely a statistical cohort. In a sense, a generation unit is a "cultural unit" in which the members (1) are bonded together by a specific range of experiences, which predispose them to a typical mode of perception, thought, and behavior; (2) feel a "common destiny" or interest just as forcefully as a socioeconomic class; and (3) manifest "identity of responses," i.e., they act or react in similar, if not identical, ways to the contingencies of life. This generation unit acts as an agent of rapid social change by challenging existing norms, values, and traditional behavior modes. Hence the theory that social change is a steady, evolutionary process heeding continuity of cultural forms must be modified in the face of the generation unit.

The counterculture was a prime example of a challenging generation unit. It exhibited all the vital characteristics of a cultural unit, particularly a separate identity (as strong as a "social-class consciousness") that pitted it against the rest of society. The broader impact far exceeded the assumptions of the slow-evolutionary-change theory. Robert Nisbet, in criticizing the theory, put the significance of the counterculture into perspective when he said: "Change in any degree of notable significance is intermittent rather than continuous; mutational, even explosive, rather than the simple accumulation of internal variations."[21]

The discontent of the counterculture generation was indeed explosive. Foremost among reasons that the young gave for their anger and alienation was their opposition to *technocracy* – a lifestyle presumably dominated by technology, instead of the other way around. This phrase became a catchall concept for everything the young found wrong with American society and Western civilization in general. It included a pervasive rejection of a number of aspects, such as the military-industrial complex, which they accused of profiteering and chicanery; the impersonality of urban-industrial life, which they felt had lost the human touch; insensitivity toward human needs and human dignity, injustices of various types, inequality of racial, ethnic, sex, and age groups; the specific inhumanity and authoritarianism of the authorities; the abusiveness of the power structure; ecological disregards resulting in devastation of the natural environment; the capitalistic-materialistic world view, which they saw as a means to dehumanize; and the futile "objective consciousness" typical of Western inquiry into the riddles of life and the universe.

How pervasive can a rejection be? Literally, no building block of Western civilization was left untouched, and not one passed muster!

Complaints and rebellion against the power hierarchy, against material destitution and social oppression are an old history story that has recurred many times and, in fact, has been a constant in American society (and Western civiliza-

---

[20] Karl Mannheim, *Essays on the Sociology of Knowledge* (New York: Oxford University Press, 1952).

[21] Robert A. Nisbet, *Social Change and History* (New York: Oxford University Press, 1969), pp. 281–82.

tion in general). The significant new feature of the counterculture was its condemnation of the very method that has contributed to combat material wants and social problems: the scientific world view. Appraised as "objective consciousness," this world view was now condemned as being too impersonal and superficial and as leading to nowhere but disaster. The alternative groping for a lifestyle and a way to gain knowledge became a vulgarized form of *mysticism* that consisted of a naive conglomerate of largely misunderstood Eastern thought,[22] immature hedonism straight from Haight-Ashbury, and some thoughts of appreciable sensitivity and insight.

The counterculture had its prophets and literary heroes. Some of them, had they been asked, would probably have declined candidacy for such status. For example, Hermann Hesse's novels were adopted variously as a door to Eastern peacefulness and mysticism (*Siddhartha*) and as a visionary example of psychedelia (*Steppenwolf*),[23] but there is serious doubt that Hesse wrote any of his works with a countercultural concept in mind. As he cautioned in his 1963 foreword to *Steppenwolf*, his perspective was artistic and psychoanalytic, and varying interpretations were outside his literary responsibility. Nonetheless, the counterculture boosted the sale of his books; of the 30 million sold worldwide nearly 12 million were sold in the United States by 1977.

Psychologist Timothy Leary gleefully grasped the nomination, became a prophet and, in fact, a martyr of the psychedelic wing of the counterculture. Fired from Harvard in 1963, along with Richard Alpert, because of unauthorized psychedelic experiments with students, he became guru of the drug culture that joined forces with the counterculture. His style, however, literary and otherwise, was so phantasmagoric and unbecomingly egotistic, even to most of the young drug users, that his role of psychedelic guru was limited to the inner circles of the newly founded International Federation for Internal Freedom and never penetrated into other segments of the counterculture. His autobiographical works, *High Priest* and *The Politics of Ecstasy*, add up to an unintentional caricature of countercultural themes delivered in an embarrassingly egomaniacal style.[24]

The counterculture selected Allen Ginsberg its poet. His style, a combination of protest, lament, and mysticism, appealed to sentiment-hungry youth who welcomed a poetic manifesto reflecting their dissatisfaction.[25]

Alan Watts, through his televised lectures, books, and private classes, became the foremost popularizer of Zen Buddhism.[26] Though his background was associ-

---

[22] Authoritative assessment of what American youth's adaptation of Hindu elements means was presented by Gita Mehta, *Karma Cola: Marketing the Mystic East* (New York: Simon & Schuster, 1981).

[23] Hermann Hesse, *Steppenwolf* (New York: Random House, 1963) and *Siddhartha* (New York: New Directions, 1951).

[24] Timothy Leary, *High Priest* (New York: World, 1968) and *The Politics of Ecstasy* (New York: Putnam, 1968).

[25] Allen Ginsberg, *Empty Mirror: Early Poems* (New York: Totem Press, 1961).

[26] Alan Watts, *This Is It, and Other Essays on Zen and Spiritual Experience* (New York: Collier, 1967).

ated with erudite studies of Oriental religion, the popularized version of his work crystallized into a simplistic and naive cult that served perfectly to enhance and reinforce the adolescent knack for rationalizing and dignifying hedonism, "dropping out," and the inability to be articulate. With its commitment to "wise silence," for example, Zen provided a convenient camouflage for the moody inarticulateness of adolescents. Although adolescents talked about it and made it a significant entry in their argot, "satori" (the achievement of inner peace and bliss) remained far from the American coast.

The wide acceptance of Carlos Castaneda's works signaled the passing of the age of ideology and the inauguration of the age of mystagogy. His works deserve this distinction on the basis of their astonishingly widespread acceptance and the religious fervor with which the young adopted his ideas, replacing the scientific world view with Castaneda's "magical view" of life and the universe. In such books as *The Teaching of Don Juan: A Yaqui Way of Life* and *Journey to Ixtlan: The Lessons of Don Juan*, he tried to persuade the young that the psychedelic vision is a way of life that is vastly more profound and insightful than the knowledge obtained through the traditional "objective" approach.[27] The setting of his presumedly factual observations was a Yaqui Indian's Sonoran environment. Although Castaneda's lore remained unverified (he refused to introduce anyone to the characters or places described, and his depiction of life in the desert creates a credibility gap for those who know it), the teachings of the shaman, Don Juan, were accepted with a singular ferocity by masses of young Americans as if they were truly verified and, in fact, as if they would open the door to a truer, albeit magical, world. This was the time for college instructors to be nonplussed by the noncritical acceptance of such "magical" and "mystic" credos, even though this acceptance meant that reliable scientific principles were totally rejected. It was not until Richard de Mille's publication of two critical tomes, *Castaneda's Journey* and *The Don Juan Papers*,[28] that Castaneda's credibility was seriously questioned— and even then fanatics tried to ignore evidence that strongly suggested Castaneda's tales to be hoaxes.

A degree of political sophistication was derived from reading the works of socialist and political scientist Herbert Marcuse, who compared Marx and Freud, accomplished amazing theoretical combinations, and offered scathing criticism of the capitalistic system.[29] Such reading of political philosophers, including Marx and Engels, was reserved for the college-educated and politically radicalized wing of the counterculture and remained esoteric matter to other segments of the movement.

[27] Carlos Castaneda, *The Teaching of Don Juan: A Yaqui Way of Knowledge* (Berkeley, Cal.: University of California Press, 1968) and *Journey to Ixtlan: The Lessons of Don Juan* (New York: Simon and Schuster, 1972).

[28] Richard de Mille, *Castaneda's Journey* (Santa Barbara, Calif.: Ross-Erickson, 1976); *The Don Juan Papers: Further Castaneda Controversies* (Santa Barbara, Calif.: Ross-Erickson, 1980).

[29] Herbert Marcuse's writings are too prolific to be listed here; the interested reader is directed to an anthology, *The Critical Spirit: Essays in Honor of Herbert Marcuse*, ed. Kurt H. Wolff and Barrington Moore (Boston: Beacon Press, 1967).

Then there were writers who were semiproponents and semievaluators of the counterculture, writing during its life span, largely applauding it, and praying for its longevity. Theodore Roszak's *The Making of a Counter Culture*[30] became the counterculture's little book of thoughts, interpretations, and prophecies, supplemented by such manifestos as Charles A. Reich's *The Greening of America*[31] and Philip E. Slater's *The Pursuit of Loneliness.*[32] These books reiterated the counterculture's assaults on American civilization, gave it a literary platform, and became part of the movement proper.

It would tax the frame of this chapter to discuss all the important writers and contributors who promoted the cause of the counterculture. Suffice it to say that they included personalities who offered political philosophy, religious orientation, educational reform, poetic protest, the psychedelic or "magical" approach, utopian constructs, and a rejection of Western science and "objective consciousness."

The diversity of these contributions is directly correlated with the diversity of the countercultural population itself, which consisted of an amorphous body with diverse motivations, orientations, and interests. Yet on one basic goal, all seemed to coalesce: to supplant Western technocracy by a "humane and just" system that would reintroduce (the question of "re-" from what and where was never clarified) sensitivity and humanity. Another agreement was the antiwar stance directed against American intervention in the political and military processes of Southeast Asia. More than any other element, this issue added cohesiveness and some degree of organization to the movement. It is a good question, albeit hardly answerable, whether or not the counterculture would have had a chance to evolve had the U.S. not been involved in the war.

Two other basic agreements seemed to run through the counterculture. One was prodrug and the other was promysticism. A majority of radical youth accepted drugs (psychedelics and marijuana) as a life-enhancing medium. A vast majority sympathized deeply with a mystic (vs. "objective") approach to life and knowledge. While youthful political activism was not an entirely new thing in American history, Roszak identified a novel dimension that became an integral part of the counterculture: the unprecedented infatuation with the occult, magic, and exotic ritual.[33]

The craving for the mystic and occult spread and took root outside the counterculture and has been growing ever since. Future historians may define this development as a significant turning point in the religious orientation of Western people. It was with the counterculture that a singular religious-philosophical syncretism arose that blended elements of Hinduism, Buddhism, Christianity, and various

---

[30] Theodore Roszak, *The Making of a Counter Culture* (Garden City, N.Y.: Doubleday, 1969).

[31] Charles A. Reich, *The Greening of America* (New York: Bantam, 1970).

[32] Philip E. Slater, *The Pursuit of Loneliness: American Culture at the Breaking Point* (Boston: Beacon Press, 1970).

[33] Roszak, *The Making of a Counter Culture*, p. 124.

and sundry aspects of the occult into a new panmysticism. Illogical and romantic as it may appear to "objective" outsiders, this mixture seems to endure and give meaning to many modern youths, particularly to those identifying with the New Age movement. However, identification with the movement is not a necessary condition for embracing the new syncretic "consciousness." For example, college students, many of whom are not even familiar with the phrase "New Age," reflect a high degree of occult-mystic inclination. Inquiring into this question over a three-year period resulted in the information presented in Table 11-1. Accordingly, in 1981 nearly 30 percent of college students believed in reincarnation, with the same proportion undecided but allowing for its possibility, and only 40 percent not believing in it. At the same time, 75 percent believed in a personal God. Half of the respondents either believed in astrology or allow for its validity. Only 8 percent of the respondents refused to believe that we are visited by UFOs directed by intelligent beings from outer space. (See details in Table 11-1.)

TABLE 11-1   Percentage distribution of religious/occult beliefs held by college students, 1979, 1980, 1981

BELIEF IN		1979 (N = 100)	1980 (N = 157)	1981 (N = 106)
Reincarnation	yes	20	23	29
	no	47	44	42
	undecided	33	33	29
Astrology	yes	14	12	12
	no	57	58	50
	undecided	29	30	38
UFOs from outer space directed by intelligent beings	yes	39	52	59
	no	20	16	8
	undecided	41	32	33
Personal God with whom you can communicate	yes	65	73	75
	no	17	12	9
	undecided	18	15	16
ESP, including clairvoyance, psychokinesis, etc.	yes	54	58	66
	no	16	20	6
	undecided	30	22	29

Source: Hans Sebald, Surveys at Arizona State University, Tempe, Arizona, 1979, 1980, 1981.

Apart from prodrug and promysticism, the diversity of the counterculture was remarkable. The counterculture incorporated the psychedelic movement, the peace and protest movement, the various liberation movements (women, homosexuals, ethnic and racial groups, etc.), radical professional groups (the radical therapists, liberal clergy, progressive academicians and educators, etc.), the New Left movement and possibly some religious-mystic movements (Hare Krishna, meditators,

Jesus movement, etc.). A conglomerate of numerous intertwining movements and organizations either totally or partly, lastingly or temporarily pursued countercultural objectives.

How did the activism manifest itself in real life, in the actual behavior of young Americans? A part of the outward expressions of the counterculture included such mass behavior as protest demonstrations, sit-ins, riots, occupations of buildings on campuses, taking hostages of university administrators to force consent to political and social demands, destruction of government property, disruption of classroom procedures, ritualistic burning of draft cards, militant confrontations with law enforcement personnel (such as culminated at Kent State University), and widespread (though more individually enacted) draft evasion and desertion from the armed forces.

Though some of these mass expressions were planned, organized, and reasonably constrained, many of them sprang from impulse and the carnival spirit, were destructive, and did not serve the nobler causes of the movement. Among the masses of protesters were many teenagers (as well as older youths) who were not trained in abstract thought and not honed in political sophistication. They were primarily attracted by excitement, the personality drama at elections and other political exhibitionisms, and the sensate experience of being bodily engulfed in the excited mass of a mob or riot. Maybe Dr. Andrew Weil's notion that the human brain, old and young, needs to be "blown" or "stoned" once in a while to clear the neurons of congestive tension is valid to such scenes.[34] Such ecstasy, presumably natural and necessary to the brain, can find implementation in the context of a mass of protesters or rioters. (Weil, who was sympathetic to the counterculture, saw in psychedelic drug use only one avenue—one he warned against—to achieve this beneficial ecstasy.) This brings to mind Gustave LeBon's classic treatise on mass psychology, which proposed that individuality is absorbed and suppressed by the crowd's raptures and action-oriented surges.[35]

Not all countercultural expressions assumed a mass character. Part of the activities consisted of rational negotiations and legitimate political campaigns, especially at election time to promote sympathetic candidates and to publicize new ideas.

A large portion of activities took place *within* the counterculture, in interaction with like-minded peers. Many of the styles and patterns of interaction deserve to be defined as subinstitutions or, as Richard Flacks called them, "counter-institutions."[36] Examples include the commune movement that stirred within the counterculture;[37] publications such as *Rolling Stone* and *High Times* (particularly

---

[34] Andrew Weil, *The Natural Mind* (Boston: Houghton Mifflin Company, 1973).

[35] Gustave LeBon, *Psychologie des Foules* (Paris: F. Olean, 1895).

[36] Richard Flacks, *Youth and Social Change* (Chicago: Rand McNally, 1971), pp. 110-20.

[37] Keith Melville, *Communes in the Counter Culture: Origins, Theories, Styles of Life* (New York: Morrow, 1975).

slanted toward the psychedelic movement) and the flamboyant underground press; musicals or rock operas such as *Hair*, *Jesus Christ Superstar*, *Godspell*, and *Tommy*; free schools; childcare centers; people's parks; credit unions; tenant organizations; "hot-line" phone services; "first-aid" psychiatric service centers (such as Terros); rock music festivals; organic food co-ops; illegal drug traffic, including growing, manufacturing, smuggling, distributing, and consuming illegal drugs; business enterprises marketing books, clothes, psychedelia, jewelry, candles, incense, posters, etc; therapeutic networks and free clinics helping youngsters with such problems as abortion, VD, drug addiction, and mental health; and peace centers serving as bases for the planning and staging of protest actions.

The pursuit of these functions and the adherence to structures to carry them out had an interesting consequence: *it territorialized the counterculture*, reinforcing youth ghettos, forming youth communities, and establishing exclusive channels of communication. The creation of jobs in subinstitutions and the sharing of economic and child-rearing responsibilities in collectives suggested viable means to refuse adult roles as currently defined in our culture and to avoid becoming absorbed by conventional social structure. Examples of youth's territorializing were (and still are to some extent) rural communes and households established in an effort to live off the land, and to live cooperatively and maximize self-sufficiency. It was hoped that in the process the pressures of competitive work, police, pollution, crowds, and the corruption of technocratic affluence could be shut out.

The movement can thus be understood first as activism directed outward, aiming at changing and reforming the "system," and secondly as an attempt to regulate interaction and to satisfy desires not met by the parent society's regular institutions. The former function distinguishes the movement from an ordinary subculture; the latter, dealing with internal structure, operates to varying degrees in both subcultures and countercultures.

These two major functions tended to conflict with each other. In fact, they deflected the main goals of the counterculture and sidetracked the whole movement. This happened because the counterinstitutions developed ever-greater exclusivity, grew into rigidity, and preserved territoriality — conditions that blocked the proclaimed goal of reforming the larger society and transcending it with the subinstitutions. In other words, the counterinstitutions and the internal organization got in the way of revolution and prevented society from being permeated with the new ideas. It is the old process of an initially revolutionary movement becoming immobilized by preoccupation with internal functions and the structures that go with them.

Not all interpretations of the counterculture are as positive and supportive as the earlier mentioned examples. Unlike Roszak or Reich or Slater, psychologist Bruno Bettelheim, historian Lewis S. Feuer, and essayist John W. Aldridge, for example, interpreted the movement not as an expression of rational, intelligent, and informed youth combatting a "sick society," but as a symptom of irrational, destructive, ignorant, and even pathological personalities who rebel against a society that is reluctant to accept their immature hedonism. To some degree, the disagreements between these assessors stem from a failure to recognize fully the diversity of the counterculture and to distinguish among different kinds of activists, both in respect to motivation and to actual form of dissent.

Feuer uses psychoanalytic theory to debunk the assumption that the youth movement was based on idealism and altruism though he allows for minor degrees of such motivations. Rather, he sees the movement as an expression of strong and largely unconscious hostility against parents in specific and adults in general.[38] Despite individual variations, history has revealed a consistent similarity among all youth movements (specifically student movements): in motivation, the social conditions that provoked them, and the course the movements run. Youth movements are characterized by largely nonmaterialistic motivations that are rarely invited by conditions of daily life but are rooted in "deep, unconscious sources" that essentially deal with a conflict of generations. Feuer overlooked a very concrete source of motivation for rebellion: the war in Vietnam, which was extremely unpopular with an appreciable proportion of the young as well as the old. The refusal to risk one's life or health and the refusal to kill or maim others [the so-called "enemies"] were certainly rational, conscious, and, in a sense, "materialistic motivations."

Bettelheim's assessment of the counterculture is even more negative.[39] He explains it as rebelliousness growing out of "permissive" (though he finds the term too vague) child rearing, particularly in upper-middle-class homes, and the result of protracted adolescence that subjects physiologically and intellectually mature youth to a stagnant moratorium that is boring, degrading, and infuriating. In addition, Bettelheim believes that a sizable segment of American adults is caught up in a youth cult that is not only immature but has the wrong reinforcing effect on young people. The cult tends to reinforce youth's rebelliousness, since its followers feel that their youthfulness not only makes them admirable but also endows them with impunity to do whatever they wish. Many adults are in awe of anything that is youthful and are therefore hesitant to react negatively toward young people. What the public often overlooks, Bettelheim fears, is that radical youth are basically "fixated at the age of temper tantrum." Needless to say, Bettelheim's claim that the "pathology" against which activists presumably fight lies in their own personalities rather than in society has as much pleased and appeased the conservative audience as it has disturbed and displeased the liberal audience.

Aldridge, the most eloquent of the critics of countercultural activism, warns against dignifying it by calling it a "culture" of any sort, feeling that if we do, we would pay homage to the infantile hedonism of youth.[40] Western societies tend to

[38] Lewis S. Feuer, *The Conflict of Generations* (New York: Basic Books, 1969).

[39] Bruno Bettelheim, "Student Revolt, The Hard Core," *Vital Speeches of the Day*, 35 (1969), 406; see also D. Dempsey, "Bruno Bettelheim is Dr. No," *New York Times Magazine*, January 11, 1970, p. 22.

[40] John W. Aldridge, *In the Country of the Young* (New York: Harper's Magazine Press, 1970).

give credence to youth's complaints as if they were legitimate matters and rational propositions, whereas actually they are largely bluffs—which often succeed because of society's pervasive guilt complexes and its pursuit of youth cult. Youth must learn that real life is not to be confused with an encounter group session, that status interaction is not necessarily bad, and that clear and hard functional work without disruption by *ad hominem* arguments is an indispensable prerequisite for society.

Sociologists Ken Keniston[41] and Richard Flacks[42] take the middle ground, seeing mature as well as immature aspects of countercultural activism and take a scientific stance in describing their findings. They have found activist youth more intelligent, independent, sensitive, concerned with moral values, idealistic, and emotionally secure than nonactivist youth. Rather than rejecting youthful activism and dissent by references to psychopathology or, on the other hand, accepting it uncritically as the dawn of a new millennium, these sociologists encourage the public to be responsive to what is legitimate and reasonable in the dissent. By engaging in a dialogue, the older and the younger generation as well as the radicals and the conservatives could help each other obtain insight and understanding. Radical youth, in the opinion of these sociologists, points the way to improvement because they react against a society that may need alternative or modified values to improve a materialistic-capitalistic civilization.

Where has the counterculture gone and what has it accomplished?

First, the youthful counterculture is not an ephemeral moment in history; it is an ongoing process that will linger to some degree as long as there exists an adolescent population that possesses the potential for rebellion, deviation, and innovation. (This argument, discussed earlier, is also advanced by Mannheim and Musgrove.) The countercultural potential is an intrinsic element of the adolescent collectivity; and, in a sense, there is a correlation between the degrees of adolescence and the degree of potential. In sum, one may say that adolescence provides for some degree of perpetual counterculture. The virulent upheaval of the 1965-72 counterculture is therefore merely a sharp upward fluctuation of the seismograph that measures adolescent unrest. Its extreme expression was probably triggered by the unusually vulnerable climate surrounding the war in Vietnam; and, interestingly enough, countercultural activism dissipated as the war declined and finally came to an end. The potential for renewed explosion remains, and the triggering of new unrest depends on processes occurring in the larger society as well as in international relations.

Second, the counterculture made impressions that will not soon be deleted. "Straight" society, in absorbing them, has been bent. Student activism, a core aspect of the counterculture, has largely abolished the old *in loco parentis* authority and promoted a clearer transition into adult status. It is largely to the credit of the agitation and demands of the counterculture that federal legislation fixed the legal

[41] Kenneth Keniston, *Young Radicals: Notes on Committed Youth* (New York: Harcourt, 1968) and "Student Activism, Moral Development, and Morality," *American Journal of Orthopsychiatry*, 40 (July 1970), 577-92.

[42] Richard Flacks, "The Liberated Generation."

adult age at eighteen. A new morality reflects the impact of the counterculture: Yankelovich's survey during the mid 1970s revealed the emergence of new cultural attitudes and the decline of some old ones. To reiterate: the new generation has a less sex-stereotyped view of human interaction; a more sensitive outlook on war, the military, and national policy; a "self-actualizing" career motivation; a psychology of entitlement that takes economic security and other privileges for granted, and expects the government to provide them; and a resistance to the old Protestant ethic.

Most importantly, the counterculture has silently spawned the New Age movement. Because the movement refrains from militancy, missionary zeal, and representation in public life, its growth and significance have largely escaped public attention. While it is unlike its progenitorial counterculture in manner and in the amount of decibels used to express an alternative lifestyle, it resembles the counterculture insofar as it lacks coherent organization, definite leadership, and a uniform platform. The core followers of the New Age are withdrawn communards who prefer a gentle and "natural" way of life and "doing one's own thing." Their lifestyle is a conscious and uncompromising result of the counterculture, and their guiding star is a philosophy that has little use for the traditional American materialism and capitalism.

It is for future historians to more fully recognize the impact that the counterculture and its New Age offshoot is having on sociocultural change in America.

THE TRUE-BELIEVER MOVEMENTS

The escape routes from alienation and meaninglessness during the 1960s and '70s jutted out into many different directions. Where they arrived depended not so much on youth's sense of direction as on three related factors: (1) the intensity of alienation; (2) the basic emotional predisposition of the individual; and (3) the coincidence of exposure. Most likely it is the basic emotional makeup of the individual that is the major prompting force to join radical and totalitarian groups.

For example, young persons who have been consistently conditioned from early years to depend on outside authority to guide them and make decisions for them are more interested in affiliations where they again can play a subservient role. If their sense of alienation and loneliness is strong enough, and if exposure (in many instances largely coincidental) provides the contact, they may lock into a movement that calls for following and obeying rather than for action and initiative. Conversely, youths whose upbringing equipped them with a sense of initiative and power may either stay aloof from radical affiliations or seek out groups that provide opportunities for independent thought.

Depending on these variables, we can observe a spectrum of group affiliations, some of them giving optimal initiative and personal freedom to their members, others denying individuality. These, then, are the broad theoretical considerations that would play a role if one wanted to answer the question of why certain youths end up in certain movements.

Another general point must be made. In our age, characterized by an intense search for meaning, the various movements are related not merely by the motivational backdrop of helping fulfill the need of an identity, but also by actual goals, interests, and style of attempting to achieve them. Movements of different appearances thus found a common framework in the counterculture. A discussion of True-Believer movements is therefore not to be understood as focusing on a completely different phenomenon from the counterculture. Some of the movements that go under the True-Believer label were in fact part of the general countercultural stream. One could even enlarge upon the definition of the True Believer and say that the counterculture as such belongs in this category. For purposes of singling out groups with a particularly doctrinaire and totalitarian climate, however, a separate discussion is necessary.

Pitirim A. Sorokin's theory of historical phases forms a cogent background for this discussion. The theory, as briefly mentioned in Chapter One, assumes that we have left an idealistic era, are currently groping in a sensate age, and are about to enter a new ideational phase. Our current unrest, symptomized by youth's search for identity, signifies the advent of an ideational civilization that will satisfy the need for an unambiguous world view.

Apparently our traditional ideational forces have declined and become meaningless for the young generations, whose alienation drives them on toward alternative realities. The old scientific reality, the "objective consciousness," is no longer sufficiently powerful to capture the imagination of youth and dispel their existential anxiety.

No movement other than the religious-totalitarian provides so complete a gratification for youth's ideational search. It is in this perspective that a number of powerful religious youth movements must be understood. The revival of mystical religion, primitive lore, spiritualism, ritual occultism, astrology, and the preoccupation with meditation is beyond a mere fad—it is youth's attempt to expand awareness beyond the limits imposed by modern science and the objective approach to life. This reaching out for new meaning is the great adventure of our age.[43]

While the search for meaning is of course a natural part of every individual's life, the followers of the True-Believer movements distinguish themselves from ordinary searchers insofar as

1. they use their lives to serve the belief instead of the reverse;
2. they make proselytizing their duty;
3. they are convinced, or at least claim to be, that their belief is the only valid philosophy in life;

---

[43] See detailed discussions in David G. Bromley and Anson D. Shupe, Jr., *Strange Gods: The Great American Cult Scare* (Boston: Beacon, 1981); Ken Levi, ed., *Violence and Religious Commitment* (University Park: Pennsylvania State University Press, 1982); and Herbert Richardson, ed., *New Religious and Mental Health* (Lewiston, N.Y.: Edwin Mellen Press, 1980).

4. they use radical means to accomplish the missions and visions of their True Belief;
5. they subordinate themselves to a totalitarian-radical organization and to leaders who demand absolute loyalty.

These characteristics illustrate that the psychological climate of the general counterculture was different only in degree and not in kind. The True-Believer movement must also be understood in terms of the *ideal type*, which means that some of the movements discussed do not meet all criteria or meet them only to some extent.

All radical youth movements have a religious core. It is the integrating, meaning-giving function at the heart of the definition of religion (from *religare*, "to bind together") that youth seek. Such movements typically possess *creed*, *cult*, and *code*; i.e., they proclaim a basic meaning, provide ritual and sensate implementation, and present guidelines for everyday life.

The cultic is instrumental in creating a sense of transcendence, the feeling of merging into a wholeness of existence, being related to others, and being integrated meaningfully into the universe. This feeling can be strong enough to envision a freedom from conventional rules of language and logic—ultimately of freedom from all the rules of society. Some movements exhibit these characteristics more explicitly than the general counterculture, and that is why we present a separate discussion here. Below are some examples.

The Jesus movement.   A movement that amassed many followers and much publicity was, and to a significant degree still is, the Jesus movement. In a sense it was a revival of a fundamentalist version of Christianity, the brunt of which was carried by the radical fervor of thousands of young Americans who proclaimed a revolution in Jesus' name.[44] Their basic message was that the Bible is absolutely true and that miracles do happen. They proceeded to spread the message with the zeal of revolutionaries. Their reliance in the crusade was on otherworldly powers; and their activism followed a timetable that was announced by Bill Bright, the founder of Campus Crusade for Christ. He forecast the saturation of America with the gospel of Christ by 1976, and that of the world by 1980; he allowed, however, that the Lord might prefer a slower pace.[45]

Studies have shown that many of the young zealots had gone through serious personal difficulties prior to their conversions, and many of them engaged in a May-December marriage of the rebellious counterculture and conservative religion.[46] Many of them switched from the fraudulent promises of drugs to the

---

[44] Flo Conway and Jim Siegelman, *Holy Terror* (New York: Doubleday, 1982). A less analytic and more personal account of confronting the Jesus cult is by Steve Allen, *Beloved Son: A Story of the Jesus Cults* (New York: Bobbs-Merrill, 1981).

[45] "The New Rebel Cry: Jesus is Coming," *Time*, June 21, 1971, p. 56.

[46] Fred L. Whitam, "Peers, Parents, and Christ," *Proceedings of the Southwestern Sociological Association*, 19 (1968), 154–58.

promises of Life Eternal and Life Meaningful. They replaced the situation ethics of the "new morality" with the Ten Commandments, apparently expecting greater psychological security from an ensconcement in a totalitarian world view. Many of them switched from being flower children to children of the Lord. In letters to editors teenagers repent their past "dope" habits, find Jesus far more rewarding to be "stoned on," and approve of Him as a "far-out guy," who works miracles.[47]

The emphasis of the new Christian movement was on the *personal relationship* with Jesus, who enters the lives of individuals and manifests Himself in miracles that still occur today. The commitment of many adolescents to the new Christianity was total and they burned all bridges behind — though they didn't have that many to burn.

This was not a uniform movement. There were the well-dressed collegians, the Campus Crusaders for Christ, maintaining booths on campus malls and taking every opportunity to speak to classes and groups. Then there were the more spontaneous and younger converts who chanted hymns, swayed to musical rhythms in ecstasy, crowded beaches for mass baptism, and proclaimed their newly found identity with jubilation, love, and eternal promises. They were also known as Street Christians, Jesus Freaks, or Evangelical hippies, and it was they who blended conservative religion with the counterculture. Their beginning is usually traced to the 1967 flower era in San Francisco, but there were almost simultaneous stirrings in other parts of the U.S. Many of the converts, though by no means all, affected the hippie style; many others, however, foreswore it as part of their new lives. And finally there were the dead-serious Children of God who foresaw doomsday for America, retreated into farm communes, adopted biblical aliases for their members, pursued proselytizing with fanaticism (they were accused of brainwashing), and spread to become an international movement.

The mass-behavior aspects of the movement would have provided a laboratory for testing the Durkheimian theory of the origin of religiosity: the contagious chanting, singing, dancing, swaying, and the reinforcing corollary of testimonials, oratory, and ritual seemed to produce in many participants a degree of ecstasy that was interpreted as religious experience by the transfixed adolescent. Durkheim's theory maintains that religiosity is predicated not by cognitive search and rational insight but by the ecstasy-arousing participation in group rituals and mass excitement. The French sociologist called attention to the power of the group in bringing forth social products which could not be explained through individual physiological or psychological process.[48]

The Unification movement. Another radical religious movement that recruited followers primarily from the young was Rev. Sun Myung Moon's international Unification Church and its college chapters, the Collegiate Association for

[47] "Letters to the Editor," *Look*, March 23, 1971, p. 6.
[48] Emile Durkheim, *The Elementary Forms of the Religious Life* (New York: Macmillan, 1915).

the Research of Principles. The youthful followers were inspired by the idea of changing the world and, as a new generation, making it a better place. The method for achieving this, according to the movement's spokespersons, is a "unification of thought" that, more than being merely a religious creed, consists of a total lifestyle. It aspires to unite the world on a spiritual basis. To pursue the conversion of college youth, the movement maintains communal living centers in the vicinity of most large universities. As is the Krishna movement, Moon's circle is a haven for ex-hippies who fled confusing promiscuity and anomie to embrace an ascetic and absolutistic lifestyle that provides security and direction.[49]

The endurance of the movement is astounding. It has weathered difficulties on all fronts, including the 1982 federal conviction of Rev. Moon on tax offenses, restrictions by local authorities, and the relentless pursuit of "deprogrammers" over more than two decades. Instead of diminishing, membership has grown steadily and by the early '80s far exceeded the reported 30,000 of the mid '70s.

At the Unification Church Training Center at Barrytown, N.Y., Moon's young missionaries are being prepared for a World Plan to rid the world of Satan, who is believed to be very much alive and active—in fact, causing possessions. The implicit belief among the believers is that Moon is the messiah (although he himself claims to be merely a clairvoyant tool of God) and that he may command absolute devotion. Numerous cases of youthful followers' alienation from their parents have been reported and the movement was accused of brainwashing young people. Press and TV reports described mental breakdowns as a consequence of intense indoc-trination and the resulting conflicts and anxieties. Some parents, realizing that they had lost control over their offspring, conspired to have them kidnapped.

The movement declares the world ripe for spiritual change, for spiritual revolution. This finds a receptive audience among adolescents who long for peace and clarity and can identify with the goals of the movement. The slogans of "spiritual revolution," "replacing America's materialistic values," and "new values of love and brotherhood"—ancient as they may sound—function as the promise for deliverance, particularly for those youths who are in extreme need of "spiritual" (speaking more correctly, emotional) guidance and deliverance.

The Divine Light Mission.   Also during the 1970s, the Divine Light Mission, headed for several years by the teenage guru Maharij Ji, rallied thousands of young Americans around the belief that there is always a Perfect Master on earth and that Moses, Jesus, Buddha, and Krishna are now succeeded by Maharij Ji, who is in charge of spreading the Divine Word to initiate modern humans into the full know-ledge of God. This was fervently believed by an estimated 60,000 young Americans.

Young people's need for a totalitarian meaning and for a spiritual leader was met by the charismatic mystique the young Oriental guru seemed to possess. This charisma was apparently powerful enough to make palatable—if not plausible—the

[49] Berkeley Rice, "Messiah From Korea: Honor Thy Father Moon," *Psychology Today*, 9 (January 1976), 36–45.

conspicuous discrepancy between the lifestyle of the guru and that of his followers. The former included airplanes, expensive real estate, mansions, a Rolls Royce, two Mercedes Benz automobiles, and so forth, whereas the latter approached the non-materialistic level of the countercultural people. Rennie Davis, of Chicago Seven fame and the most celebrated of the guru's converts, explained the discrepancy by pointing out that Maharij Ji was divine, the Lord, and that his followers gladly wait on him.[50]

Again, the movement used the elements of mass behavior to inspire followers. There were secret rituals, pageantry (e.g., the three-day "Millennium 1973" that attracted 25,000 devotees to the Houston Astrodome), public commitments, and an uncomplicated, grandiose World Plan for salvation and deliverance from all problems. That masses of young Americans found credence in something so un-original and simplistic is testimony to the depth of their starvation for meaning and identity.

The Krishna movement. Youth's search for meaning and order has found Krishna a source of bliss.[51] The American public has become somewhat accustomed to the chanting head-shaven, saffron-robed youths found standing and swaying as if in a blissful trance in public places. Accustomed is not the proper way of describing the public reaction, however, since it usually consists of a mixture of uneasy emotions, including a vague embarrassment and alienation that is usually reserved for something slightly repulsive and untouchable—such as the primitives' awe of the insane. Be this as it may, the Hare Krishna disciples exhibit a singular courage to appear and openly behave in a way so radically different from that of the Western churchgoing believers.

The Hare Krishna movement takes its strength from asceticism and, strangely simple as it may sound, from chanting and dancing. Its participants conceptualize "the illusion" that the physical world reported by our senses is real and potentially satisfying and call this illusion *maya*. This assumption offers to the Krishna devotee the same challenge that sin offers to the revival preacher. Krishna, to the believer, is the name of God in His highest manifestation. Chanting His name and His qualities drives away this illusion and is the source of absolute bliss.

The personality cult of the movement used to focus on Swami Bhaktive-danta, the spiritual master and inspirer of the International Society of Krishna Consciousness. His death in 1977 did not slow down the movement. Instead, it continued to grow (nationally and internationally) since then, manifesting its vitality by completing in 1980 a "Palace of Gold" on a two-thousand-acre spread in the hills of West Virginia, winning a New York State Supreme Court judgment in a deprogramming case, untiringly soliciting in airports and other public places, which

---

[50] David Snell, "Goom Rodgie," *Saturday Review*, September 2, 1974, p. 19.

[51] J. Stillson Judah, *Hare Krishna and the Counterculture* (New York: Wiley-Interscience, 1974).

netted them injunctions by various local authorities, and producing out of their own ranks effective new leadership.[52]

Few of the thousands of followers, including full initiates, part-time chanters, and temple worshippers, are over 30, and a large proportion are in their teens. Their lives include vegetarianism; abstention from drugs, alcohol, and sex (except for purpose of reproduction within the marital relationship); adoption of Sanskrit aliases; up to 12 hours of daily chanting and dancing in public places; and what modern Americans would call an outspokenly sexist philosophy. Females (or as they would put it, "living entities that assume the female organism") are always considered inferior to males. The female devotee's only purpose in life is to serve her husband.

Many of the Krishna devotees have come from the hippie movement, where they lived in communes, were into drugs (many admit to LSD trips during that stage), and lived promiscuously. Conversion to Krishna Consciousness radically reversed the latter two aspects and led to the condemnation of Leary and others as false prophets and to a new "puritanism" unmatched by any other current movement.

The power of conversion is illustrated by a participant-observation study by Joseph Damrell, who describes the unintentionally comical conversion of a commune to the Krishna creed: a typically drug-infested (dealing and "tripping"), hedonistic hippie commune tried to pass itself off as a religious group using marijuana as a "sacrament" (thereby intending to gain impunity before the law) and in the process of charading became serious about Krishna ideas, ultimately converted, refashioned the commune into a temple, and radically altered their former ethics.[53]

The Meditation movement. The most powerful and numerous among the different meditation groups is the Transcendental Meditation movement. TM practitioners increased by leaps and bounds during the '70s, starting with perhaps 100,000 at the beginning of the decade and ending with about 800,000.

TM's student branch, Students International Meditation Society, addresses itself to college students and has probably established a chapter on every large campus in the U.S. The founder, Maharishi Mahesh Yogi (again the focus of personality cult), has control over the vast network of teachers and initiators and has established a business enterprise that would do honor to a successful industrial magnate. From the angle of most devotees, however, it is not business (notwithstanding the relatively high initiation fee, costs for "retreats," "residence courses," teacher's training, etc.) but a True Belief and the answer to all problems. Again, we notice the all-encompassing solution that meditation promises. Given that there is

[52] "Religion," *Time*, September 15, 1980, p. 71.

[53] Joseph Damrell, *Search for Identity: Youth, Religion and Culture* (Beverly Hills: Sage Publications, 1978).

little doubt that transcendental meditation can function as hygiene for the human brain, leading to relaxation and thus to a more comfortable and healthier life, the philosophy of transcendental meditation has been expanded to visualize "levels of consciousness," the highest of which is God Consciousness—which brings us straight back to Krishna Consciousness.

Like the Krishna chant, transcendental meditation uses the medium of a repetitive word to induce trance and relaxation—called "bliss." This time, however, the word is called a *mantra* and is repeated silently in one's mind, usually without the benefit of an immediate group (though group meditation is a favorite, too).

Unlike the Krishna devotees, meditators keep cult and ritual at a minimum (though there are Hindu rituals and prayers at the time of initiation), do not base communal living on it, and essentially adapt meditation to the fast pace of American life without retreating to it more than twice daily for 20 minutes each time. In general, meditators exhibit a more adaptive attitude, make meditation serve other functions in their lives, are not radically oriented, and, unlike members of other movements, they meet the earlier mentioned characteristics of the True Believer movement only in a few aspects. This Oriental import has in fact been adapted to scientific and Puritan values because, as a literal prime claim, "it makes you *work* better."[54]

This exercise in brain hygiene, however, has assumed more and more the nature of a totalitarian philosophy that claims to possess the solution for all of humankind's problems. In line with this assumption a World Plan has been prepared, according to which every population center should have a World Plan Center and enough teachers (ultimately one per 1000 population) to bring transcendental meditation to everyone. Maharishi International University (formerly Parsons College) has a hefty enrollment of devotees studying the Science of Creative Intelligence and forming a potential pool for teachers of meditation.

It must be emphasized that the benefits of meditation seem to have a sound scientific basis insofar as they include relaxation and the consequent freeing of extra nervous energy.[55] The attributes of a True Believer movement come into sharper focus only when the theology of God Consciousness is added: a level of consciousness that presumably can be achieved through consistent meditation and that will mean the deliverance of humankind from all evil.

The Psychedelic movement. Close to the core of the counterculture, the psychedelic movement could be singled out as a True-Believer movement because it tried to make converts, assumed to have found a lifestyle of bliss and superior insight, and practiced ritual and cultism to provide the emotional solidarity of the

[54] A simple in-group statement of what TM is was presented by Denise Denniston and Peter McWilliams, *The TM Book* (New York: Price, Stern, Sloan, 1975).
[55] The psychosomatic benefits of TM were extolled by psychiatrist Harold Bloomfield *et al.*, *TM* (New York: Delacorte, 1975).

like-minded and the persecuted.[56] Presumably, its essential *raison d'être* was the pursuit of internal freedom and the exploration of the inner reaches of the human mind. This ideology of the mystical experience must be understood against the background of what was perceived as an insensitive and overobjectified civilization; it was a withdrawal from Western objectivism to the inner dimensions of visions and beatitude.

The movement, which started in the late 1950s and early 1960s, had its major prophet in Aldous Huxley,[57] soon found its gurus in such figures as Timothy Leary and Richard Alpert, not long thereafter acquired armies of "martyrs" (including Leary and Alpert), founded the International Federation for Internal Freedom with its short-lived esoteric quarterly, *The Psychedelic Review*, and established centers for research and the psychedelic experience. The movement gradually spilled over into the unorganized masses of unprepared adolescents, attracted followers who were less interested in research and insight than in the thrill of the new and forbidden and in the benefits of belonging to an in-group. Soon the movement became coterminous with the hippie movement. What attracted the vast majority of adolescent followers was more the identity derived from submerging into an underground movement than a serious interest in finding the doors to higher levels of consciousness (including the elusive "cosmic consciousness" promised by the earlier and more serious pioneers of the movement).

There was also the promise—mostly fraudulent as it turned out—of *instant* gratification and insight through such drugs as LSD, mescaline, and psilocybin. The philosophy of instantness was perfectly suited for the adolescent mind whose hedonism was not yet harnessed by the experiences of life. This attitude was a natural extrapolation of society's philosophy of "better living through chemistry" and the habit of taking recourse to chemicals for almost any conceivable problems or ailments. The psychedelists expanded the practice to the realm of the mental and spiritual and also based their mystical pursuits on chemical promises.[58]

Insight and knowledge, alas, defy chemical instantness. Nonetheless, the movement continued, vociferously covered up its abortive experiment and, instead of the mystical function of psychedelics, increasingly accented the gregarious bonds among the followers. By the mid 1970s, the psychedelic movement was largely dissipated, at best an empty shell that was merely sporadically inhabited by stragglers who had not yet reconciled themselves with the historical fact that the hippie-psychedelic movement had largely become defunct. We can thus see that this movement, from its inception in the 1950s to its demise in the 1970s, has gone through the fervor of a religious movement, the rebellion associated with the

---

[56] Orrin E. Klapp argues cogently the appropriateness of defining the psychedelic wave as a social movement in *Collective Search for Identity* (New York: Holt, Rinehart & Winston, 1969), pp. 170–176.

[57] Aldous Huxley, *Doors of Perception* (New York: Harper & Row, Publishers, 1954).

[58] Hans Sebald, "The Pursuit of 'Instantness' in Technocratic Society and Youth's Psychedelic Drug Use," *Adolescence*, 7 (Fall 1972), 343–50.

counterculture, the indiscriminate following of masses of unsophisticated teenagers, to merely sporadic and individual experimentations.

Archconservative movements. It would be misleading to assume that a True-Believer movement must always be innovative, revolutionary, and threaten society with the overturn of existing mores and institutions. A True-Believer movement may consist of archconservatives who defend the *status quo* and who, if necessary, are willing to do so by radical means. Though their motivation is not so much a search for identity, it is the defense of an identity they already have, want to keep, and feel is the only true source of wisdom. They are similar to the radical searchers for meaning insofar as they try to convert others; have some sort of a World Plan, a vision of salvation that applies to all humans regardless of whether they know or like it (in the first instance they have to be told, in the second instance, persuaded or coerced); subordinate their personal lives to the goals of the True Belief; and become obedient followers of charismatic leaders.

This kind of movement is usually carried by adults, which is only logical, for in order to conserve something, one first has to have something. Youth, by age limitation, are not in a position to be conservative about their own values; they can only adopt values and join other conservatives. This, of course, is done every day in the U.S. and around the world. Were this not true, no established organization, sect, or cult would survive. There is an ongoing process of recruitment from the ranks of the young, and a sizable proportion of American youth throws in with the meanings and premises of such conservative groups—be they Pentecostalists or the Moral Majority—and find their identity in such fashion.

COMMON FEATURES

Although the labels differ, the functions of the various True-Believer movements are very similar, if not identical. All of them present a total meaning of life; provide the emotional succor of belonging to a community of the destined, elect or persecuted; make possible a transcendental feeling that opens the cage of self-isolation; make ecstasy possible through rituals and group raptures; define evil; suggest a World Plan that spells out the way to salvation; engage in a personality cult and make idols of their leaders; and strongly proselytize, often winning converts who have already a history of search or affiliation with radical or deviant groups.

TRENDS AND OUTLOOK

Since the 1970s, the waves of youthful activism and radicalism, once of shattering power, have calmed. Resignation and privatism have set in. The Establishment has once more withstood the onslaught of youth's restlessness, rebellion, and demand for meaning. Neither side has won the battle; the larger society has been affected by the counterculture and has bowed to some of its criticisms; and the younger generation, before as after, finds itself ensconced in an essentially postindustrial system that keeps them in holding pens in the youth ghettos of adolescence. Provided that no new national or international crises disrupt the relative calm of the early '80s, American youth most likely will, though grudgingly, stick to books and lectures to get an education and will pursue careers with "self-actualizing" potential. To ameliorate banal existence and appease the worst of the craving for a sense of destiny, they will be attracted to a range of pop mysticism, including the occult, astrology, and spiritualism—unfailing signs of their alienation from existing institutions.

The cultic experiences will continue, but will not necessarily become more prevalent.[59] It appears that with the early '80s a stagnation period has set in, with youth having settled on a certain plateau of alienation and separatism.

Sooner or later, the vast majority of rebellious youth will be swallowed up by the social structure of society and find positions that will soothe the hurt of adolescence and make them miraculously forget all about it. In fact, soon after they anchor their personal identities in the adult social structure, *they* in turn will be the older generation against which the resentment of the younger generation (including their own offspring) will be directed. So much for the erstwhile countercultural youth!

This illustrates the power of the Establishment's social structure, the arrangement of positions, which, once entered, have a way of surreptitiously and imperceptibly changing attitudes and outlook to convert countercultural individuals into defenders of the "system."

However, the reentry principle fails to apply to a minority of countercultural people. Certain young adults appear unable to fully reenter the mainstream of American society. Not addressing herself so much to bonafide activists, Amira Wallach completed 105 follow-up studies of persons who, during the 1960s and '70s, had identified themselves as hippies and had been heavily into drugs (an average of thirteen different kinds, including daily marijuana).[60] She discovered that by the late '70s the subjects could be categorized into three groups: reentry, semireentry, and nonreentry into mainstream American society. The young adults were assessed on six variables—drug use, occupation, education, residential stability, interpersonal relationships, and therapy—and had to meet the norms and expectations of the dominant society on at least five variables to be considered reformed. The forty-three persons who were considered as having reentered came from large, stable families and felt more attached to their families. Of the sample, they had been the lightest drug users and largely nondelinquent. The thirty-five semireentries were least competent in establishing an economically independent lifestyle; one third of them were on welfare. They had considerable personality

[59] Andrew J. Pavlos, *The Cult Experience* (Westport, Ct.: Greenwood Press, 1982).

[60] Amira Wallach, "Straggling Back: Yesterday's Flower Children are Growing Up," *Human Behavior*, Vol. 7, February 1978, p. 36.

problems and came from families where role models had been unstable. The twenty-seven nonreentries were, unlike the other two groups, almost all males. They were lowest in educational achievement, with most not having completed high school. Their drug use was heaviest (including opiates) and their employment record highly unstable. These people stayed in the hippie subculture, or in a substitute thereof. To Wallach, "the hippie movement seems like a prolonged adolescence that some participants outgrew and some didn't."[61]

Focusing on a sample of young adults who had been sophisticated activists rather than mere hippies, James M. Fendrich traced the socioeconomic careers of the former over ten years.[62] He found that almost all of them gyrated toward the public sector of the job market, where the largest proportion of them were concentrated in university teaching positions (primarily social sciences). The second largest concentration was found in the social service and creative occupations. They became social workers and freelance writers. These positions allow them the role of societal critics and many of them continue to express political concerns as they attempt, especially as teachers, to influence young people. Their new style of activism is less raucous. Being more subtle, it often claims immunity from criticism by merit of the traditional sanctity accorded the role of the educator.

The integration of erstwhile dissident youth into the adult structure is highlighted by "reform" of such notorious counterculture figures as Abbie Hoffman and Jerry Rubin. They now channel their fervor and aggressiveness into the business world of America, intent on making money, intent on becoming "successful." Hoffman was a leader of the 1960s underground Yippie movement, preaching revolution against the American Establishment, dealing in drugs, being convicted, escaping from justice and going underground for seven years. With opportunistic flair, he timed his reappearance in 1980 to coincide with the publication of his autobiography, *Soon to be a Major Movie Picture* (Putnam; $13.95), with the movie rights sold to Universal for $200,000.[63] Rubin, another leading figure of the Yippies, mocked the U.S. political system in 1968 by trying to run a pig for President. As one of the Chicago Seven defendants, he was convicted of inciting the riots at the 1968 Democratic Convention. Now he wears a businessman's suit, draws an impressive, nonproletarian salary as a securities analyst in a respectable New York firm, and proclaims what would cheer the Moral Majority as well as the Republican Convention: "The challenge of the '80s is to bring back the entrepreneurial spirit."[64]

There are additional examples. Rennie Davis, another revolutionary who rejoined middle America, has become an insurance salesman. Bobby Seale, tired of rebellion, is now researching a cookbook on barbecuing. Former rebel Tom

[61] Ibid.

[62] James M. Fendrich, "Activists Ten Years Later: A Test of Generational Unit Continuity," *Journal of Social Issues*, 30 (Fall 1974), 95–118.

[63] "A Yippie Comes in from the Damp," *Time*, September 15, 1980, p. 22.

[64] "Rubin Relents," *Time*, August 11, 1980, p. 23.

Hayden, with substantial support from his movie-actress wife, changed his political manners and in 1982 decided to run for the California state assembly.[65] The list of famous persons, whose rebelliousness once made headlines across the nation and who now lead bourgeois lifestyles could be continued.

The immediate reaction of young adults who have suffered (or at least witnessed) the defeat of their counterculture usually is retreatism and renunciation of the world, and the pursuit of personal salvation. Even younger youths, not knowing what it was all about, tend to follow their example for awhile, imitating their privatistic ways and what is "in" until in the years ahead a new mood may arouse them to a new cause. And what that will be, no one can safely predict.

No observer of youth should make the mistake of believing that the counter-cultural upheaval was unique and will not recur. The motivation for it continues to exist and is only temporarily anesthetized by privatistic diversion. If there is any truth in Sorokin's historical-sociological theory, our sensate age screams for a resolution, and demands will again be couched in a radical and countercultural framework.

The currently existing ideation of American civilization apparently does not satisfy youth's hunger for meaning. They reject what they see. And what they see consists largely of technology and science, which they immediately mistake as an ideation. As such, they find it inadequate and unacceptable.

What has happened is that the decline of Western ideation is mistakenly ascribed to the failure of Western science to provide an answer. Young people incorrectly demand from the scientific credo a statement of meaning of life. When they receive no answer, they reject science altogether. They fail to recognize that science is a tool, not an answer. So they try to supplant it with the mystic, believing that they find something better and purer that way. Little do they realize that the "pure" and the "magical" can manifest themselves in such holocausts as the Nazi attempt at genocide that used science as a means; and little do they realize that it was not science, but rather emotion and faith that used "purity of blood and thought" as a basis for such action.

The alliance between the mystic and the scientific is not the doing of science but the consequence of an aberrant and all-too-desperate search for meaning and identity. The revolt against science was a mistaken dethronement. The coup threw out the servant because the lord couldn't be found.

SUMMARY

The radical or countercultural youth movement differs from the general teen and pop subculture in dimensions that range from static to dynamic, faddist orientation to action orientation, coexistence to intolerance, entertainment to activism.

[65] "People," *Time*, July 12, 1982, p. 51.

Alienation is probably the most generic concept for understanding youth's unrest and dissatisfaction. Youth is vulnerable to the elusiveness of tradition, an elusiveness caused by rapid sociocultural changes; to the ideational void imposed by anomie; to the meaninglessness derived from upper-middle-class youth's satiation of material needs and the boredom of extra leisure time to the nearly universal pain and frustration of socialization (augmented by postindustrial conditions).

Youth activism and radicalism in our age are essentially a search for alternative realities that make more sense and offer clearer identities than the present system. The response to alienation differs widely. Utopias, countercultures, True-Believer movements, and retreatism appeal to alienated youth.

The prime example of the search for an alternative lifestyle was the counterculture, a composite of various movements which agreed on a stance that was antitechnocratic (including science and the "objective consciousness"), antiwar, prodrug, and promystic. The evaluations of the counterculture ranged from enthusiastic endorsement as a presumably mature and sensitive collectivity to clinical rejection as a presumably immature and pathological expression; a number of sociologists took the middle ground, encouraging a dialogue that might benefit American society. The movement's activities can be divided into activism directed outward and into internal maintenance functions that regulate interaction and the subinstitutions — with the latter tending to interfere with activist functions.

The New Age movement of the '80s is a more philosophical, more retreatist, and nonmilitant extension of the counterculture. It is putting to actual test an alternative lifestyle the counterculture largely only talked about, and is synthesizing Oriental religion with a small-community or commune philosophy.

The True-Believer movements provide a radical and essentially religious environment, ideally suited for youths with extreme identity needs. The True Believers use their lives to serve the belief instead of vice versa. They proselytize, assume they possess the only true philosophy, use drastic means to achieve their goals, and give unquestioned loyalty to leaders. Examples include the Jesus movement, the Unification movement, the Divine Light Mission, Krishna Consciousness, the Meditation movement, the psychedelic movement, and archconservative movements. All present a total meaning of life, provide a community, induce transcendentalism, use group ecstasy, define evil, have a World Plan for salvation, engage in personality cults, and pursue conversions.

Although the counterculture has subsided, the potential for renewed youth upheaval is immanent in the adolescent condition, the anomie of Western civilization, and the thirst for a total ideation. In the meantime, youth have withdrawn to privatistic pursuits that include "self-actualization" and an interest in the occult and the mystic.

Chapter 12

Adolescence

in Perspective

AN ERA OF YOUTHFUL DISSENT

In almost all modern societies adolescence has evolved so extensively that it appears to be an inevitable component of the human life cycle. However, adolescence is an invention of urban-industrial life and not a universal such as infancy, childhood, adulthood, and old age.

The epitome of adolescence evolved in postindustrial society, which has generated armies of adolescents who, even into their twenties, march to their own peculiar tune and maintain a moratorium on a range of adult characteristics.

If we assume an era to be composed of several generations, then we can say that our era is one of youthful unrest that includes the raucous counterculture of the late '60s and early '70s. Most modern industrial societies have been shaken by the rebellion of the young and their recession from traditional culture during that period. While the rebellion has subsided, the recession is lingering. The upheaval was nearly global. Youth demanded recognition of new ideas and instant implementation of reforms. A United Nations study during the height of the counterculture identified over fifty different countries that were racked by youth revolts.[1] Twelve-to-twenty-five-year-olds, amounting to 500 million worldwide during those years,

---

[1] AP Report, United Nations Headquarters, February 14, 1969.

were a force to be reckoned with. The younger generation seemed, by and large, to have lost confidence in the capacity of the older generation to guide affairs without assistance and planning from the young, who believed their views were worth considering.

VIEWS OF ADOLESCENCE

The youthful stirring of our age has received various interpretations—from enthusiastic welcome to clinical condemnation. Historian Theodore Roszak heralded it as a counterculture that promised a gentler, more sensitive, and natural life. Psychologist Bruno Bettelheim countered by exposing it as expressions of basically narcissistic, immature, and pathological attitudes. Psychologist Edgar Z. Friedenberg, educator Paul Goodman, and many others perceived it as the assertion of a basically creative and renovating spirit trying to cleanse the obsolete Establishment of dysfunctional waste. Sociologist Lewis Feuer saw in it little that warranted hope for betterment, and essayist John W. Aldridge described it as a symptom of a generation unaccustomed to hard work, clear thought, and a realistic outlook.

Sociologist Frank Musgrove felt that adolescence is one of the least efficient inventions of modern industrial age, for it wastes a resource which society cannot easily do without—the imagination and energy of its youth. Adolescents are potentially mature, creative human beings who differ from their elders largely because they are not allowed to participate in adult activities. The resulting frustrations make them rebellious and often destructive inverts who join ranks to confront the Establishment with seemingly illogical dissent. Sociologist Karl Mannheim, concurring to some degree, visualized a useful, if not indispensable, function in adolescent dissent: a force checking society's follies and blind spots, and a perennial challenge to seek more just and complete ways of meeting personal and social needs. Adolescents thus form a catalytic element in society.

To many sociologists and psychologists, the question, "Why youthful dissent in our time?" is reduced in essence to the acuteness of the *adolescent experience* in our time and, more basically, to the fundamental meaning of *adolescence* itself. Again, we observe positive and negative interpretations. Hence, Friedenberg defines adolescence as a creative period during which young persons learn who they are and what they really feel, during which they become persons in their own rights, capable of deeply felt relationships with other individuals.

But many others equate adolescence with "teenagerism," consider it a disease without which the young as well as the old would be happier. This interpretation is fostered by a number of factors: first, by the extensiveness of adolescence, stretching into the twenties and making large numbers of youth appear useless and parasitic; second, by the intensity of adolescence, bringing out disturbed, confused, and searching behavior; and third, by the collectivization of adolescent disturbance, advancing a dissentful, alienated, and alienating culture of its own.

This does not fit the traditional view that youth should be a preadult stage and that young people are apprentices going through an awkward yet learning and preparatory phase before taking their places in the adult world. Long, drawn-out adolescence and millions of cultist members of the teenage subculture seem to defy this view. Indeed, most teenagers no longer possess this preparatory feeling. They behave as if they have arrived, bearing testimony to the fact that adolescence has evolved as a phase in its own right within the life span of the modern individual. The ingredients of the youth subculture assume a semipermanent quality, particularly since much of it is adulated and imitated by the rest of society, including adults. The heroes, songs, music, styles, and fads appear more all-American than the world of jobs and professions looming somewhere out there—the encounter with which is continually postponed.

THE BACKGROUND

Whatever one might say about adolescents, it must be clear that it was not they who determined adolescence as the interim phase between childhood and adulthood. The forces combining to forge the conditions that gave rise to adolescence include the peculiarities of urban-industrial society's social structure and the generally anomic culture of modern Western civilization.

Two fundamental causes of adolescence can be identified. One can be traced to the original fissure in the social structure, which opened during the Industrial Revolution because of increasing requirements for education and training. Having eliminated the direct transition from childhood to adulthood, the fissure broadened over the years into a new phase, bringing along a generation gap. This break in the passage between statuses is the social-structural cause of adolescence, laying down the *necessary* cause. The *sufficient* cause arrived with the increasingly secular and anomic lifestyle of most industrialized societies, which deprived the young of cultural meanings that traditionally proved helpful in achieving orientation in life. Without these cultural meanings, the individual's reliance on the social structure, especially on the adult division of labor, for personal identity increased acutely— ironically, again affecting the young most disadvantageously, since they found themselves in preadult-structural circumstances.

The deriving of personal identity from a specific position within the social structure is a relatively recent innovation and is correlated with the weakening of cultural control. This means that as the persuasiveness of the cultural ethos decreased and became too nonspecific for life-orientation, the importance of the vocational or professional position for meaning and behavioral orientation increased —identity-genesis and identity-reinforcement shifted from the general cultural ethos to the vastly more specific and discrete social position. This shift constitutes an attempt to reanchor identity and can be understood as a natural reaction to un-structuredness and uncertainty. People need clearly defined norms and expectations that enable them to engage in meaningful, predictable, and in fact, viable behavior. Clearly, a life situation offering noncompelling cultural guidelines and highly diversified and discrete adult positions must be frustrating to young people, and it is prone to create a hotbed of unrest.

It follows from such conditions that adolescents form a pool of vulnerable individuals who starve for new (vs. outgrown familial) object fixation, and that as such they are convenient targets for demagogues. Modern history is replete with examples in which newly dedicated youth were drawn into devastating causes, "serving" their country or their True Belief, and were exploited literally to the last drop of blood—theirs as well as their adversaries'.

In a sense, part of the responsibility of a democratic society is to refuse to give in to its youth's constant pressure for deliverance from anomie and to reject infusing them with absolutistic credos, giving them collective causes, involving them in totalitarian programs—in short, to reject dominating their lives. Anomie unintentionally curtails that temptation. But, of course, in the process it conjures up a host of other problems.

This thought will be briefly pursued later. Here, however, we are interested in the causal backdrop of adolescence. The two major causes—one structural and the other cultural, one operative by commission and the other by omission—contain interrelated conditions.

Some of the conditions arise from the combined impact of social-structural discontinuity and cultural nonspecificity, exerting adolescence-generating influence, and should be briefly reviewed.

With the rise of urban-industrial conditions, the division of labor increased in specificity to the point where common cultural ground was obscured. An alienating factor was introduced. Young people no longer intimately witnessed the work of adults; the place of residence and the place of work were separated.

The conditions of postindustrial life further deepen the adolescent experience. As an important factor, the labor market repulses early entry. Mechanization and automation have made production and service possible with a minimum of labor. Young people are not needed—a fact cloaked by rhetoric dignifying prolonged education and bemoaning the dropout rate. But the gimmick is flimsy, and most adolescents cannot help but feel that they are not needed or wanted. They recognize high school, and increasingly college, as holding pens and see little meaning in them. This puts undue strain on educational institutions, which find it difficult to motivate and inform at the same time.

Postindustrial ability to cater to liberal consumption patterns and render an abundance of service unheard of during previous generations has resulted in a peculiar mental state among the young, particularly among the middle class. Called the psychology of entitlement, it not only expects instant gratification but also assumes that society owes one a financially secure and psychologically happy ("self-actualized") life.

The postindustrial conditions of delayed entry into the labor market and liberally offered consumption in fact allow the vast majority of American youth to remain preadult for so long, and thus to form a pool of potentially dissenting individuals.

American culture has been accused of lacking compelling ideation that would provide meaning and a cause for the young, and of thereby contributing to the sustaining cause of the interim between child and adult status. This accusation should not, however, be understood as denying the existence of all or any cultural values. The American culture *does* suggest a number of strong values, but not in the form of an integrated ethos that is as totalitarian, action-oriented, and cause-suggestive as the kinds of ethos experienced by teenagers in other countries or in different historical periods. The very nature of the American ethos stresses individuality and democracy; the burden of deciding on a cause, on life meaning, and on goal aspirations is thereby placed in the hands of the individual rather than in the action programs of a nationwide *Hitler-Jugend*, *Komsomol*, or Red Guard. A noncompelling and individualistic ideation such as the modern American ethos taxes the imagination and creativity of youth to a far greater extent than the totalitarian regime that presents ready-made programs and identities. The price paid for the freedom of self-exploration and unique identity is a longer search—a prolonged adolescence.

In addition to the noncompelling nature of the American ethos, several values are beset with negative or ambivalent elements; for example, the cultural view of pubescence is largely evasive, semitaboo, and often negative. Another cultural dilemma is the disjunction between biological maturity and social maturity: The adolescent period between pubescence and the accordance of adulthood is lengthened because of the progressively lower age at puberty. Furthermore, American culture does not offer a rite of passage in the form of a public ceremony proclaiming the transition into adulthood.

Other confusing elements of American culture are value schisms requiring the young to determine which norms and expectations apply in what situation and at what time. American culture is diverse and inconsistent enough to offer for each value an opposing one. These include the polar values of competition vs. cooperation, work vs. leisure, piousness vs. free-thinking, individualism vs. conformity, sexuality vs. chastity. Another schism includes such adult-child polarities as responsibility vs. nonresponsibility, sex vs. sexlessness, and dominance vs. submission.

American culture is also characterized by anomic elements that fail to specify norms for achieving culturally suggested goals. Thus a lower-class teenager may be exposed to values such as material success, but may lack feasible, legitimate norms for attaining the goal. The reaction to the unstructured condition is a gravitation toward a subcultural environment with norms and values the adolescent can meet.

The greater the amount of technological innovation, the greater are the modifying effects on social life. This principle affects the relationship between generations, because rapid technological and social changes constantly alter conditions and render the adjustments of one generation at least partially invalid for the next generation. One could thus say that the faster the rate of sociocultural change, the greater the degree of intergenerational conflict. This conflict can be seen in the

differences between the norms and values held by the older and younger generations.

Besides suffering from a general cultural lag, parents also suffer from specific
knowledge lags, for it is virtually impossible for them to keep up with the latest
information provided by fast-moving science and technology. Children and adolescents, who keep abreast of latest knowledge under the intellectual guardianship of
teachers and experts, are better informed than their parents in many aspects.

Cultural and knowledge lags are not the only negative experiences of modern
parents. Social scientists and educators have voiced doubts concerning the pedagogic qualifications of American parents and have even ascribed to them the responsibility for typical teenage behavior. If one adds the threat of population explosion
to this parent-deprecatory syndrome, then parenthood appears no longer as an asset
but as a liability to society. One parental reaction to this realization was an
apologetic *mea culpa*, and parents, desiring to establish rapprochement between
the generations, resorted to communication, information, and equality. This
idealistic approach largely failed, for it neglected to assess realistically the nature of
socialization, which is not conducive to an equalitarian relationship between
socializer and socializee. Another reaction was to reassert traditional authority.
This reaction came with the awareness that teenagers, in spite of their up-to-date
technological knowledge, lack insights into life's problems — the mature solutions of
which require more than classroom learning and technical know-how.

Significant in intergenerational friction is a clash of psychological dispositions
that has been called the "clash of inferiority complexes." On one side, parents are
constantly exposed to the American "youth cult" that creates feelings of inferiority
in the face of declining strength, prowess, and youthful appearance. On the other
side, young people feel inferior in the face of many restrictions that limit activities
and privileges. The interplay between the complexes results in a cumulative,
mutually reinforcing cycle that perpetuates reciprocal resentment.

The shift from the consanguine to the nuclear family created a drastic reduction of concrete adult models. It also brought about a reduction of familial peers.
Clan association was replaced by association with peers whose background experiences and attitudes frequently differed greatly. Over time, this body of peers evolved
into an influential collectivity forming a corporate identity apart from, and often
opposed to, the family. Association wih nonfamilial peers thus encourages modern
youth to maintain independent subcultures.

The contemporary vagueness in cultural precepts and emphasis on individual
freedom have burdened marriage and the family with a heretofore unknown
intensity of personality functions. Gratification from marital and familial affiliation, however, is often curtailed by individualism and secularism, which tend to
neutralize the beneficial effects of familism. The effects of individualistic and
secular philosophy are also observable in the abrogation of the placement function
of the family: The adolescent is now largely on his or her own in determining career
and social standing. There is even suspicion that the primariness of group interaction of the modern family has shifted slightly toward secondariness.

For the adolescent, the combined effect of these changes in family structure and function is the tendency to become involved in peer subcultures, to make family-independent career decisions, and to become engaged in nonfamilial career preparation—all circumstances and tendencies that place the youth in subcultural environments and make his or her transition into adulthood more complex. The function of the peer group, however, also includes bridging the gap between childhood and adulthood, learning to get along with others, testing one's wits, and establishing autonomy from the family.

Modern family life has also given rise to a perversion of motherhood defined as Momism. In this situation, frequently characterized by a father who is remote or absent from the socialization process, the mother seeks fulfillment of neurotic needs through the child. A prevalent mode is the "perfect" mother who tries to make motherhood a "success"—and in the process produces a personality condemned to lifelong adolescence.

Modern mass media are powerful socializers of young people. Among them, TV has become the most ubiquitous influence. By age eighteen, young Americans on the average have spent more time watching the screen than attending school. This makes more than merely academic the questions of TV's ingredients and their effects on the audience; we are dealing with impingement on human nature.

The style of communication and socialization via TV is vastly more symbolic and abstract than the style that prevailed in the traditional family. The new qualities are highly susceptible to the presentation of the unreal and the violent. These two themes worry many parents, educators, and social scientists because, unlike the educational and informative functions of the medium, they are suspected of stimulating immature and possibly even violent imitation. But the definitive verdict has not yet been reached. Research is still trying to come up with unambiguous conclusions. What can be said with some degree of certainty is that certain control forces act to curb unwise imitation of TV fare: parental influence and socialization measures, the limited availability of the means necessary to carry out violent plots and images, the influence of other American norms and values balancing the more destructive ones, and the conditional arousal of anger and hostility that would motivate the imitation of violence. Imitation of violence or unrealism does, however, occur in situations where absence of all control variables coincides—situations that do not arise frequently.

TV reinforces the teenage subculture by catering to it through adoption of teen standards, tastes, and fads. Many programs, in fact, are specifically aimed at the teen population and are part of the business syndrome capitalizing on the youth cult.

TV has functions that undeniably further the knowledgeability of young people. Information covering a vast spectrum is offered. For example, events that happen somewhere in the nation or the world are almost instantly communicated, potentially enhancing youth's understanding of life and the world. The instantness and realism of witnessing happenings from around the globe may in part explain youth's quick arousal to action and political protest. However, here again looms danger. The sensational aspects seen on the screen often obscure more complex and hidden political reasons and maneuvers that lie behind the reported action, and the young are led to engage in naive political activism.

Timeless difficulties are associated with youth's unfolding into culturized human personalities: roles have to be learned and an identity established.

But are we here expressing a slightly antiquated bias? Some of the recent writing in social psychology suggests a different formula—one that has presumably resulted from a vastly changed social milieu and that has displaced formulas conducive to developing relatively stable roles and a core identity. Erving Goffman in his latest works has abandoned role concepts previously applied to understanding human relationships, in favor of infinitely ephemeral, symbolic, and ritualistic etiquette that regulates human encounters on a situational basis.

If this is true, the younger generations learn to become human beings in a significantly different way, one based not on lasting or semipermanent role definitions, but on principles of efficiency and expedience. This would replace traditional human intimacy with anonymity, sharing with exchange, and the sense of social communion with self-actualization.

Perhaps the difficulties and disturbances in the interaction between the sexes is a symptom of the new style of self-development: It is no longer based on pervasive cultural blueprints, but on individualistic characteristics. Roles are abandoned to make room for idiosyncratic makeup. The brunt of this development (or revolution) was, of course, borne by females. Underlying the activities of women's liberation is the more fundamental attempt to achieve a different concept in personality development. That we witness it first in the case of women is due to the antiquated limitations inherent in the stereotypical status.

As a result of respecting personal uniqueness and abstaining from imposing *a priori* roles on others, the ritual of encounter must necessarily be nonspecific, nonintrusive, and nonpersonal. If it is too specific or personal, it may violate a person's unique self-definition. The old role concepts run that danger. The new impersonal rituals steer clear of it.

Modern adolescents therefore learn a different style of human interaction, with a premium on communication and efficiency, and pay the price of increasing interpersonal alienation.

The foregoing points attempted to summarize the major antecedent conditions of adolescence and to explain why the second half of the twentieth century is characterized by acute adolescent symptoms.

Continuation of the analysis of adolescence leads logically to the next point: the *consequences* of adolescence. The major sociological consequence of adolescent discontinuity expresses itself in collective behavior and presents a relatively novel social problem. It seems safe to conclude that there has never before been so massive a recession of the young from the adult society into their own subsociety, which is not only different but opposed to adult standards. Manifestations of their subcultural life are manifold and can be observed in distinct and recurrent fads, styles, hero worship, attitudes, values, argot, and material implementation. Many of these subcultural expressions have been insufficiently researched, and the only sources of information are often popular media through which teenagers express themselves directly, such as songs, dances, fashion, and teen magazines.

More seriously, youth has made a decisive impact on the political lifestyle of the nation. The counterculture was the epitome of modern adolescence—with its follies as well as its good points. It contained both senseless rebelliousness and valuable commentary, attacking valuable traditions as well as corruptions and perversions of the Establishment. Furthermore, we have not yet heard the last word from the counterculture: it is not dead, only dormant.

RESEARCH NEEDS

Sociological research into adolescent and teenage behavior reflects uneven tendencies, with great interest and coverage in some sectors and little or no interest in others. Teenage marriages, for example, have received extensive attention, and sociologists have prolifically described when, where, whom, and why teenagers marry. On the other hand, there has been great neglect of inquiry into advertising and attempts to form the opinions of children and teenagers toward purchasing. In view of the affluence of young Americans, this question is of more than academic value.

A conspicuous lack of knowledge exists about collective behavior. Its study calls for scrutiny of the development and fluctuations of subcultures, fads, crazes, and hero worship. For example, such fervent activities as teenage dancing have not yet been systematically studied. The precise dimensions of the teen subculture, or of the subculture generally, are still a mystery to most social scientists. (To stimulate discussion, a systematic approach was suggested by this author. See Chapter 9.) Exactly what takes place at the dawn of subcultural formation, when teenagers engage in so-called "exploratory gestures?" What mechanisms operate as younger teenagers learn subcultural norms and values from older peers? What exactly are the channels and processes of subcultural transmission?

Also needing research is the relationship between teenagers and the various mass media. What is the social corollary of teenagers who expose themselves to certain fare of the mass media? How does it affect them? How do teen styles and tastes affect the producers of mass media fare? Although some of the questions have been researched, more investigation is needed, especially concerning the influence of teen tastes on the media's productions. A mass medium largely ignored by research is the teen magazine. Not until content analyses have been applied is there any way of knowing whether we have missed a source of insight into teenage life.

Among the unanswered questions concerning teenage affluence are questions not so much of *what* they buy—there are exhaustive itemized lists on teen consumptions—but of *why* and *how* they acquire certain items. Answers to the "why" might provide a link to the understanding of subcultural reinforcement and the nature of peer standards. Answers to the "how" would fill in information on how much and by what means teenagers acquire financial power.

The issue of intergenerational conflict has been presented here more on the basis of hypothesis, inference, and nonsystematic content analysis than on the basis of reliable studies. There is enough *general* evidence to safely allow the assumption that intergenerational conflict does in fact exist; but *specific* correlations, social variables, and accentuating circumstances are relatively unknown.

How does a "generalist" teenager decide on a "specialist" future career? The questions surrounding this issue are multitudinous, and its specific aspects, such as how the transition is affected by the home or educational institutions, should be investigated.

Whereas research has paid ample attention to the circumstances that obscure the lower-class child's intelligence, it has neglected the fact that upper-class upbringing often obscures a child's low intelligence. Inquiry might reveal that the adolescent's display of socially approved manners and conformity to etiquette tend to be defined as intelligent behavior.

A question that has seldom been asked concerns the kind of social institutions that administer the *coup de grace* to the adolescent period and the manner in which they effect the transition to the adult status. The adult-initiating and adult-reinforcing roles of such institutions as the military, the labor force, marriage, civic clubs, political parties, and community organizations should be examined. It could be hypothesized that the degree of involvement in these institutions is directly correlated with changes in self-perception. Correlations should be checked against such intervening variables as time of entry into institution, personal motivation, kind of program offered, and institutional responsibilities assumed. Knowledge accrued could be used to restructure programs and activities to increase their effectiveness in helping older adolescents make the final transition into adulthood and to reinforce his or her adult identity.

The problem of identity is intricately connected to virtually all the above issues. Inquiry should focus on youths who experience generational mobility when they enter into careers different from those of their parents and face discontinuity of familiar patterns. Considering that a majority of boys and girls take up jobs or careers dissimilar to those of their parents', this becomes a timely research objective. Also to be examined is the role of the family of orientation as a value-instilling agency in the face of weak and nondescript cultural premises: Under what familial, peer, school, or religious circumstances does family influence balance cultural *anomie*? Under what family conditions does either peer or parental identification prevail? Which familial conditions make the young vulnerable to indoctrination by mass media, and which give the young immunity against imitation or internalization of mass media models?

Finally, there are questions concerning the diversity of the adolescent experience. Though some minority groups, such as blacks and lower-class teenagers, have been researched fairly exhaustively, other groups such as the Chicanos of the southwest and the Puerto Ricans of the east coast have been neglected. Also, more social psychological research is needed to fully understand the culture shock American Indians undergo on, near, and away from the reservation.

These research suggestions do not exhaust all needed inquiry. They are meant primarily to alert the beginning student to research possibilities and to stimulate formulation of research propositions.

OUTLOOK

Nothing will stop the continued forays of adolescence into the purviews of the Establishment — unless a radical reversal of urban-industrial conditions commands a halt and turns society back to earlier forms of technology and commerce. But this is improbable and would happen only if the world should tumble into an unprecedented holocaust that destroyed the technological achievements forged by many generations.

In societies with advanced adolescence, like the United States (where Ken Keniston found it necessary to interject "youth" between adolescence and adulthood), unrest will continue, though it will periodically seem deceptively peaceful. Societies that have not yet felt the rebellious power of their young will soon taste the bitter fruits of what the elders thought were the sweet seeds of increasing industrialization and long-awaited affluence. Countries surprised by what they may deem uncalled-for dissent and ungratefulness will especially include the developing countries where, until now, most youth made a swift transition from childhood to adulthood. It may also include some nations in which totalitarian and doctrinaire oppression has obscured chronic youth disaffection. Youth's sense of relative deprivation (fostered through improved international communication) will break through and symptomize itself through demands and deviations that no simple police state can roll back. Some of these countries may include Communist societies, where decreasing revolutionary fervor and increasing industrial affluence create growing demands for personal freedom and self-actualization. Adolescence is already alive in these countries, sustained by the discontinuity of the social structure and is merely awaiting sufficient cultural leeway to raise its dissentful head.

Indeed, a United Nations study predicted that during the 1980s generational conflict will assume proportions not previously imagined and that youth will begin to predominate in world affairs.[2] The report, the first detailed review of global youth problems by the United Nations, noted that many young people resort to antisocial behavior because of frustration, but concluded that in general the world's youth wants to participate in national development. What to many looms as a dangerous worldwide youth rebellion, can also be understood as a potential for

---

[2] Ibid.

global betterment. The talent, drive, and openmindedness inherent in the young of the world (estimated to run approximately 700 million for the world's twelve-to-twenty-five-year-olds at the beginning of the '80s) could be marshalled into building a healthier and more peaceful world.

In developing countries, youth participation will come to be particularly significant. On one side, it will represent a tremendous political opportunity to raise the country to new levels of achievement and national growth; on the other side, it will mean a recurrent political threat for governments whose record of achievement may not be to the liking of its younger generation.

In the United States, the near future of the mood of the young will be quiet and characterized by retreat to privatism and the attempt to find self-fulfillment within a conventional career. But this does not mean that the young cannot be turned on to a cause—be it a dissenting, a patriotic, or a cosmopolitan one. If we extrapolate youthful sentiments of the recent past and, to some extent, of the present, the future cause may well turn out to again be a dissentful one. All it would take would be the Establishment throwing a bone of contention in youth's direction (as, for example, renewal of the disliked draft registration which caused some disturbance during the early '80s), and counterculture symptoms could flare up with renewed vehemence.

In the meantime, the '80s have started out with a calm home front. The counterculture achievements appear to have found a plateau on which to rest. Antiwar protest is largely abstract, directed toward the question of nuclear armament and nuclear weapons deployment, and far from being as fervent as it was during the Vietnam crisis. The liberality of youth's sexual morality is still pervasive, but seems to be slowly responding to inherent limitations—limitations emanating from the need for relational security and exclusive intimacy. Hard economic conditions of the nation (if not the world) have stopped further deterioration of the work ethic—it may in fact have recovered a slim margin of the ground lost during the '60s and '70s. Likewise, political disillusionment is slowing down. Politically interested youths are becoming less polarized, and the aggressiveness of both the left and the right is lessening. The precepts of women's liberation are penetrating deeper, though in a less raucous way, into the American population, and more people are accepting the role-free status of women, or, for that matter, of humans generally.

The generation gap will continue; and no bridges are in sight. If we give credence to such expert prognosticators as Urie Bronfenbrenner (a founding father of Head Start and consultant to Washington), the generation gap will be reinforced by continued, if not increased, age segregation. On the basis of widespread studies (including international comparisons) he contends that age segregation poses problems of great magnitude for the Western world in general and for American society in particular. If the institutions of our society continue to remove parents, other adults, and older youths from active participation in the lives of children and if the resulting vacuum is filled by the age-segregated peer group, "we can anticipate increased alienation, indifference, antagonism, and violence on the part of the young generation in all segments of our society—middle-class children as well as the disadvantaged."[3]

Bronfenbrenner discusses a five-point reform or prevention plan, believes that the family by itself can do little to bring the necessary change, and that other institutions in our society must be activated to break the vicious isolation of our young in their subcultural environment. Institutions such as school, government, business, and church shut out the young and relegate them to an amoral, antisocial milieu, which breeds rebellion and dissent.

Unfortunately, cold statistical trends suggest that such age segregation will continue. Teenage work, early marriage, and traditional ways of assuming adult responsibilities are declining. Instead, formal education has become the norm— and a way of life shutting off the young from productive participation in the mainstream of American society. The number of young people remaining in school has increased, the steepest rise occurring among eighteen- and nineteen-year-olds, a development that is probably linked directly to the proliferation of community colleges during the past decade. Though formal schooling has almost entirely pre-empted other more traditional routes to adulthood, it does nothing either for those who have dropped out or for those who graduate but gain little from school.

Interestingly, the tendency will undoubtedly persist for much of the adult population not only to acquiesce to growing teenage influence but even to imitate adolescents. Teenagers are linked to the adult world by such institutions as family, church, and education. They have come to exert an ever-increasing degree of influence over the operation of these institutions, and specific teen subinstitutions have evolved within or alongside the parental institutions. This trend is exemplified by youth services reflecting teen lingo and behavior and by acceptance of student participation in school administration. The trend giving youth a voice in the operation of previously adult institutions will continue, gain strength, and spread to still other adult realms.

Teen fads and styles will continue to be exploited by business and industry to establish brand loyalties and to predict collective moods. Predictably, the American economy is bound to stimulate artificial wants, and adolescents will continue to compensate for psychological insecurity by craving material possessions. Material implementations create status, enhance personal significance, and build social power within one's peer group. Due to national economic difficulties, the spending behavior of youth in the 1980s appears, however, slightly subdued when compared to the affluent behavior of youth during the 1970s. Whether youthful spending will regain its previous fervor depends on further national and international developments.

[3] Urie Bronfenbrenner, *Two Worlds of Childhood: U.S. and U.S.S.R.* (New York: Russell-Sage Foundation, 1970), pp. 116–17.

WHAT PRICE ADOLESCENCE?

The outlook on the youth scene—indeed, on our total postindustrial way of life—seems to hinge on what is going to happen in the cultural realm. The eminent feature of our postindustrial society is the disjunctive change in various realms of life, symptomizing the absence of a strong ideology to hold the different structures, institutions, and ideas together. The divergence of the old techno-economic structure and the cultural ethos is the most crucial example of modernism's disharmony. Daniel Bell called it the contradictions of modern capitalism whereby, on one side, our capitalistic system requires ever greater application of rationality to solve problems of organization, efficiency, and production and, on the other side, the emerging culture emphasizes emotionality, the sensate, and hedonistic self-centeredness.[4] As these two approaches grow stronger, the incompatibility between them becomes greater.

The irony of the evolving divergence is that the new values are blind to the hand that feeds them. The very fruits produced by the capitalistic ethic of work and self-discipline, which have enabled people to demand inner fulfillment and social and sexual abandon, may now prove fatal to that ethic. This paradox threatens to undermine the very existence of Western Society. Only a revitalization of our cultural ideas can prevent the disintegration of postindustrial society.

Youth plays an active role in this crisis. It most fervently advances the self-destructive outgrowth of latter-day capitalistic culture, while the older generation is more inclined to implement the techno-economic apparatus and cling to the traditional Protestant ethic that is coupled with it. Historically this meant that on the personal level the two realms, the techno-economic and the cultural, were joined to produce a single character structure—the Puritanical. Now, with the unjoining of the two realms, a different character structure emerges.

In other words, the younger generation is spinning off a sensate and self-centered cultural credo from the traditional techno-economic system (which we generally call capitalism)—a process that is driving a wedge between our technical and industrial institutions and our cultural beliefs and attitudes. The inherent danger of this divergent process lies in the destruction of the philosophy that generated and upheld the economic system that created superindustrialism. With the fading of this philosophy, we will undermine the working order of our techno-economic system and ultimately destroy it.

How soon the forecasts of this macrosociological notion will come true, and whether they will come true at all, is speculation at this time. But even the remote possibility of its happening is justification for making it part of this discussion. The horrendous social and cultural upheavals that would result from youth's decisive abdication as successors of the Protestant ethic are hardly fathomable at this time.

---

[4] Daniel Bell, *The Cultural Contradictions of Capitalism* (New York: Basic Books, 1976).

But, certainly, they would change our lifestyle as we know it today. Daniel Bell, the prophetic sociologist, warns that the changes would abrogate the standard of living, economically, as well as culturally.

This again demonstrates that adolescence is a many-edged sword cutting in many directions, some constructive and others destructive. Undermining a system, the fruits of which we desire, by aberrant values may be judged destructive; but the freedom to experiment with different lifestyles and to carve out a unique identity by merit of the adolescent moratorium can be considered constructive.

But what if this freedom results in destruction, in the casting away of the tools necessary to achieve coveted products and services?

The risk stands! and there may not be a solution to this danger. This contradiction of adolescence must be accepted if the adolescent moratorium is to make sense. It would be a fatal mistake to tolerate adolescence merely on the basis of outcomes that are palatable to the current social order. To try and engineer outcomes would negate the very essence of adolescence, which is experimenting, finding new solutions, and creating unique identities. Adolescence may well be a phenomenon containing an inseparable duality: if we eliminate one ingredient, we also forfeit the other. The freedom inherent in adolescence can only be preserved if we grant it an unfettered scope of functions. If we attempt to cast adolescence into a mold determined by our desires or fears, then we have, *ipso facto*, annihilated the experimentalist and explorative freedom of adolescence—and adolescence as such.

What attempts at solving adolescent unrest can lead to has been amply illustrated by the totalitarian youth of equally totalitarian regimes. Those youths did not necessarily destroy the values of their own society but they became the instrument that devastated the lives of other peoples.

In sum, the contradictions of adolescence are not solvable. The risk of a drastic outcome is the price that must be paid for the experiment. We can only hope that the experiment will result in something that will enhance and dignify the lives of all.

ADOLESCENCE AS IDENTITY
AND GROWTH: CRUCIBLE
AND DELIVERANCE

Adolescence is a many-splendored thing. Like a kaleidoscope, it takes on different colors and designs depending how one looks at it. And each appearance bears its own truth.

The list of differing perceptions of adolescence is endless, but some of the major interpretations include a modern pathology, the tyranny of immature tastes, the happiest and freest time in life, the most depressing and unhappy period, a time of trial-and-error experimentation, a primarily delinquent period, the most creative phase, the age of conformity to the peer group, a subcultural existence, a moratorium on adult responsibilities, the age of rebellion and dissent, the time of sexual prowess and exuberance, the time of learning and training, the time of serving one's community, the time of being with one's parents, the time of insecurity and search, and the crisis of identity.

Adolescence is all of these things! Not to obscure the manifold nature of the adolescent experience dictated the open framework in which this book was couched. It allowed recognition of the many aspects of adolescence and avoided distortion of its portrait by refraining from undue theoretical encapsulation. Nonetheless, some critics might lament the fact that the book eschewed a unitary theoretical approach — as perhaps would have been reflected in a Freudian, behavioristic, problem-oriented, or lifespan-oriented framework. But the Procrustean bed is a maiming gift, and this author is unwilling to give it.

Whatever the kaleidoscope shows, all images have one thing in common: the transition to adulthood. And as such, the crisis of identity functions as the crucible out of which the young will emerge, hopefully intact in mind and body and ready to assume a productive life.

To those who worry excessively about modern adolescence, nostalgically reciting past and presumably adolescence-free days and wishing to replace adolescents with a "cause"-oriented national youth, let them be reminded of the perennial folly of the sorcerer's apprentice, who conjured up a phenomenon that could not be called back.

It is easy to point to cultures which have been spared the affliction of adolescence. They seem to fall into two categories, and in each the adolescent-free members pay a substantial price for their privilege. The dictatorship does not allow selectivity in identity and thus minimizes the struggle of the young to acquire an identity. Identity comes in a ready-made package, neatly labeled and often attractively wrapped. These youths function well, at least as far as the society and its leaders are concerned. The primitive or tribal society has traditional roles that are handed down unaltered from generation to generation, removing the responsibility from the young of finding or creating their true identities.

On the other side, the democratic ethos grants to each member of society the right to and the responsibility for one's identity, as long as it does not jeopardize others. This freedom undoubtedly places a gigantic burden on the adolescent as well as on those who live with him or her. But all the trouble may pay off. In fact, it usually does: The troubled adolescent of yesterday turns out to be the responsible, integrated adult of today. The freedom for self-search begets the patience and generosity to encourage others to do likewise. And a chain reaction is established that becomes part of the democratic tradition, a tradition that is as irksome as it is imperative for the preservation of a democratic ethos.

Imposed alternatives for the process of adolescent self-search would mean a regression to some sort of mental servitude that is secure — but secure too soon.

Author Index

Addams, Jane, 16
Adelson, Joseph, 110, 134, 218, 227, 229
Adler, Freda, 52
Aldous, Jr., J., 134, 218
Aldridge, John W., 20, 121-123, 294, 295, 312
Allport, Gordon W., 35
Allport, Steve, 299
Altheide, David L., 213
Amneus, Daniel, 39
Anderson, J. W., 38
Ariès, Philippe, 12
Aristotle, 110, 111
Armory, Cleveland, 251
Ausubel, David P., 83

Bachman, Gerald, 192
Baldwin, James M., 58
Bales, Robert F., 43, 140
Bandura, Albert, 133-134, 190, 191, 193, 198, 218
Barclay, A., 175
Barnes, Richard, 55
Barzun, Jacques, 253
Bell, Daniel, 17, 67, 106, 324-325
Belson, William A., 195
Bem, Sandra, 54-55
Bender, Lauretta, 39, 76-77

Benedict, Ruth, 92, 100-102
Bengston, Vern L., 110
Berelson, Bernard, 150
Beres, D., 39
Berger, Bennett M., 152
Berger, Brigitte, 68
Berger, D. G., 213
Berger, Peter L., 68
Bernard, Jessie, 78
Bertrand, Alvin L., 166, 173
Bettelheim, Bruno, 46, 71, 76, 123, 279, 294, 295, 312
Bird, Caroline, 164
Blitsten, Dorothy R., 42
Bloomfield, Harold, 304
Blos, Peter, 123
Blum, Lucille H., 261
Boulding, Kenneth, 2
Boylen, K. W., 84
Brake, Mike, 281
Brim, Jr., Orville, 150
Broder, Paul, 172
Bromley, David G., 298
Bronfenbrenner, Urie, 43, 125, 132, 145, 151, 154, 322, 323
Bronson, Gordon W., 212
Brooks, John, 257
Brown, Charles H., 213

Brown, Daniel G., 43
Brownstone, Jane E., 229
Diunei, Jerome S., 101
Buckley, Hilda M., 257
Burgess, Ernest W., 15, 35
Burke, Carl F., 118

Calderone, M. S., 48
Campbell, W. J., 204
Cantor, Pamela, 51
Casler, Lawrence, 241
Castaneda, Carlos, 290
Cavan, Sherri, 286
Cervantes, Lucius F., 171, 175, 235
Champion, Dean J., 264
Cline, Victor B., 196
Cloward, Richard A., 220-221
Cohen, Albert K., 210, 221, 222
Cole, Luella, 85
Coleman, James S., 40, 71f., 75, 110, 131,
    156, 163, 171, 216, 227, 276
Connor, Walter D., 24
Constantine, Larry L., 119
Conway, Flo, 285, 299
Cook, Bruce, 285
Cooley, Charles H., 40, 58, 78, 131, 143
Cooper, Hal, 262
Cottle, Thomas J., 123-124
Crain, Alan J., 44
Cramer, James A., 264

Damrell, Joseph, 303
Davis, Kingsley, 38, 108, 150
DeFleur, Lois B., 200
DeFleur, Melvin L., 200
Demant, Vigo A., 204
Demerath, Nicholas, 150
DeMille, Richard, 290
Dempsey, D., 295
Denenberg, Victor H., 77
Denisoff, R. Serge, 213, 254
Deniston, Denise, 304
Denzin, Norman K., 40
Dion, Karen K., 203
Dodson, Fitzhugh, 147
Dominick, Joseph, 196
Douvan, Elizabeth, 134-135, 218, 227, **229**
Dragastin, Sigmund E., 3
Dunivant, Noel, 172
Durkheim, Emile, 103, 300

Eicher, Joanne B., 265, 266
Elder, Jr., Glen H., 3
Elkin, Frederick, 110, 217
Ellis, Albert, 240
Engels, Friederich, 280, 290
Erikson, Erik H., 4, 36, 56f., 62, 146, 212
Eron, Leonard, 192

Fairchild, H. P., 207
Farber, Bernard, 129
Faris, E., 35
Fass, Paula, 14
Fendrich, James M., 308
Feshbach, Seymour, 193
Feuer, Lewis S., 294, 295, 312
Flacks, Richard, 109, 121, 281, 293, 296
Foster, George M., 150
Freeman, Derek, 91
Freeman, Ronald, 150
Freud, Sigmund, 4, 35, 36, 43, 44, 290
Friedenberg, Edgar Z., 14, 110, 162, 179, 312
Frisbie, Charlotte J., 92
Fromm, Erich, 36, 280

Galbraith, John Kenneth, 17
Gallegos, Rudolfo N., 240
Gardner, Joyce, 153
Gerbner, George, 188-190
Gergen, Kenneth, 62
Gesell, Arnold, 35, 91
Gibran, Kahlil, 188
Gillis, John R., 14
Ginsberg, Allen, 289
Ginzberg, E., 67, 212
Glass, H. Bentley, 150
Glasser, William, 100
Glick, Paul C., 48
Glock, C. Y., 279
Goertzel, Ted, 230, 241
Goffman, Erving, 61ff., 318
Gold, H., 134-135, 218
Gold, Ray, 255-256
Goldfarb, William, 38-39
Goode, William J., 39
Goodman, Paul, 121, 162, 179, 312
Gordon, Milton M., 207
Goren, Kathleen J., 202
Goslin, D., 134, 218
Gottlieb, David, 14, 163, 180, 248
Gould, Harley N., 84
Gould, Julius, 256
Gould, Mary R., 84
Gove, Walter G., 50
Grafton, Samuel, 260
Green, Arnold, 146, 147, 217
Greenberg, Bradley, 196
Griessman, B. Eugene, 32
Grinder, Robert E., 53
Gross, Larry, 189
Gross, Leonard, 144
Grotberg, Edith H., 76
Gutierres, S. E., 202

Haan, Norma, 249
Hall, G. Stanley, 90-92
Hall, Irma Nelson, 85

Harris, Linda H., 169
Hartley, Ruth E., 147
Harvey, O. J., 77
Hass, Aaron, 93
Hathaway, Starke R., 167, 169, 170, 173, 174
Hatt, Paul K., 75
Hauser, Philip, 150
Havighurst, Robert J., 4, 5
Hayakawa, S. I., 204
Hechinger, Fred M., 119, 122
Hechinger, Grace, 119, 122
Hendin, Herbert, 149
Henton, Comradge L., 83
Hesse, Hermann, 289
Higginson, J., 84
Hill, Reuben, 134, 150, 218
Hinton, Sam, 253
Hirsch, Paul, 190
Hobart, Charles W., 137, 144
Hoffer, Eric, 8, 149, 280, 281
Hoffman, Abbie, 308
Hoffman, L., 43, 49, 76, 134, 218
Hoffman, M., 134, 218
Hollingshead, August B., 166
Holt, John, 161, 180
Horner, Matina, 49
Howard, Kenneth I., 49, 51, 218-219, 242-243
Howard, Sidney C., 146
Howe, Paul E., 86
Hudgins, Garven, 147
Hughes, Michael, 50
Hurlock, E. B., 7
Huxley, Aldous, 305

Ickes, William, 55
Ilg, Frances L., 91
Ito, Paul D., 84

Janis, Irving L., 199
Jencks, Christopher, 169-170
Jessor, R., 48
Jessor, S., 48
Jourard, Sidney, 240
Judah, J. Stillson, 302

Kamstra, Jerry, 285
Kandel, Denise B., 110
Kantner, John E., 47, 93
Kark, E., 84
Keating, John, 39, 130, 147
Keim, Albert N., 159
Kellner, Hansfried, 68
Keniston, Kenneth, 9, 19, 279, 296, 321
Kenrick, Douglas T., 202
Kerouac, John, 285
Kett, Joseph F., 10

Kiil, V., 84
King, K., 47
Kirkpatrick, Clifford, 113
Klapp, Orin E., 281, 306
Kluckhohn, Clyde, 10
Knott, Virginia B., 85
Kolb, William L., 257
Komarovsky, Mirra, 46, 50, 54
Kornhauser, William, 280
Kotlyar, Alexandre, 25
Krauss, Karen, 229, 231, 232, 235, 237
Kuo, You-Yuh, 27

LaGrone, Don M., 74
Lamb, Michael E., 39, 130
Larson, William R., 169
Laslett, Peter, 129
Lasowick, Lionel M., 147
Lear, Martha W., 146
Leary, Timothy, 290
LeBon, Gustave, 294
Lee, Robert, 280
Lefkowitz, Monroe M., 192
LeMasters, E. E., 187
Lennard, Henry L., 188
Leonard, George B., 163, 180
Lerman, Paul, 253
Lerner, Max, 59
Lesser, Gerald S., 110, 201
Levi, Ken, 299
Levin, H., 147
Levine, Saul V., 152
Levy, David M., 146
Lewis, Oscar, 152
Liebert, Robert M., 186
Lindesmith, Alfred R., 40, 188
Lindsey, Gardner, 10
Lipset, Seymour M., 125, 284
Locke, Harvey J., 15
Long, Elton, 32
Lyle, Jack, 185
Lyle, Jerolyn R., 76
Lynn, David B., 43, 147

Macaulay, Thomas B., 13
Maccoby, Eleanor E., 43, 125, 147, 187, 189, 199
McCord, Joan, 44
McCord, William, 44
Mace, David R., 154
Mace, Vera C., 154
McLamore, Dale S., 32
McLuhan, Marshall, 201
McWilliams, Peter, 304
Malinowski, Bronislaw, 102, 152
Mannheim, Karl, 108, 109, 132, 283, 287, 288, 296, 312
Marcia, James E., 56

Marcuse, Herbert, 290
Martin, Bernice, 213-214, 259
Marty, Martin, 279
Marx, Karl, 280, 290
Maslow, Abraham, 36-37
Masserman, Jules H., 215
Matteson, David R., 53
Mead, George H., 40, 45, 58
Mead, Margaret, 91, 110, 146, 150, 152, 201, 212, 276
Mehta, Gita, 289
Melville, Keith, 293
Meredith, Howard V., 85
Merker, M., 95
Merten, Don, 252, 267
Merton, Robert K., 39, 42, 103
Michelson, N., 83
Michener, James, 124
Miles, Catherine C., 45
Miller, Arthur, 119
Miller, Sherod, 136
Miller, Walter B., 167, 220
Mills, Clarence A., 85
Monachesi, Elio D., 167, 169, 170, 173, 174
Moore, Barrington, 130, 140, 290
Morgan, Thomas B., 269, 270
Morrison, D. E., 279
Morrow, Lance, 253
Mowrer, Orvall H., 43
Murray, J. M., 276
Musgrave, P., 197
Musgrove, Frank, 282, 296, 312
Myerhoff, Barbara G., 169

Nelson, Edward A., 252
Newfield, J., 19, 20
Nisbet, Robert A., 39, 124, 288
Noble, Grant, 188
North, Cecil C., 75
Norton, Arthur J., 48

Obers, S. J., 39
Oettlé, A. G., 84
Offer, Daniel, 49, 51, 110, 218-219, 242-243
Ohlin, Lloyd E., 220-221
Opie, Iona, 250
Opie, Peter, 250
Ostrov, Eric, 49, 51, 218-219, 242-243
Otto, Herbert A., 240, 256

Packard, Vance, 74
Palmer, C. E., 87
Park, Robert E., 61
Parker, Edwin B., 186
Parsons, Talcott, 43, 46, 140, 171, 216
Pavlos, Andrew J., 307
Peterson, Ann C., 83
Peterson, R. A., 213

Piaget, Jean, 36-37
Pines, Maya, 38
Poremba, Chester D., 172
Prince, C. H., 35

Radler, D. H., 227
Ramey, James W., 14, 124, 152
Rasch, G., 84
Reich, Charles A., 19, 110, 291, 294
Reiss, Ira, 230
Remmers, H. H., 227
Rice, Berkeley, 301
Richardson, Herbert, 298
Richardson, Stephan A., 77
Riesman, David, 60
Roach, Mary E., 257
Robinson, John, 192
Rogers, Carl, 36
Rogers, D., 218
Rogers, Everett, 150
Rosen, Bernard C., 169
Rosenbaum, Edward, 252
Ross, Dorothea, 192
Ross, Sheila A., 192
Roszak, Theodore, 9, 18, 19, 20, 110, 124, 246, 291, 294, 312
Rousseau, Jean-Jacques, 13, 91, 180
Ryan, Mary S., 257

Sarrel, P., 48
Sarrel, S., 48
Saunders, Lavelle E., 138
Saur, William, 136
Schaflander, Gerald M., 283
Schaller, Joseph, 74
Schiller, Maria, 86
Schnitzer, Phoebe K., 49
Schramm, Wilbur, 185, 187, 190, 203-205
Schreiber, Daniel, 174
Schwartz, Gary, 252, 267
Schwartzman, John, 148
Sears, R. R., 147
Sebald, Hans, 40, 44, 45, 54, 69, 98, 145, 148, 170, 187, 199, 208, 228, 230, 231, 232, 234, 236, 244, 266, 279, 281, 282, 286, 292, 305
Sexton, Patricia C., 146
Shafer, Susanne M., 53
Short, Jr., James F., 221-222
Shupe, Anson D., 298
Siegelman, Jim, 285, 299
Simpson, G., 103
Singer, Robert D., 193
Slater, Philip E., 19, 291, 294
Smallwood, A. L., 84
Smith, Brewster, 150
Smith, Ernest A., 40
Snell, David, 302

Snow, Robert P., 193
Socrates, 13
Solomon, Philip, 261
Sorokin, Pitirim A., 31, 280, 298, 309
Spaulding, J. A., 103
Spitz, R. A., 39
Spock, Benjamin, 117
Staats, Arthur W., 214
Staats, Carolyn K., 214
Stamm, Caroline S., 44
Stein, Maurice R., 130
Stein, Peter J., 48
Stern, Stanley, 204
Stoller, Frederick, 240
Strauss, Anselm L., 40
Strecker, Edward, 146, 149
Streib, Gordon F., 153
Sullivan, H. S., 42

Terman, Lewis M., 45
Teselle, Sallie, 152
Thomas, L. Eugene, 134, 218
Thurber, Emily, 44
Thurnher, Majda, 110
Toch, Hans, 280
Toffler, Alvin, 17
Tseng, M. S., 168, 178
Tuchman, Barbara, 12

Ullman, Paul S., 42, 43
Urbano, Paul D., 124

Ven Gennep, Arnold, 95
Veysey, Laurence, 152
Vidich, Arthur J., 130

Wallach, Amira, 307
Walsh, Maurice N., 31
Waterman, A. S., 180
Waterman, C. K., 180
Watts, Alan, 289
Weil, Andrew, 293
Weis-Bentzon, M., 84
Westley, William A., 110, 217
Whitam, Fred L., 299
White, Becky, 170
White, Daniel M., 130
Whorf, Benjamin, 10, 252
Wilkins, Joan A., 185
Williams, Paul A., 80
Williams, Percy, 174, 169
Williams, Jr., Robin M., 216–217
Willis, Richard H., 229
Windeshausen, Nicholas H., 80
Wofenden, R. C., 84
Wolff, Kurt H., 290
Won, George, 119
Wuthnow, Robert, 287–288
Wylie, Philip, 146
Wyzanski, Charles E., 119

Yamamura, Douglas, 119
Yankelovich, Daniel, 50, 97, 110, 243, 245, 297
Yarnell, H., 39
Yinger, Milton J., 207, 279
Young, Anne M., 167
Young, Michael, 150

Zajonc, Robert, 198
Zamoff, Richard B., 76
Zelnick, M., 47, 93
Zimmerman, Carl C., 140

Subject Index

Abortion, 138
Activism and radicalism. *See* Counterculture
Adolescence
  affluence and, 19–21, 78–82
  alienation and, 27, 132, 175, 279–283,
    297, 307–309
  automobile and, 275–276
  as autonomy process, 132–135, 235–236
  causes of, 2, 27–32, 127, 313–314
  communication skill and, 5, 136f., 141, 318
  cross-cultural, 6–8, 11, 12, 21–28, 91, 95,
    99–102
  culture and, 66–68, 70, 89–105
  definition of, 2–11
  developing countries and, 28–32, 322
  diversity of, 32, 127–128, 165–172,
    175–179, 220, 246
  economic conditions, 5–6, 14, 16, 69,
    78–82, 97–98, 175–179, 281
  education and, 71–73, 156–183
  family life and, 117–155
  future of, 321–323
  historical evolution of, 12–16
  life span, 2–3, 238, 313
  mass media influence, 184–205
  normative, 2
  reference groups, 39–41, 230–237
  religion and, 118–119, 127, 134, 246, 286,
    289–292, 297–306
  research needs, 319–321
  rural-urban migration and, 15–16
  as self-fulfilling prophecy, 2, 10, 134
  significant other, 42–44
  social change and, 21, 31–32, 106–113,
    114–117, 125, 128–155, 159–164, 238,
    245–247, 274–275, 278–297, 306–309,
    312–319, 321–326
  social structure and, 66–68, 71–78, 307
  television influence on, 131, 132, 145, 174,
    184–205, 317
  universality of, 28–32
Affluence, teenage, 19–21, 78–82
Alienation, 27, 93, 175, 279–284, 297,
  307–309
  counterculture and, 283, 285
  developmental estrangement, 280
  positive functions of, 282–283
  social change and, 280
Alternative lifestyles, 284–286, 297,
  307–309, 310
Amish, 32, 72, 73, 127, 152, 159, 165
Anomie, 18–19, 23, 67, 68, 102–103, 152,
  281, 285, 310, 314, 315
Apprenticeship, 12, 28, 68–69, 160

Archconservative movements, 306
Argot, 25, 27, 118, 124, 207, 208, 250–254
Australian adolescents, 24, 205
Austrian adolescents, 24
Authority
  authoritative, 124–125
  parental, 42–44, 117–126, 130, 132–135,
    138–139, 144, 150–151, 163, 175, 316
  rational vs. irrational, 112–113

Bar mitzvah, 95–96
Beatles, 269, 271
Beatniks, 285
Birth control, 115, 116, 138–139, 229
Black youth, 157, 167–168, 176
Blousons noirs, 23
Bohemians, 285
Brazilian adolescents, 27
Bulgarian adolescents, 26

California Conservation Corps, 248
Campus Crusade for Christ, 299
Careers
  preparation for, 49, 67, 71–75, 163–164,
    175–179, 182, 247, 248
  women and, 52–55, 136
Cars, adolescents and, 82
Chaoten, 23
Chicano youth, 167
Childrearing, 75–78, 91, 99, 102, 108–113,
    117–126, 123–125
  authoritarian, 120–126
  permissive, 91, 117–120, 123–125
  social class and, 125
Chinese youth, 26, 29–30
Clash of inferiority complexes, 113, 316
Cohabitation, 48, 237, 276
Communes, 151–154, 240, 275, 286
Communication skill, 5, 136f., 141, 154, 318
Communist countries, adolescence in, 24–27,
    321
Counterculture, 1, 9, 19–22, 97, 98, 120,
    125, 246, 247, 278–310
  activists' backgrounds, 9, 281, 307–309
  activists reentering society, 307–309
  alienation and, 279–283, 297, 307–309
  definition of, 278–279
  drugs and, 289, 307
  evaluation of the, 294–296, 312–313
  extent of, 311–312
  mystic/magical attitudes, 246, 289–292,
    307
  political attitudes, 288–291, 293
  subinstitutions, 208–209, 286, 293–294
  trends, 306–309, 322
Crowd behavior, 270–271, 293
Cults. *See* True Believer movements

Culture
  causes of adolescence, 28–32
  identity and, 18, 28–32, 34, 43, 57–63, 67,
    313, 315, 318, 326
  influences on adolescence, 89–105
  Protestant/work ethic, 17–21, 71, 97,
    106–107, 117

Dating, 231, 232, 237, 266, 273–274
Day-care centers, 47, 76, 132, 144
Delinquency, 100, 132, 169, 170–172, 175,
    220–222
  crosscultural, 21–27
  female, 52, 222
  gang, 13, 14, 15, 21, 212, 222
  school vandalism, 171–172, 221
Developing countries and adolescence, 28–32,
    322
Developmental theory, 35–46, 90–92, 280
Divine Light Mission, 301f.
Divorce, 128, 129, 135, 140
Draft, 23, 322
Drinking, 5, 24, 144, 266
Drug use, 24, 148, 222, 275, 285, 289, 291,
    299, 304–305, 307

Economic attitudes, 245–247, 324–325
Education, 71–73, 112, 116, 120, 123,
    156–183
  academic attitudes, 173–174, 241, 242
  criticism of American, 13, 161–164,
    169–170, 179–182
  custodial, 13, 18, 19, 161–164, 314
  family influences on, 168–170
  gender differences, 52–53, 157, 160,
    167–170, 174
  high-school dropout, 164–175
  learning disabilities, 172–174
  longer, 73, 160–161
  mandatory, 13, 161–163, 171
  nonfamilial, 72f., 159–160
  "pushouts," 168, 172
  racial/ethnic minorities, 157, 160, 167–168
  school vandalism, 161, 171–172, 221
  socioeconomic differences, 165–169,
    181–182
  television, 181, 199–201, 317–318
  trends, 156–159
English adolescents, 21, 27, 176
Entitlement, psychology/philosophy of, 19,
    107, 117, 245–246, 314, 324f.

Fads
  affluence and, 78–82
  business and, 79–82, 323
  clothing, 120, 257–258
  dancing, 255, 260–261

Fads (*Continued*)
  definition of, 22, 256
  hair style, 120, 261–263
  hero worship, 267
  music, 213–214, 254, 258–260
  Punk, 22, 25, 258, 270, 271, 284
  subcultural reinforcement, 22, 265
Familism, 43, 115, 135–145, 232
Family, 74–78, 127–155
  alternative structures, 151–154
  changing functions, 135–145
  changing structure, 128, 316
  law, 138–139
  personality function, 139–142, 145
  single-parent, 128–129
  status ascription, 137
Father absenteeism, 42–44, 130, 141, 147,
    175
Fear of success, 49–50
Fetishism, 260
Filipino adolescents, 27
Freie Deutsche Jugend, 29–30
French adolescents, 23–24, 27, 176
Friendship, patterns of, 229, 237, 265–267

Gangs, 13, 14, 15, 21, 212, 222
  female, 222
Gender role. *See* Role learning
Generalized other, 45, 58
Generational conflict/gap, 106–126, 132–135,
    315–316
  continuous nature of, 238, 307
  subculture and, 264
  television and, 201
  theory of, 107, 110–111
German adolescents, 22–23, 26, 27, 29–31,
    48, 86, 144, 160, 176, 182, 187
Gesellschaft für Sport und Technik, 30

Halbstarke, 24
Halo effect, 112, 126
Hero worship, 265, 267–273
Hippies, 21, 257, 285–286
Hitler-Jugend, 29–31, 315
Hutterites, 32, 127, 152

Identification
  with heroes, 271–273
  with parents, 43–44, 74
  with subculture, 82, 211, 257, 317
  with television characters, 184–185, 188,
    190–199, 201, 203, 205
Identity, 30ff., 34–65, 126, 127, 185, 201,
    261, 307. *See also* Personality
  crisis, 4, 33, 56ff., 326
  cultural influence, 18, 29–32, 57–63, 67,
    313, 315, 326
  development, 55–63, 70, 136

  social structure and, 29–32, 67, 313
  theories of, 55–63, 318
Illegitimate births, 129
Immigration, 14–15
Incest, 169
Indian (American) youth, 92, 95, 101–102
Indian (Asian) youth, 27
Industrial Revolution, 12ff.
Inferiority complexes
  adolescent, 113, 114
  parental, 111, 113, 114
In loco parentis, 6, 112, 120, 139, 163, 296
Instantness, pursuit of, 69–71, 117, 186, 260,
    282
Institutional homes, 38–39, 75–78
Intergenerational conflict. *See* Generational
    conflict
Isolate child, 37–38
Isomorphic interpenetration, 46
Israeli kibbutz, 152
Italian adolescents, 176

Japanese adolescents, 27, 176
Jesus movement, 299–300
Jewish adolescents, 95–96
Job Corps, 178
Juvenile. *See also* Delinquency
  definition, 8
  detention, 172

Kent State University, 124
Knowledge explosion, 111–113
Komsomol, 29–30, 315
Krishna movement, 301–304

Language, teenage. *See* Argot
Learning disabilities, 172–174
Legal age, 5–7, 138
Life span theory, 3, 7, 326

Magazines, teenage, 213, 230, 254–255
Marxian theory, 18, 280, 290
Masculinity/femininity. *See* Role Learning
Mass media, 116, 184–205. *See also*
    Television
  books, 189
  magazines, 213, 230, 254–255
  movies, 184, 186, 188, 191, 194, 195, 198,
    202
  personality development and, 44, 59–60,
    188, 190–199, 201, 203, 205
  radio, 254
  television, 131, 132, 145, 174, 184–205,
    254, 317
Meditation movement, 303–304
Menarche, 83–87, 92
Mental health, 74, 77–78
Military families, 74

Minority group youth, 32, 127–128, 157, 167–168, 176
Mobility, 19, 73–75, 141–142
Mods, 21
Momism, 145–149
Moral attitudes, 242
Motherhood
    choice of, 53–54
    working mother, 76, 132
Movies, 184, 186, 188, 191, 194, 195, 198, 202. *See also* Television, Mass media
Multi-personae, 55–63

Nature-nurture controversy, 90–92
New Age movement, 286, 287, 292, 297, 310
New Wave, 22
Nutrition, 82–87

Parents
    authority of, 42–43, 130, 132–135, 138–139, 144, 150–151, 163, 175, 316
    -child rapprochement, 177–121
    vs. experts, 111–113
    as role models, 130–131, 178
    -youth interaction, 37–44, 109–114, 117–126
Peace Corps, 248, 249
Peace movement, 98, 322
Peer influence, 131–135, 159–161, 170–172, 175, 227–242, 251–254, 257–273, 316
Personality
    concept of, 35ff.
    development, 34–65
    human nature, 142–145
    mass media influence on, 184–186
    multi-personae, 55–63
    other-directed, 60, 199
    persona dramatis, 63
    sociopathic, 78
    theories of, 35–46, 55–63
Philosophy of entitlement, 19, 107, 117, 245–246, 314, 324f.
Political attitudes, 134, 243–245, 288–291, 293, 322, 324–325
Popularity, value of, 227–229
Postindustrialism, 1, 16–20, 21, 48, 66–88, 106ff., 111, 160, 164, 206, 311–314, 324
Pregnancy, teenage, 138, 139, 174, 177, 240
Premarital sex, 47–48
Primary/secondary groups, 37–41, 142–145
Prostitution, 222
Protestant ethic, 17–21, 71, 97, 106–107, 117, 152, 245–246, 297, 324–325
Psychedelic movement, 304–305
Puberty, 5, 6, 83–87, 92, 95, 96, 116, 315
Pubescence. *See* Puberty
Puerto Rican adolescents, 167
Punk style, 22, 25, 258, 270, 271, 284

Raggare, 24
Reality therapy, 100
Recapitulation theory, 90–92
Red Guard, 29–30, 315
Reference groups, 39–41
    parents vs. peers, 109, 131–135, 170–175, 230–237, 263, 288
Religious behavior/attitudes, 118–119, 127, 134, 240, 246, 286, 289–292, 297–306
Rite of passage, 10, 68, 94–96
Rockers and mods, 21
Role learning, 4–5, 34, 94–96, 99–102. *See also* Personality, Identity
    culture and, 18, 44–46
    gender role, 4–5, 42–55, 57, 115, 130, 136, 175, 318
    modern modifications of, 135–136
    multiple personae, 55, 59–63
    persona dramatis, 63
    stereotypes, 201–202
Romanticism, 12–13, 229, 238–239, 268. *See also* Hero worship, Values
Rousseauan philosophy, 13, 91, 180
Runaway, 129
Rural-urban migration, 15–16
Russian adolescents, 24–26, 29–30

Samoan youth, 91, 152
Schools. *See* Education
Self-actualization, 37, 97, 106, 117, 135, 137, 307, 310, 321
Sesame Street, 200
Sex role. *See* role learning
Sexual behavior/attitudes, 93–94, 99, 101, 114–117, 123–124, 186, 222, 229–230, 237–241, 261, 269, 274, 275
    variant, 237–238
Sexual Revolution, 114–117
Significant other, 42–44, 60
Skinheads and Suedeheads, 21–22
Social change. *See also* Postindustrialism
    adolescence and, 21, 31–32, 106–113, 114–117, 125, 128–155, 159–164, 238, 245–247, 274–275, 278–297, 306–309, 311–319, 321–326
Social-class differences, 32, 83–87, 125, 127, 146, 165–172, 175–179, 181, 220–222, 227–229, 246, 255, 281
Socialization, 106–126. *See also* Childrearing, Role learning
Social movements
    adolescence and, 108–110, 278–310
Social structure
    anomie and, 28–32
    causes of adolescence in, 3, 16, 28–32, 66–69, 103
    identity and, 28–32, 67, 130, 313
    multispecificity, 18, 19, 66–69

Sociosomatics, 82–87
Stilyagi, 24
Structural functional analysis, 11
Students for a Democratic Society, 283
Styles. *See* Fads
Subculture, teenage
  adolescent paradox and 223–224
  affluence and, 19–21, 78–82
  age of members, 87
  anti-intellectualism, 241–242
  argot/lingo, 118, 124, 207, 208, 250–254
  behavioristic model, 214–215
  charisma in, 208, 209, 267–273, 301
  counterculture differing from, 278–279
  culture-transition model, 213f.
  definition, 207–209
  delinquent, 220–222
  dimensions of, 206–277
  diversity of, 219–223
  drug use, 24, 222, 263–264, 275, 285,
    289, 291, 304–305
  etiology of, 206–225
  fads, 81–82, 207–208, 255–263
  groupies, 269
  identity and, 82, 211, 257, 284, 317
  mass communication, 207, 208, 213–214,
    254–255. *See also* Mass media
  psychogenic model, 212f.
  solidarity/espris de corps, 207, 251, 254,
    263–264, 304–305
  status criteria, 208, 209, 251, 264–267
  subinstitutionalization, 208, 209, 224, 263,
    274–277, 286, 293–294
  theories concerning, 110–111, 133–135,
    215–219, 223–224, 278
  values/norms, 207, 208, 216, 227–250
Suicide, 24, 51–52, 103, 148, 149, 169
Swedish adolescents, 24, 27
Swiss adolescents, 27

Taiwanese adolescents, 27
Teenager, defined, 8–10
Television, 131, 132, 145, 174, 190–199,
    203–204, 213–214, 254. *See also* Mass media
  creativity and, 174, 188, 203–204
  exposure to, 185–187, 191, 203–204, 317
  functions, 145, 186–205
  gender-differentiated responses, 192f.

identification with characters on, 184–185,
    188, 190–199, 201, 203, 205
  imitation, 190 199
  subculturally reinforcing, 214, 254, 317
  unrealism and, 186–189, 199, 201–203
  violence and, 186, 189–199
True believer movements, 31, 148, 297–306,
    310, 314

Unification Church, 300–301
United Nations youth survey, 311, 321
Urban-industrial life. *See also*
    Postindustrialism
  causes of adolescence in, 1–2, 12ff., 28
Urban Youth Service Corps, 178

"Val-speak," 253
Values
  commitment to society, 242, 247–250
  conflicts, 96–102, 315
  dichotomies, 96–102, 315
  economic, 17–21, 71, 97, 106–107, 117,
    152, 245–246, 297, 324–325
  religious, 118–119, 127, 134, 240, 246,
    286, 289–292, 297–306
  subcultural, 207, 208, 216, 227–250, 252
Vandalism, 171–172, 221
VD, 139
Vietnam War, 22, 23, 98, 119, 174, 243–245,
    298
Vista, 248
Volunteerism, 242, 247–250

Women's liberation, 44, 47ff., 52, 114–117,
    146, 201, 238, 260, 322
Work ethic. *See* Protestant ethic
Working-/lower-class youth, 21, 165–172,
    175–179, 220, 246

Yippie movement, 308
Youth. *See also* Adolescence
  cult, 113–114
  definition of, 8, 9, 19, 321
  earnings, 5–6, 14, 16, 78–82, 97, 175–179,
    281
  law and, 5–7, 138–139
  national programs, 29–31, 247–250, 326
  retreatist, 285ff.
  unemployed, 175–179
Yugoslav adolescents, 27